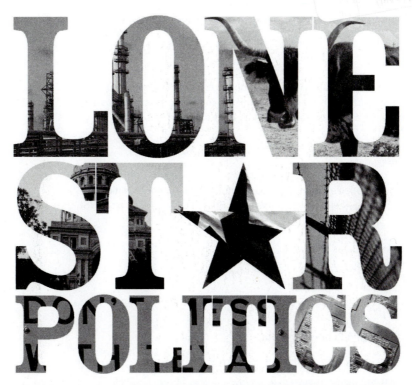

LONE STAR POLITICS

Tradition and Transformation in Texas

Ken Collier ★ Stephen F. Austin State University
Steven Galatas ★ Stephen F. Austin State University
Julie Harrelson-Stephens ★ Stephen F. Austin State University

CQ PRESS

A Division of SAGE
Washington, D.C.

CQ Press
2300 N Street, NW, Suite 800
Washington, DC 20037

Phone: 202-729-1900; toll-free, 1-866-4CQ-PRESS (1-866-427-7737)

Web: www.cqpress.com

Cover design by Jeffrey M. Hall, ION Graphic Design Works
Composition by Naylor Design, Inc.

∞ The paper used in this publication exceeds the requirements of the American National Standard for Information Sciences—Permanence of Paper for Printed Library Materials, ANSI Z39.48-1992.

Printed and bound in the United States of America

13 12 11 10 09   2 3 4 5 6

Library of Congress Cataloging-in-Publication Data

Collier, Kenneth E.,
    Lone star politics: tradition and transformation in Texas / Ken Collier, Steven Galatas,
Julie Harrelson-Stephens.
        p. cm.
    Includes bibliographical references and index.
    ISBN 978-0-87289-506-5 (alk. paper)
    1. Texas–Politics and government. I. Galatas, Steven. II. Harrelson-Stephens, Julie. III. Title.

    JK4816.C65 2008
    320.4764–dc22   2008005715

To our loving and patient spouses:

Sandy Benavides Collier,

Rebecca Suzanne Galatas,

Mark Stephens

About the Authors

Ken Collier is associate professor at Stephen F. Austin State University, with a PhD from the University of Texas at Austin. He is the author of *Between the Branches: The White House Office of Legislative Affairs* and is currently researching presidential speechwriting and gubernatorial elections. He has published articles in such journals as *Journal of Politics, White House Studies, Presidential Studies Quarterly, Public Choice,* and *Social Science Quarterly.*

Steven Galatas is assistant professor at Stephen F. Austin State University, with a PhD from the University of Missouri. He has published articles in *Journal of Politics, Public Choice,* and *Party Politics.* His research and teaching concern comparative elections, voting behavior, and campaign finance.

Julie Harrelson-Stephens is assistant professor at Stephen F. Austin State University, with a PhD from the University of North Texas. She has coedited, with Rhonda L. Callaway, *Exploring International Human Rights: Essential Readings* and has been published in *Conflict and Terrorism* and *International Interactions.*

Brief Contents

Contents

Maps, Boxed Features, Tables, and Figures

Maps

Boxed Features

Tables

Figures

Preface

As has often been said, there is no State in the Union whose history presents such varied and romantic scenes as does that of Texas. This alone would recommend it to the general reader and the earnest student. But there is in addition to its interest a weighty reason why every school in the State should give Texas History a place in its course of study. No one who learns well the lessons taught can fail to become a better and wiser citizen.[1]

Anna J. Hardwicke Pennybacker
A New History of Texas for Schools (1888)

Mrs. Pennybacker's "new" history of Texas presents a traditional view of Texas history. The copy we used originally belonged to Earl B. Persons, the great-uncle of one of the authors. In the century since young Earl Persons first read this quotation in his schoolbook, Texans have written some new history and revised some old history. Mr. Persons served in World War I before taking part in the rise of the oil business in Texas, a time when he saw his pastures become more valuable for the oil under them than the cattle that grazed on them. The next generation of Texans saw America through World War II, the Cold War, and the space race directed from NASA in Houston. That generation grew up on *Texas History Movies*, a comic version of Texas history, sponsored by an oil company. Another generation saw the high-tech boom take root in Texas. Today's young Texans often shun books and learn their Texas history from the Internet.

The economic, demographic, and political changes in the state brought new ways of life to its citizens. Over the past century, as Texans moved from the countryside into the cities, ranches and farms gave way to cities and suburbs as the natural habitat of Texans. As small towns gave way to the more impersonal big cities, Texans found themselves living closer and closer together, meaning that they would have to cooperate more with neighbors and fellow citizens. The farmer's lonely but simple commute from farmhouse to field has been replaced by long treks to work on crowded superhighways. For Texans of an earlier time commerce meant the weekly trip into town to sell goods, buy supplies, and check the mail. Networking meant occasionally gathering at the local coffee shop to swap information over breakfast.

Today, in the course of their daily work, many Texans are in constant contact with other Texans, other Americans, and other people from around the world. Many Texans have trouble working when their Internet connection goes down even briefly.

Clearly, we Texans aren't what we used to be. However, our image of ourselves has not changed quite as much as the circumstances of our lives. During the century since Mrs. Pennybacker's words, Texans have looked again at our history and found a much more nuanced view of our conflicts with the Mexican government during the revolution and with the U.S. government during and after the U.S. Civil War. While scholars have reviewed and revised the stories of Texas, Texans have often clung to the more romantic version of our history.

Our state's government is in the unenviable position of having to keep pace with all these changes while still remaining true to our traditions and legends. Texas government needs to be a lean, modern government, managing the affairs of over 23 million Texans while still retaining a small-town feel and the frontier spirit. Today's government must be nimble enough to respond to global competition and regional hurricane devastation. Today's governors should be able to ride a horse and manage their own e-mail.

One of the most remarkable things about teaching Texas politics is that, while so many Texas students only take it because it's required and so many instructors have doubts about teaching it, the subject is actually pretty enjoyable. Generations of textbooks have stepped into the breach between these reluctant participants, often with mixed results. Textbooks about Texas politics are often rather dry, when the study of Texas politics should actually be very interesting, as our state's history is full of legends, criminals, preachers, hucksters, and even comedians. Somehow, when it's all said and done, the life is too often taken out of Texas politics, and we think that's a true Texas tragedy.

We hope to breathe a little of that life back into the study of Texas politics. We can't engage in storytelling for storytelling's sake. However, any effort to put together a dry, story-free, (i.e., "serious") textbook on Texas politics would lead us to forget the role that the state's legends and myths play in shaping how Texans think and how our politicians behave. You can't tell the story of Texas without revisiting a few tall tales, debunking some persistent myths in the state, and captivating the readers with the true stories that are often more interesting than the legends.

Reading between the Lines of Lone Star Politics

ur book was written by Texans but published by CQ Press in Washington, D.C. We designed our text to work well when partnered with CQ Press's other offerings or when used as a text that can stand on its own.

The plan for the book is relatively simple. We open with an introduction to the state and its history in Chapter 1. While much of this story will be familiar to many readers, we feel it bears repeating, to bring focus to the political history of the state and to refresh the memories of Texas students who haven't seen much of their state's history since middle school. Building on the state's history, Chapter 2 examines the birth and rebirth of the state through its constitutions. The chapter emphasizes that while the Texas Constitution continues to evolve, it has not been able to keep pace with a rapidly changing state. Chapter 3 looks at how the Texas Legislature is elected and how it functions. As the heart of Texas democracy, the legislature is a fine example of how changes have been slow to come. Next, Chapter 4 visits the Texas governor's mansion to see if the executive office is ready to keep up with the state. Chapter 5 explores the justice system in Texas. Chapter 6 looks at local government in Texas. Chapter 7 examines how Texans elect their officials, and Chapter 8 looks at how Texans work together through parties and organized interests. Finally, Chapter 9 investigates what the government produces: policy. We'll also use that chapter to conclude the book and revisit a few themes.

Featuring Our Features

his text is designed to draw readers into the key issues of politics in Texas. Several features of the text are designed to bring the reader's attention to an issue, often in a new light.

Texas Legends

John Steinbeck observed after his first visit to Texas, "Like most passionate nations Texas has its own history based on, but not limited by, facts." [2] We have made a discussion of "Texas legends" a recurring feature of this text. When we look at the characters and stories that fill Texas politics, we often find that Texas's legends differ from reality. These legends play a role in shaping Texans' self-image whether or not they can be proven true. One historian, who suggested that the real Davy Crockett surrendered rather than died fighting like Fess Parker's portrayal in Disney's version of the Alamo, was told by one angry reader that the "Fess Parker image has done more for children than your book can." [3] Discussing what has been termed the "Texas creation myth," one writer concluded, "the mythic Alamo of the American collective imagination has become far more important than the Alamo of tedious historical fact." [4] It is odd that Texans have allowed Crockett, Bowie, and other legends of the Alamo to be recast. Many of the men who defended the Alamo were brave, but their lives were not necessarily family fare. For example, Jim Bowie partnered in a slave-smuggling ring with pirate Jean Lafitte before Bowie came to Texas. [5] William Travis abandoned a young son and a pregnant wife before he came to Texas.

That these men and women lived hard lives and made serious errors is not the point of retelling their stories. Texas is a place where people have come to start over and find a new identity. The celebrated "Baron de Bastrop" was really a Dutchman named Philip Hendrick Nering Bögel who invented the title when he arrived in San Antonio with very little money. When Moses Austin came to Texas in 1820 to win the right to form colonies in Texas only to be sent packing by a Spanish governor who distrusted foreigners, it was the baron who persuaded the governor to forward Austin's proposal to the Spanish government. As one author put it, "He was among the first, but certainly not the last, loser to come to Texas to reinvent himself and emerge in prominence." [6] The flaws in Texas's leaders remain evident today. George W. Bush was honest—if not always specific—about the mistakes in his past. Despite those flaws, Texans twice chose him as their governor before recommending him to the nation.

Even after the legends of our history reinvented themselves, we Texans have reinvented our own history. Our recollection of history is less fixed than we care to admit. After the Texans won the Battle of San Jacinto with the battle cry, "Remember the Alamo," the Alamo itself would lie in neglect for half a century, a forgotten monument that was used to store onions and potatoes before being restored and elevated as "the shrine of Texas Liberty."

Our explorations of Texas legends are not an attempt to resolve the debate between views of "Disneyland Davy" and other versions of Texas history. Texans need not be sidetracked by the debate about whether their state's heroes were perfect. They were not. Neither were the founders of the United States. What we need to understand is how important these images are to the people of Texas. Describing the "passionate nation" that is Texas, John Steinbeck noted that "[r]ich, poor, Panhandle, Gulf, city, county, Texas is the obsession, the proper study and the passionate possession of all Texans." [7]

The aspirations embedded in our myths play a role in how the state approaches change. Because our legends are about who we once were, retelling these stories now reminds us who we are today and keeps us from drifting too far from our values. At the same time these legends can tell us a great deal about who we want to be and where our hopes come from. As Steinbeck wrote, "I have said that Texas is a state of mind, but I think it is more than that. It is a mystique closely approximating a religion." [8]

Winners and Losers

Politics involves the distribution of goods and by its nature produces winners and losers. While Texas's history, culture, and predilections may seem vague and distant to students today, the politics that spring from them have ramifications that are very real for the citizens of the state. This text is intended to encourage students to think critically about Texas politics, identify problems, and look ahead to solutions. In every chapter we will be looking at who gets what from government by looking at winners and losers in Texas politics. This is especially valuable in studying Texas political history because the victories won by a group in one era most often lay the groundwork for the next battles. Texas is in a constant state of change, and citizens need to consider what needs to be changed and how their fellow Texans might be affected by the changes.

Texas versus . . .

We will occasionally pause to compare Texas to other states, often focusing on those states that provide the most dramatic or interesting contrast to Texas. We want to illustrate how Texas is different and why that difference is significant. Because most citizens of a state seldom consider their options, we felt it was important to illustrate the possibilities of state government and to illustrate the consequences of choices that people face. Comparisons were selected to provide examples from potentially familiar settings, like Louisiana or California, to settings that Texans may have little exposure to, like Vermont or North Dakota. Hopefully, students will come to appreciate why Texas is just a little bit different. Thus, our comparison of Texas to other states is a good place to highlight critical thinking. We pose a set of questions to encourage students to look at options and ponder what would best serve the state.

Companion Web Site and Instructor Resources

Students and instructors also will benefit from a variety of ancillaries. A companion Web site, available at http://lonestar.cqpress.com, provides chapter summaries, interactive flashcards of key words, practice quizzes, and annotated hyperlinks to a wealth of online resources and readings. Instructors adopting the text can download test bank questions covering each chapter, along with PowerPoint lecture slides.

Acknowledgments

bviously, we didn't do this by ourselves. We did make all the mistakes. However, a small band of dedicated people tried their best to detect these mistakes and set us right.

Don Gregory served as our research assistant early in this project. He provided us a wealth of old Texas texts and sent many interesting clippings. His research skills were exceptional, and we expect that he will do quite well in political science. We also enjoyed assistance from Joe Ericson. We believe that Joe served as a political advisor to Stephen F. Austin himself. We also benefited from many small favors from other colleagues. We thank Laurie Dodson of the Texas Municipal League for her assistance with statistics and resources on city government in Texas. She was also helpful in translating the legalese of local government administration into political science terms. Debra Gaston, Nacogdoches County elections administrator, provided invaluable consultation regarding elections processes and procedures in Texas.

Far from Texas, the good people at CQ Press labored to keep us on schedule and under control. Despite the fact that they never found the pictures we wanted of the "Los Conquistadors Coronado Burro Ride" at the Six Flags Over Texas amusement park (or hid them from us if they did), we would like to thank Charisse Kiino, Kristine Enderle, Anna Socrates, Allyson Rudolph, and Jennifer Schroeder for their benevolence, patience, and diligence. We'd also like to thank the reviewers who saw the path through the errors and awkwardness of an early draft and offered up a balance of criticism and encouragement: Frank Codspoti, Cy-Fair College; Rick Henderson, Texas State University; Glen Hunt, Austin Community College; Patricia Jaramillo, University of Texas at San Antonio; Franklin Jones, Texas Southern University; Heidi Lange, Houston Community College; James Startin, University of Texas at San Antonio; and Nikki Van Hightower, Texas A & M University.

The work of this text is still not done. We look forward to hearing from readers about ways to improve the text. We welcome you to send your comments to kcollier@sfasu.edu.

Notes

1. Mrs. Anna J. Hardwicke Pennybacker, *A New History of Texas for Schools* (Tyler, Tex., 1888), v.
2. John Steinbeck, *Travels with Charley: In Search of America* (New York: Bantam Books, 1961), 226.
3. James E. Crisp, *Sleuthing the Alamo: Davy Crockett's Last Stand and Other Mysteries of the Texas Revolution* (New York: Oxford University Press, 2004), 142.
4. Ibid., 144.
5. Ibid., 17.
6. James L. Haley, *Passionate Nation: The Epic History of Texas* (New York: Free Press, 2006), 70.
7. Steinbeck, *Travels with Charley,* 226.
8. Ibid., 227.

Big Tex, the world's tallest talking cowboy, greets visitors to the State Fair of Texas, the nation's largest state fair. Big Tex was originally the world's largest Santa Claus before he was re-outfitted in 1952 as the symbol of the state fair.

CHAPTER 1

Introduction: "Gone to Texas"

After watching immigrants stream across the border into Texas year after year government officials on the Texas side began to worry that their state was being transformed into a part-Mexican, part-Anglo society that would prove unmanageable and ungovernable as the growing number of immigrants asserted their political power. Some immigrants had entered lawfully, patiently working their way through the government's cumbersome process, others came without regard to the laws, exploiting a border that was too long and too remote to be effectively monitored. Most of the new immigrants proved to be hard-working and enterprising additions to the Texas society and economy. A few others, however, had crossed the border to escape legal and financial problems back home and seemed more interested in making a quick buck. Many immigrants brought their families along for a chance at a better life or planned to bring them over as soon as they made enough money, but a few contributed to criminal enterprises or squandered their wages on alcohol and vice while eventually abandoning their families. Established residents worried that they would become foreigners in their own country or doubted that their new neighbors would ever prove to be anything but a challenge since many newcomers refused to assimilate or adopt the politics and culture of their new home. Many of the new arrivals stubbornly clung to their native tongue; some even began to demand that official business be conducted in it.

The government felt that much of the problem lay on the other side of the border. Some of these immigrants seemed to be entering the state to foment change and many had strong political ties to political leaders back home. Some, like Sam Houston, who had been governor of Tennessee, were close political and personal friends of U.S. president Andrew Jackson. Davy Crockett, also a product of Jackson's Democratic Party in Tennessee, had served in the U.S. Congress and was one of the leading political figures of the day. It seemed likely that his political ambitions followed him to Texas.

Many of the early Texans who later fought for independence from Mexico came to Texas against the expressed wishes of the Mexican government. Whereas early American colonists along the Eastern seaboard settled among, and then pushed aside, the more loosely organized Native American populations, early Texans violated a border officially recognized by the American government as they brushed aside Mexican law. The immigration issue—then as today—represents a challenge of governing a rapidly changing state. Immigrants today generate a great deal of tax money for the state through sales and income taxes, but can also cost the counties and local governments a great deal in services. Immigrants contribute greatly to the economic success of the state by meeting the demand for inexpensive labor but often do so at the expense of American labor.

The location of Texas at the crossroads between new and old has been one of the few constants in the state. Texas has relished its growth, but often disparaged the new citizens that contributed to it. Texans have enjoyed the prosperity that growth brings, but reluctantly accepted the new Texans and the changes they brought.

While change may be inevitable, a society is rooted by the stories citizens share and hand down from generation to generation. We Texans are especially attached to our state's history and particular legends of larger-than-life people and events. Stories from Texas history are more than dramatic scenes we retell and recreate for entertainment; these stories define who we are and remind us of our values. Texas's unique relationship with its history is reflected in a favorite theme park, "Six Flags over Texas," an amusement park originally constructed around Texas history themes, which at one time featured rides such as "LaSalle's River Boat Adventure" in the French section and "Los Conquistadors Coronado Burro Ride" in the Spanish section.

Legends are stories passed down for generations, but are often presented as history. While not always entirely true, legends play an important role in politics. Legends reveal a desire to be culturally connected to our fellow citizens and to a larger entity, and they also tell us a great deal about who we want to be.

So somewhere between legend and reality lies the Texas of today. Texas simultaneously projects the most rustic frontier image while providing a home for many of the most innovative businesses in the world. The gap between the state's political heritage and future was never more evident than when Governor Rick Perry opened his 2006 reelection bid with an ad that depicted longhorn cattle being herded down a city street lined with modern skyscrapers. This leaves our elected officials acting like cowboys while thinking like engineers.

This chapter charts the contours of this gap, by first looking at Texas history and geography with an eye toward the traditions and transformations that have shaped the state's politics. We examine the legends behind Texas politics and compare ourselves to some other U.S. states. Then we conclude the chapter by focusing on the state of Texas today—its people, economy, culture.

As you read the chapter, think about the following questions:

★ What role do legends play in the political culture of Texas?
★ How does Texas's size affect its political institutions?
★ To what extent do changing demographics and economic diversification shape the state of Texas?
★ Why is there a tension between the rapidly changing nature of Texas and Texas's legends?

Texas Geography

he land mass of Texas defines the state's image as much as it determined the course of its history. With a land area totaling 263,513 square miles it is the second largest state, behind Alaska's 663,276 square miles. From east to west the state spans 773 miles and 801 miles from north to south. The 785-mile drive from Marshall to El Paso takes a traveler from the Piney Woods of East Texas to the arid desert of West Texas. Driving the 900 miles north from Brownsville to

Texline takes you from the border of Mexico and the Gulf of Mexico to the borders of Oklahoma and New Mexico. The Texas Gulf Coast consists of shoreline and marshy areas while the Trans-Pecos region includes the arid desert of the Big Bend and Guadalupe Peak, the highest point in Texas at 8,749 feet.

Texas runs the full gamut from urban to rural. Texas's most populous county, Harris County, which contains Houston, had 3,866,207 residents in 2006, making it more populous than almost half of the states in the United States. Texas also has some of the nation's least populated counties, with Loving County's 677 square miles in the Panhandle occupied by only sixty residents. Texas has eight counties with populations under 1,000 and about one-third (eighty-eight) of Texas counties have populations under 10,000.

Texas's size creates more than bragging rights. V. O. Key, a native Texan and one of the founders of modern political science, pointed out that the geographic size of the state has limited the face-to-face interactions needed to develop closely-knit political organizations. While this helped inoculate Texas from the large party machines that corrupted politics in many places in the nineteenth century, it has also inhibited the formation of beneficial groups that would bring together more benevolent forces from across the state.

The state's size makes campaigning expensive for candidates trying to win votes statewide and has left the state's politicians more dependent on those capable of financing a statewide campaign. The sheer size of the state has also rewarded a dramatic style. As V. O. Key observed after surveying the electoral history of his home state, "Attention-getting antics substituted for organized politics." [1] In the absence of closely-knit state political networks, and given Texans' fondness for independence, the path to power for the political "outsider" may be a little bit easier. The ability to quickly grab the imagination of voters has given Texas politics a colorful cast of characters rivaled by few other places. Texas's political candidates are often larger than life and while change has been a constant in Texas politics, subtlety is often lacking.

Size has contributed to the state's mentality in other ways. With its seemingly endless supply of land, Texas represents limitless potential to many. At the same time, Texas offers an escape, thus reinforcing a sense of independence and freedom. With Texans dispersed all over the state, history and legends become even more important. The vast geographic distances and the differences in human geography cause many to wonder what makes all these people from all these places into such fiercely loyal Texans. What binds this state so tightly is its history. As John Steinbeck wrote, "there is no physical or geographical unity in Texas. Its unity lies in the mind." [2]

While Texas's history unites its citizens, it also represents a long string of transitions that often brought conflict between new and old ways. As we will see, the Texas political system has often resisted the needs and wishes of new arrivals because those that came before were reluctant to give up the power they earned or fought for. While not unique to this state, Texas history may most vividly demonstrate the hard road of change.

History: The Birth of Texas Traditions

he first wave of change began about 12,000 years ago, when humans, who had drifted across the Bering Strait land bridge into North America starting 20,000 years ago, eventually found their way into Texas. These earliest

Map 1: State of Texas

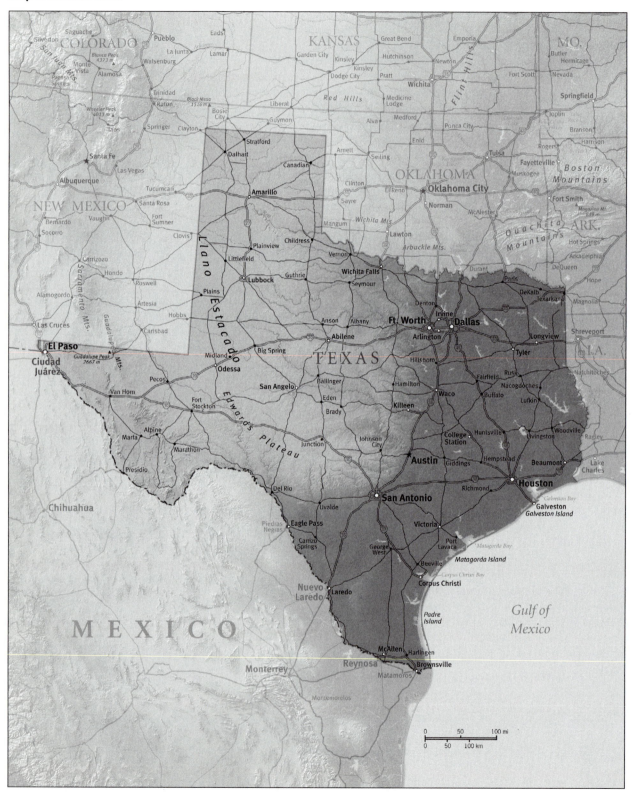

Texans hunted mammoths before these large animals became extinct. Later, bison became a primary food source in the grassy plains that covered present-day West Texas. As changes in the climate began to warm the plains, the land could no longer support the large mammals that the predominantly hunting tribes depended on and hunter-gatherer tribes became more prevalent.

As with native people from other parts of the continent, the native American tribes of Texas were diverse. About 1,500 years ago, the Caddo people developed agricultural tools and practices that gave them a more stable food supply, less need to roam, and more time to form a society with social classes and trading relations with other tribes. By 1500 an estimated 200,000 Caddos inhabited a society extensive enough to lead some to call them the "Romans of Texas."[3] Along the Gulf Coast the Karankawa tribe relied on fish and shellfish for much of their diet. While they have been called cannibals, the Karankawas ate only their enemies and were so shocked to learn that the Spanish survivors of the Narváez Expedition had cannibalized each other that some Karankawas expressed regret for not killing the Spanish explorers when they first came ashore.[4] Coahuiltecan tribes roamed the area southwest of the Karankawas, surviving on a diverse diet of whatever they could gather or catch. As a result of moving about the prairies in small hunter-gatherer bands, these tribes lacked the cohesive society that bound tribes like the Caddos. In contrast, the Apaches—who inhabited parts of what would become the Texas Panhandle—lived in large, extended families in a peaceful and well-ordered society.

Christopher Columbus's first voyage brought great change to the Texas region as the Spanish empire in America began to take root in the Caribbean, Central America, and the Southwest. As would many others after them, the conquistadores Álvar Núñez Cabeza de Vaca and later Hernando Cortéz visited the region seeking wealth. One of the most significant instruments of change the Spanish brought with them was the horse. Even though the Spanish forces would never be a large enough presence to transform the region, the horses they brought would change Indian society by giving some tribes the means to move their camps more quickly and become more effective hunters and warriors.

The French, led by René-Robert Cavelier and Sieur de La Salle, managed only a brief presence in Texas. La Salle who, in the words of one historian, had "the sort of personality and behavior that led many to question his mental stability"[5] had an ambitious plan to build a series of posts down the Mississippi River to the Gulf of Mexico, claim all of the land drained by the Mississippi, and name it Louisiana in honor of the French king Louis XIV. La Salle's incursions into Texas failed and La Salle himself would be killed in an ambush. However, while the French settlements failed, La Salle's adventure caused the Spanish to increase their settlement of East Texas to counter any future French arrivals.

Although relative newcomers themselves, the Spanish, as the Indian tribes before them, were suspicious of the motives of new arrivals and sought to bar outsiders as they struggled to find enough of their own people to settle the area. For much of the eighteenth century, the Spanish continued to gradually establish themselves in Texas through a system of missions and presidios (forts). The missions were designed to bring the Indians to God while pushing the French out. Native Americans in the area showed little interest in converting to Catholicism, and the Spanish had to supplement their religious outposts with the presidios. Given the high costs of maintaining these forts, Spanish investments in the area proved inadequate and by the 1790s there were fewer than 3,200 Spanish-speaking people in Texas.

While not as famous as the Alamo, the San José y San Miguel de Aguayo Mission is regarded by many observers as the "Queen of the Missions" because it is the most complete and beautiful of the five Spanish missions in San Antonio.

Building a border wall to keep immigrants out of Spanish territory was out of the question, but Spanish officials declared in 1795 that local officials should take "the utmost care to prevent the passage to this kingdom of persons from the United States of America."[6] In one of the first recorded verbal assaults on immigrants, one Spanish official colorfully warned that the American immigrants "are not and will not be anything but crows to pick out our eyes."[7]

Despite the efforts of Spanish officials, the tides of change proved too strong to resist and eventually the Spanish government resorted to giving citizens of the United States land grants to settle in Louisiana (before the territory was acquired by France in 1800). While recruiting Anglo settlers from the United States to serve as a buffer against intrusion by the U.S. government seems self-defeating, the Spanish government had little choice. Many in Spain realized that closing off Texas was futile and Spanish officials hoped that abandoning Florida and negotiating the Adams-Onís treaty of 1819 to establish clear boundaries between Spanish and U.S. claims would divert American interests away from Texas long enough to build a strong Spanish presence in Texas.

The Spanish legacy in Texas can be seen on any Texas map, where every major river in Texas except the Red River bears a Spanish name. Spanish rule also left a different kind of mark as a result of a 1778 Spanish proclamation that all unbranded cattle became property of the King, leading to the practice of branding to identify cattle.[8]

The roots of the organized Anglo settlement of Texas in the early nineteenth century can be traced to the last years of Spanish rule in Texas. A Missouri resident, Moses Austin, visited Texas in 1820 in hopes of winning the legal right to form colonies in the area. Unfortunately, the return trip took its toll on Austin after his horses were stolen, and Austin soon died after returning to Missouri. Before he died he expressed the hope that his son Stephen would carry on the endeavor. Stephen F. Austin originally had little interest in serving as an *empresario* (an entrepreneur that made money colonizing areas) and Texas initially was a somewhat unwanted inheritance before he came to see the potential of the land and warmed to the task.

Empresario

an entrepreneur who made money colonizing areas of the Mexican territories.

Mexican Independence

The next round of change began on September 16 (still celebrated by many Tejanos—Texans of Mexican origin—as Diez y Seis de Septiembre) when Father Miguel Hidalgo y Costilla launched the Mexican War of Independence against Spain through his revolutionary "Call of Hidalgo" (also known as the "Grito de Dolores"), which called for endowing those born in the New World with the same rights as those born in Europe. Mexican independence would end Spanish control of Texas, but it did not end the desire of local authorities to stop the growing trickle of immigrants from the United States. The fledgling Mexican government eventually approved Stephen F. Austin's colonization plan in the hope that legal settlers brought by authorized empresarios like Austin would become loyal to the Mexican government rather than their U.S. roots.

By 1824 Austin had assembled the 300 families allowed under his initial contract and began to settle in Texas. While these colonists suffered more than their share of mishaps, Austin's colonies prospered so much that he received four additional contracts to bring settlers over the next seven years. However, the same opportunities that drew legal settlers to the colonies of Austin and other empresarios also drew illegal immigrants unwilling to deal with the encumbrance of law. Soon Austin and other empresarios found themselves laboring to protect their legal colonies from a flood of illegal squatters.

By the 1830s there were about 10,000 Anglo settlers in Texas. Some came to Texas hoping to make money quickly in land speculation, but most were subsistence farmers looking for a chance to own their own land and control their own destiny. Some were fleeing financial ruin brought on by the Panic of 1819 in the United States while other settlers came to Texas fleeing justice in American states. Tensions between the Anglos and the Mexican government developed because of differences in political culture and the Mexican government's insistence on Spanish as the official language. In addition, many of these settlers were Protestants who resented the Mexican government's requirement that they become Catholics. Finally, many of these southern settlers wanted to use their land to produce cotton, a cash crop that depended heavily on the labor of the approximately 1,000 slaves they owned, creating a conflict with the Mexican government's opposition to slavery. The risk of losing their slaves kept many wealthy southern plantation owners from moving into Texas.

The Texas Revolution

The tension between the Mexican government and the Anglo settlers eventually built to the most dramatic political transformation—revolution. Initially, Anglo settlers were divided on the issues of revolution and independence. Stephen F. Austin and many of the established settlers advocated a moderate course, asking for separate statehood within the Mexican nation. Mexico's constitution required that Texas have a population of 80,000 before becoming a state, a number far greater than the 30,000 who inhabited the area at the time. During the early 1830s the Mexican government granted some of the Anglos' other requests: the right to trial by jury and the official use of the English language. Despite these concessions, many Anglos remained unhappy.

Tejanos were in a difficult position. In the 1820s about 4,000 Tejanos inhabited the region, including many former soldiers stationed in the area who remained after leaving military service. Many Tejanos had become community leaders and owned large ranches. While Anglo settlers were unhappy about life under the Mexican government, Tejanos were uneasy about the possibility of living under the rule of Anglo settlers, many of whom considered Mexicans and their culture to be inferior. At the same time, Tejanos shared the concerns of Anglo settlers who did not want a central government in Mexico City controlling their fate and hampering their economic development.

The politics of the independence movement was often chaotic. As Mexican president Santa Anna became less flexible toward the Texans and sent troops to enforce his laws, the Texans began to mobilize politically, calling for a meeting to organize their response. They termed their meeting a "Consultation" of the people of Texas to avoid drawing the ire of Mexican officials with the label "convention," which implied the authority to rewrite the constitution. When the Consultation assembled on

November 1, and November 13, 1835, it passed the Organic Law creating a government with a governor, lieutenant governor, and a General Council with representatives for each geographic district. Henry Smith, the leader of the more radical group favoring immediate independence, was elected governor by a 30–22 vote, beating out Stephen F. Austin who clung to a more moderate course. Perhaps Texans should have worried—Smith had married two sisters only to be widowed twice before marrying the third sister who was a twin of his second wife. Smith's political relationships died even more quickly than his romantic relationships as Smith resisted compromise and suspended the General Council. Meanwhile, the council impeached him, leaving the government paralyzed.

The military was hamstrung because the council created a regular army under the command of Sam Houston without formally bringing the volunteers already in the field under Houston's command. The volunteers were notorious for their autonomy and lack of discipline, as Austin would find out on November 23 when he ordered them to attack Béxar only to have his order refused.

Voters on February 1 elected representatives to serve as delegates to a new convention to begin deliberations on March 1, 1836. Shunning most of the men who had served in the earlier Consultation and General Council, Texans chose younger men, many of whom were newcomers, as nearly half of the fifty-nine delegates had lived in Texas less than two years. They met in the town of Washington (on the Brazos River) in part because local business owners provided a building without charge. There the delegates adopted without debate a Declaration of Independence, drafted by George C. Childress, who had been in Texas for less than eight months. The convention continued meeting until March 17 and the completion of the Constitution of the Republic of Texas. The constitution protected slavery and permitted a freed slave to live in Texas only with the permission of the Texas Legislature. A government ad interim, composed of the members of the constitutional convention, was empowered to run the affairs of the state. One of the first orders of business was the election of David G. Burnet as Texas's first president. For vice president the convention selected Lorenzo de Zavala who had served as Mexican minister to Paris under Santa Anna but left his post when Santa Anna claimed dictatorial powers in 1835.

While united by their struggle against the Mexican government, the revolutionary leaders of Texas often fought among themselves even after independence was won. After Houston's ankle was shattered in the Battle of San Jacinto on April 21, 1836, President Burnet denied the general permission to leave for New Orleans to seek medical treatment. Burnet eventually relented when the boat's captain refused to take anyone if he was not allowed to take Houston.

The Republic of Texas

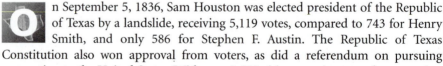n September 5, 1836, Sam Houston was elected president of the Republic of Texas by a landslide, receiving 5,119 votes, compared to 743 for Henry Smith, and only 586 for Stephen F. Austin. The Republic of Texas Constitution also won approval from voters, as did a referendum on pursuing annexation to the United States. With over 3,000 citizens voting to seek annexation and with fewer than 100 objecting, Texas's interest in joining the United States would be clear from its first day of independence.

The government was temporarily located in Columbia, but would soon move to a new town located on Buffalo Bayou that backers, much to the new president's

Sam Houston

By the time he became a Texan and led Texas to independence, Sam Houston had gone through two wives and lots of alcohol and was, in the words of Texas historian James L. Haley, "considered in respectable circles as unsavory as he was colorful."[i] However, no one better reflects the reality that the greatness of Texas's legends can be found in less-than-perfect people, as Houston guided Texas through some of its most dramatic transitions.

In his youth Houston generally preferred sneaking away to live among the Indians to working in the family business. Houston distinguished himself during the War of 1812, serving bravely and winning the admiration of General Andrew Jackson. Houston followed Jackson, his new mentor, into politics and was sometimes mentioned as a successor to President Jackson. However, his first marriage abruptly ended in 1827 in the middle of his term as governor of Tennessee and just two months after his wedding. His marriage over and his political career in ruins, Houston went to live again among the Cherokees. During this time he took a Cherokee wife, without entering into a formal Christian marriage. Over time Houston's state of mind deteriorated and his Indian hosts eventually stripped him of his original Indian name ("The Raven") and began to call him Oo-tse-tee Ar-dee-tah-skee ("The Big Drunk").[ii] After abandoning his second wife and returning to public life in America, Houston narrowly avoided jail after assaulting a member of Congress who had insulted his integrity. Brought before Congress to face charges, Houston delivered an impassioned defense on his own behalf, allegedly because his lawyer, Francis Scott Key, was too hungover to speak.

During the Texas Revolution gossips frequently attributed Houston's disappearances to drinking binges rather than military missions. Some questioned his bravery and military leadership during the war. Many Texans wanted Houston to turn and fight the Mexican Army sooner, despite Houston's protest that his troops were undertrained and outnumbered. While most Texans sided with Houston after his victory at San Jacinto, criticisms of his conduct of the war would reappear in political campaigns for the rest of his career.

After leading Texas through the Revolution, Houston continued to play a major role in the state's changes while serving as Texas's first president during its years as an independent nation. Houston struggled in the years after the Texas Revolution to protect the Tejanos who had served alongside him during the war. Similarly, his years among the Cherokees and his continued fondness for them left him at odds with many Anglos who preferred to see Native Americans driven off or killed.

After playing a central role in winning Texas's entry into the United States, Houston's final political act would be the struggle to keep Texas from seceding and joining the Confederacy. Houston disliked slavery and defied state law by freeing his own slaves. He had been one of few southern senators to speak out against slavery, a sentiment that led the Texas Legislature to vote against his return to the Senate. His final departure from politics came when he refused to support the secession of Texas in the American Civil War and, as a result, was forced by the legislature to resign his governorship. If Texans had followed Houston's leadership, the lives of many Texas soldiers would have been saved and the state spared post–war Reconstruction.

Houston finally settled down after marrying his third wife and finding redemption, but he never denied his faults. When asked if his sins had been washed away at his river baptism, Houston joked, "I hope so. But if they were all washed away, the Lord help the fish down below."[iii]

However numerous his sins, Houston's principles make him a much more heroic historical figure than many of his more sober peers. From the moment Houston arrived in Texas he became a central figure in the transformation of the state and for thirty years he guided Texas through its most turbulent times. While Houston might not be able to be elected today, he did more to shape modern Texas than any other person.

i. James L. Haley, *Passionate Nation: The Epic History of Texas* (New York: Free Press, 2006) 107.
ii. James E. Crisp, *Sleuthing the Alamo: Davy Crockett's Last Stand and Other Mysteries of the Texas Revolution* (New York: Oxford University Press, 2004) 29.
iii. Haley, *Passionate Nation*, 277.

delight, suggested be named Houston. The new capital city, like much of the republic, was improvised; the legislature met in an unfinished capitol building with tree branches forming the roof.

While the period of Texas independence was relatively brief, it was neither simple nor quiet. The population of Texas doubled. Just after the revolution Texas had about 30,000 Anglos, 5,000 black slaves, 3,470 Tejanos, and 14,500 Indians. By 1847 the "white" population (including 12,000 to 14,000 persons of Mexican descent) had soared to 102,961 with 38,753 slaves, and 295 freed blacks.

Change continued during Texas's days of independence. While the Republic's second president, Mirabeau B. Lamar, helped develop the Texas education system, his administration proved disastrous for the Indian tribes living in Texas. Houston had worked to build friendships with Texas's tribes, but Lamar sought to eradicate them. During the three years of the Lamar administration, the Republic of Texas's debt skyrocketed from two to seven million dollars and the value of its currency plummeted. Lamar opposed annexation by the United States at a time when the United States was expressing doubts of its own. Sam Houston returned to the presidency only after a bruising political battle. Once back in office, Houston helped make peace with the Indians and brought fiscal sanity back to government, spending one-tenth of what Lamar had.

The path to statehood would not be as simple as Houston hoped. In the United States Northern interests in the U.S. Congress, led by John Quincy Adams, balked at bringing another slave state into the nation. Houston managed to stir U.S. interest by making overtures toward European powers—a course of action designed to make the United States jealous and wary of possible foreign intervention so close to its borders. As threats from Mexico continued into the 1840s, Texas turned to England and France for help in obtaining the release of Texas soldiers imprisoned in Mexican jails. Sam Houston also positioned Texas for future bargaining by claiming for the Republic land reaching west and north as far as Wyoming, including portions of the Santa Fe Trail used for trade between the United States and Mexico. The legislature passed a bill that claimed all the land south of the forty-second parallel and west of Texas to the Pacific, as well as portions of Mexico, a claim that would have made Texas larger than the United States at the time.

Texas Statehood

The issue of annexation of Texas eventually became a central issue in the 1844 U.S. presidential election when James K. Polk, the candidate backed by Andrew Jackson, campaigned for the acquisition of Texas. Texas's expansive claim to territory was resolved when Henry Clay crafted a compromise that got Texas to accept its present borders in return for a payment of $10 million. While the joint resolution inviting Texas to join the United States passed the U.S. House easily, it barely squeaked through the Senate, 27 to 25. John Quincy Adams and Texas's opponents made one final last-ditch effort to stop admission of Texas by asserting that the admission of Texas through a joint resolution was unconstitutional because that method of admission was not spelled out in the U.S. Constitution.

Texas called a convention for July 4, 1845, to approve annexation and draft a constitution that accommodated Texas's new role as a U.S. state. The only vote in the Texas Legislature against entering the United States came from a Richard Bache, who allegedly voted against annexation because he had come to Texas to escape his ex-wife and did not care to live in the same country with her again.[9] Texas was able to retain ownership of its public lands, a term of annexation that other new states did not enjoy. The U.S. Congress accepted the state's new constitution in December and President Polk signed the bill on December 29, 1845. Texas formally entered statehood on February 19, 1846.

An interesting part of the residual folklore of Texas history is the notion that the state holds the right to secede, and if it so chooses, reenter the United States as five separate states. The origins of this folklore come from a compromise designed to overcome objections in the U.S. Congress to the original annexation of Texas. The joint resolution that admitted Texas to the Union provided that Texas could be divided into as many as five states. New states north or west of the Missouri Compromise lines would be free, and in those states south of the compromise lines, a popular vote would determine the legality of slavery. However, the power to create new states ultimately rested with the U.S. Congress and the right to divide was not reserved to Texas.

J. Pinckney Henderson earned the honor of serving at Texas's first governor after winning election by a large margin. Texas sent Sam Houston and Thomas Jefferson Rusk to serve as the state's first two U.S. senators. Texas's only Jewish member of Congress for 130 years was among its first: David Kaufman of Nacogdoches, a Philadelphia-born Jew who had worked as a lawyer in Mississippi before coming to Texas, distinguishing himself as an Indian fighter, and then serving two terms as the speaker of the Republic of Texas's legislature. Kaufman was only the second Jewish member of the U.S. House, taking office the year after Lewis C. Levin became the nation's first Jewish representative in 1845. Passed over in the selection of Texas's first congressional delegation was Anson Jones, who had been sworn in as president of Texas on December 9, 1844. Jones was embittered by this perceived slight and set about putting together his own volume of the history of the Republic, published a year after Jones shot himself on the steps of the old capitol in Houston.

Americans who had resisted admission of Texas for fear of provoking war with Mexico soon saw those fears realized when fighting broke out in 1846. Many historians believe that U.S. president James K. Polk orchestrated the war by ordering General Zachary Taylor into territory near the mouth of the Rio Grande that Mexican officials claimed was part of Mexico. Mexico responded by declaring a defensive war on April 23, with the United States responding with its own declaration of war on May 13. The war ended after troops under the command of U.S. General Winfield Scott moved into Mexico City. The **Treaty of Guadalupe Hidalgo** was signed on February 2, 1848, recognizing the Rio Grande as the official boundary between the Texas and Mexico. While the treaty offered assurances that the rights of the Mexican citizens who suddenly found themselves citizens in America's new territory would be protected, this promise proved fragile.

The rapid population growth following Texas's annexation further transformed the state. However, not every group grew at an equal rate. Despite the general population surge, the Tejano population declined, and by the 1847 census the 8,000 Germans in Texas were the largest ethnic minority in the state which had a total population of about 142,000, including 40,000 slaves, and only 295 free people of color. Even though the Tejanos had fought for independence, many were forced to move to Mexico as the clash of Mexican and Anglo cultures intensified, and for one of the few times in its history Texas saw people moving away.

Treaty of Guadalupe Hidalgo signed on February 2, 1848, this agreement between the United States and Mexico ended the Mexican American War and recognized the Rio Grande as the boundary between Texas, now part of the United States, and Mexico.

Texas in the Confederacy

The rise of cotton farming in Texas increased the importance of slavery to the Texas economy as production of cotton grew from 40,000 bales in 1848 to 420,000 bales in 1860.[10] By 1860, Texans held 182,566 slaves, compared to the total population of 604,215.[11] While much of Texas was becoming dependent on slave labor, Sam Houston battled slavery, and in 1855 became one of the few southern members of Congress to publicly oppose it. Once again, Houston's personal popularity would be undone by an unpopular stand on the burning issue of the day. In 1857, two years before his term expired, the Texas Legislature voted to not return Houston to the Senate. Houston responded to the insult by running for governor in 1857. Over the course of this campaign, he traveled over 1,500 miles, visited forty-two cities, and gave endless speeches, many as long as four hours. Despite the effort, Houston lost the election to Hardin R. Runnels by a vote of 32,552 to 28,678. Houston's loss came in part from his association with the anti-immigrant "Know Nothing" party that hurt him with voters of Mexican and German ancestry who would otherwise have sympathized with his anti-slavery stance.

After serving out the remainder of his Senate term, Houston left the U.S. Senate in 1859 to once again run for governor, hoping that when the South seceded from the Union, he could lead Texas back into becoming a separate nation. Houston defeated Runnels 33,375 to 27,500. However, over the objections of Governor Houston, a convention on February 1, 1861, voted overwhelmingly in favor of secession and a few weeks later, voters statewide approved a secession ordinance by a three to one margin. The Secession Convention approved a requirement that all state officers swear an oath of loyalty to the Confederacy. After Houston refused to take the oath, the governor's office was declared vacant.

The Confederate regime in Texas was a disaster for several groups. Not only were free blacks victimized, Germans were targeted because of their opposition to slavery. Tejanos saw their land seized and many chose to align themselves with the Union, with some enlisting and becoming the heart of the Union's Second Cavalry while others fought as pro-Union guerrillas. Many pro-Union Anglos were forced to flee the state. William Marsh Rice, whose wealth would one day endow Rice University, had to leave Houston and move his businesses to Matamoros in Mexico.

Reconstruction in Texas

Northern rule arrived with the end of the Civil War on June 19, 1865, when Union forces under General Gordon Granger arrived in Galveston bringing a proclamation ending slavery in Texas. Thus, June 19 became "Juneteenth," the day in which the slaves in Texas were actually freed, despite Lincoln having signed the Emancipation Proclamation in January 1863. While many of the transformations in Texas history were marked by new citizens coming in from outside the state, the end of slavery meant that former slaves found themselves as new citizens in their old state. Joining with a small number of Anglo Republicans, African Americans helped bring about change in the state by electing Republicans to statewide offices and constitutional conventions.

Freedom proved a mixed blessing for the "freedmen." While they might technically be free, they were far from social equals and they had to endure intimidation and exploitation. State law would not recognize any marriage involving African

American Texans until 1869. While the Freedmen's Bureau was created to help former slaves, the bureau's efforts were sometimes limited by administrators who may have supported the end of slavery while doubting the goal of racial equality. Texas, like other southern states, passed "Black Codes" designed to limit the rights of the former slaves. In Texas, any person with one-eighth or more of Negro blood could not serve on a jury or vote. With local law enforcement often in the hands of Confederate sympathizers, African Americans relied on Union troops for protection. As elsewhere in the former Confederate states, the Ku Klux Klan became a vehicle for terrorizing former slaves and those sympathetic to their cause, as well as "carpetbaggers" (people from the North who came south to assist or cash in on Reconstruction) and "scalawags" (Republicans of local origins).

In January 1866, Texans elected delegates to a convention to draft a new state constitution that would win the state readmission into the United States. However, the Texas Legislature seemed to have missed the news that the South lost the war and refused to ratify the Thirteenth Amendment (ending slavery) and Fourteenth Amendment (guaranteeing equal rights) and instead drafted a framework of laws limiting the rights of freed slaves. The Constitution of 1866 failed to meet the demands of the "Radical Republicans" who had won control of the U.S. Congress in the 1866 election. While much has been made of the influx of "carpetbaggers," the political transition in Texas resulted less from the influx of outsiders from the Northeast than it did from freed slaves gaining the right to vote when supporters of the Confederacy lost their right to vote or hold office after Congress passed the Second Reconstruction Act. With most white Democrats purged from office and voting lists, the next constitutional convention was dominated by Republicans who accounted for seventy-eight of the ninety delegates. The resulting Constitution of 1869 contained many provisions granting rights to freed slaves that made it unpopular with the secessionists: the rights to vote, run for office, serve on juries, testify in court against whites, and attend public schools.

The End of Reconstruction and Rise of the "Redeemers"

exas politics was transformed again when Reconstruction ended and more Confederate sympathizers were allowed to vote. The Democrats (the party of the white Confederate sympathizers) won control of the legislature in the election of 1872. Like the emancipation of the slaves, this transformation of Texas politics did not come from new Texans, but resulted from the renewal of citizenship of old citizens. Republican E. J. Davis was widely despised by Democrats who considered him at best a symbol of northern oppression after the war, and at worst incredibly corrupt. Once in control of Texas government, the Democrats proclaimed themselves "Redeemers" and removed the last remnants of Republican rule. On August 2, 1875, the Texas Legislature authorized a new constitutional convention and elected three delegates each from the state's thirty senatorial districts. None of the ninety members of the 1875 convention had been members of the convention that drafted the 1869 constitution and the partisan composition was dramatically different. Seventy-five members were Democrats while only fifteen were Republicans. At least forty were members of the Patrons of Husbandry, or "the Grange," an economic and political organization of farmers. Voters ratified the constitution on February 15, 1876, by a vote of 136,606 to 56,652.

The rise of the Redeemers and the impact of the Grange are especially important transitions in Texas politics, since the constitution of this era would remain in force long after the politics and politicians responsible for it had vanished. Texas would continue to change and grow, but the Texas Constitution has not been replaced and has only been mended with piecemeal changes through individual amendments allowing only minor alterations to the basic design of 1876. The twenty-five years after the Civil War spawned the cowboy imagery that Texans still relish. It was during this brief period of frontier that Texas saw large ranches tended by rugged cowboys pushing large herds of cattle. Even then, the image of Texas as the "Old West" was based on the lives of only a small number of Texans living at the time. Although Texans hold the legend of the cowboy in high esteem, actual cowboys found life much less glamorous. Most were young. About one-third were Hispanic or African American. The ranch owners generally regarded these cowboys as common laborers on horseback and the men who rode the range and drove the cattle were paid less than the trail cooks.[12] By the 1890s the fabled trail drives would end, finished by drought, quarantines, barbed-wire fencing across the open range, and competition from the railroads.

The state government encouraged immigration in the last half of the nineteenth century to help settle and populate the western part of the state and help drive off Indian tribes. Some state officials saw immigration as a means of encouraging white settlers and farmers to counteract the increase in former slaves becoming sharecroppers. Germans flooded into Texas, going from 41,000 in 1870 to 125,262 in 1890, at a time when Texans of Mexican ancestry numbered only 105,193. While Texas west of Austin may have resembled the Wild West, most Texans resided in the eastern portion of the state, which resembled the "New South" that was emerging elsewhere out of the former Confederate states and was characterized by railroad networks and urbanized cities like Dallas.

Although glamorized in movies and television shows today, cowboys, or *vaqueros,* led a hard life and were often shunned by civilized society.

Era of Reform

s Texas transitioned from the farming and ranching of the nineteenth century to the industrial and oil economy of the twentieth century, the state began to struggle with the limits of the Constitution of 1876. In 1890 Attorney General James Stephen Hogg decided that his office lacked the resources to adequately enforce regulations on the state's railroads. Hogg's call for the creation of a railroad commission would become a centerpiece of his campaign for governor. The railroads labeled Hogg "communistic," but his reforms proved popular and his election represented the first stirrings of the reform movement in Texas. The creation of the Texas Railroad Commission was proclaimed as a way to produce fair competition, but the commission was often used to restrict out-of-state railroads and protect Texas-based businesses from international competitors.

Frustrated by the lack of responsiveness from the Democrats to their needs, farmers organized the People's Party, more commonly known as the Populist Party. While the populists were short-lived, their call for radical reforms like public ownership of the railroads and their willingness to reach out to black voters rattled the political order. After the populists were absorbed into the Democratic Party, the progressives would take up the role of reform party. In contrast to the populists' narrow base in agricultural communities, the progressives would emerge in the 1890s as a broader reform movement attacking both the railroads that bedeviled the farmers and the big industries that challenged urban labor.

While progressive candidates for governor won elections, their legislative victories would be limited. Thomas Campbell won the governorship in the election of 1906 only to see much of his progressive agenda hijacked or sidetracked by the legislature. Most crucially, Campbell was unable to win approval of statewide referendum and recall. Legislation requiring that insurance companies invest 75 percent of their premiums in Texas did change the way insurance companies operated, but mainly benefited Texas businesses and drove foreign insurers from the state.

The progressive movement in Texas would be consumed by the alcohol prohibition issue, in part because Texas politics lacked the large corporations and big city political machines that energized the efforts of progressives in the north. Much of the prohibitionists' efforts took place at the local level, especially winning local option elections to outlaw drinking. In 1891 the Texas Legislature put a prohibitionist constitutional amendment before the state's voters. The campaign was intense and voters turned out at more than twice the rate they had in the last gubernatorial election and they narrowly rejected the amendment by a 237,393 to 231,096 vote.

While the emergence of a new Texas early in the twentieth century and the reforms of the progressive movement captured the attention of many voters, others remained fixated on the old issues of race and the Civil War. In 1912 Governor Oscar Branch Colquitt struggled in his reelection bid because he had criticized the state textbook board for rejecting a history book because it contained a photograph of Abraham Lincoln. Meanwhile, voters flocked to see Colquitt's opponent William Ramsay who played upon southern sentiments in his speeches and had bands play "Dixie" during campaign events. Prohibition was a hotly contested issue on its own and reflected old racial hatreds as alcohol was portrayed as a vice of the Germans and Mexicans.

No one better reflects the failures of Texas progressives to produce reform in Texas than James E. "Pa" Ferguson. While the rest of the Texas political system obsessed over prohibition, "Farmer Jim" shunned the issue and instead won office with promises of capping how much rent tenant farmers could be charged by their landlords. Ferguson's tenant farmer law would be ruled unconstitutional but he remained a hero to the state's small farmers. Ferguson could be charming, but his politics were often petty. For example, he used appointments to the board of Prairie View Normal and Industrial College to remove principal Edward Blackshear who had supported a political rival. Ferguson took his personal political fight to the University of Texas when he demanded the removal of William J. Battle, the president of the university. When asked his reason for wanting Battle's removal, Ferguson proclaimed, "I don't have to give any reason. I am Governor of the State of Texas." [13] Later, Ferguson vetoed appropriations for the university. When Ferguson was elected to a second term in 1916, his battle with the university and its allies grew into a conflict that would bring him down. On July 23, 1917, the Speaker of the Texas House called for a special session to consider impeachment, and in August the Texas House voted on twenty-one articles of impeachment, including charges dealing with Ferguson's personal finances, especially bank loans. The Senate found him guilty on ten charges, primarily those dealing with his finances. While impeachment removed Ferguson from the governor's office and disqualified him from holding other public office, Texas was not so easily rid of Ferguson's influence.

The departure of Ferguson made passing prohibition easier and the presence of military training camps in Texas led to the argument that patriotism required that the state protect young recruits from liquor. Initially, the Texas Legislature simply made it illegal to sell alcohol within ten miles of a military base. The next year, in May 1919, Texas voters approved an amendment to the Texas Constitution that brought prohibition to Texas a year before it came into effect nationwide.

As with other states, prohibition in Texas proved to be unworkable as many Texans refused to give up alcohol. The legislature contributed to the failure of the initiative by providing very little funding for the enforcement necessary to make prohibition a success. Organized crime thrived on the revenue that illegal alcohol distribution and sales brought and allegedly worked with prohibitionists to keep alcohol illegal. During prohibition over 20 percent of all arrests in the state were related to prohibition. [14] Galveston became a major center for liquor smuggling as foreign ships anchored along "Rum Row," a line just beyond U.S. territorial waters where boats dropped anchor to distribute alcohol just out of the reach of American law.

While voters were approving prohibition, they also rejected an amendment that would have embraced the progressive reform of allowing women to vote in all elections. Some of the resistance was based solely on gender considerations, but some voters believed that granting equal rights to women would open the door to "Negro rule" and socialism.

Texas changed economically during this period, but this was a flood of oil, not new citizens. While the presence of oil in Texas had been noted since Spanish explorers used natural tar seeps to patch their boats, oil's impact on Texas would not be fully realized for centuries. A few wells were drilled in Texas in the 1890s, but the state lacked the refinery capacity to make use of the oil. After the first refinery was built in Texas, interest in oil exploration increased, but Texas was still a minor producer. That would change in 1901 when the Spindletop oil rig near Beaumont hit oil and gas, eventually producing 100,000 barrels of oil a day. Investors began streaming into Texas in search of oil and by 1928 Texas led the nation in oil production and provided 20 percent of the world's oil. By 1929 oil had replaced "King Cotton" as the largest part of the Texas economy.

Just as oil investors transformed much of the Texas countryside and economy, oil revenues had a huge impact on Texas government, contributing almost six million dollars to state accounts by 1929 and reducing the need for other state taxes. Texas's other major business was lumber, which grew dramatically early in the twentieth century, eventually topping 2.25 billion board feet in 1907 before overcutting slowed production. Highway construction boomed in Texas, and by the end of the 1920s Texas had almost 19,000 miles of highway. Fruit trees were introduced into South Texas, providing a new segment of the economy and planting the seeds for future immigration as seasonal, migratory labor was needed to harvest these fruits. By the 1920s Texas was showing signs of a strong, diverse economy, a situation that would be undone by the Great Depression.

The Great Depression and the New Deal in Texas

y the late 1920s, Texans were beginning to show a little independence from the Democratic Party. The state went for a Republican presidential candidate for the first time in 1928 when Texans shunned Democrat Al Smith, a Catholic New Yorker who drank. However, many Texans regretted their votes for Republican Herbert Hoover as Texas was hit hard by the Depression that many blamed on Hoover. As many as one-third of farmers in some areas were driven from their farms by the Depression and the Texas oil boom did little to spare the state. Overproduction of oil caused prices to fall as low as three cents a barrel. When the Railroad Commission refused to act to reduce overproduction, Governor Ross S. Sterling declared martial law and used National Guardsmen to shut down the East Texas oil fields. The desperation of the times brought about the repeal of prohibition, with "wets" arguing that repeal would aid recovery.

Burdened with a depressed economy and the overproduction of oil and cotton, Governor Sterling ran for reelection only to face the "Pa" Ferguson legacy in the form of his wife, Miriam "Ma" Ferguson, who trounced Sterling at the ballot box. While the Fergusons finally left the governor's office for the last time in 1935, it wouldn't be long until another character, Wilbert Lee "Pappy" O'Daniel, would usher in a new brand of populist politics. O'Daniel, a former sales manager for a flour mill, became known statewide as the host of a radio show that featured the music of the Light Crust Doughboys mixed with inspirational stories. Purportedly encouraged by listeners' letters urging him to run—although some suggested that wealthy business interests and a public relations expert had done the urging—O'Daniel declared his candidacy, proclaiming the Ten Commandments as his platform and the Golden Rule as his motto. He won the Democratic nomination without a runoff and, facing no real opposition, won the general election with 97 percent of the vote.

Although a colorful personality on the campaign trail, O'Daniel accomplished little of importance once in office, where he lacked the skill to work with legislators and tended to appoint less-than-qualified people to office. After winning reelection to the governorship in 1940, O'Daniel shifted his sights to Washington, D.C., when the death of Senator Morris Sheppard created a vacancy in 1941. O'Daniel won the special election to replace Sheppard, narrowly edging out a young ex-congressman named Lyndon Johnson in a disputed election.

Transitions to the Twenty-First Century

 exas spent the rest of the twentieth century in transition, shedding some old habits. Even with the landmark *Brown v. Board of Education* Supreme Court decision in 1954, Texas managed to resist desegregation, despite the Court's mandate of "all deliberate speed." Many Texas schools remained segregated well into the early 1970s when federal courts ordered Texas schools to desegregate. In 1954 Texas women belatedly won the right to serve on juries, but further progress toward equality was slow. In the 1960s only six women served in the Texas Legislature while the state failed to ratify the national Equal Rights Amendment (ERA). However, in 1972 voters approved an equal rights amendment to the state constitution and the legislature voted to ratify the ERA (although it would fail to get the required two-thirds states nationally). In 1975 Liz Cockrell was elected mayor of San Antonio, making her the first woman mayor of a major Texas city.

By the 1960s the partisan legacy of the Civil War was finally beginning to wear off. In 1961 John Tower was elected to the U.S. Senate, becoming the first Republican to win statewide office since Reconstruction. With the Republican Party showing signs of viability, many conservative Democrats shifted their allegiances to the Republican Party in state elections, after years of dividing their loyalty by voting for Republicans in national elections while supporting Democrats for state and local offices, a practice labeled **presidential republicanism.** An example is Governor John Connally, who, although friendly with Lyndon Johnson and elected governor as a Democrat, served in the cabinet of Republican president Richard Nixon and eventually sought the presidency as a Republican candidate. Texas did not get its first Republican governor until the 1978 election gave William P. Clements an upset victory. While Clements' narrow victory was the only statewide race the Republicans won that year, it was a significant step as Texas Republicans began to succeed on their own. Once conservatives saw that they could win elections under the Republican banner, they began to shift their party affiliation. By the 2000 elections, Republicans dominated, winning every statewide office on the ballot.

Texas Today

 or generations, waves of people have come to Texas to find new lives for themselves, while in the process bringing new life and new traditions to the state. Texas has always been the meeting ground for different ambitions and cultures. These cultures have clashed, blended, and evolved into a complicated modern state that can be a challenge to govern.

Political culture is the shared values and beliefs about the nature of the political world that give us a common language that we can use to discuss and debate ideas.[15] The **individualistic** **political culture** that many observers attribute to Texans holds that individuals are best left largely free of the intervention of community forces like government which should attempt only those things demanded by the people it is created to serve.[16] The individualistic subculture is most dominant in western parts of the state, where frontier living fostered independence and a general distrust of government. In contrast, the **traditionalistic** **political culture** sees government as having a limited role concerned with the preservation of the existing social order. The traditionalistic culture can be seen in parts of Texas like East Texas that were more heavily influenced by the traditions of the old South. Finally, the **moral-**

Presidential republicanism
the practice in the South of voting for Republicans in presidential elections, but voting for conservative Democrats in other races, a practice that continued until animosity over Reconstruction faded and the Republicans demonstrated their electability in the South.

Political culture
the shared values and beliefs of citizens about the nature of the political world that give the public a common language as a foundation to discuss and debate ideas.

Individualistic political culture
the idea that individuals are best left largely free of the intervention of community forces like government and that government should attempt only those things demanded by the people it is created to serve.

Traditionalistic political culture
the idea, most prevalent in parts of Texas most like the old South, that government has a limited role concerned with the preservation of the existing social order.

istic **political culture** sees the exercise of community forces as sometimes necessary to advance the public good. In this view government can be a positive force and citizens have a duty to participate. While this view can be found in many places in New England and other parts of the United States, it is rare in Texas.

The sheer size and diversity of Texas makes any discussion of political culture difficult. The idea of a political culture is further clouded by the growth of the state's urban areas, the influx of citizens from other states, and the rise of electronic communication. Traditional analyses of political culture in Texas have suggested that traditionalistic culture dominates in East Texas and weakens as you move west, with individualistic culture becoming more prominent as you reach the Panhandle. However, Mexican immigrants bring their own brand of traditionalistic culture, while immigrants from other states have often brought moralistic values into the state. Now national media and the Internet increasingly bring every point of view into Texas homes.

In reality, Texas does not have a single culture. The state is richly diverse and the mixing of cultures that come to Texas have produced new cultures unique to Texas. In no place is this unique mixture more evident than in Laredo's annual George Washington Birthday celebration, a month-long festival created in 1896 to bring an American-style celebration to unite the city's diverse roots. Today, Mexican food and colonial gowns both star in the celebration of the city's bicultural roots and Laredoans and their guests move easily from jalapeño eating contests to formal colonial pageants. In that sense Laredo perfectly embraces the tradition of change that defines Texas.

A Tradition of Change

exas has a tradition of change. For hundreds of years people left their old lives to build new ones in Texas, leaving behind them signs declaring, "Gone to Texas." While these generations of new Texans have brought different languages and culture, all of these arrivals brought one thing—change. Change brought by new arrivals has defined Texas since the 1500s when newly arrived Spanish explorers turned the Caddo word for friend (*techas*) into *Tejas,* a term describing the Caddo tribe.[17] In the centuries since, waves of people have come to Texas seeking opportunity and bringing change.

The changes brought by new arrivals have not always been welcome by the old Texans. When Coronado's expedition arrived and proudly proclaimed to the Zuñi Indians who lived in Texas that the tribe now enjoyed protection as subjects of the Spanish king, the Zuñis answered with a volley of arrows.[18] The Zuñis' arrows bounced off the Spanish armor and today, immigrants arriving from across the nation and around the world generally receive a better reception. Still, new arrivals have often been seen by many Texans as competitors and not partners in the state's future.

New arrivals have been a constant of Texas politics and the state's population increased about one-hundredfold since joining the United States, growing at an average of just over 40 percent each decade (see Table 1.1). Change is especially difficult for any political system that must meet the needs of a large, diverse, and ever-changing population. Political systems tend to represent the status quo—and established groups are inherently threatened by changes to the government's base of power. Because politics is, in the words of a classic definition, about who gets what, newcomers compete against the established residents, leaving the government to

Table 1.1 Population and Percentage of Growth in Texas since 1850

CENSUS	POPULATION	PERCENTAGE OF GROWTH
1850	212,592	
1860	604,215	184.2%
1870	818,579	35.5%
1880	1,591,749	94.5%
1890	2,235,527	40.4%
1900	3,048,710	36.4%
1910	3,896,542	27.8%
1920	4,663,228	19.7%
1930	5,824,715	24.9%
1940	6,414,824	10.1%
1950	7,711,194	20.2%
1960	9,579,677	24.2%
1970	11,196,730	16.9%
1980	14,229,191	27.1%
1990	16,986,510	19.4%
2000	20,851,820	22.8%
2005	22,859,968	9.6%

Source: U.S. Census Bureau.

resolve the conflict and determine who wins and who loses. Politics becomes a battle between the old and the new, and this battle is often repeated in Texas. The most dramatic example of such a battle was the Texas revolution that resulted when the Mexican officials refused to meet the needs of Anglo settlers.

A current snapshot of Texas reveals growing diversity. While about 83 percent of residents describe themselves as "white," this category includes both Anglos and Hispanics. Overall, Texas has about 50 percent whites of non-Hispanic origins, 35 percent of Hispanic origins, 12 percent African American, and about 3 percent Asian. The rural nature of Texas has been transformed, and today about 80 percent of Texans live in 1,210 cities or suburbs. Texas has three of the nation's ten largest cities—Houston, Dallas, and San Antonio—and five of the ten fastest growing counties in the United States.

Texans often quip they are the buckle in the "Bible Belt," reflecting on the fact that Texas is home to over 5 million evangelical Protestants. While the state's 4.5 million Baptists are a large presence, the state is also home to almost 4.4 million Catholics. In fact, Catholics outnumber Southern Baptists in every major urban area except Dallas-Fort Worth.[19] Texas also is the home to a large number of congregations ranging from the Amish to Hindus.

The Texas economy is as diverse as its people. While the state still has more farms (229,000 farms encompassing about 129,000,000 acres) and ranches than any other state, more Texans work in the information industry than agriculture. Ranching and farming remain the image of Texas, but residents today are also engaged in providing virtually every kind of product and service.

Even as Texas grapples with changes within its borders, it has also had to deal with competition from overseas. While Texans have always relished their independence, the state today must work to ensure its place in a growing global economy. Even Texas farmers must look overseas as they attempt to cultivate foreign markets for their products while warding off foreign competitors.

While the wealthy Texas oil baron or cattle rancher is a familiar image in movies and television, Texans fall below the national average on many measures of wealth. Compared to the national average, Texans have a lower per capita income ($39,967 versus $43,318 in 2003), a higher poverty rate (15.2 percent versus 12.5 percent), and a lower rate of home ownership (63.8 percent versus 66.2 percent). The income disparity depicted in Figure 1.1 illustrates that while Texas may be a land of great wealth, it is also a land of great need. One study found that Texas ranked first or second in income inequality, depending on whether you measure inequality between the highest income group and the bottom income group or between the highest and middle income groups.[20]

Texas's years of change are not over, as the state continues to change rapidly. In the 1990s, the Texas population grew by 22.8 percent and Texas grew another 9.6 percent between 2001 and 2005. Texas is now second in population with 22,859,968 residents in 2005, though it is still well behind California's 36,132,147 residents. The growth rate in some Texas cities, such as Frisco, was an amazing 400 percent in this period.

Texans must brace themselves for more change. Texas, California, and Florida are expected to account for almost half of the nation's growth from 1995 to 2025.[21] Texas's growth will likely come from a balance of internal immigration (about 1.8 million people moving from other states), international immigration (about 1 million people coming to Texas from other nations), and "natural growth" (adding about 5.7 million people as Texans have babies and live longer).

Thus, the state, whose constitution was authored by isolated farmers who had formed the Grange as a way of connecting with other farmers, today is a booming high-tech center with citizens connected by the Internet. Visitors arriving in the Texas capital expecting to find cowboys astride horses on the open plains are more likely to find computer engineers and game programmers stuck in traffic.

Figure 1.1 Income Distribution

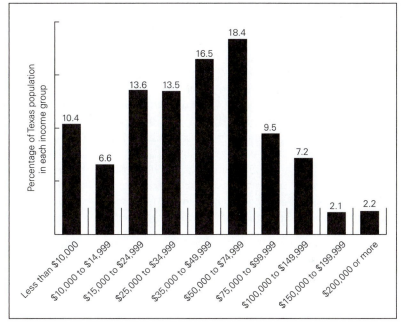

Source: U.S. Census Bureau, "Texas: 2000," August 2002, http://www.census.gov/prod/2002pubs/c2kprof00-tx.pdf.

Winners and Losers

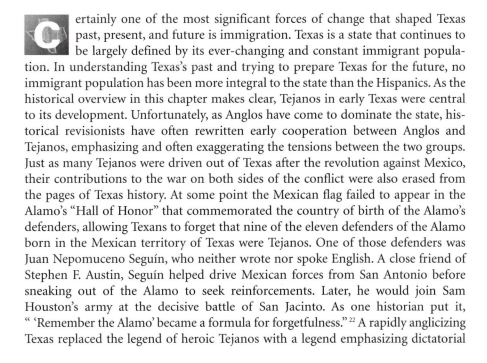

ertainly one of the most significant forces of change that shaped Texas past, present, and future is immigration. Texas is a state that continues to be largely defined by its ever-changing and constant immigrant population. In understanding Texas's past and trying to prepare Texas for the future, no immigrant population has been more integral to the state than the Hispanics. As the historical overview in this chapter makes clear, Tejanos in early Texas were central to its development. Unfortunately, as Anglos have come to dominate the state, historical revisionists have often rewritten early cooperation between Anglos and Tejanos, emphasizing and often exaggerating the tensions between the two groups. Just as many Tejanos were driven out of Texas after the revolution against Mexico, their contributions to the war on both sides of the conflict were also erased from the pages of Texas history. At some point the Mexican flag failed to appear in the Alamo's "Hall of Honor" that commemorated the country of birth of the Alamo's defenders, allowing Texans to forget that nine of the eleven defenders of the Alamo born in the Mexican territory of Texas were Tejanos. One of those defenders was Juan Nepomuceno Seguín, who neither wrote nor spoke English. A close friend of Stephen F. Austin, Seguín helped drive Mexican forces from San Antonio before sneaking out of the Alamo to seek reinforcements. Later, he would join Sam Houston's army at the decisive battle of San Jacinto. As one historian put it, " 'Remember the Alamo' became a formula for forgetfulness."[22] A rapidly anglicizing Texas replaced the legend of heroic Tejanos with a legend emphasizing dictatorial

Texas versus Vermont

Texas and Vermont illustrate the diversity of states within the United States. Vermont, a Northeastern state, got its start when Ethan Allen and the Green Mountain Boys rebelled against attempts by New York and New Hampshire to exert control over the region after the American Revolution. On January 15, 1777, the independent Republic of New Connecticut was declared; later the name was changed to the Republic of Vermont. Vermont sent ambassadors to France, the Netherlands, and the United States. In 1791, Vermont entered the United States as the fourteenth state to balance the admission of slave-holding Kentucky as the fifteenth state.

While both Texas and Vermont share a history of independence before joining the United States, the comparisons end quickly. Geographically, Vermont is quite small, at 9,250 square miles. Vermont's size is smaller than the combined area of the largest two Texas counties (10,957 square miles is the combined area of Brewster and Pecos counties in West Texas). Vermont's landscape is dominated by the Green Mountains, abundant forests, and plentiful rivers and streams. As the second largest state by area, Texas covers a vast territory that varies tremendously in land formations, water resources, and natural resources.

The demographics of the two states also illustrate this diversity. Settled by English settlers and some French colonists from nearby Quebec, Vermont remains among the most homogeneous states in the United States. In 2005, Vermont held the distinction of being one of the whitest states in the United States; Texas, in contrast, was among the most racially and ethnically diverse states.

Texas versus Vermont: Ethnic Makeup of the State

POPULATION GROUP	TEXAS	VERMONT
White	48.5%	95.8%
Hispanic/Latino	34.7%	1.1%
African American	11.9%	0.9%
Asian American	3.6%	1.2%
Other	1.3%	1.0%

Source: Population Division, U.S. Census Bureau, "Estimates of the Population by Race Alone or in Combination and Hispanic or Latino Origin for the United States and States," July 1, 2005.

Mexican rulers seeking the expulsion of the Anglos. The role played by Tejanos was largely ignored.

The Tejano population of Texas declined from the time of the revolution until a repressive regime in Mexico, coupled with decades of revolution within that country, created a new wave of immigrants into Texas. This tripled the Mexican population in Texas from 1900 to 1920. While these immigrants played important roles in cotton production, they were often not welcome and took their place somewhere between Anglos and African Americans, not being accepted into either community. Techniques such as "white primaries," which were used to exclude African Americans from voting, were eventually also employed against Tejanos. As the state has continued to change, and immigrants have continued to move into Texas, Hispanics have been increasingly marginalized in the political process, as well as in the history books.

One of the enduring legends of early Texas history is how Anglo order and hard work saved the state from Mexican chaos. According to this view it was immigrants from the United States who, in the words of one public school textbook from the 1880s, "changed Texas from a wilderness into a civilized state: Mexico had nothing but fear and hatred." [23] Like other legacies, this historical "truth" ignores some aspects

Vermont also consistently ranks as one of the smallest states in population. In 1850, the first census in which Texas participated, Vermont had a slightly larger population than Texas. Immigration during that decade saw Texas surpass Vermont in population by the next census in 1860, when Texas already had over 600,000 residents. Vermont only reached that level of population in 2000, the same year that Texas recorded over 22 million residents.

Large cities are found throughout Texas; three of the nation's ten largest cities are located in Texas. Vermont's largest city, Burlington (38,358), is so small that it would rank as the seventieth largest city in Texas. Even the images of the two states generate contrasts. Texas is the land of open plains, oil wells, cattle, gun-slinging cowboys, and big-time football. Vermont is the land of maple syrup, ice cream, fall foliage, and quaint towns.

Obviously, to be able to govern a diverse population spread over a vast geographic area, with extensive mineral wealth, Texas requires a fundamentally different approach than Vermont. In many instances, Texas politics is vastly different in practice than Vermont's political system. However, these differences may not be exactly what we expect.

Thinking Critically

In several places, this textbook presents discussion, tables, and figures to offer comparisons between Texas and other states. At this point, think about the heritage and demographics of your community or hometown.

- Is your community more like a typical Texas or Vermont community?
- What have your experiences in politics been like?
- How would they compare to those in a state like Vermont?

of history and exaggerates others. So far, Hispanics have been the losers of this historical legend.

By 1930 the Tejano population of Texas had begun to rise with the rest of the population, reaching almost 684,000. Reflecting the return of Tejanos to Texas politics, the League of United Latin American Citizens (LULAC) was formed in Corpus Christi in 1929. LULAC quickly became a major factor in Texas politics. In 1956 Henry B. González became the first Tejano in over half a century to hold a seat in the Texas Senate. During the 1957 legislative session González set the record for a filibuster in the Texas Senate as he fought laws backing segregation in Texas public schools. In 1961 González would break ground again by winning a seat in the U.S. House of Representatives. By that time half a dozen Tejanos were serving in the Texas Legislature and a Tejano was serving as mayor of El Paso. Tejanos won their first statewide office when Dan Morales was elected attorney general in 1992. Hispanics are both the largest and fastest growing minority in the state and today hold a variety of statewide offices. As Tony Sanchez's unsuccessful but highly visible bid for the governorship in 2002 indicated, many Texans are ready for a Hispanic governor. Hispanics are increasingly successful in organizing and exerting political pressure in Texas. As this population continues to increase and successfully organize their interests within the state, Hispanics are in a position to be the winners in a future Texas.

Today Texas is again dealing with an immigrant population whose numbers are increasing so rapidly that they form a majority in some parts of the state. The struggle to deal with this change is part of what defines Texas as a state today. As we will see throughout this text, legends tend to be static and are often at odds with the changing nature of the state. The story of Texas that is a primarily Anglo story and ignores other minorities in the state remains the dominant legend in Texas's history books today. Throughout the rest of this book we will continue to explore this tension between legend and change.

Conclusion: The Lone Star in Transition

n the new millennium, Texas faces new challenges as it continues to change. The rising political clout of Republicans, Hispanics, and women at the close of the twentieth century has been only partially reflected in changes to the Texas political system. At the same time, Texas now faces many political issues that have been long deferred by the state's leaders. The funding of the state's public schools, in dispute for over a decade, was only partially resolved by a special session of the legislature in 2006. Texas continues to grapple with air quality, an issue that the state hadn't even started to address until 1965. Toll roads and mass transit have become major issues as the state tries to manage its growing cities and the heavy truck traffic generated by new trade agreements with Mexico.

In 2004, Republicans redistricted the state of Texas to correct what they saw as the under-representation of their party in the U.S. Congress. Hispanic leaders have struggled to elect officials in proportion to their share of the population. Despite some highly visible women representing the state in the U.S. Senate or as Texas comptroller, women remain dramatically underrepresented in state offices, composing only 20 percent of the Texas Legislature in 2007. The struggle of Republicans, women, and Tejanos exemplify the dilemma that changes in the state's politics often lag behind other changes—demographic, social, and economic—in the state.

Like all democracies, Texas government takes its flavor from the people it represents. While sharing a common history, Texans often take different lessons from that history. As this chapter demonstrates, the meaning of "Texan" has changed dramatically over the state's history, and today the meaning of the word conjures a different image in each corner of the state. Despite the changes in those who call themselves Texans and where they live, the basic structure of Texas government has remained largely unchanged.

While Texans relish their colorful history, the state today must work to ensure its place in a competitive global high-tech economy. A constitution written in 1876 by isolated Texas farmers who had little interest in government, growth, diversity, big business, or the modern world leaves behind a government that must struggle to meet the needs of a state that is rapidly growing and increasingly diverse with an economy driven by large multinational corporations on the cutting edge of the information age.

Change does not make the state's history less important. The rapid changes occurring in the state today make understanding our history even more important as Texans grapple with difficult issues like immigration. Following the legacy of a Declaration of Independence written by men who had lived in the state only a few years, Texans must both acknowledge the potential contributions of new arrivals and protect what previous generations have created. In the following chapters we'll look at how Texas politics and government has adapted to the waves of changes in its history and how well it is prepared for the changes ahead.

Key Terms

empresario
individualistic political culture
moralistic political culture
political culture
presidential republicanism
traditionalistic political culture
Treaty of Guadalupe Hidalgo

Explore this subject further at http://college.cqpress.com/lonestarpolitics, where you'll find chapter summaries, practice quizzes, key word flash cards, and additional suggested resources.

Delegates to the 1875 Constitutional Convention, who wrote our current constitution. The convention was dominated by Democrats, many of whom were members of the Grange party interested in keeping government small and protecting the rights of farmers. Six African Americans were also elected as delegates to the convention.

CHAPTER 2

Texas Constitution

Most Texans believe that "if it ain't broke, don't fix it," and apply that to the myth that the Texas Constitution still works. Our current constitution was written in the era of cowboys and cattle drives. Today's Texas is one of computers and commuters. Many governors and politicians have continuously called for a new constitution. As early as 1922 Gov. Pat Neff urged the legislature to write a new state constitution, arguing that the 1876 constitution had become a "patch-work," after only thirty-eight amendments.[1] As of 2007, the Texas Constitution has been amended 456 times. Other Texans, ever distrustful of government, have repeatedly opposed overhauling the constitution.

In 1999, two legislators, state senator Bill Ratliff, R-Mount Pleasant, and state representative Rob Junell, D-San Angelo, took on this myth. According to these legislators, "Times have changed, the world has changed and this significant document should be revised in order to continue serving Texas as a guide through the future."[2] In spite of most Texans' resistance to a new constitution and despite government's typical inertia, according to these legislators, it was time to fix, not simply patch, the Texas Constitution. "There is widespread belief among Capitol watchers that the Texas legislature is incapable of dealing with major substantive changes in the absence of crisis."[3]

Ratliff and Junell faced an uphill battle when they proposed a new constitution that would solve a Texas-sized problem—specifically, the current constitution's outdated provisions written over 100 years ago tie the hands of the legislature. Ratliff and Junell's proposed constitution expanded the powers of the governor, created a gubernatorially-appointed cabinet, established term limits for the legislative branch, merged the two high courts in the state, and eliminated the election of state judges in favor of gubernatorial appointments followed by retention elections.

Ratliff and Junell argued that the current constitution is clearly broken and imposes an intolerable cost on the state. Ratliff suggests that "[voters know] that any document you have to try to amend 20 times every other year is broke. It's sort of a Texas tragedy, actually, that we can't seem to come to grips with the fact that we need a new, basic document going into the next century and the next millennium."[4] Moreover, the cost of frequent elections necessary to amend the constitution is considerable: "voter fatigue and the temptation for special-interest groups to push amendments that aren't in the public interest."[5]

The more the state changes, the more outdated the constitution becomes. As Texas has continued to change and diversify, our government is mired in an unyielding constitution. Ratliff sums up the democratic costs of retaining our current constitution:

To fix it piece by piece, line by line in an era where when you try to fix it, someone wants to tack on something else that's of their particular interest, is not working. One day, the people will simply stop going to the polls to vote on constitutional amendments until we fix it. Maybe that's what they've already done.[6]

Ratliff and Junell's proposal, like earlier movements for constitutional change, failed to gain enough popular support. The proposal died in committee and was never voted on by the full Texas Legislature. Texans have consistently rejected rewriting the current document, instead favoring incremental revision, which just exacerbates the mess we're in.

So how has this happened and why does it keep happening? To better understand the predicament in Texas we examine the principles underlying a constitutional government. We first outline the federalist structure of the national government and how Texas fits into that structure. We then survey how the Texas Constitution has evolved over time, reflecting our rich history and culture. Finally, we discuss the problems of the current constitution and examine the prospects for constitutional reform.

As you read the chapter, think about the following questions:

★ What is the purpose of a constitution?
★ How does federalism affect policies in Texas?
★ To what extent have Texas's previous constitutions contributed to the state's current constitution?
★ What are the problems with the current Texas Constitution?

Constitutional Government

Constitution

a written document that outlines the powers of government and the limitations on those powers.

A constitution is a written document which outlines the powers of government and limitations on those powers to protect the rights of citizens. Ideally, a constitution should be a brief, flexible document that confers broad grants of power to the government. Written constitutions have become the norm in modern times and confer legitimacy on countries. The government, in turn, works within the boundaries of the constitution, as it goes about day-to-day operations. The legislature, for example, passes laws that do not violate the basic principles outlined in the constitution. The more fundamental the constitution's provisions, the less likely it will need to be updated over time. The U.S. Constitution, for instance, has lasted over 200 years, with Congress passing and repealing more specific laws to reflect the changing times. Ideally a constitution should protect citizens' rights while being broad enough to adapt with changing times.

Our country's founders believed that a constitutional or written government was necessary to prevent tyranny of the government. James Madison wrote in *Federalist* No. 51 that "If men were angels, no government would be necessary. If angels were to govern men, neither external nor internal controls on government would be necessary. In framing a government which is to be administered by men over men, the great difficulty lies in this: you must first enable the government to control the governed; and in the next place oblige it to control itself." The founders, concerned with tyranny often displayed by the monarchs at the expense of the people, set out to create a new form of government. The U.S. Constitution checked potential tyrants in several ways: by creating different levels of government (federalism), separating power among different branches of government (separation of powers), and empowering the people to check the government (popular sovereignty).

The idea of **popular sovereignty,** or creating a government where the power to govern is derived from the will of the people, is a critical aspect in limiting tyranny. This idea is in sharp contrast to the prevailing norm 200 years ago when the U.S. Constitution was written. Monarchs ruled with little concept of popular representation in government, instead claiming a divine right to rule derived from the will of God. With the memories of a rebellion against a monarch fresh in their memories, the founders included popular sovereignty in the preamble to the Constitution, which begins "We the people." In Texas, popular sovereignty is manifest in the popular election of almost all state officials, including members of the legislative, executive, and judicial branches. Texas voters must also approve amendments to the state's constitution, further extending popular rule to the country's fundamental law.

As an additional protection for individuals against tyranny, a constitution may place limits on governmental action to curb potential abuses. In the U.S. Constitution, most of these limits are contained within the Bill of Rights.

The United States invented modern constitutional government and the U.S. Constitution is a model of brevity and flexible language. It remains relatively short, has been amended only twenty-seven times, and outlines the fundamental functions and limits of government while leaving the legislature to pass more specific legislation.

Of course, such an ideal constitution is rarely achieved. The Texas Constitution by contrast is extremely long and specific, creates a relatively weak government, and undergos constant amendment as the government tries to keep up with a rapidly growing and changing state. The current Texas Constitution, Texas's sixth since its independence from Mexico, reflects Texas's historical experience under Mexico and Spain, its reaction to the Civil War and Reconstruction, and the still prevailing preference for limited government. The current constitution also represents the federal nature of the United States government.

Popular sovereignty
a government where the power to govern is derived from the will of the people.

The Federal System of the United States

ederalism—the sharing of powers between two levels of government—is a uniquely American creation. The North American colonies had relatively little influence in decisions made by the central government back in London. The founders were frustrated over lack of representation in the British government, and they believed that governmental tyranny could be checked by separating the powers of government. In an attempt to limit the potential for tyranny, the framers divided powers among the branches of government, as well as between the levels of government. The federalist concept specifies a division of powers between the central or national government and the lower levels of state government.

In creating a federal system, the framers compromised between two alternative ideal systems: unitary and confederal. **Confederal systems** are governmental arrangements where the lower units of government retain decision-making authority. The United States experienced a confederacy twice: first under the Articles of Confederation, and later, in the short-lived Confederacy created by southern states during the Civil War. In both cases, the states retained decision-

Confederal system
a type of government where the lower units of government retain decision-making authority.

Unitary system
a type of government where power is vested in a central governmental authority.

Federalism
a form of government based on the sharing of powers between the national and state governments.

Vertical federalism
the distribution of power between the national and state governments.

Supremacy clause
the section in the U.S. Constitution that guarantees that the national government is the supreme law of the land, and national laws and the national constitution supersede state laws and state constitutions.

Reserved powers
the specification in the Tenth Amendment that all powers not delegated to the national government belong to the states.

Delegated powers
the powers listed in Article I, Section 8 of the U.S. Constitution that are expressly granted to the national government.

making authority, leaving a relatively weaker national government. A modern day example of a confederacy is the United Nations, where member countries can participate in various treaties, choose to opt out of treaties, or withdraw from the organization at any time.

Unitary systems, by contrast, vest power in a central government and lower units of government only have power that is granted to them by the central government. For instance, the North American colonies had only the powers granted to them by the British government. Today, about 75 percent of governments remain unitary, making this the most prevalent type of government in the world. An example of a unitary government close to home is the relationship between Texas and its lower governmental units, the cities and counties. Cities and counties in Texas are granted only limited law-making authority by the state constitution and the state legislature.

The founders, having experienced both a unitary and confederal government, created an alternative form of government known as federalism. **Federalism** is based on the sharing of powers between the national and state governments and represents a compromise between a unitary and confederal system. The U.S. Constitution creates a federal system by vesting certain powers in the national government while reserving other powers for the states. Theoretically, dividing power among levels of government prevents the national government from imposing "one-size-fits-all" standards that may not make sense for a particular state or region. On the one hand, federalism allows states to experiment with different laws and results in flexibility as different states pass laws that represent differences in their political culture. On the other hand, federalism imposes significant costs on the United States, since different levels of government fight over policy areas, often at the taxpayer's expense. The founders believed that the prevention of tyranny was more important than the inefficiency that different levels of government create.

Vertical Federalism

Although the founders generally believed that dividing powers among levels of government would be beneficial, the exact division of power within our federal system is unclear. **Vertical federalism,** or the distribution of power between the national government and the state governments, was highly contested in our early history. The difficulty in describing the federal nature of the U.S. government is best exemplified by juxtaposing the supremacy clause and the reserved powers clause of the U.S. Constitution. The **supremacy clause** guarantees that the national government is the supreme law of the land. Thus, the U.S. Constitution and national laws supersede state laws and state constitutions. States can make laws within their territory so long as those laws do not conflict with national laws or the U.S. Constitution. On the other hand, the Tenth Amendment reserves for the states all powers not delegated to the national government. This provision creates a class of powers called **reserved powers,** although the Supreme Court has interpreted these powers narrowly in recent times.

The U.S. Constitution gives the national government exclusive authority over coining money, establishing a navy, declaring war, and regulating interstate commerce. These **delegated powers** expressly granted to the national government are listed in Article I, Section 8 of the U.S. Constitution. The U.S. Constitution also outlines explicit roles for the states including conducting elections, as well as selecting electors for the Electoral College, establishing voter qualifications, and

Figure 2.1 Distribution of Powers between the National Government and the States in the U.S. Constitution

DELEGATED POWERS (to the national government)

Admit new states to the Union

Coin money

Conduct foreign affairs

Declare war

Establish courts inferior to the Supreme Court

Make laws that are necessary for carrying out the powers vested by the Constitution

Raise and maintain armies and navies

Regulate interstate and foreign commerce

CONCURRENT POWERS (shared by the national government and the states)

Borrow and spend money for the general welfare

Charter and regulate banks; charter corporations

Collect taxes

Establish courts

Establish highways

Pass and enforce laws

Take private property for public purposes, with just compensation

RESERVED POWERS (to the states)

Conduct elections and determine voter qualifications

Establish local governments

Maintain militia (National Guard)

Provide for public health, safety, and morals

Ratify amendments to the federal constitution

Regulate intrastate commerce

DENIED POWERS (to the states)

Abridging the privileges or immunities of citizens or denying due process and equal protection of the laws (14th Amendment)

Coining money

Entering into treaties

Keeping troops or navies

Levying import or export taxes on goods

Making war

Source: Adapted from Christine Barbour and Gerald C. Wright, *Keeping the Republic*, 2nd brief ed. (Washington, D.C.: CQ Press, 2006).

approving constitutional amendments. Moreover, Article I, Section 10 of the U.S. Constitution explicitly prohibits states from entering into treaties, coining money, or granting letters of marque or titles of nobility, among other things. Other powers, such as the power to tax and spend, to establish courts, or to charter banks are **concurrent powers** shared by the national and state governments.

Concurrent powers

powers such as taxing and spending, the ability to establish courts, and charter banks that are shared by the national and state governments.

Horizontal Federalism

Horizontal federalism

refers to the relationship between the states.

Privileges and immunities

the constitutional requirement that states may not fundamentally treat citizens of other states differently than their own citizens.

Full faith and credit clause

the constitutional requirement that court judgments or legal contracts entered into in one state will be honored by other states.

Extradition

the constitutional requirement that states deliver someone suspected or convicted of a crime in another state back to that state so they can face trial or sentencing.

Fiscal federalism

use of national financial incentives to encourage policies at the state level.

Categorical grant

national money given to states and local governments that must be spent for specific activities.

Horizontal federalism refers to the relationship between states. Certain provisions within the U.S. Constitution regulate the relations among states. The founders specified certain state obligations to other states, in part, to create a sense of national unity among the states. For instance, states are required to grant the same **privileges and immunities** to citizens of other states as they grant to their own citizens. This provision means that states may not fundamentally treat citizens of other states differently than their citizens. The privileges and immunities clause makes travel between states easier and prevents discrimination against citizens of other states. However, exceptions to the privileges and immunities clause have been recognized in two cases.[7] First, states may deny the right to vote to nonresidents of the state. Thus, the laws of one state cannot be unduly influenced by citizens from neighboring states. In addition, states may distinguish between residents and nonresidents in the distribution of certain state-subsidized benefits that may differ from state to state, such as in-state tuition rates or welfare payments. This exception has been deemed reasonable, since "individuals could benefit from subsidies without being subject to the taxes that pay the subsidies."[8] States are further required to recognize acts, records, and judicial decisions of other states according to the **full faith and credit clause.** This means that court judgments or legal contracts entered into in one state will be honored by other states. Thus, you cannot escape debt or child support payments by moving states. Finally, the U.S. Constitution requires that states deliver someone suspected or convicted of a crime in another state back to that state so they can face trial and sentencing. This process, known as **extradition,** was designed to keep criminals from escaping justice by moving from state to state.

The Evolving Idea of Federalism

Creating a new type of government generated a considerable amount of uncertainty. It is clear that the founders sought to produce a system of government where powers are shared between two levels of government. It is considerably less clear exactly what that distribution of power looked like. From its inception, the idea of federalism has generated a good deal of controversy, culminating, in part, in a civil war less than a century after the republic was founded. Very few policy areas have escaped this tension. Today the United States continues to grapple with exactly which powers are given to the national government and which should be reserved for the states. Sentimental attachment to the idea of federalism is often usurped by a preference for efficiency and uniformity. The result is that over time, the power of the states has eroded significantly. Most notably, states have historically enjoyed policy control over issues such as police power, marriage, education, and election laws. Yet in the last half a century, the national government has begun to encroach on policy areas traditionally reserved for the states.

Perhaps the most significant tool the national government uses to gain control of state policy areas is money. With the creation of a national income tax, the national government enjoyed a significant increase in tax revenues. Since that time, the Congress has used its financial advantage to control issues that were traditionally considered state policy areas. Use of financial incentives to encourage policies at the state level is referred to as **fiscal federalism.** The national government has awarded three types of grants to state and local governments. The **categorical grant** is money given to states and local governments that must be spent for specific activities. When the national government specifies how the money is to be spent, it can then set national policy goals in traditionally state-controlled policy areas. Republican administrations created **block grants** in an attempt to return policy control back to the states. Theoretically, block grants are given to state and local governments for a broader purpose and impose fewer restrictions on the states regarding how the grant money is to be spent. In the 1970s, President Richard Nixon reorganized existing categorical grants into block grants to continue the flow of money from the national government to the states while allowing the states to exert more discretion on how the money was spent. The Nixon administration created a third type of grant, called **general revenue sharing,** that transferred money from the national government to the states with no rules on how the money was spent. Although the latter two forms of grants are a popular means of reviving state power, they have been politically difficult to achieve. Members of Congress prefer to allocate money attached to specific policies, making it easier for them to take credit for the resulting goods provided to their home states.

One example of the national government using grants to intrude on state policy issues occurred in the 1980s when Congress wanted to establish a national drinking age. Congress, faced with increasing pressure from the relatively new Mothers Against Drunk Driving group, and absent clear constitutional authority to establish a national drinking age, passed legislation that would take away 10 percent of a state's federal highway funds if the state did not raise its drinking age to twenty-one within two years. South Dakota sued the national government, arguing that the policy amounted to coercion and was a blatant intrusion on states' rights. In *South Dakota v. Dole,* the Supreme Court ruled that the national government could reasonably attach conditions to national grants. In a dissenting opinion, Justice Sandra Day O'Connor concurred with South Dakota that the law violated the spirit of federalism, arguing that "[t]he immense size and power of the Government of the United States ought not obscure its fundamental character." [9] This case illustrates how the national government, conferred with limited enumerated powers, has used its substantial tax base to considerably increase its policy authority over time.

One controversial way that the national government has infringed on state policy areas is its reliance on unfunded mandates. **Unfunded mandates** occur when the national government passes legislation that imposes requirements on state and local governments, which bear the cost of meeting those requirements. Some examples include requirements that all states, including Texas, ensure equal access to public facilities for disabled persons, guarantee civil rights, provide public assistance for single parents, and enforce clean air standards. [10] In each of these cases, the states and local governments must pay for a significant portion of these regulations, imposed on them by the national government.

Currently, the states' customary authority over marriages is at the forefront of the debate over federalism. Traditionally, states have enjoyed almost complete control over rules governing marriage, including defining licensing requirements, establishing an age of consent, providing for common law marriages, and determining general guidelines for divorce. Recently, this control has been challenged by issues regarding same-sex marriages. In 2000, Vermont became the first state in America to approve civil unions. Three years later, Massachusetts became the first state to allow same-sex marriage. Under the full faith and credit clause of the U.S. Constitution states have honored marriages performed in other states so long as they do not violate the state's own marriage guidelines. The new law in

Block grant
created by Republicans, these national funds are given to state and local governments for a broader purpose and they impose fewer restrictions on the states regarding how the money is to be spent.

General revenue sharing
transfers of money from the national government to the states with no rules on how the money is spent.

Unfunded mandates
when legislation is passed by the national government imposing requirements on state and local governments, in which those governments bear the costs of meeting those requirements.

Massachusetts caused a national uproar as opponents of same-sex marriage feared that the full faith and credit clause would result in legalizing gay marriages across the United States. The national government responded by passing the 1996 Defense of Marriage Act, which allowed states to adopt legislation excluding same-sex marriages in their territory. With this act, the national government is explicitly attempting to relieve the states of their obligation to grant full faith and credit to public acts in other states. At the state level, many states began to pass state laws explicitly denying the validity of same-sex marriages within their state. Texas followed suit in 2005, when voters overwhelmingly approved a constitutional amendment defining marriage as a union between a man and a woman. However, the national government may still assume control of this issue in the future. The U.S. Supreme Court could conceivably rule that the Defense of Marriage Act is an unconstitutional breach of a state's full faith and credit obligation. There have also been several attempts by the U.S. Congress (most recently in 2006) to amend the Constitution to ban same-sex marriage. So far, though, these attempts have failed to pass in either house.

As we can see, after two hundred years, federalism in the United States continues to evolve. States have also continued to become more involved in the day-to-day lives of their citizens. Nevertheless, state constitutions vary greatly in their length and specificity, the amount of power they confer to each branch of government, and the structure of their state judiciary, among other things.

Texas Constitutions

Texas's constitutions, including the current document, reflect its experience as a province of Spain and later Mexico. During the time that Texas was part of the Spanish empire, its population was relatively sparse and there was no written constitution. Nevertheless, centuries of Spanish rule left an indelible mark on Texas law. In contrast to English common law, property rights for women were well defined under Spanish law, including the right to hold property, the right to half of all property accumulated during a marriage, and the right to manage their own financial affairs.[11] In addition, Spanish law traditionally protected a debtor's home and farming equipment from seizure for repayment of debt, and this protection has persisted throughout Texas's history under the homestead provisions.

Under Mexican rule, Texas, as part of the state of Coahuila y Tejas, experienced its first federal constitution. Texans were always somewhat frustrated with their limited voice within the Mexican government. Most Texans felt underrepresented in the state of Coahuila y Tejas where Texans held only two of the state's twelve legislative seats. Anglo-Texans also resented certain aspects of Mexican rule, in particular the establishment of Catholicism as a state religion. Officially Texans were required to join the Catholic Church. Texans also were unhappy with the constitutional provisions prohibiting slavery, although they largely ignored these provisions. In general, Texans favored local control of government and distrusted centralized government, a preference we continue to see today. However, it was Santa Anna's abolition of the Mexican constitution, and assumption of dictatorial powers, which undoubtedly made independence from Mexico inevitable. On April 21, 1836, Texans defeated Santa Anna at the Battle of San Jacinto, and both sides signed the Treaty of Velasco, granting Texas its independence.

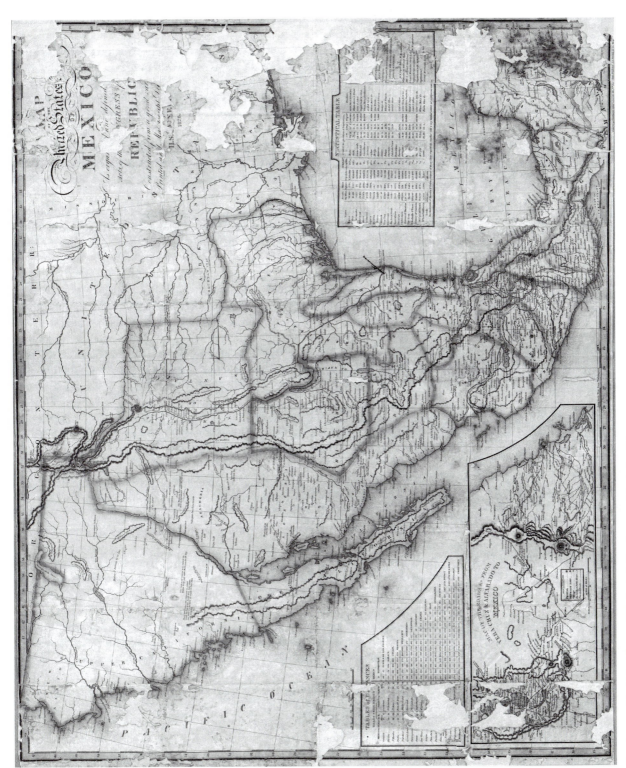

Historic map of the United States of Mexico including the state of Coahuila y Tejas.

Immigration Rights

When Texans declared independence from Mexico, they brought up a wide list of complaints including fairness in the judiciary, lack of adequate political representation, and a state-imposed religion. White Texans were frustrated with Mexican laws that seemed to ignore their needs. Texas was given only two seats in the legislature and the Mexican judicial system often seemed to disregard the concerns of the new settlers. But much of the Texans' frustration with Mexico was that Mexico simply didn't represent the cultural preferences of its white settlers. Immigration issues were high among the grievances that fueled Texans' impetus to separate from Mexico.

The Mexican Texans' concern with immigration might seem strange to modern-day Texans. Ironically, much like the way the modern economy of Texas depends on its immigrant population, Mexican Texas depended on immigration for the security of the sparsely populated state. Under Spain and the early years of the Mexican Republic, immigration laws were quite liberal. However, Mexican authorities were increasingly concerned with the growing influence of Anglos in Texas. Although Mexico initially sought to encourage European immigration, it eventually sought to halt American immigration with the Law of April 6, 1830, although a significant number of Americans continued to enter Texas illegally.[12]

Anglo immigrants to Texas under Mexico faced a variety of difficulties arising from their inability to speak or write Spanish. Indeed, among the complaints of the Anglos about the judicial system was their inability to understand the laws or Spanish law books. Stephen F. Austin, in an attempt to avoid revolution, wrote to the Mexican government that "[w]ith only two measures Texas would be satisfied, judges who understand English . . . and trial by jury."[13] The basic difficulties of English-speaking immigrants living under a Spanish-speaking government was a primary concern of Anglos in Texas. One of the demands Texans made at the Consultation of 1832 was that the Mexican government create bilingual primary schools, with instruction in both English and Spanish. In 1834, Santa Anna, responding to the unrest in Texas, passed several reforms including making English the official language of the state of Coahuila y Tejas.[14] Unfortunately, Santa Anna soon abolished the constitution and assumed dictatorial powers in Mexico. Once independent, Texans would not forget their experiences under Mexico and they resolved to have their new constitution and all subsequent laws passed translated into Spanish.

Anglo Texans' experiences as an immigrant minority were manifested in the Constitution of 1836, which established extraordinarily liberal immigration policies. It declared that "All persons, (Africans, the descendants of Africans, and Indians excepted,) who were residing in Texas on the day of the Declaration of Independence, shall be considered citizens of the Republic."[15] Furthermore, the constitution provided that a future immigrant "after a residence of six months, make oath before some competent authority that he intends to reside permanently in the same, and shall swear to support this Constitution, and that he will bear true allegiance to the Republic of Texas, shall be entitled to all the privileges of citizenship."[16]

Before Texas declared its independence from Mexico, Anglo Texans complained that they were inadequately represented in Mexico. Thus, the framers of the new Texas constitution sought to allow immigrants to vote, regardless of citizenship. The current Texas constitution allowed "male persons of foreign birth" to vote in the state, so long as they had "resided in this State one year next preceding an election, and the last six months within the district or county in which he offers to vote" and "shall have declared his intention to become a citizen of the United States."[17] Originally, the constitution was designed to ensure that future immigrants could easily and reasonably attain both citizenship and the right to participate in the government. This provision remained in force until 1921, when Texans, by a slim majority (52 percent in favor; 48 percent opposed), approved a constitutional amendment allowing only citizens to vote.

Hispanics in Texas today fight for many of the same rights that Anglos demanded under Mexican rule a century ago. Immigrants in Texas today make similar demands for easing citizenship requirements and for language rights. Anglo Texans today, apparently sufficiently distanced from their own experience as an immigrant population, have, in many cases, forgotten the difficulties they faced in being the immigrant minority. But historically, the immigration issue was critical in the independence movement of Texas.

The Republic of Texas—The Constitution of 1836

No episode contributes to the mythical history of Texas more than its brief period as an independent country. Delegates from across the state met at Washington-on-the-Brazos to write a constitution for the future Republic of Texas. Of the fifty-nine delegates, almost half had been in Texas less than two years and most of them had emigrated from southern states. The constitutional convention occurred in the midst of the revolution, and delegates hurriedly wrote the new constitution, well aware that the revolution might arrive at their doorstep at any moment.[18] The resulting document was largely influenced by the U.S. Constitution in that it was relatively brief and flexible, provided for three branches of government, and established a system of checks and balances. The president was elected to a three-year term, prohibited from serving consecutive terms, and appointed commander-in-chief of the Texas military. A bicameral legislature was established with one-year terms in the House and three-year terms in the Senate. The short legislative terms and the nonconsecutive presidential term reflected Texans' distrust of government in general, an attitude that continues to dominate Texas politics today. At the end of the constitution was a Declaration of Rights, which enumerated individual rights similar to those found in the national Bill of Rights, such as freedom of speech, press, and religion. While White and Hispanic males were given a broad range of freedoms, free persons of African descent were prohibited from residing in the state without the consent of the Texas legislature.

There were, however, some notable differences between the U.S. Constitution and the Republic of Texas Constitution. For instance, Texas's constitution was distinctly unitary rather than federal in nature, since the Republic of Texas did not create lower units of government with any independent power. Reacting to the establishment under Mexican rule of Catholicism as the state religion, the Republic's constitution prohibited priests from holding office. Perhaps the most important feature of the new constitution was its legalization of slavery, a provision that had irreversible consequences for both Texas and the United States. Immigrants moving to Texas were permitted to bring their existing slaves with them, and Texas slave owners were prohibited from freeing their slaves without the consent of the legislature. However, the constitution stopped short of allowing the slave trade in Texas.

Texas voters overwhelmingly supported the new constitution as well as annexation by the United States. However, annexation was not immediate. There were two significant obstacles to Texas joining the United States. The first was the precarious nature of Texas's claim of independence. Upon his return to Mexico, Santa Anna renounced the Treaty of Velasco and reiterated Mexico's claims to Texas. Any attempt by the United States to annex Texas could potentially provoke a war with Mexico. Second, Texas's constitutional protection of slavery made annexation controversial within the United States. Abolitionists objected to the addition of another slave state, at the same time other slave states saw the admission of Texas into the United States as a guarantee of the future of slavery. Initially, at least, the annexation of Texas was largely unpopular in the United States, particularly outside of the South. Thus, the initial annexation treaty failed to receive Senate ratification. Eventually, though, the idea of **Manifest Destiny** gained popularity in the United States. James Polk campaigned for the presidency based on expanding the United States through immediate annexation of Texas and expansion into Oregon. In 1845, Texas was finally admitted into the United States. According to the annexation agreement Texas would retain responsibility for its debt as well as the rights to its public land. In addition, Texas could divide itself into as many as five states as the population continued to expand, and then be admitted to the U.S. under the provisions of the national constitution.

Some of the greatest legends in Texas are built on this brief period of independence. Today Texans speak fondly of a time when they were masters of their own domain. According to popular imagery, Texas's time as an independent country makes Texas exceptional among the states. In truth, the Republic of Texas, though unique, was also relatively short-lived, poor, and unproductive. Much of Sam Houston's presidency was spent trying to convince the United States to annex Texas, while simultaneously attempting to secure international recognition of Texas's independence by the United States, Great Britain, and France, as well as trying to procure financial aid from these governments.[19] As noted above, Texans overwhelmingly preferred joining the United States. It was the United States that hesitated on bringing Texas into the union. Offshoots of this legend continue to prevail throughout the state. For instance, many Texans believe that Texas is permitted to fly its flag at the same height as the U.S. flag as an indication of the unique status of Texas. In truth, all states can fly their flags equal to the U.S. flag.

Statehood—The Constitution of 1845

Once Texas was admitted into the United States, a new constitution was necessary. The statehood constitution continued to specify separation of powers and a system of checks and balances while recognizing the federal nature of the United States. The terms for legislators were lengthened to two years for the Texas House and four years for the Texas Senate, although the legislature would now meet biennially, in other words, every other year. The governor's term was shortened to two years, and the governor was prohibited from serving more than four years in any six. The governor's appointment power was expanded to include the attorney general, the Supreme Court judges, and district court judges, in addition to the secretary of state. Texans' experience under both Spain and Mexico was evident in the guarantees of property rights for women and homestead provisions in the new constitution.

The new constitution reflected the experience of Texans in other ways as well. Most Texans were in debt and highly distrustful of creditors, and indeed many individuals, including Stephen F. Austin, came to Texas to try to get out of debt. Thus, the statehood constitution established guarantees against imprisonment for

Manifest Destiny

the belief that U.S. expansion across the North American continent was inevitable.

debt. The bill of rights was moved to the beginning of the constitution, an indication of the importance Texans placed on individual freedom and limited government. Most of the Republic's constitutional guarantees, such as freedom of speech and press and protections for the accused were continued. At the same time, the provisions protecting slavery and prohibiting the Texas legislature from emancipating slaves remained. Voting rights for African Americans and women were not considered in the deliberations, although there was a vigorous debate over enfranchising all free "white" men. Historically, the category of "white" had included both Native Americans and native Mexicans, though some of the delegates expressed concern that the term might now be used to exclude those populations.[20] In the end, the right to vote was conferred on "[e]very free male person who shall have attained the age of twenty-one years . . . (Indians not taxed, Africans and descendants of Africans excepted)."[21] In addition, the constitution mandated that one-tenth of the state's annual revenue be set aside to create a permanent school fund. Overall, the statehood constitution was relatively brief and flexible. Daniel Webster, a U.S. senator at the time, referred to the framers of this constitution as the "ablest political body assembled in Texas," producing the best constitution of the day.[22]

With the election of Abraham Lincoln as U.S. president however, secessionist movements erupted in many southern states, including Texas. Although the movement to secede was strong in Texas, Governor Sam Houston led a substantial opposition. Indeed when Texas voted to secede a few months later, several counties in Central Texas and North Texas, as well as Angelina County in East Texas, voted against secession. In the rest of East Texas, where slavery dominated the economy, there was almost universal support for secession. There was, however, significant opposition to secession is certain parts of the state. For instance, the Central Texas frontier relied on protection from the U.S. Army, and the ethnic German population there opposed slavery, making secession less popular. Secession was also unpopular in North Texas, where slavery was virtually absent.[23] Nonetheless, on February 23, 1861, Texas voted to secede and joined the Confederate States of America.

Secession and the Confederacy—The Constitution of 1861

Joining the Confederacy meant that a new constitution was needed. However, the 1861 Confederate constitution was primarily a revised version of the 1845 statehood constitution, replacing references to the United States with references to the Confederate States of America. One notable difference was that under the Confederate constitution, slavery received even stronger protection. In the statehood constitution, the legislature was prohibited from emancipating slaves without compensating their owners and owners were prohibited from emancipating slaves without permission of the legislature. In the 1861 constitution, both slave owners and the state legislature were prohibited from emancipating slaves under any circumstance. Otherwise the Confederate constitution kept the same general governmental structures as the 1845 statehood constitution.

The First Reconstruction—The Constitution of 1866

With the end of the Civil War, Texas needed a new constitution that recognized the new political reality of the defeated Confederacy and reconstituted Union. Lincoln assigned a provisional governor, A. J. Hamilton, who immediately called for a con-

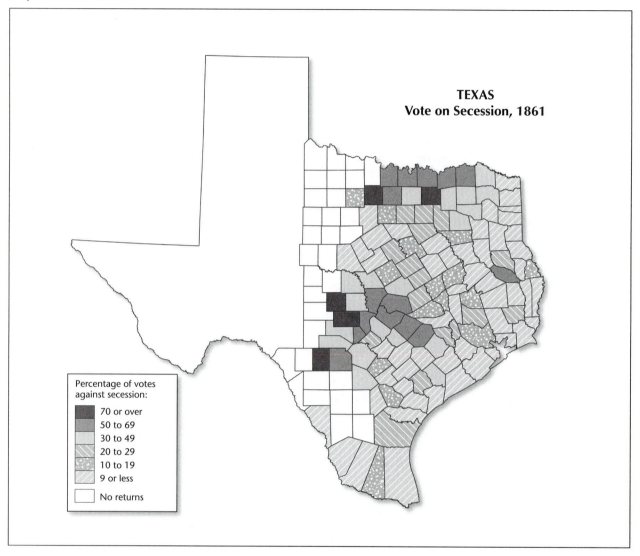

TEXAS
Vote on Secession, 1861

Percentage of votes against secession:

- 70 or over
- 50 to 69
- 30 to 49
- 20 to 29
- 10 to 19
- 9 or less
- No returns

stitutional convention. Adult white males who swore an oath of allegiance to the United States of America could participate in electing delegates to the convention. Once again, the approach of the drafters at the 1866 constitutional convention was to amend the 1845 statehood constitution, rather than write an entirely new constitution. The 1866 constitution specifically renounced secession, repudiated the debts associated with fighting the Civil War on the side of the Confederacy, and acknowledged that slavery was "terminated by this State, by the Government of the United States, by force of arms." [24]

Although slavery was ended, African Americans were not granted voting rights in the 1866 constitution and other provisions expressly prohibited them from holding office. In addition, the scope of the governorship was altered. Positions that had been previously appointed by the governor, such as the attorney general and state level judges, would now be elected. The governor's term was extended to four years, with the stipulation that the governor serves no more than eight years in any twelve-year time period. In addition, the governor was granted a line-item veto for appropriations bills. Perhaps the most significant contribution of the 1866 constitution was a clause that made it legal for individuals to acquire the mineral rights of their property.[25] In the end, though, this constitution was short-lived as Radical Republicans gained control of the national Congress and passed Reconstruction Acts designed to punish southern states.

The Second Reconstruction—The Constitution of 1869

The Reconstruction Acts passed by Congress divided the South into military districts and assigned military leaders. Texans were required by Congress to write a new constitution in which African Americans would realize full political rights, as well as ratify the Thirteenth and Fourteenth Amendments, in order to end military rule in the state. Moreover, the Radical Republicans who gained control of Congress prevented ex-Confederates, including anyone who had held a political office during the Confederacy, from either participating as delegates at this convention or voting on the resulting constitution. The result was that only six of the ninety delegates that participated in the 1866 constitutional convention attended the 1869 convention.[26] The delegates then, most of whom were unionist Republicans, were viewed with suspicion and resentment by the majority of Texans who had supported the Confederacy. Thus, the 1869 constitution is perhaps best viewed as an anomaly in Texas's constitutional development, as many of its provisions were more radical than the average Texan preferred. For instance, the office of the governor was again given broad appointment powers, including appointing Texas's Supreme Court and district court justices, as well as the attorney general and the secretary of state. The governor's salary was increased and the line-item veto was retained. The 1869 constitution also created a plural executive that consisted of eight offices, including the governor. Perhaps a more radical development for Texans was the 1869 constitution's institution of a broader range of social services and corresponding taxes than Texans had previously experienced. For example, the constitution created a road tax, which would fund bridge building and road improvements in Texas. In addition, this constitution made elementary education compulsory and funded it with one-fourth of the state's annual tax revenues, along with a poll tax and monies from the state's public lands. The constitution guaranteed adult males the right to suffrage, regardless of race, color, or previous condition, and outlawed both slavery and systems of peonage. The delegates also proposed the creation of a new state of West Texas, although this was ultimately defeated.[27]

To protest the exclusion of ex-Confederates while including African Americans in the creation of the 1869 constitution, many Democrats boycotted the election to ratify this constitution. Nonetheless, in November 1869, the participating voters approved the new constitution and Republican E. J. Davis was elected governor of Texas. The climate in which the new 1869 constitution was written would have lasting effects. After all, the national Congress had mandated many of the provisions of the new constitution and many Texans had not participated in the election of the convention members, the election to ratify the constitution, or the subsequent election of Governor Davis. Davis would remain the only Republican elected as governor in the state until the 1970s. Because the events surrounding the 1869 constitution occurred during a period of military administration of the state, the legitimacy of both the new constitution and the new governor was doubted by most Texans from the outset.

E. J. Davis

According to Texas legend, Texas needed the "Redeemer" constitution of 1876 to cleanse the state of the despotism endured under Republican governor E. J. Davis. Davis represented the more extreme branch of the Republican Party and narrowly won the gubernatorial election in 1869 with the backing of black voters. This connection to ex-slaves no doubt helped to alienate former slave owners. In the eyes of many, Davis ballooned the debt, declared martial law in much of the state with his control of the state militia and state police, and sold out the state's farmers to big business, including railroads, at the expense of the mainly agrarian population. And to add insult to injury, when it became clear that Republicans would likely lose the next election, Davis postponed the legislative election and initially refused to leave office after losing the governor's race. This version of events allowed Texans, still stinging from their loss of the recent "War of Northern Aggression," to blame the North for the economic decline of the state, erase from memory the Confederates' military defeat, and give birth to the legend of Democrats as redeemers who saved the state from a corrupt "foreign" invader.

However, if we examine some of the particulars of this story, we get a much more complicated history. Davis sought to create a compulsory education system for all children throughout the state. Any compulsory educational system with its accompanying taxes would have been seen as exorbitant, but it was also the first time that tax dollars would pay for the education of African Americans in the state, and it was the education of African Americans that led to the claims of waste.

It is true that Davis increased the debt of the state, but this is only half of the story. The state of Texas had been financially devastated by the Civil War and would have faced a lack of revenue regardless of who occupied the governor's office. Davis advocated an expansion of social services, which would necessarily translate into higher state taxes. The Republican policies were no doubt more progressive than most Democrats were comfortable with. That does not necessarily translate into wastefulness or dishonesty, though. Moreover, both taxes and state debt were actually higher under the succeeding Democratic administration.[i]

Davis also used the state police and the state militia to deal aggressively with lawless areas in the state. Texas still had large expanses of frontier to protect and there was a good deal of resistance remaining from the Civil War. For instance, Davis declared martial law in Hill County in January 1871, following the arrest of the state police who had attempted to arrest the son of the largest landowner in the county for killing a freedman and his wife.[ii] Similarly, racially motivated attacks and murders in Limestone County along with a mob threatening the state police led Davis to declare martial law there in 1871. So, while it is true that Davis used expanded police pow-

E. J. Davis would prove to be one of the most controversial governors in the state's history. The taint of illegitimacy in the state was impossible for Davis—and for the next century, the Republican Party—to overcome. After Reconstruction ended and former Confederates were again eligible to vote, Democrats won back control of the state legislature and the governorship, when Davis was defeated by Democrat Richard Coke in the 1873 gubernatorial election. Once Davis was ousted from office, Texans immediately set out to write a new constitution. Appeasing Davis's critics, the new constitution appeared to prevent such a tyrant from ever again gaining so much power in Texas. Others saw Texans leaping at the first opportunity to replace the constitution that the national government and the Republican Party had imposed on them. Either way, Texans were once again writing a constitution.

ers to maintain order in the state, often the disorder was motivated by whites attempting to dominate the newly freed African American minority and reject the authority of the Republican-dominated state government and police.

Given that many Democrats were disenfranchised during punitive Reconstruction, Davis knew that Republican control of both the governorship and the legislature would be short-lived. Although Davis postponed the legislative and Congressional elections, when they finally did take place the Democrats won overwhelmingly. The new Democrat-controlled legislature passed a law calling for the election of state and local offices, including the governor, to be held on December 2, 1873. In that election, Davis was overwhelmingly defeated by Democrat Richard Coke. However, the validity of the election was challenged by Republicans in the *Ex parte Rodriguez* case in the Texas Supreme Court. The 1869 constitution stated that "[a]ll elections for State, district and county officers shall be held at the county seats of the several counties, until otherwise provided by law; and the polls shall be opened for four days, from 8 o'clock, a.m., until 4 o'clock, p.m., of each day."[iii] Democrats argued that the constitution allowed the legislature to change either the allotted time or the place of the election. Republicans argued that the semi-colon after the phrase "provided by law" created two independent clauses and though the legislature could change the location of the polls, it could not change

the time allotted for the elections. The Texas Supreme Court sided with the Republicans and earned the moniker "the Semi-colon Court." According to the Texas Supreme Court, Coke's election was thus invalid. Democrats ignored the ruling and inaugurated Coke. Davis, unwilling to resort to force to protect his position, vacated the office.

In many ways vilifying the Davis administration extended the tensions of the Civil War, as Democrats blamed Republican unionists for all of the state's problems. That we still see many textbooks repeat the one-sided view of the Davis administration even today is a testament to the pervasiveness of the anti-Republican and anti-northern myth.

---

i. Janice C. May, *The Texas State Constitution: A Reference Guide* (Westport, Conn: Greenwood Press, 1996); see also Randolph B. Campbell, *Gone to Texas* (New York: Oxford University Press, 2004).
ii. For more details of this incident, see *Handbook of Texas Online,* www.tsha.utexas.edu/handbook/online/articles/HH/jchka.html, accessed on June 20, 2007.
iii. Texas Constitution (1869), art. 3, sec. 6.

The Current System—The Constitution of 1876

The current constitution of Texas emerged from the tangled mess left by the demise of Radical Republican rule and the return to power of the Democrats. The 1876 constitution creates three branches of government, with separation of power between the branches of government and a system of checks and balances. Texas's constitution is based on the idea of popular sovereignty, evidenced in the preamble: "Humbly invoking the blessings of Almighty God, the people of the State of Texas do ordain and establish this Constitution." The constitution also embodies the principle of federalism in recognizing that Texas is free, "subject only to the Constitution of the United States."[28]

Several clashes created the context for the current Texas constitution. First, the Civil War and the subsequent Reconstruction created resentment toward Northern Republican interests throughout the South. The Reconstruction era in Texas saw the creation of a constitution and election of politicians, while excluding the majority of Texans from participation in either activity. Second, a preference for independence and individual freedom along with a deep-seated distrust of government has always characterized the state's political culture. With the exception of the 1869 constitution, Texas has continuously sought to restrict the powers of government in general. While the current constitution represents the most extreme attempt at restricting Texas government, all of the constitutions, with the exception of the 1869 constitution, sought to create a government that would generally stay out of the lives of average Texans. The current constitution, in reaction to the comparatively progressive 1869 constitution, goes farther than any previous constitution in creating a document that specifies exactly what the government can and cannot do. Delegates to the convention that created the current constitution were overwhelmingly Democrats who distrusted government, favored local control, preferred fiscal restraint, and wanted to fix the perceived injustices of the Republican-created 1869 constitution. Third, the delegates who wrote the current constitution were primarily concerned with protecting agrarian interests, as most Texans in 1876 engaged in farming. Indeed, close to half of the delegates were members of the Grange party, an organization created to protect the interest of farmers. These farmers were interested in limiting the power of the railroads that they relied on to deliver their crops and livestock to market. The Davis administration's policies aided the expansion of the railroads in Texas, which led to the exorbitant rail rates that frustrated the farmers in the state. The resulting constitution is one of specific limitations on governmental power, rather than a fundamental set of laws.

Table 2.1 Articles of the Current Texas Constitution

PREAMBLE	
Article 1	Bill of Rights
Article 2	The Power of Government
Article 3	Legislative Department
Article 4	Executive Department
Article 5	Judicial Department
Article 6	Suffrage
Article 7	Education
Article 8	Taxation and Revenue
Article 9	Counties
Article 10	Railroads
Article 11	Municipal Corporations
Article 12	Private Corporations
Article 13	Spanish and Mexican Land (repealed August 5, 1969)
Article 14	Public Lands and Land Office
Article 15	Impeachment
Article 16	General Provisions
Article 17	Mode of Amending the Constitutions of this State

Individual Freedom

Texans have always placed a high value on individual freedoms. Since 1845, a Bill of Rights has been the first article in each Texas constitution, demonstrating the importance Texans place on individual freedom. The current constitution carries over rights from the previous constitution, such as freedom of speech, press, and assembly, along with the right to bear arms. It also includes protections against unreasonable search and seizure, cruel and unusual punishment, and guarantees a trail by jury.

Texans' experiences during the Civil War also influenced the writers of the current constitution. Because Lincoln had suspended habeas corpus during the war, so that people who were suspected of disloyalty could be arrested and held indefinitely without being charged, the authors of the current constitution specified that the right to habeas corpus shall never be suspended. The authors kept the provisions for freedom of religion while adding a requirement that state officeholders "acknowledge the existence of a Supreme Being." Moreover, the current constitution prohibits public money from being used for the benefit of "any sect, or religious society, theological or religious seminary." Prohibitions against imprisonment for debt and community property and homestead provisions were retained.

Texas versus California

The states of California and Texas seem to provide natural comparisons. Both states have large, racially and ethnically diverse populations, are experiencing rapid population growth, and are substantially urbanized. In addition, both states possess constitutions that date from the 1870s. However, the differences between the two states are readily apparent. The current Texas constitution is a reaction to the Civil War and Reconstruction. By contrast, the California Constitution reflects some aspects of the Populist and Progressive Era politics that influenced the United States from the 1870s until the 1910s. The shorter California Constitution possesses fewer than 55,000 words, compared to the Texas Constitution, which has more than 93,000 words. Though their document is shorter, Californians have exercised their right to amend their constitution 513 times, over 50 times more than Texans have.

Civil liberties provide a key difference in the two state constitutions. Take for example the issue of free speech. The California Constitution states, "Every person may freely speak, write and publish his or her sentiments on all subjects, being responsible for the abuse of this right. A law may not restrain or abridge liberty of speech or press." [i] This language is similar to the Texas Constitution, which states that "[e]very person shall be at liberty to speak, write or publish his opinions on any subject, being responsible for the abuse of that privilege; and no law shall ever be passed curtailing the liberty of speech or of the press." [ii] While the language is similar, courts in California have interpreted the language to mean a near absolute right to speech, including the right to speech in private spaces like restaurants and shopping centers that are open to the public. Thus, residents of California are occasionally subject to protests, rallies, and debates when visiting the local grocery store or hardware store. Similar provisions in California spell out a more detailed and expansive concept of freedom of the press. Texas courts in comparison have tended to reject a broad interpretation of the free speech clauses of the Texas Constitution, favoring some limits on speech rights in publicly accessible but privately owned spaces like restaurants.

Additional differences reflect the experiences that divide Texas and California. Texans' right to free exercise of religion is addressed in four different sections of the constitution, including a strict prohibition on public money given to religious organizations; California has a single clause that addresses the topic of religious expression. Texans enjoy a broad concept of the right to bear arms and protection from quartering of soldiers, while the California Constitution lacks any language on either subject. In contrast, Californians enjoy extensive rights to fish on public lands, whereas the Texas Constitution is silent on this issue. In California, "cruel or unusual punishments" are outlawed, leading the California Supreme Court in 1972 to become the first to ban the death penalty; although a constitutional referendum restored the death penalty several years later. The Texas Constitution specially mentions the death penalty and the capital felonies that may carry the death penalty. Finally, the Texas Constitution was amended in 2005 to define marriage as a union between one man and one woman; California's document does not define marriage.

Thinking Critically

- Does the way that the two constitutions handle the issues of freedom of speech, right to bear arms, right to fish, and cruel or unusual punishment fit your images of Texas and California?
- Does one constitution appear to be more protective of civil liberties than the other?
- How much do you think that the courts' interpretations have to do with how civil liberties in each state are applied?
- Do you think extending free speech to private but publicly accessible areas like shopping centers seems reasonable?

i. California Constitution (1879), art. I, sec. 2(a).
ii. Texas Constitution (1876), art. 1, sec. 8.

The Legislative Branch

The legislative branch is composed of a Texas House of Representatives with 150 members and a Texas Senate with 31 members. The current constitution imposes several explicit limitations on the legislature. Members of the House continue to be elected every two years, while the terms of the senators were shortened to four years. Originally, the constitution spelled out the legislator's salaries, and increasing salaries required a constitutional amendment, which had to be approved by the electorate. This constitutional restriction persisted until 1991, when the constitution was amended to create the Texas Ethics Commission to set legislative salaries, subject to voter approval. The constitution also restricts the legislature to biennial sessions for only 140 days. While the legislature is restricted to a relatively short session, thirty-day special sessions can be called by the governor, who sets the agenda for those sessions.

Much of the Texas Constitution is a list of things that the legislature is specifically prohibited from doing. For instance, the constitution spells out the types of taxes the legislature can and cannot levy. It explicitly prohibits the state from passing a property tax and sets ceilings on the amount of property taxes that local governments can collect. The constitution further forbids the government from imposing a state income tax without approval by a majority of voters. The legislature is additionally prohibited from passing a bill that contains more than one subject, and is required to place the subject of the bill in the title. A reading of the current constitution makes clear that the main goal of the framers was to expressly limit the government rather than creating a broad governing mandate.

The Executive Branch

One of the most outstanding features of the current Texas constitution is the creation of a fractured and severely limited executive. According to Article IV of the constitution, the executive branch is divided between a governor, lieutenant governor, secretary of state, comptroller, land commissioner, and attorney general.[29] Thus, in contrast to the United States executive, the Texas Constitution creates a plural executive. Moreover, most offices that had been appointed by the governor would now be elected, in order to further limit the power of the governor. In fact, the only major appointment left to the governor is the secretary of state. The delegates of the constitutional convention also shortened the term of office for the governor, decreased the governor's salary, and limited the number of terms that a governor could hold office. Later amendments would increase the governor's term to four years and remove the term limits. Clearly, though, one of the main goals of the delegates creating the current constitution was to limit the power of the governor.

The Texas Judiciary

Article V of the Texas Constitution creates a judicial branch with county courts, commissioner's courts, justice of the peace courts, district courts, and appellate courts, as well as "such other courts as may be provided by law." It also specifies the creation of two high courts, a Supreme Court to hear final civil appeals, and a Court of Criminal Appeals to hear final criminal appeals.[30] Moreover, the constitution specifies the election of all state judges. The result is a judiciary whose members are constantly raising campaign funds in order to get reelected. This is in sharp contrast to the federal judiciary, which is appointed for the purpose of creating an independent judiciary.

Civil Rights

Two of the most controversial subjects at the 1876 constitutional convention dealt with suffrage and education. One Reconstruction reform that could not be undone was the extension of suffrage to African Americans in Texas, which was now mandated by the U.S. Constitution. There were those at the convention, however, who favored a poll tax in order to vote, ostensibly in an attempt to disenfranchise African Americans in Texas. However, the Grange and other poor farmers objected to the poll tax, which would also disenfranchise poor whites in Texas. In the end, the convention delegates defeated the poll tax. They refused to grant women's suffrage. Interestingly, the current constitution protects voters from arrest on their way to and from the polls on Election Day.

Perhaps more controversial than voting was the educational system that had been mandated in the Constitution of 1869. During the Reconstruction period, education was compulsory, regardless of race, and was paid for with tax revenue. At a time when the Texas economy had been devastated by the Civil War, a majority of Texans saw such a widespread educational system as excessive. Opposition to this system was widespread, as white landowners objected to paying for the education of African American children, and farmers in general favored local control of education, which could be tailored to the needs of particular communities while corresponding to crop cycles.[31] Thus, the 1876 constitution ended compulsory education and required segregated schools. In 1972, the Texas Constitution was amended to guarantee equality under the law regardless of "sex, race, color, creed or national origin"—the so-called Texas equal rights amendment. A similar amendment failed to pass in the U.S. Congress. More recently, in 2005, Texas voters overwhelmingly voted to define marriage as only "the union of one man and one woman."

Distrust in Government

The most prominent feature in the current Texas constitution is the general distrust of government. Article I underscores the attitudes of most Texans that "[a]ll political power is inherent in the people, and all free governments are founded on their authority . . . they have at all times the inalienable right to alter, reform or abolish their government in such manner as they may think expedient." We see evidence of Texans' distaste for government throughout the document. For example, the circumstances under which the government can tax and incur debt are spelled out in the constitution. In order to keep the government small, the powers, terms, and salaries of the executive and legislature are severely limited. Instead, the framers of the Texas Constitution created a system where political power is retained by the people. An example of the power entrusted to the Texas voter is the use of the **long ballot** in which almost all positions in the state are elected. This distrust of government continues to pervade Texans' attitudes today, and is one of the main reasons why a complete constitutional revision has failed to get support in the state.

Long ballot
a system in which almost all of the positions in a state are elected rather than appointed.

Criticisms of the Texas Constitution

 he current Texas constitution was written in 1876, for a state that was completely different than modern-day Texas. The population in the 1880s was slightly over 1.5 million people, whereas in 2006 Texas's population was

Texas versus Massachusetts

The Massachusetts Constitution of 1780, predating the U.S. Constitution by nearly ten years, is the oldest written constitution still in use not only in the United States but also anywhere in the world. The framers of the Massachusetts Constitution included three heroes of the American Revolution: John Adams, Samuel Adams, and James Bowdoin. These larger-than-life heroes established a pattern that many states now follow for state constitutions: a preamble, a declaration of the rights of citizens, a framework for government, and amendments to the constitution. The virtues of the relatively broad language of the Massachusetts Constitution have served the state well, as opposed to the highly specific and technical language of the Texas Constitution. Fewer constitutional amendments (120 total) have been passed in Massachusetts than almost half of the states, certainly fewer than Texas's 456 amendments. Also unlike Texas, Massachusetts still uses the original document, while Texas is on its fifth constitution since statehood (and its sixth if you add the short-lived Constitution of the Republic of Texas).

Thinking Critically

- Why do you think the Massachusetts Constitution is a model for other states?
- What aspects of the Massachusetts Constitution seem unusual to you?
- What aspects seem familiar?
- Do some features in the Texas Constitution seem preferable to you?

A Constitutional Comparison of Massachusetts and Texas

FEATURE	MASSACHUSETTS	TEXAS
Year adopted	1780	1876
Word length	36,700	93,000
Amendments	120	456
Major sections	4	17
Executive offices elected		
Governor	Yes	Yes
Lieutenant Governor	Yes	Yes
Secretary of State	Yes	No
Attorney General	Yes	Yes
Treasurer/Comptroller	Yes	Yes
Other	Yes (1)	Yes (2)
Legislature	General Court	Texas Legislature
Senate		
Size	40	31
Length of term	2 years	4 years
House		
Size	160	150
Length of term	2 years	4 years
Judiciary	Appointed	Elected
Statewide referendum to amend constitution	Yes	Yes
Statewide referendum to make general laws	Yes	No
Initiative petition to amend constitution	Yes	No
Initiative petition to make general laws	Yes	No

approaching 24 million. While Hispanic and African American populations comprised the two largest minorities in Texas in the 1880s, the Hispanic population has increased significantly since then, while the African American population has declined, and other minorities such as Asian immigrants have a greater presence in the state today. Economically, Texas in 1876 was agrarian with small farms and ranches dominating the state. Today, the state's economy is one of the most diverse in the United States and continues to diversify. Texas has a substantial aerospace and defense industry, a significant telecommunications and computer sector, along with important centers of finance, shipping, energy, and other big business. Thus, it is not surprising that the current constitution is considered outdated and inadequate for such a large and diverse state.

The desire of the framers to eliminate the last vestiges of Reconstruction, rather than the goal of writing a long-lasting constitution, shaped the current constitution. One of the most frequently cited criticisms is the amount of specific detail in the current constitution. The Texas Constitution is a long list of specific rules rather than a set of fundamental legal principles for state law. For instance, in 2003, Texans approved twenty-two constitutional amendments, including one permitting cities to donate their surplus fire-fighting equipment to volunteer fire departments. Similarly, of the sixteen constitutional amendments voters passed in November 2007, one was a proposal to create and fund a cancer research institute. While both of these amendments may be commendable, they are the sort of specific policymaking we would ideally see from a legislature, rather than embedded in a constitution.

Writing this sort of specific detail into the state's constitution means that Texas has the second longest constitution in the United States, one that is unorganized and unwieldy. The problem is compounded because enacting statutes often requires amending the state constitution rather than passage in the legislature. This ironically means that the constitution continues to grow; it is now approximately 93,000 words.

In addition, the constitution severely limits the government. The formal power of the executive is limited, making Texas's governor one of the weakest executives in the United States. Moreover, the legislature's session is limited to 140 days every other year. While that may have been desirable in 1876 agrarian Texas, today Texas is the second largest state with an increasingly diverse population and economy. Extremely low legislative pay, which is spelled out in the constitution, means that average Texans could not afford to take the job. Instead of creating a citizen legislature, the Texas legislature is dominated by wealthy individuals and big business. Finally, election of judges in Texas creates a climate of mistrust in the Texas judiciary, with judges constantly having to raise money for reelection. The result is a judiciary that most Texans believe is overly influenced by money.

Amending the Constitution

The current Texas constitution outlines the process by which it can be amended. Both houses of the Texas Legislature must approve any proposed amendments by a two-thirds vote. Once approved, the amendment must be published twice in major newspapers, and posted in each county courthouse thirty days prior to the election. Finally, the amendment must be approved by a simple majority of voters. The Texas Constitution has been amended 456 times, making it one of the most frequently amended constitutions among the states.[32]

The overwhelming majority of proposed amendments are approved by electors; 87 percent of all proposed amendments have been adopted since 1985. Almost all constitutional amendments are put on the ballot in odd years, or in special elections. Unfortunately, the voter turnout during the special elections is significantly lower than during general election years. Since 1985 the average turnout in elections with constitutional amendments is 8.67 percent of the entire voting age population.[33] Voter turnout remains alarmingly low even when the proposed amendment is relatively popular or controversial. For example, in 2007 when 88 percent of voters approved school tax relief for the elderly and disabled in Texas, only 7 percent of potential voters actually participated in that election. In 2003, voters approved twenty-two constitutional amendments, including a

Table 2.2 Comparison of State Constitutions

STATE	NUMBER OF CONSTITUTIONS	DATE OF CURRENT CONSTITUTION	APPROXIMATE WORD LENGTH
Alabama	6	1901	310,328
Alaska	1	1959	15,988
Arizona	1	1912	28,876
Arkansas	5	1874	59,500
California	2	1879	54,645
Colorado	1	1876	45,679
Connecticut	4	1965	16,608
Delaware	4	1879	19,000
Florida	6	1969	38,000
Georgia	10	1983	25,000
Hawaii	1	1959	20,774
Idaho	1	1890	23,239
Illinois	4	1971	13,200
Indiana	2	1851	10,230
Iowa	2	1857	12,500
Kansas	1	1861	12,246
Kentucky	4	1891	23,911
Louisiana	11	1975	54,112
Maine	1	1820	13,500
Maryland	4	1867	46,600
Massachusetts	1	1780	36,700
Michigan	4	1964	27,000
Minnesota	1	1858	11,547
Mississippi	4	1890	24,323
Missouri	4	1945	42,600
Montana	2	1973	13,218
Nebraska	2	1875	20,048
Nevada	1	1864	21,377
New Hampshire	2	1784	9,200
New Jersey	3	1948	22,956
New Mexico	1	1912	27,200
New York	4	1895	51,700
North Carolina	3	1971	11,000
North Dakota	1	1889	20,564
Ohio	2	1851	36,900
Oklahoma	1	1907	79,133
Oregon	1	1859	63,372
Pennsylvania	5	1968	27,503
Rhode Island	2	1986	10,908

Table 2.2, continued

STATE	NUMBER OF CONSTITUTIONS	DATE OF CURRENT CONSTITUTION	APPROXIMATE WORD LENGTH
South Carolina	7	1896	22,300
South Dakota	1	1889	27,703
Tennessee	3	1870	13,300
Texas	**5**	**1876**	**93,000**
Utah	1	1896	11,000
Vermont	3	1793	8,295
Virginia	6	1971	21,319
Washington	1	1889	50,237
West Virginia	2	1872	26,000
Wisconsin	1	1848	14,392
Wyoming	1	1890	31,800

Source:The Book of the States 2005 (Lexington, Ky: Council of State Governments, 2003), vol. 37, table 1.1, 10.

controversial limit on medical malpractice lawsuits, with a mere 12 percent turnout rate. In 2005, 76 percent of voters approved a constitutional amendment defining marriage as only a union between a man and a woman. An amendment this controversial was based on a 14 percent voter turnout. Amending the fundamental state law with such low turnout rates raises serious questions about the nature of popular sovereignty in Texas.

Constitutional Revision

Distrust of government has generally translated to suspicion of change in Texas. The current constitution has been criticized since its inception. Demands for constitutional revision have been almost continuous in Texas, with calls for constitutional conventions occurring in 1913, 1917, 1949, 1957, and 1967.[34] However, it wasn't until the early 1970s, in reaction to the Sharpstown Scandal, a banking and stock fraud scandal involving officials at the highest levels of government, that Texas came close to substantial constitutional revisions. The legislature created a constitutional revision commission which proposed sweeping changes to the current constitution. The proposal included annual sessions for the legislature, increasing the power of the governor, creation of a single high court, and changing the selection process of the judiciary. The proposed document would have contained only 14,000 words and would have reduced the number of articles from seventeen to eleven. The final proposal was considered a well-drafted constitution and contains many of the changes constitutional experts continue to propose today. In the end, though, a joint meeting of both houses of the legislature failed by three votes to get the two-thirds vote necessary to pass. In its next regular session, the legislature revived most of those proposals in the form of eight amendments to the constitution, but Texas voters overwhelmingly rejected each of the amendments.

Another serious attempt at significant constitutional revision came in 1998, spearheaded by Sen. Bill Ratliff and Rep. Rob Junell. The Ratliff-Junell proposal also reduced the document to about 18,000 words, granted expanded appointment

Table 2.3 Texas Constitution of 1876: Amendments Proposed and Adopted, 1879–2007

YEAR PROPOSED	NUMBER PROPOSED	NUMBER ADOPTED	YEAR PROPOSED	NUMBER PROPOSED	NUMBER ADOPTED
1879	1	1	1951	7	3
1881	2	0	1953	11	11
1883	5	5	1955	9	9
1887	6	0	1957	12	10
1889	2	2	1959	4	4
1891	5	5	1961	14	10
1893	2	2	1963	7	4
1895	2	0	1965	27	20
1897	5	1	1967	20	13
1899	1	0	1969	16	9
1901	1	1	1971	18	12
1903	3	3	1973	9	6
1905	3	2	1975	12	3
1907	9	1	1977	15	11
1909	4	4	1978	1	1
1911	5	4	1979	12	9
1913	7	0	1981	10	8
1915	7	0	1982	3	3
1917	3	3	1983	19	16
1919	13	3	1985	17	17
1921	5	1	1986	1	1
1923	22	1	1987	28	20
1925	4	4	1989	21	19
1927	8	4	1990	1	1
1929	7	5	1991	15	12
1931	9	9	1993	19	14
1933	12	4	1995	14	11
1935	13	10	1997	15	13
1937	7	6	1999	17	13
1939	4	3	2001	19	19
1941	5	1	2002	1	1
1943	3	3	2003	22	22
1945	8	7	2005	9	7
1947	9	9	2007	17	17
1949	10	2			

Source: www.tlc.state.tx.us.

power to the governor, increased the length of legislators, terms while imposing term limits, created a salary commission, appointed by the governor to set compensation for legislators (without voter approval), and reorganized the judiciary with a single high court and gubernatorial appointment of judges, followed by a retention election. The Ratliff-Junell proposal unceremoniously died in the legislature from neglect. As with previous attempts at constitutional revision, Texans resisted change and chose to continue to patch up the old constitution. The constitution remains mired in legislative detail and Texas remains unwilling or unable to create a constitution designed for the diversity and complexities of the state.

Absent a constitutional convention, constitutional revision can occur in a variety of other ways. In Texas, constitutional revision has been accomplished primarily through amending the constitution. This incremental change in Texas, while not ideal, has been necessary since many Texans resist more sweeping changes, such as wholesale revision through constitutional conventions. Theoretically change could also be accomplished with the voter-led initiative and referendum. An **initiative** occurs when voters gather signatures on a petition in order to place either statutes or constitutional amendments on a ballot. A **referendum** allows voters to cast a popular vote on statutes passed by the legislature. These two voter-led mechanisms are consistent with Texans' legendary preference for limited government and popular control. So it is particularly surprising that the Texas Constitution does not have provisions for either procedure. While Texans' preference for limited government may be notorious, in this case it is apparently trumped by Texas's equally entrenched resistance to change. In the end, prospects for constitutional change seem limited. Most Texans, even as they acknowledge the problems with the current constitution, still distrust more the potential problems of a new constitution.

Table 2.4 Voter Turnout during Special Elections and Off-Year Elections, 1981–2007

YEAR	VOTER TURNOUT AS A PERCENTAGE OF THE VOTING AGE POPULATION
2007	8.64
2005	13.8 (Gay marriage amendment)
2003	9.30
2001	5.60
1999	6.69
1997	5.32
1997	8.45 (Special education)
1995	5.55
1993	8.25
1991	16.6 (School tax reform)
1989	9.33
1985	8.24
1983	6.19
1981	8.07

Source: Texas Secretary of State, www.sos.state.tx.us/elections/historical/70-92.shtml.

Initiative

a mechanism that allows voters to gather signatures on a petition in order to place statutes or constitutional amendments on a ballot.

Referendum

a mechanism that allows voters to cast a popular vote on statutes passed by the state legislature; the legislature can place measures on the ballot for voter consideration.

Winners and Losers

 n Texas, the general distrust of government and resulting resistance to change has created an environment where the fundamental law is unyielding—a difficult situation for one of the nation's most rapidly changing states. The authors of the current Texas constitution distrusted the Reconstruction government, a government they saw as the government of an occupying army, and reacted by creating a constitution intended to limit the power of government, curb the potential for abuse from business and preserve the power of citizens in the state. Ironically, the constitution generated such a high democratic cost to Texas citizens that the goals of the framers were guaranteed to fail. In an effort to safeguard the power of individuals, voters in Texas face a long ballot, and are literally overwhelmed by the number of offices and constitutional amendments put before them at each general election. Instead of ensuring popular control of government, such a burden on citizens ensures voter fatigue and apathy. When citizens don't play their role to keep government in check, professional politicians and narrow special interests fill in the gap.

The winners of the current constitutional rules tend to be big business interests. Business in Texas can dominate both the elections of officials and the approval or defeat of constitutional amendments, as overwhelmed voters simply opt out. The voters comprise the losers of the stagnant Texas constitution. The voters who continue to distrust government and therefore resist changing the political system end up with a state where business and political interests often override popular concerns. They cling to the myth that the Texas Constitution "ain't broke" in the face of mounting evidence to the contrary.

Moreover, the short biennial legislative sessions stipulated in the constitution create a government that has not kept up with the increasing complexities of the state. The goal of the framers was to create a legislature dominated by citizen legislators. By keeping the legislative sessions fixed and biennial, and the salary small, the framers hoped to preclude the creation of a professional legislature. Instead these constitutional impediments guarantee that the legislature is dominated by people who depend on business corporations or legal firms for their salary, entities that often have interests in state legislation. The constitution has created a legislature that is indebted to big business and special interests rather than one concerned with representing the people.

The election of judges in Texas, when most citizens are overwhelmed by the number of officials on the ballot, also creates an environment whereby citizens' interests may be marginalized in favor of big business interests. Judges must raise significant amounts of money to be elected in the state, while most citizens are simply not paying attention to judicial elections. Big business and other special interests are willing to fill that gap. In general the Texas Constitution as it currently stands does not effectively empower the people in the state, and the general distrust of government and change means the people do not favor changing the constitution.

Conclusion: Tradition of Mistrust and Time for a Change?

Texans continues to cling to a constitution written over one hundred years ago, when Texas was largely dominated by agriculture. The state of Texas has undergone constant and dramatic change since the constitution was written and there is no sign that change will be slowing down. Gone are the days of the rugged frontier. In today's Texas you are more likely to see a computer chip than a longhorn. As Texas continues to change, Texans cling to the myth that the constitution continues to serve the citizens of the state. Mistrust of government overrides concerns over an unresponsive governmental structure. Texas continues to face increasingly complex issues but Texans' tradition of mistrust undermines the ability of the government to respond to the state's transformations. Relying on its outdated constitution will not serve Texas in the future.

Key Terms

block grant
categorical grant
concurrent powers
confederal system
constitution
delegated powers
extradition
federalism
fiscal federalism
full faith and credit clause
general revenue sharing
horizontal federalism
initiative
long ballot
Manifest Destiny
plural executive
popular sovereignty
privileges and immunities
referendum
reserved powers
supremacy clause
unfunded mandates
unitary system
vertical federalism

Explore this subject further at http://college.cqpress.com/lonestarpolitics, where you'll find chapter summaries, practice quizzes, key word flash cards, and additional suggested resources.

Seen from the visitor's gallery, the Texas House of Representatives meets during its regular session. Directly behind the Speaker's desk at the front of the chamber is a display containing the remains of the flag from the Battle of San Jacinto.

CHAPTER 3

Texas Legislature

I n January 2007, the Texas Legislature met for its biennial regular session. As part of its regular business, the Texas House of Representatives conducted the normal opening of session, including the election of the Speaker of the House. Tom Craddick, R-Midland, was reelected as Speaker of the House, one of the most powerful positions in the Texas state government. Craddick won with a lopsided vote of about 80 percent of the 150 members of the Texas House of Representatives. Although carrying 80 percent of the vote might suggest overwhelming support for Craddick, his campaign to get reelected as Speaker had been difficult, including strong opposition from members of his own party. When the Texas House began to consider legislation in earnest, further resistance to Craddick's exercise of power coalesced. By May an open rebellion brewed.

Craddick's leadership led to the unusual discussion to remove him as Speaker. The chief complaint was Craddick's style, which was criticized for being autocratic and win-at-all-costs. On May 26, opponents in the House attempted to unseat Craddick using a procedural motion.[1] Craddick even refused to permit one opponent—Rep. Fred Hill, R-Richardson, who sought to make a motion to oust Craddick—to speak on the floor of the House. Under the procedural rules for the Texas House of Representatives, Hill's motion to remove Craddick as Speaker was "privileged" and required that the member be recognized by the Speaker in order to make the motion. At one point in the debate, Craddick's opponents tried to physically seize the Speaker's podium to stop Craddick. In the wake of this rebellion and Craddick's unwillingness to let an opponent address the House, the House parliamentarian and assistant parliamentarian resigned.[2]

Rep. James Keffer, R-Eastland, even requested an advisory opinion from the Texas Attorney General regarding the constitutional basis for removing the Speaker. Craddick argued that, according to the Texas Constitution, the House could only remove him as Speaker in a vote every two years at the beginning of a regular session or through the regular impeachment procedure. Craddick also claimed that the power of the Speaker to recognize members or allow the introduction of a motion is absolute.[3] In effect, Craddick's position ensured that he would remain in office until after the next election in 2008. His opponents countered that the Texas Constitution and the bylaws of the Texas House of Representatives allows "legislative officers" such as the Speaker to serve at the pleasure of the House and are subject to replacement at any time. Precedent allows for the removal of a sitting Speaker, as happened in 1871, when Ira Evans was removed from the position for denouncing a change in Texas election law that was supported by the majority.[4]

Why does the battle between Speaker Craddick and his opponents matter? The battle is not just about rules, procedures, and interpretations. This episode illustrates the importance of leadership and organization in the Texas House of Representatives. The Speaker is a very powerful position, possessing the ability to shape which bills become laws and who controls committees. The Speaker may reward allies and punish opponents. Craddick's allies liked what they got, his opponents did not. A revolt seemed to be the only way to change the workings of the Texas House.

In this chapter, we examine the Texas Legislature in relation to other state legislatures, including issues like the size of the chambers, the nature of bicameralism, types of state legislatures, and qualifications for office. Then, we explore the meaning of representation, examine who is a representative, and consider just how representative the Texas Legislature actually is. A discussion of elections to the Texas Legislature follows, with a focus on the election system, the issue of redistricting, and the impact of the Voting Rights Act of 1965. Next, legislative organization is discussed by examining the structure and function of chamber leadership, party organization, and committees in the Texas Legislature. Finally, the chapter concludes with an examination of the legislative process or "how a bill becomes a law" in Texas.

As you read the chapter, think about the following questions:

★ How does Texas's size affect the representative nature of the legislature?
★ To what extent does Texas have a citizen legislature?
★ What limits are placed on the Texas Legislature?
★ Who is included in the leadership structure in the Texas Legislature?
★ What are the obstacles to a bill becoming a law?

The Texas Legislature in Context

The U.S. Congress, as the legislative branch of the U.S. government, serves as a model for most legislative branches of state governments. Texas is no exception to this rule. The legislative branch in Texas is usually referred to as the Texas Legislature or simply *the* Legislature. The Texas Legislature is **bicameral,** consisting of two separate chambers or houses. The lower house is most frequently called the House of Representatives, and the upper house is often called the Senate. References to "upper" and "lower" houses developed from the British Parliament where the House of Lords represented the nobility of the "upper class" and the House of Commons represented the ordinary citizens of the "lower class." These terms carried over into the American, and Texan, experience. States vary slightly in the names of the two chambers. For example, in Virginia, the lower house is called the House of Delegates. Most states, however, employ the naming convention that Texas also uses. Forty-nine states possess a bicameral legislature in the state government. Only Nebraska possesses a single-chamber, or unicameral, state legislature.

The decision to have a dual-chambered state legislature reflects not just a simple desire to mirror the U.S. Congress. James Madison suggests in the *Federalist Papers* that the protection of liberty from passionate majorities rests in part with dividing the power of the legislature.[5] Requiring any new law to pass in two chambers makes it more difficult for a majority to abuse its power. This "divide and subdue" technique of allocating the power of the legislature across two chambers is enhanced

Bicameral

a legislature that consists of two separate chambers or houses.

when each chamber is chosen by a different means. For example, the members of the U.S. House of Representatives are chosen by popular vote based on small geographic districts, while the U.S. senators are chosen by statewide popular vote. Another reason, historically, to have a bicameral legislature is to represent different levels or groups. Originally, state governments were directly represented in the U.S. Congress because state legislatures at one time chose the members of the U.S. Senate.

Historically, some states mirrored the relationship between the two houses in the U.S. Congress by making counties the basis of representation in the upper house of the state legislature. However, with 254 counties, Texas never really used each individual county as the basis of representation in the Texas Senate. Moreover, the use of counties for representation in the upper house of state legislatures is no longer employed in any state. The U.S. Supreme Court rejected counties and local governments as a basis for representation in state legislatures in *Baker v. Carr* (1962), ruling that the Equal Protection Clause of the Fourteenth Amendment asserts the principle of "one person, one vote."[6] The *Baker* decision meant that the population of state legislative districts must be roughly equal and may not differ in population by more than, give or take, 5 percent. Using counties as the basis of representation for state legislatures clearly violated this concept since counties can and do vary tremendously in population size. For example, if counties were used to determine the make-up of the Texas Senate, Harris County in metropolitan Houston would contain one senator for 3.4 million people, while Loving County in West Texas would contain one senator for its 60 residents. Obviously, people in Loving County would be significantly overrepresented compared to those living in Harris County. In *Reynolds v. Sims* (1964), the U.S. Supreme Court extended this logic by requiring that both houses of state legislatures represent the population of a state on a one-person, one-vote basis.[7]

The forty-nine states with bicameral state legislatures have an upper house that is smaller than the lower house. However, the size of the chambers is not proportional to the population of the state. Large population states like Texas, Florida, or California do not always have the largest state legislatures.

What may matter more is the relationship between the number of citizens and the size of the legislature. Where there are more legislators relative to the population, each legislator represents fewer people; in some sense the legislator is closer to the people. As shown in Table 3.1, the relationship between the size of the state legislature and the number of representatives is a bit more complex than might be expected. In Texas, with the eleventh largest legislature and the second largest population, each member represents around 130,000 people. When comparing the ratios of representation to population, Texas ranks 49th in the United States. Thus, Texans are less represented in their own state legislature than almost every other state. Only California has fewer state representatives per person than Texas. Of course, the relative sizes of both houses of legislature change the dynamic a bit. The Texas Senate's 31 members each represent over 750,000 people, but in the Texas House of Representatives the ratio is 156,733 per member.

States vary in the size of their legislature and ratio of legislators to people because each individual state determines the size of the state's legislature. Often this number is set in state constitutions and therefore is difficult to change as the state population grows. The Texas Constitution sets the size of the Texas Senate at thirty-one members. Originally, the Texas Constitution set the minimum for the Texas House of Representatives at ninety-three and gave the legislature the power to add additional seats. As the population of Texas grew, the size of the Texas House of Representatives grew to Texas-sized proportions to meet this growth in population. Finally, a practi-

Table 3.1 Size of State Legislatures

STATE	TOTAL MEMBERS OF THE STATE LEGISLATURE				POPULATION PER LEGISLATOR		POPULATION	
	UPPER HOUSE	LOWER HOUSE	TOTAL MEMBERS	RANK	RATIO	RANK	IN MILLIONS	RANK
New Hampshire	24	400	424	1	3,101	1	1.315	41
Pennsylvania	50	203	253	2	49,174	38	12.441	6
Georgia	56	180	236	3	39,678	32	9.364	9
New York	62	150	212	4	91,066	46	19.306	3
Minnesota	67	134	201	5	25,706	23	5.167	21
Massachusetts	40	160	200	6	32,185	28	6.437	13
Missouri	34	163	197	7	29,614	24	5.843	18
Maryland	47	141	188	8	29,872	26	5.616	19
Connecticut	36	151	187	9	18,743	17	3.505	29
Maine	35	151	186	10	7,108	6	1.322	40
Texas	**31**	**150**	**181**	**11**	**129,878**	**49**	**23.508**	**2**
Vermont	30	150	180	12	3,467	2	0.624	49
Illinois	59	118	177	13	72,497	44	12.832	5
Mississippi	52	122	174	14	16,730	13	2.911	31
North Carolina	50	120	170	15	52,100	40	8.857	10
South Carolina	46	124	170	15	25,418	22	4.321	24
Kansas	40	125	165	17	16,752	14	2.764	33
Florida	40	120	160	18	113,062	48	18.090	4
Indiana	50	100	150	19	42,093	34	6.314	15
Iowa	50	100	150	19	19,880	18	2.982	30
Montana	50	100	150	19	6,300	5	0.945	44
Oklahoma	48	101	149	22	24,020	20	3.579	28
Michigan	38	110	148	23	68,216	42	10.096	8
Washington	49	98	147	24	43,510	35	6.396	14
Louisiana	39	105	144	25	29,778	25	4.288	25
North Dakota	47	94	141	26	4,511	3	0.636	48
Alabama	35	105	140	27	32,850	29	4.599	23
Virginia	40	100	140	27	54,593	41	7.643	12
Kentucky	38	100	138	29	30,478	27	4.206	26
Arkansas	35	100	135	30	20,822	19	2.811	32
West Virginia	34	100	134	31	13,567	10	1.818	37
Ohio	33	99	122	32	94,082	47	11.478	7
Tennessee	33	99	122	32	49,500	39	6.039	17
Wisconsin	33	99	122	32	45,549	36	5.557	20
California	40	80	120	35	303,817	50	36.458	1
New Jersey	40	80	120	35	72,708	45	8.725	11
Rhode Island	38	75	113	37	9,451	8	1.068	43
New Mexico	42	70	112	38	17,455	16	1.955	36

Table 3.1, continued

STATE	TOTAL MEMBERS OF THE STATE LEGISLATURE				POPULATION PER LEGISLATOR		POPULATION	
	UPPER HOUSE	LOWER HOUSE	TOTAL MEMBERS	RANK	RATIO	RANK	IN MILLIONS	RANK
Idaho	35	70	105	39	13,962	12	1.466	39
South Dakota	35	70	105	39	7,448	7	0.782	46
Utah	29	75	104	41	24,519	21	2.550	34
Colorado	35	65	100	42	47,530	37	4.753	22
Arizona	30	60	90	43	68,511	43	6.166	16
Oregon	30	60	90	43	41,122	33	3.701	27
Wyoming	30	60	90	43	5,722	4	0.515	50
Hawaii	25	51	76	46	16,908	15	1.285	42
Nevada	21	42	63	47	39,619	31	2.496	35
Delaware	21	41	62	48	13,758	11	0.853	45
Alaska	20	40	60	49	11,167	9	0.670	47
Nebraska	49	0	49	50	36,081	30	1.768	38

Source: Kendra A. Hovey and Harold A. Hovey, *CQ's State Fact Finder* (Washington, D.C.: CQ Press, 2007). Data compiled from tables on pages 18, 103, 104.

cal limitation on the ratio between legislators and population is the fact that extremely large legislatures are difficult to organize. If Texas used the same ratio as New Hampshire, where each member of the state legislature represents just over 3,000 people, Texas would need over 73,000 members of the state legislature. In general, there is a trade-off between representation and efficiency, as larger legislatures tend to be less efficient.

Most state legislatures meet annually. The Texas Legislature is only one of nine legislatures that does not meet yearly for a regular session. State legislatures in Arkansas, Massachusetts, Montana, Nevada, North Dakota, Oregon, South Carolina, and Wisconsin also meet biennially.[8] While the state constitutions of Minnesota and North Carolina stipulate that the legislatures are supposed to meet every other year, these legislatures are allowed to divide the regular session across two years, allowing the legislature in practice to meet annually for regular business.[9]

When in regular session, the Texas Legislature meets for 140 days, making the length of the session the fourteenth longest in the country. Eight states, including large population states like Illinois, Michigan, New York, Ohio, and Pennsylvania, do not limit the length of state legislative sessions.

The length and frequency of legislative sessions directly influences the ability of the legislature to work. Legislatures that meet annually are more likely to manage the state budget, handle new issues, and review actions of the executive branch. The infrequency of legislative sessions in Texas reflects in part the general distrust of government consistent with Texas's political culture and values.

The Texas Legislature is not limited to meeting during its regular session every two years. The legislature may hold special sessions limited to thirty days. However, the power to call special sessions in Texas does not rest with the legislature. Only the governor may do so. In addition, the governor determines the topics that the legislature may discuss during special sessions.

When the legislature is in regular session or special session, members of the legislature possess certain rights and privileges that they do not possess otherwise. For example, the Texas Constitution states that "Senators and Representatives shall, except in cases of treason, felony, or breach of the peace, be privileged from arrest during the session of the legislature, and in going to and returning from the same."[10] Another right of members is designed to allow members an expansive freedom of speech while engaged in legislative debate: "No member shall be questioned in any other place for words spoken in debate in either House."[11] Essentially, what is said in the legislature supposedly stays in the legislature. Of course, what is said in the legislature may still come back to haunt a member at the next election.

Typologies of State Legislatures

ased upon factors such as the length of legislative sessions, compensation for legislators, and professional resources, state legislatures may be classified into three types: citizen, professional, and hybrid. A **citizen legislature** attempts to keep the job of being a state legislator as a part-time function that many or most citizens can perform. Typically citizen legislatures meet every other year or for only a few weeks each year. Compensation is minimal for legislators, and in some cases amounts to no more than reimbursement for travel expenses and some meals. Staffing and other professional resources are minimal. North Dakota and Rhode Island are examples of citizen legislatures. In contrast, a **professional legislature** meets annually, often for as long as nine months a year. Members of the legislature are well compensated, averaging $68,599 among the eleven states classified as professional.[12] Generous allowances are also given for members of the legislature to hire and keep extensive staff members including secretarial support and research staff. California and New York have professional legislatures. Given the size and scope of state government, especially in high population states, the development of professional state legislatures is not surprising.

In between these two extremes are hybrid legislatures. In states like Louisiana or Missouri, the legislature typically meets annually for a couple of months. Members of the legislature receive some compensation. Average compensation for states with this type of legislature is $35,326.[13] In addition, members of the legislature receive some funds to hire a small personal staff.

The base pay for members of the Texas Legislature is only $7,200. Members also receive $128 per day while the legislature is in session for personal expenses, meaning that they earn a total of $25,120 in years with a regular session. This salary is especially restrictive for representatives from outside Austin, who must pay for a place to live in the capital during the session. To help compensate for the relatively low pay, members of the Texas Legislature enjoy one of the most generous retirement plans among the fifty state legislatures. To qualify a legislator must serve eight years in the legislature. At age 60, they can start receiving the retirement benefit on leaving the legislature. Legislators may start receiving retirement benefits at age 50 if they have served at least twelve years in the legislature. The pension formula is based on 2.3 percent of the base compensation to state district judges times the length of service in the legislature.[14] In 2005, the salary of the district judge was $125,000. This would make the minimum benefit $23,000 per year after eight years of service in the legislature. In addition, members of the legislature may contribute up to 8 percent of their salary per year while they serve in the legislature toward their pension. Addi-

Citizen legislature

a legislature that attempts to keep the job of being a state legislator as a part-time function that many or most citizens can perform. Normally it provides minimal compensation, offers few staffing resources, and operates with short or infrequent legislative sessions.

Professional legislature

a legislature that meets annually, often for nine months a year, compensates its legislators with a professional-level salary, and provides generous allowances to hire and keep support and research staffs.

tional support comes in the form of staffing resources, including an allowance of $25,000 per month for members of the Texas Senate or $8,500 per month for members of the Texas House of Representatives.

Therefore, when considering the total compensation provided to legislators, including pension and staffing resources, the Texas Legislature is usually classified as a hybrid legislature. Note that absent the generous retirement benefits, the Texas Legislature is structurally similar to a citizen legislature. The low level of pay means that most legislators cannot support themselves during their legislative career and must maintain other forms of income for many years before vesting into their retirement. The largely citizen nature of the Texas Legislature is consistent with the mythology of Texas which suggests that government should be staffed by average citizens in order to keep legislators honest and serve the people better. In reality, legislators in Texas hold jobs outside the legislature that allow them to have time off when the legislature is in session, often in professions or industries that have a vested interest in state policy.

Qualifications for Office and Length of Terms

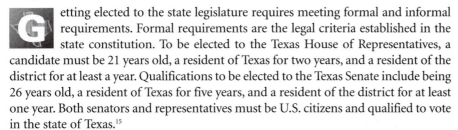 etting elected to the state legislature requires meeting formal and informal requirements. Formal requirements are the legal criteria established in the state constitution. To be elected to the Texas House of Representatives, a candidate must be 21 years old, a resident of Texas for two years, and a resident of the district for at least a year. Qualifications to be elected to the Texas Senate include being 26 years old, a resident of Texas for five years, and a resident of the district for at least one year. Both senators and representatives must be U.S. citizens and qualified to vote in the state of Texas.[15]

However, some informal elements appear to exist as well. For example, every current member of the state legislature is elected using a party affiliation. Thus, members of the state legislature identify themselves to voters as either a Democratic candidate or a Republican candidate. So, one informal requirement is **party affiliation.** Of course, receiving a party label typically means that the candidate competed in a primary election to win the right to campaign as the party's candidate in the general election. Another, extra-constitutional requirement is competing in a **party primary.** (A detailed discussion of primary elections is found in Chapters 6 and 7.) To compete in a party primary requires candidates to be well financed; candidates need to be able to campaign for the party's nomination, and if successful in the primary, campaign in the general election. Thus, a third extra-constitutional requirement of party affiliation exists. Of course, independent candidates do occasionally win election to the legislature without a party label or a primary election. However, this situation is quite rare.

Common to legislatures, the Texas House of Representatives and the Texas Senate possess the legal right to refuse to seat a legislator after the election. Rarely does this come into play. However, several decades ago a representative from Gillespie County was elected as a write-in candidate. The losing candidate appealed to the Texas House of Representatives not to seat the winner because he had not competed in the primary, never announced his candidacy, and never paid a filing fee. The House refused to consider the appeal.[16] The ability to decide whether an election is valid is a power of the legislature. As stated in the Texas Constitution, "Each House shall be the judge of the qualifications and election of its own members; but contested elections shall be determined in such manner as prescribed by law."[17]

Party affiliation
a candidate's identifiable membership in a political party, often listed on an election ballot.

Party primary
an electoral contest to win a political party's nomination for the right to appear as their candidate on the ballot in the general election.

Terms of office for members of the Texas House of Representatives are two years. Texas senators are elected every four years, but the elections are staggered so that one-half of the Texas Senate is chosen every two years. An exception to this rule involves **redistricting.** After the release of the U.S. Census data and the redistricting process to adjust election districts for the legislature is completed, the entire Texas Senate is elected at the next election. Then by lottery, one-half of the Texas Senate is up for reelection in two years, shifting to a four-year term at the next election. The other half immediately begins serving a four-year term. This process is highly unusual for state legislatures in the United States. Only Illinois and New Jersey have a similar arrangement.[18] Typically, terms in office are fixed and are not affected by the redistricting process every decade. Most states have legislatures in which the lower house serves a two-year term and the upper house serves a four-year term.

The timing of elections to the state legislature also deviates significantly by state. Some states hold elections simultaneously with elections for the U.S. president and Congress. Other states hold elections to coincide with mid-term elections to the U.S. Congress, for example, in 1998 and 2002. A few states, including Louisiana, conduct elections to the state legislature in the year before elections for U.S. president, such as 1999, 2003, and 2007. In Texas, elections for the state legislature occur simultaneously with U.S. presidential elections and with mid-term elections to the U.S. Congress.

In the 1980s, states began imposing **term limits** on the number of terms that a person could serve in the state legislature. Usually these term limits were a result of **citizen initiatives,** or petition drives, rather than self-imposed limits that the legislature itself enacted. Currently, fifteen states have term limits on the length of time that a person serves in the state legislature. Arkansas, California, and Michigan have the most restrictive limits on the amount of time someone serves in the state legislature: six consecutive years for the lower house of the state legislature and eight consecutive years for the upper house. Texas does not have term limits on the state legislature. Proponents of term limits suggest that term limits encourage **turnover** in office by requiring incumbents, those currently in office, to step down after a specified number of terms or years in office. Turnover is viewed as important to prevent "careerism" among politicians who make serving in the elected office their primary occupation and lose touch with the average voter.

Do term limits increase turnover in office? Evidence from the 2006 elections suggests that term limits do promote turnover in office. Looking at turnover in the state legislature among the fifteen states with the highest rates of turnover in their legisla-

Table 3.2 U.S. Congress and the Texas Legislature: A Comparison

CHARACTERISTIC	U.S. CONGRESS		TEXAS LEGISLATURE	
	U.S. SENATE	**U.S. HOUSE**	**TEXAS SENATE**	**TEXAS HOUSE**
Size of chamber	100	435	31	150
Term in office	6 years	2 years	4 years	2 years
Staggered terms	Yes	No	Yes	No
Minimum age for election	30	25	26	21
Resident of state	Yes	Yes	5 years	2 years
Resident of district	N/A	Yes	1 year	1 year

Source: Compiled by author.

The Texas Capitol in Austin sits among an impressive set of grounds. The capitol building itself is a source of a Texas legend. According to legend, the building was designed to be slightly taller than the U.S. Capitol in Washington, D.C. However, this legend is subject to debate. The Texas capitol is allegedly taller only if the capitol is measured from the highest tip of the statue at the top of the dome to the lowest level at the back of the building, essentially a partially exposed basement level.

ture, twelve have term limits. California and Nebraska had the highest rates of turnover, at 40.8 percent. Both states have term limits on their state legislatures. By comparison, Texas ranked number 28 in the United States in turnover. Sixteen percent of seats in the Texas Legislature changed hands in that election. Of the fifteen states with the lowest rates of turnover, only Louisiana had term limits on the state legislature.[19] Again, proponents of term limits point toward the higher rate of turnover in states with term limits as a indication that term limits end careerism by politicians and return state legislatures to citizen control.

One interesting effect of term limits seems to be a reduction in the numbers of women serving in state legislatures in some states like Missouri, Ohio, Arizona, and Florida. Ironically, the expectation was that term limits would increase the number of women representatives because more open seats would be available. It appears that when female legislators are term-limited out, often the candidates recruited to run in the open seats are not women. In fact, states without term limits, like California, Maryland, and Virginia, have demonstrated increases in women in the legislature.[20]

Theories of Representation

Representation
the relationship between an elected official and the electorate.

Delegate
this approach sees elected officials as agents of the majority who elected them to office and believes that officials should carry out, to the extent possible, the wishes of the majority.

Trustee
this approach holds that the electorate has entrusted their elected officials, who understand the issues more broadly than the electorate, to act in their best interests.

Politico
this approach is a hybrid of the trustee and delegate theories and holds that on important issues, representatives should follow the wishes of the electorate, but on other issues, the representative has leeway.

Bills
proposed new laws or changes to existing laws brought before a legislative chamber by a legislative member.

One of the key functions of a legislature is **representation**. There are three views of the relationship between the people and their representatives. According to the **delegate** approach, the people elect a representative to present the views of the district.[21] The legislator as delegate is expected to carry out specific tasks and hold specific positions, regardless of personal beliefs, on issues like public school funding, crime, abortion, etc. Essentially, the representative becomes the agent of the majority who elected him or her to office, though majorities can shift as the issues change. In contrast, the **trustee** approach begins by assuming that elected officials have access to information that voters do not. As a result, the representative understands issues from a broader perspective of the best interests of the entire district, state, or country. In this case, the people trust their representative to make the best choices for them when voting in the state legislature. Therefore, the representative, who is better educated about the issue, may go against the wishes of the majority. Finally, the **politico** approach asserts that a representative follows the wishes of the voting majority on the most important issues, but on other issues, the representative has more leeway.[22] In the latter case, the representative's personal beliefs may conflict with those of the majority and the representative then must choose between their conscience and their constituency.

In the United States, representation is connected to the Single-Member District Plurality (SMDP) election system that is used to elect both houses of the state legislature. This election system implies a certain type of representation: geographic. Texans, and indeed, most Americans, assume that a representative must represent a specific geographic area. The Texas Senate consists of thirty-one members elected from thirty-one geographic areas of Texas. So, state senator Kirk Watson of Austin is expected to reflect the views of people from Austin and parts of Travis County. For the 150 members of the Texas House of Representatives, the size of the district that each member represents is even smaller. For example, Rep. Linda Harper-Brown represents most of the city of Irving, just northwest of Dallas.

The advantage of geographic representation is the direct connection between the representative and the voters. The voters living in a specific geographic area, an election district, can know exactly who their representative is. On the other hand, this theory assumes that a representative can reflect the view of every person, or at least a majority of the people that elected him or her. Of course this is not always possible. The number of issues and **bills** on which a legislator must vote is too numerous and too complex. Also, voters often come from a variety of social and economic backgrounds, races or ethnicities, religious backgrounds, and other factors which shape their understanding of politics. A single representative is unlikely to be able to reflect all of these factors.

An alternative approach to representation is the microcosm theory, which asserts that the legislature should mirror the broader society. John Adams, the second president of the United States, believed that a legislature should look like the people as a whole.[23] The aim is to have the legislature be as close to a perfect representative sample as possible.[24] Essentially, while each individual member cannot truly represent the

Map 3: State House Districts

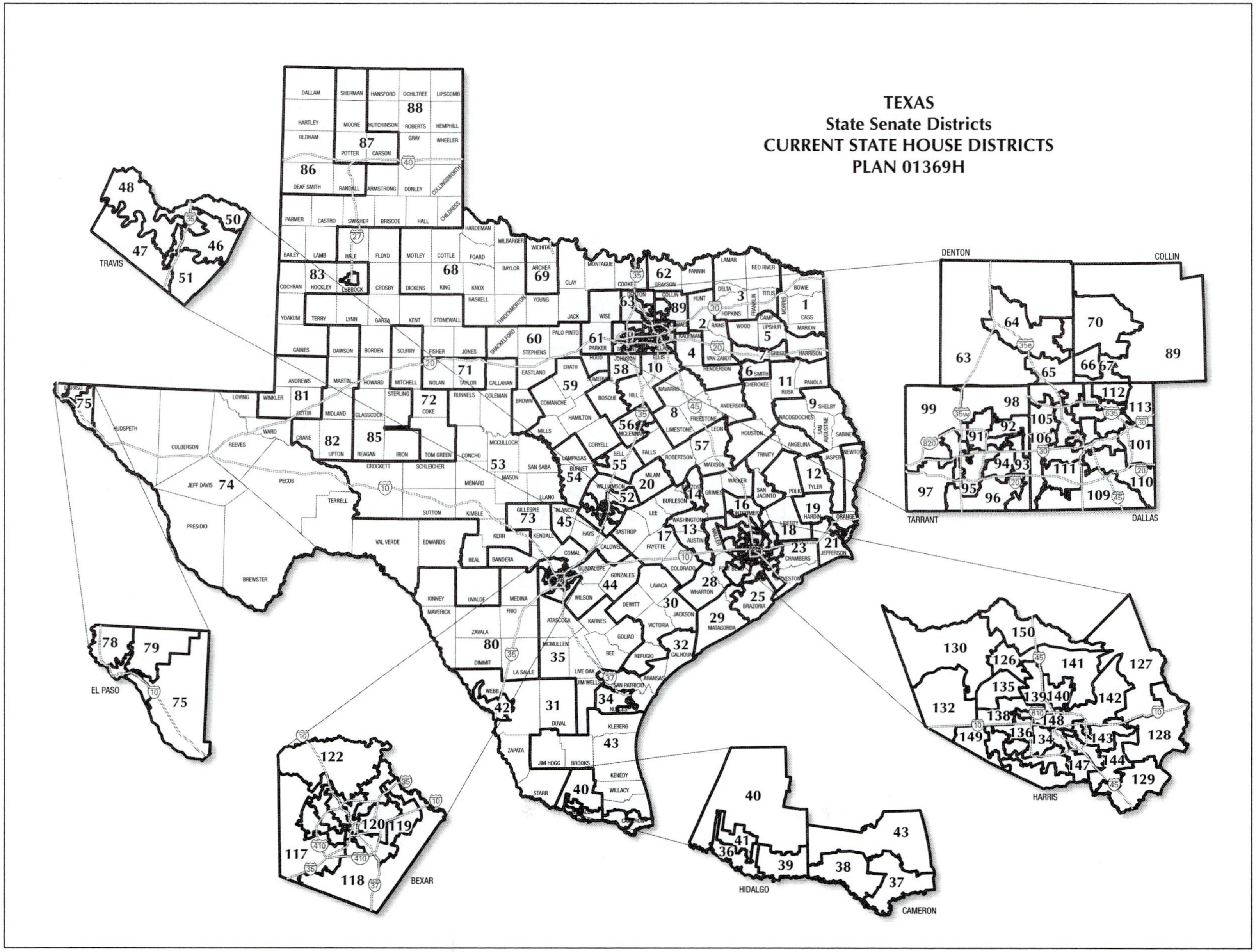

TEXAS
State Senate Districts
CURRENT STATE HOUSE DISTRICTS
PLAN 01369H

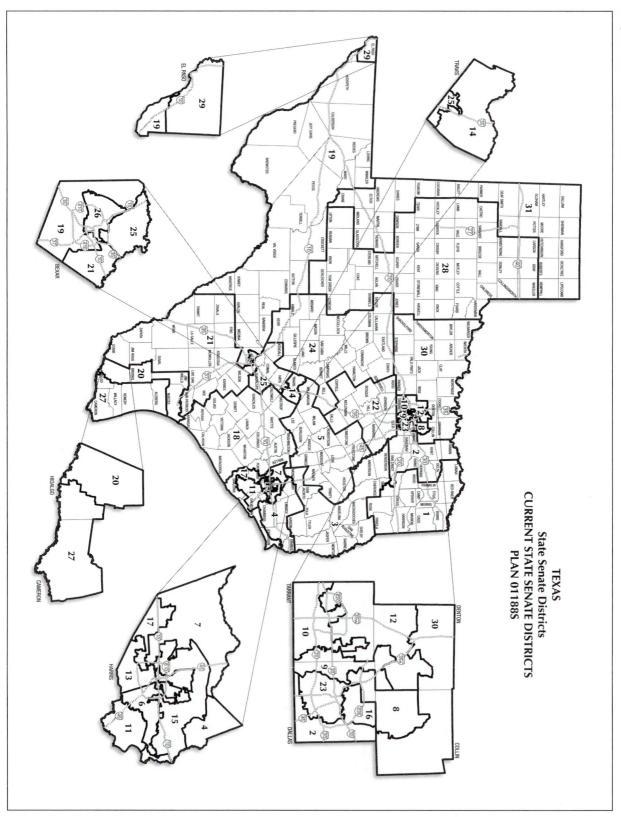

TEXAS
State Senate Districts
CURRENT STATE SENATE DISTRICTS
PLAN 01188S

Table 3.3 How "Representative" Is the 2007–2008 Texas Legislature?

	TEXAS SENATE		TEXAS HOUSE OF REPRESENTATIVES		TEXAS POPULATION
	NUMBER	PERCENTAGE	NUMBER	PERCENTAGE	PERCENTAGE
Sex					
Male	27	87.1%	118	78.7%	49.4%
Female	4	12.9%	32	21.3%	50.6%
Race/Ethnicity					
Caucasian/White	24	77.4%	110	73.3%	71.9%
Hispanic	5	16.1%	28	18.7%	35.5%
African American	2	6.5%	12	8.0%	11.0%
Education					
High school or less	0	0.0%	14	9.3%	68.7%
Two-year degree	0	0.0%	3	2.0%	6.1%
Four-year degree	15	48.4%	60	40.0%	17.0%
Graduate study	16	51.6%	73	48.6%	8.2%

Source: Adapted from Legislative Reference Library, "80th Legislature (2007)–Statistical Profile," www.lrl.state.tx.us/legis/profile80.html, accessed August 1, 2007; Texas State Directory, Inc., *Texas State Directory: The Comprehensive Guide to the Decision-Makers in Texas Government* (Austin, TX: Texas State Directory Press, 2007); U.S. Census Bureau, *2005 American Community Survey,* http://factfinder. census.gov, accessed July 11, 2007.

public at large, collectively the legislature represents the whole population. In this approach, the Texas Legislature should "look like" Texas in the gender, racial, and educational make-up of the legislature, among other factors. However, the legislature currently does not truly mirror the population as a whole. In general, the Texas Legislature is better educated than the public as a whole. The legislature also underrepresents women, as well as racial and ethnic minorities.

Microcosm theory focuses attention on the demographic nature of representation. This demographic focus is an advantage because it raises awareness about whether the legislature looks like the larger society. Assuming that issues like the income, educational, racial, religious, and gender characteristics of members of the legislature shape the decisions that they make, microcosm theory offers a starting point to address whether the legislature is truly representative of the population.

Winners and Losers

 n creating the Texas Legislature, the framers of the Texas Constitution were thinking of who wins and who loses in politics. The idea behind a citizen legislature was to ensure that citizens do not become losers and protect citizen interests rather than allowing special interests to dominate the legislature. Unfortunately in Texas there are several institutional constraints which preclude a true citizen legislature. The low level of compensation inevitably forces most legislators to have outside sources of income. Those individuals with higher levels of education, higher incomes, and more flexible work schedules may be in a more favorable position to serve in the Texas Legislature. Given the relatively high cost of campaigns, leg-

Barbara C. Jordan

Barbara Jordan's career in Texas politics represents both personal and institutional victories. Jordan graduated from Boston University Law School, but her first two efforts at winning a seat in the Texas House of Representatives were foiled by a system that chose the twelve members of the Texas House from Harris County at large through a county-wide vote that diluted the political strength of minorities. Under this system, even though about 20 percent of Houstonians were African American, none of Harris County's representatives were black. However, the *Baker v. Carr* (1962) and *Reynolds v. Sims* (1964) U.S. Supreme Court decisions required that members of the state legislature had to be elected from districts that were roughly equal in population, thus putting an end to the at-large system. Helped by the newly drawn single-member districts mandated by the Court's decisions and by the removal of the poll tax as a barrier to voting, Jordan was elected to the Texas Senate in 1966, where she became the first woman to serve in the Texas Senate and the first African American to serve since 1881.

Initially, Jordan faced insults from some legislators who called her "Mammy" or "the washerwoman" behind her back.[i] However, Jordan's intelligence and political skills won over many of her fellow legislators and the Texas Senate unanimously elected her as president pro tempore in 1972. Later in 1972, Jordan became the first black woman from the South to win election to the U.S. House of Repre-sentatives.

While in the U.S. Congress she became an important player in the impeachment of President Richard Nixon, delivering a speech in which she declared, "My faith in the Constitution is whole; it is complete; it is total. And I am not going to sit here and be an idle spectator to the diminution, the subversion, the destruction, of the Constitution." In 1976 she became the first African American woman to deliver the keynote address at the Democratic National Convention, delivering what many observers consider one of the best speeches given at a party convention.

While much of what Barbara Jordan accomplished resulted from her character and intelligence, her political career would not have been possible without the Supreme Court opening the door to more representative legislative bodies through its redistricting decisions that protected the representation of minorities.

i. James L. Haley, *Passionate Nation: The Epic History of Texas* (New York: Free Press, 2006), 545.

islators also need to be able to spend time fundraising to get reelected. The average citizen simply can't afford to take the job. Thus, the effort to maintain a "citizen" legislature may result in a legislature that does not really "look like" Texas.

The lack of a true citizen legislature also brings up the question of how representative the Texas Legislature actually is. Evaluating the legislature based on microcosm theory suggests that the legislature is unrepresentative, particularly in terms of gender. It is also problematic that Hispanics and African Americans in the state tend to be largely underrepresented. On the other hand, representation of minorities has improved recently and may continue to do so. Moreover, the Single-Member District Plurality system does tend to favor minority representation of African Americans and Hispanics. The use of this system, coupled with federal legislation like the Voting Rights Act of 1965 and with Supreme Court decisions, results in an election environment that advances minority representation.

Electing the State Legislature

lections to most state legislatures are similar to elections to the U.S. House of Representatives. Typically, states employ the Single-Member District Plurality. Under SMDP, the state (or the entire nation for the U.S. House of Representatives) is divided into a number of election districts equal to the membership of the chamber. Thus, for elections to the Texas Senate, the state of Texas is divided into thirty-one districts. Each district elects one and only one person to the chamber. For the Texas House of Representatives, the state is divided into 150 districts. Voters cast a single vote for the most preferred candidate on the ballot. For general elections in Texas, like most other states, the candidate with the most votes wins the election and the seat in the legislature. This approach is called a **plurality election.** Other states use Single-Member District Majority (SMDM) and require that the winning candidate receive a majority of the vote, or 50 percent of the vote, plus one additional vote. In a **majority election,** if no candidate receives a majority on the initial vote, a **run-off election** is held, usually two weeks to one month later. This election features only the top two candidates from the initial election, thus guaranteeing a majority outcome. A variation of this approach is called the **instant run-off.** In this election, voters indicate, in addition to their first choice, who they prefer as a second choice. If no candidate receives a majority at the initial election, the second place votes are considered, and a winner is determined by adding the first and second place votes.

The main advantage to Single-Member District Majority elections is the fact that the winner is selected by the majority of the voters who show up. Texas uses a Single-Member District Plurality system for general elections to the state legislature, U.S. House of Representatives, and U.S. Senate. Note that Texas's primary elections for state and local offices and primary elections for U.S. Senate and U.S. House of Representatives use the Single-Member District Majority system.

Single-Member District versus Multi-Member District

Some states use the **Multi-Member District (MMD)** system to elect their state legislature. In an MMD system, the state is divided into many election districts, but each district elects more than one person to the state legislature. Voters normally cast a single vote for their most preferred candidate on the ballot. After the votes are counted, then the candidates with the highest vote totals equal to the number of seats in the district are elected. The advantage of the MMD system is that candidates from more than one political party (or faction of a political party) are able to win a seat from the district.

For the Texas Senate, the requirement to use the SMDP system began in the original wording of the Constitution of 1876.[25] Election districts for the Texas House of Representatives were a combination of SMDP and MMD: MMD were used when a county contained enough people to have more than one member of the Texas House of Representatives. However, one impact of the Voting Rights Act of 1965 (VRA) was to shift states like Texas away from a MMD system to a SMDP or SMDM system.[26] The MMD system appeared to depress representation among African Americans and Hispanics especially.[27] By using the SMDP or SMDM system, minority voters can be concentrated into smaller population election districts. As a result, more minorities are elected to the legislature and candidates become more responsive to minority voters. Since the 1970s, Texas has used the Single-Member District Plurality system for both houses of the Texas Legislature.

Plurality election
the candidate with the most votes wins the election.

Majority election
an election where a candidate is required to receive 50 percent of the vote, plus one additional vote to be declared the winner. Winning the most votes is not sufficient.

Run-off election
an election to decide the winner that is held after a majority election fails to yield a clear 50 percent winner in the initial balloting.

Instant run-off
if no candidate receives a majority at the initial election, the second place votes are considered, and a winner is determined by adding the first and second place votes.

Multi-Member District (MMD)
an election system in which the state is divided into many election districts, but each district elects more than one person to the state legislature.

Texas versus North Dakota

Texas and North Dakota could not be more different. Texas is the second largest state in population, while North Dakota, with 636,000 people, ranks as the 48th largest state; only Vermont and Wyoming have fewer people. Population growth rates in Texas place the Lone Star State as one of the fastest growing states in the United States, while North Dakota ranks near the bottom. Texas is a highly urbanized state, while North Dakota remains essentially rural.

Another difference between the two is found in the election process for the North Dakota state legislature. Like a handful of other states, North Dakota chooses its lower house through a Multi-Member District (MMD) system. Each voter casts a vote in his or her election district. Instead of the top vote getter winning the seat, the top two vote getters win seats in the North Dakota State House of Representatives. The ninety-four members of the North Dakota State House of Representatives are selected every four years from forty-seven election districts. Elections are staggered so that odd-numbered districts elect their representatives in an election and two years later, even-numbered districts choose their representatives.

Because each district elects more than one representative, the possibility of candidates from both political parties getting elected occurs. The results from the 2006 elections to the North Dakota House of Representatives illustrate this result.

Also, the MMD system may encourage greater party competition. Parties have a greater incentive to run candidates. Getting elected in North Dakota means coming in either first or second, not just in first place. Of course, parties also have an incentive to run more than one candidate in each district. In contrast to Texas, as discussed in Chapter 7, North Dakota has relatively few districts in which the two major parties do not compete. In 2006, only three districts (12.5 percent) contained only Republican or only Democratic candidates.

Split Results in the 2006 Elections to the North Dakota House of Representatives

RESULT	PERCENTAGE OF DISTRICTS
Two Republicans elected	42%
One Republican, one Democrat elected	33%
Two Democrats elected	25%

Source: North Dakota Secretary of State, "General Election–November 7, 2006," http://web.apps.state.nd.us/sec/emspublic/gp/electionresultssearch.htm, accessed July 21, 2007.

Thinking Critically

- Do you think the MMD system in North Dakota encourages greater party competition?
- What do you think are advantages of the MMD system?
- What do you think are the advantages of the SMD system?
- Are there any drawbacks to either system?
- Which system would you prefer?
- Do you think Texas should maintain its SMD system of elections for the Texas House of Representatives? Why or why not?

Redistricting Games

One of the challenges of any Single-Member District System is the regular need to redraw district lines. This need to shift district lines reflects the fact that population changes occur. More importantly, population change occurs at uneven rates within the state. If election district lines for the state legislature remain fixed, then over time, some areas are going to have many more people per representative than other areas. Consider the fact that Nacogdoches County in eastern Texas, home of the oldest city in Texas, had a population of 9,614 residents in 1870, just prior to the creation of the current state constitution. That same census found that Dallas County had 13,314.[28] By 2000, Nacogdoches County, with a population of 59,203,[29] was nowhere near the population of Dallas County at 2,218,899.[30] In 1876, Dallas County and Nacogdoches County were equally represented in the Texas House of Representatives, with one member each. Obviously, if redistricting never occurred, Nacogdoches County would be drastically over-represented in the state legislature today and Dallas County would be drastically under-represented. This situation violates the principle of **one person, one vote.** Clearly the resident of Nacogdoches in an election would carry greater weight than the resident of Dallas. Redistricting, the redrawing of election district lines or boundaries, normally occurs every ten years after the results of the U.S. Census are provided to the states.

The Texas Legislature has responsibility for drawing the lines for its own election districts, as well as those for the state Board of Education and the U.S. House of Representatives from Texas. Counties, cities, and other local governments also redistrict every ten years, but these governments are responsible for their own redistricting. The state legislature must abide by a number of federal rules and guidelines for drawing election districts. First, the landmark VRA and similar laws attempt to ensure the representation of minorities who historically faced discrimination. While the VRA initially applied to African Americans, the law has expanded to include Asian Americans, Native Americans, and Hispanics. A key provision of the VRA is that the federal government must approve any change to election laws in states with a history of discrimination. Second, to boost the number of minorities that win election to the state legislature, the federal government encourages the creation of **majority-minority districts.** A majority-minority district is an election district in which the majority of the population comes from a racial or ethnic minority. In Texas, the creation of majority-minority districts focuses on establishing majority African American or majority Hispanic districts. In *Hunt v. Cromartie* (1999)[31] the U.S. Supreme Court ruled that while race can be a factor in drawing Texas's district lines, race cannot be the only factor involved. Drawing district lines for partisan advantage remains acceptable as long as the principle of one person, one vote established by the U.S. Supreme Court in *Baker v. Carr* is followed.

The Texas Constitution imposes its own restrictions on redistricting seats in the Texas Legislature. First, districts must be contiguous. Second, districts must respect county boundaries as much as possible. Finally, the state must now use the SMDP system. MMD is not permitted.

Historically, state legislatures in many states simply added new seats as populations within the state grew and shifted. Growing counties were rewarded with more seats, while those with declining populations or no population growth did not lose representation. Texas followed this pattern in the late 1800s and early 1900s. Between 1921 and 1951, the Texas Legislature never redistricted nor added new seats, despite periods of rapid population growth in some parts of the state and population decline in other areas. The Texas Constitution specified that the Texas Senate contain thirty-one members, and the Texas House of Representatives originally held ninety-three members. Since a 1999 amendment to the Texas Constitution, the membership of the Texas House of Representatives has been set at one hundred and fifty.[32]

Either the legislature itself or an independent commission can be used to draw election districts for state legislatures. Many states, like Georgia, allow the legislature to draw and redraw district lines. Obviously, this ability of members of the state legislature to define their own election districts clearly allows incumbents to draw district lines to their political advantage, a process referred to as **gerrymandering.** Other states, like Iowa, create **nonpartisan or bipartisan independent commissions**

One person, one vote
shorthand term for the requirement by the U.S. Supreme Court that election districts should be roughly equal in population.

Majority-minority districts
an election district in which the majority of the population comes from a racial or ethnic minority.

Gerrymandering
the practice of incumbents creating very oddly shaped electoral districts to maximize their political advantage in an upcoming election.

Nonpartisan or bipartisan independent commissions
a system of drawing electoral district lines that attempts to remove politics from the process of redistricting.

Legislative Redistricting Board (LRB)

created by a 1948 amendment to the Texas Constitution, this group steps in if the state legislature is unable to pass a redistricting plan or when a state or federal court invalidates a plan drawn by the legislature; this group comes into play only for plans to redistrict the state legislature.

to draw the district lines. These states attempt to remove politics from the process and perhaps more importantly to remove the members of the state legislature from drawing their own district lines.

In Texas, the state legislature is responsible for redistricting, with one important modification. If the legislature is unable to pass a redistricting plan, the process is handed over to the **Legislative Redistricting Board (LRB).** The LRB, created by a 1948 amendment to the state constitution, is composed of the lieutenant governor, the Speaker of the Texas House of Representatives, the attorney general, the comptroller of accounts, and the commissioner of the General Land Office. The LRB develops a plan for redistricting that is submitted to the state legislature for approval. The LRB also becomes involved in redistricting the state legislature when a state or federal court invalidates a plan approved by the state legislature. However, the LRB only redistricts the state legislature. The task of drawing election districts for the members of the U.S. House of Representatives from Texas remains the exclusive domain of the state legislature.

In 2000, Texas faced the unusual situation of divided control over the state legislature, with Republicans controlling the Texas Senate and Democrats controlling the Texas House of Representatives. This transition occurred with the rise of the Republican Party and the end of the era of Democratic Party dominance. An impasse developed. The two chambers could not reconcile their differences to pass a final redistricting plan. When the legislature was unable to pass a redistricting plan, the LRB developed the proposal, which became the basis of redistricting the Texas Legislature. This plan was authored by Republican attorney general John Cornyn and passed on a 3–2 vote in the LRB with support from Comptroller Carole Keeton Rylander and Land Commissioner David Dewhurst. The plan ensured that Republicans increased their majority in the Texas House of Representatives.[33]

However, redistricting for U.S. House of Representatives seats became a contentious issue. With the Texas Legislature unable to come to a consensus, the federal courts stepped in and drew the lines to favor both Democratic and Republican incumbents. Following the 2002 elections, Republicans gained control of the Texas House of Representatives and retained control over the Texas Senate. With Republicans now in charge of both houses of the state legislature and the governorship, Speaker of the U.S. House of Representatives Tom DeLay, R-Sugarland, proposed to Republican leaders in the state legislature a plan to redistrict Texas. DeLay sought to increase the number of Texas seats controlled by Republicans. After intense debate in the state legislature during the regular session, Gov. Rick Perry called the Texas Legislature into special session three times in order to accomplish this redistricting. In the middle of this political drama, Democratic members of the Texas House of Representatives fled to Oklahoma to block the ability of the legislature to meet. Shortly after their return, some Democrats in the Texas Senate camped out in New Mexico in an attempt to prevent a quorum to conduct business. However, the state legislature did eventually pass a mid-decade redistricting plan. In the 2004 elections, the new district lines yielded Republicans twenty-one of the thirty-two Texas seats in the U.S. House of Representatives.

A mid-decade redistricting of the U.S. House of Representatives seats by the Texas Legislature, without being ordered to do so by a court, was unprecedented in recent history. Almost immediately, the redistricting plan was challenged in federal courts. The court cases identified three issues for the U.S. Supreme Court to examine. First, did the mid-decade redistricting violate the U.S. Constitution? Second, did the new districts disenfranchise minority voters, violating the Voting

Redistricting in Texas leaves the process in the hands of the Texas Legislature and the Legislative Redistricting Board (LRB), all elected officials with a vested interest in engineering district lines. For members of the legislature, protecting incumbents of both parties or securing gains for their party in the legislature can be important. For members of the LRB, assisting their party in gaining or retaining control of the legislature also matters. However, the implications for wider issues like partisan control over state delegations to the U.S. House of Representatives are apparent from the recent battles in Texas.

Arizona voters in 2000 approved Proposition 106, which amended the Arizona Constitution to create an independent commission to oversee redistricting for the state legislature and U.S. House of Representatives. The Arizona Independent Redistricting Commission consists of five persons.[i] By law, two members are Democrats, two members are Republicans, and one member is independent. All five must have maintained the same party affiliation, or no affiliation in the case of the independent, for at least the previous three years. In addition, all five members cannot have served as a public official, a lobbyist, a campaign worker, or a political party official in the three years prior to their appointment. Nominees are compiled by another independent commission charged with making nominations to Arizona appellate courts and are presented to the leadership of the Arizona Legislature for final appointment.

Proposition 106 contains explicit language to specify how the commission carries out the redistricting process.[ii] For example, the initial mapping of electoral districts cannot consider party affiliations of voters or the history of voting in existing districts. The commission must follow the guidelines of the Voter Rights Act of 1965, other legislation passed by Congress, and relevant rulings by the courts. District lines are to be compact and to respect the boundaries of existing communities, counties, and cities. Also, districts are expected to be competitive between Democratic and Republican candidates. This provision is tested only after the initial plan is developed. Thus, highly gerrymandered districts that clearly favor one party or another are not possible in Arizona.

Thinking Critically

- How does the Independent Redistricting Commission system of Arizona attempt to depoliticize the redistricting process?
- Does Arizona's system accomplish this goal? Why or why not?
- Has redistricting affected your hometown? Would you like to see your state adopt such a plan?

i. Arizona Independent Redistricting Commission, "Frequently Asked Questions," (2007), www.azredistricting.org/?page=faq, accessed August 1, 2007.
ii. Arizona Independent Redistricting Commission, "Proposition 106," (2007) www.azredistricting.org/?page=prop106, accessed August 1, 2007.

Rights Act of 1965? Third, were the district lines drawn in such a partisan manner as to violate earlier U.S. Supreme Court rulings? In 2006, the U.S. Supreme Court issued a decision in *LULAC v. Perry* (2006),[34] which stated that mid-decade redistricting was permissible and held that the Texas districts were not drawn in an excessively partisan manner so as to completely dilute Democratic voters. Finally, the courts did find that some of the district lines violated the Voting Rights Act of 1965, primarily by reducing the strength of Hispanic voters in at least one district. These unacceptable district lines were redrawn to solve the problem identified by the courts. Thus, the transition to Republican Party control over the Texas Legislature ushered in a new era of partisan politics. Redistricting battles shifted from the tradition of defending the reelection chances of incumbents of both parties to securing partisan control over the U.S. House of Representatives and the Texas Legislature for the majority party.

Legislative Organization

The system of organizing a legislature to conduct everyday business is the purpose of legislative organization. In doing so, the legislature attempts to provide processes to carry out functions such as developing new bills, or proposed new laws. Legislative organization also helps with revising existing laws and overseeing activities of the executive branch. Legislative organization consists of the chamber leadership, party organization, and committee structure. Each aspect of legislative organization shapes the legislative process in powerful ways.

Chamber Leadership

Leadership of each chamber of the Texas Legislature is important. The leadership, including the presiding officers and **party caucus chairs** possess important powers to shape and to model the agendas of the chambers. This ability to control the agenda influences the likelihood that a bill becomes a law.

The presiding officer of the Texas Senate is the **lieutenant governor.** The lieutenant governor is directly elected by the voters of the state, so the senators lack control over the choice of their presiding officer. If the lieutenant governor's position is vacant, as when Lt. Gov. Rick Perry became the governor after Gov. George Bush was elected president of the United States, then the Texas Senate can appoint a new lieutenant governor. The Lieutenant Governor exercises immense power in the Senate, including the power to assign bills to committee and to appoint, without limitation, members of the standing committees of the Texas Senate and the chairs of the standing committees. However, the lieutenant governor votes in the Texas Senate only to break a tie. The lieutenant governor also serves on the LRB and the **Legislative Budget Board (LBB).** The LBB develops a proposed state budget for the legislature to consider. When the lieutenant governor is unable to attend sessions, the **president pro tempore** takes over as the presiding officer. The president pro tempore is elected by the membership of the Senate.

The **Speaker of the House** presides over sessions of the Texas House of Representatives. The Speaker is elected by the membership of the House as the first order of business at the beginning of the legislative session in January following the elections for the entire state legislature in December. Although the election is by secret ballot, candidates for the position of Speaker campaign for weeks before the vote is taken. Historically, this process involves a system of members of the Texas House of Representatives signing cards pledging their support to a candidate before the legislature meets. Thus, a candidate for the Speaker position knows pretty much which members of the Texas House of Representatives are going to vote for her or him before the balloting occurs.[35]

Unlike in the U.S. House of Representatives, the vote for the Texas Speaker is usually bipartisan and lopsided. For example the January 2007 election of Speaker Craddick was 121 in favor and 27 against;[36] Craddick's predecessor, James "Pete" Laney, was unanimously elected in 1999.[37] From the end of Reconstruction in the 1870s through the 1980s, the lopsided votes reflected the reality of Texas politics: the Democratic Party controlled the chamber. As a result, the Republicans in the House often found that supporting the eventual Democratic winner created opportunities for Republicans to have bills and amendments that they favored considered by the majority party. A more pragmatic reason exists for members of both parties to support the Speaker. The powers of the Speaker are extensive, thus maintaining a favor-

---

Party caucus chairs
the party leaders, whose main job it is to organize party members to vote for legislation on the floor.

Lieutenant governor
the presiding officer of the Texas Senate, elected directly by the voters.

Legislative Budget Board (LBB)
the group that develops a proposed state budget for legislative consideration.

President pro tempore
a presiding officer elected by the members of the Texas Senate, who takes over when the Lieutenant Governor is unavailable.

Speaker of the House
the presiding officer of the Texas House of Representatives.

able relationship with the Speaker is important, and therefore the tradition of lopsided votes continues. For now, the transition to Republican control over the Texas House of Representatives has not produced a shift in the bipartisan support for the election of the Speaker because the powers of the Speaker, regardless of party affiliation, remain extensive.

Powers of the Speaker include presiding over debates and controlling debates by deciding whether to recognize a member to speak or introduce a motion, as illustrated in the vignette at the beginning of the chapter. The Speaker's power also involves the interpretation of the standing rules by which the legislature operates, a power that may be used to help some legislators and hurt others. The Speaker serves on the LRB and appoints part of the membership of the LBB. In addition, the Speaker appoints some standing committee members, the chairs of standing committees, and members of conference committees from the Texas House of Representatives. The Speaker may also create select committees and interim committees. Thus, the Speaker has the ability to influence the size and shape of election districts and the items included in the state budget.

The Speaker also assigns bills to the committees. To be in favor with the Speaker helps ensure a member of the House of Representatives favorable consideration of pet bills and favorable committee assignments. However, unlike the Lieutenant Governor in the Texas Senate, the power to appoint committee members is limited, since one-half of the makeup of standing committees is determined by seniority. The Speaker appoints a **Speaker pro tempore** to preside when the Speaker is unable to be at the Capitol.

Speaker pro tempore
akin to the president pro tempore in the Texas Senate, this officer presides when the Speaker is unavailable.

Unlike some other states, Texas provides no other compensation to members of the state legislature holding positions of leadership. Typically, when the lieutenant governor serves as a presiding officer, no additional pay is given. However, other positions do receive additional pay in other states. For example, Oklahoma provides $12,364 per year to the majority party and minority party leaders in both houses of the Oklahoma legislature. Utah gives $1,500 to the party whips. North Dakota gives between $5 and $250 per day the legislature is in session, depending on the position. New York provides over twenty different leadership positions with between $9000 and $34,500 depending on the position. In fact, only Arizona, New Mexico, South Dakota, and Texas offer no additional compensation to members of the legislature who assume leadership positions.[38]

Party Organization

The political parties provide a basis for organizing the legislature. Because political parties join together people with similar political beliefs, the parties assist in aligning support or opposition to bills, including **structuring the vote.** Parties sometimes play an important role in the selection of committees and the organization of the work of committees. Parties can also form a base of support for the election of the Speaker of the House. At the most basic level, the party functions as the **party caucus.** The party caucus normally is simply the members of a specific chamber of the legislature who belong to a political party. However, the historic dominance of the Democratic Party in Texas meant that party caucuses were unneeded, and like other single-party states, patterns of behavior among legislators reflected divisions within the Democratic Party itself. In the Texas House of Representatives, the creation of the Democratic Party caucus in 1981 signaled a shift in the party system within the legislature. Rising numbers of Republicans

Structuring the vote
the way in which political parties align support or opposition to bills.

Party caucus
the organization of the members of a specific legislative chamber who belong to a political party.

sparked a reaction among Democratic members to increase awareness of policy issues, discuss bills, and discipline party members.[39] Although more cohesive in voting than the Democrats, Republicans did not formally create a party caucus until 1989. The transition to a more competitive two-party legislature led the Democratic Party, at that time still in the majority, to institutionalize in order to stave off a Republican challenge.

Today, both parties maintain party caucuses in the Texas House of Representatives to provide communication among members of the caucus, to discuss bills before the Texas House of Representative, and to raise money for campaigns.[40] The Republican Caucus in the Texas House of Representatives also maintains a policy committee that reviews bills under consideration and makes recommendations to the caucus on whether to support the bill, how to amend the bill, or how to defeat the bill.[41] Each party caucus also elects a party caucus chair. The party caucus chair is elected by the caucus to oversee the day-to-day operation of the party. The party caucus chairs in the Texas Legislature do not play as active and important a role as their counterparts in the U.S. Congress. The Republican Party Caucus also has **floor whips,** individuals who remind members of the party's position on the bill and encourage members to vote with the rest of the party caucus. Because the Texas House of Representatives is larger than the Texas Senate, party organization is more developed and more relevant in the Texas House of Representatives.

A study of the party caucuses in state legislatures suggests that, relative to other states, party cohesion is relatively weak in Texas.[42] However, this study occurred before the emergence of a Republican majority in the legislature. Under Democratic Party dominance, party cohesion mattered less and legislators could afford to be more independent-minded. The individualistic aspects of Texas political culture also suggest that voters may expect their legislators to exert a degree of independence from their party. Additionally, the powers and influences of the Speaker and lieutenant governor in their respective chambers produce their own centralized system of legislative organization.

Special Caucuses

Sometimes members of the state legislature form **special caucuses,** organizations of members of the state legislature who share a common interest. These caucuses may contain members of both chambers of the Texas legislature and may have Democratic and Republican members. These groups meet regularly to discuss topics of mutual interest to them and to their constituents. Examples include the Rural Caucus, Sportsmen's Caucus, Environmental Caucus, and the Mexican American Caucus. Among the best known is the Texas Legislative Black Caucus (TLBC). One study of the TLBC suggests that the caucus enjoys a high degree of **cohesion,** that is members of a political party or special caucus voting together on a bill or resolution. During the 1980s and 1990s, when the TLBC membership voted together as a bloc, the caucus was able to influence legislation related to the group's shared interests.[43]

Special caucuses are important in the legislative process because they provide opportunities for members of the legislature to network on common interests. At a meeting, the members informally discuss bills before the legislature. In some cases, authors of bills or other interested individuals may address the caucus. The caucus may also provide a springboard for amendments and other changes to legislation.[44]

Floor whips
individuals who remind legislators of their party's position on a bill and encourage members to vote with the rest of the party caucus.

Special caucuses
organizations of members of the state legislature who share a common interest or have constituencies with a common interest.

Cohesion
members of a political party or special caucus voting together on a bill or resolution.

Committees

A more formal form of organization with a direct influence over legislation is the committee system. Like the U.S. Congress, the Texas Legislature possesses **committees** that assist the legislature in accomplishing its work. The presence of committees allows, among other things, a division of labor, so that bills may be reviewed in detail before being considered by the entire chamber. Four types of committees exist in the Texas Legislature: standing, conference, joint, and interim.

Standing committees are the most important type of committee. These committees are considered permanent because they typically exist across sessions and elections. Standing committees are chamber exclusive, meaning that each standing committee is associated with a specific chamber of the legislature and is made of members from only that chamber. Standing committees are functionally divided. Each committee handles bills in a specific area of policy, although there are some exceptions. For example, every bill in the Texas House of Representatives that involves spending tax revenue must pass through the Appropriations Committee regardless of the subject of the bill. The Texas House Ways and Means Committee handles every bill involving changes in tax law, the rate of taxation, and the types of taxes levied. In the 2006–2007 legislature, there were fifteen standing committee in the Texas Senate and thirty-nine in the Texas House of Representatives.

Committees
a formally organized group of legislators that assists the legislature in accomplishing its work, allowing a division of labor and an in-depth review of an issue or a bill before review by the entire chamber.

Standing committees
permanent, chamber-exclusive formal work groups that typically exist across sessions and across elections.

Table 3.4 Standing Committees in the 80th Texas Legislature

TEXAS HOUSE OF REPRESENTATIVES		TEXAS SENATE
Agriculture and Livestock	Insurance	Administration
Appropriations	Judiciary	Business and Commerce
Border and International Affairs	Juvenile Justice and Family Issues	Criminal Justice
Business and Industry	Land and Resource Management	Education
Calendars	Law Enforcement	Finance
Civil Practices	Licensing and Administrative Procedures	Government Organization
Corrections	Local and Consent Calendars	Health and Human Services
County Affairs	Local Government Ways and Means	Intergovernmental Relations
Criminal Jurisprudence	Natural Resources	International Relations and Trade
Culture, Recreation, and Tourism	Pensions and Investments	Jurisprudence
Defense Affairs and State-Federal Relations	Public Education	Natural Resources
Economic Development	Public Health	Nominations
Elections	Redistricting	State Affairs
Energy Resources	Regulated Industries	Transportation and Homeland Security
Environmental Regulation	Rules and Resolutions	Veterans Affairs and Military Installations
Financial Institutions	State Affairs	
General Investigating and Ethics	Transportation	
Higher Education	Urban Affairs	
House Administration	Ways and Means	
Human Services		

The appointment process for members of the standing committees varies between the Texas House of Representatives and Texas Senate. As mentioned above, the lieutenant governor appoints the members of the standing committees in the Texas Senate. In the Texas House, the process is a bit more complicated. Seats on standing committees are assigned based upon seniority for the first committee assignment, while the second (or third) committee assignment is made at the discretion of the Speaker of the House.

The membership of the committees has undergone tremendous transition over the past few decades. Prior to the 1980s, so few Republicans were in either chamber of the legislature that placing Republicans on every standing committee proved difficult. As Republicans gained strength in the Texas House of Representatives, Republicans who courted favor with a Democratic Speaker often found themselves receiving favorable positions on committees. In the 1980s and 1990s, Republicans often were overrepresented in committees and even chaired a number of standing committees.[45] This situation stands in sharp contrast to the party-oriented system of the U.S. Congress and many state legislatures where committee seats are divided so that the party makeup of the committee mirrors the overall strength of the party in the chamber, the majority party is guaranteed a majority of seats on every standing committee, and the majority party holds all of the committee chairs. The control of committee membership and chairs ensures the majority a degree of control over the legislative process since every bill passes through at least one standing committee.

Beginning in the 1990s, committee assignments began to shift in the Texas House of Representatives toward a more party-centered model similar to the U.S. Congress. However, this transition is incomplete at best. The Speaker of the House retains powers over committee assignments and continues some bipartisan appointments to reward supporters. Every member of the Texas House of Representatives sits on two or three committees, and Texas Senate members sit on at least four standing committees.

Presiding over each standing committee is a committee chair. Committee chairs are quite powerful. The committee chair sets the agenda for the committee, determining the order in which bills sent to the committee are considered. The chair also establishes the length of debate and the amendment process for each bill. As a result, the committee chair may schedule bills that he or she supports early in the legislative session to ensure that those bills are considered first by the committee. Likewise, the committee chair may move bills that she or he does not support to the end of the committee's calendar, effectively ensuring that the committee runs out of time before the bills are considered. The committee chair also decides other aspects of the agenda, like the time devoted to hearings and oversight. This power over the agenda, and the flow of legislation in and out of the committee, gives the chair of a standing committee tremendous control over the legislative process.

Standing committees perform several important functions for the legislature, including **mark-up** and **amendment** to bills. Amendments are formal changes to the bill during the committee process. Mark-up is when the committee goes line-by-line through a bill to make changes without formal amendments. Because a committee is not required to report every bill to the whole chamber, committees may kill a bill by having a majority of the members on the committee vote against a bill or by not acting on a bill before the legislative session ends.

Another function of the standing committees in Texas is to conduct **oversight** of the executive branch agencies. Oversight occurs when the legislature reviews

Mark-up

when the committee goes line-by-line through a bill to make changes without formal amendments.

Amendment

formal changes to a bill during the committee process.

Oversight

when the legislature reviews policies and decisions of the executive branch to make sure that the executive branch is following the intentions of the legislature.

policies and decisions of the executive branch to make sure that the executive branch is following the intentions of the legislature. Because some laws passed by the legislature provide only general guidelines to the executive branch, the specific agency that carries out the law often has discretion to determine exactly how to implement the law. For example, the state legislature in 2005 passed a law requiring state universities in Texas to set the minimum number of hours required for a bachelor's degree at 120 hours.[46] Most degree programs at many Texas public universities required more than 120 hours. To make these changes, systems like the University of Texas and independent state universities like Midwestern State University developed plans to reduce the hours required for degrees to 120 hours. The standing committees responsible for higher education in the state legislature review progress toward the 120-hour degree program every two years during the regular session of the legislature.

In addition, new administrative regulations are subject to review by standing committees. For example, if the Texas Department of Parks and Wildlife decided to impose a user fee of $5.00 on everyone who tries to fish at a state park, the legislature could review this decision the next time the legislature met in regular session. The standing committees lack the power to require changes in new regulations and can only issue an advisory opinion.[47] However, executive agencies take these opinions seriously. Keeping the legislature satisfied avoids having the committee, or the legislature, develop new laws to replace administrative regulations.

Committees have the authority to hold hearings when acting on legislation and overseeing the executive. These are meetings of the committee at which experts, invited guests, organized interests, officials from other branches, officials from other levels of government, and private citizens are allowed to address the committee about issues before the committee. The work of standing committees in all of these functions is enhanced by the research and report-writing of committee professional staffs.

The second type of committee is necessary because the Texas Legislature contains two chambers. Bills may be passed in different versions in each chamber simply because the two chambers are different in their membership. As a result, when a bill passes both houses in different versions, a single version must be agreed to by both houses before the bill goes to the governor. A committee called a **conference committee** reconciles the differences in the Texas Senate and Texas House versions of the bill. Conference committees contain ten members, five from the Texas House and five from the Texas Senate. Normally some of the members of the standing committees who considered the original bill serve on the conference committee that reconciles the bill. The committee meets on a limited basis to reconcile the differences on a single bill. After producing a single, reconciled version of the bill, the committee disbands. The bill is then reintroduced to both chambers for consideration.

A third type of committee is the **joint committee.** These committees are normally temporary committees created by agreement between the lieutenant governor and the Speaker of the Texas House of Representatives. These committees exist for a special purpose. Once the reason for the creation of the committee is resolved or settled, then the committee normally disbands. Joint committees, sometimes called select committees, contain members of both chambers. The Select Committee on Operation and Management of the Texas Youth Commission is an example of a joint committee. The committee is investigating allegations of improper activity by employees of the Texas Youth Commission. Once the investigation is complete, the

Conference committee
an official legislative work group that meets on a limited basis to reconcile the different versions of a bill that has passed in the Texas House and Senate.

Joint committee
temporary legislative work group created by agreement between the lieutenant governor and Speaker of the Texas House of Representatives for a special purpose; sometimes called a select committee.

committee makes recommendations to the legislature about changes to the policies and practices of the commission.

A final type of committee is the **interim committee.** Interim committees are important because the Texas Legislature does not meet each year. During periods when the legislature is not in session, interim committees may be created to provide oversight of the executive branch and to monitor public policy. Typically, interim committees mirror the division of duties and responsibilities used for the standing committees. Often, the committee studies specific problems or conducts research into specific issues as instructed by the state legislature.

Legislative Process

f course, a primary function of the Texas Legislature is making new laws and updating existing laws. Therefore, the legislative process, or how a bill becomes a law, is an important part of the legislature.

Bills must be **introduced,** by a member of the chamber in which the bill is considered. Because a bill must pass both houses of the Texas Legislature, one practice is for the author of a bill to seek out members of both chambers to help co-sponsor the bill, generating interest in the bill and support for the bill after introduction. Members of the legislature and their staff are important sources of bills. Most bills originate in the Texas Legislative Council, the professional staff of the legislature. However, organized interests, who often have greater resources, access to lawyers, and experience in "legalese" or the language of bills and laws, write bills also.

Bills may be pre-filed before the start of each legislature session, but any new bill may be introduced up to sixty days after the start of the legislative session. To introduce a bill after the sixtieth day requires agreement by 80 percent of the members of the chamber present. Any bill dealing with the state budget must be considered by the Texas House of Representatives first. Budget bills must be introduced by the thirtieth day after the legislative session opens. Any bill that impacts the state budget must include the cost involved, a projection of future costs, the source of revenue, and the impact on local governments.[48] Texas also requires statements of the impact of the bill on the equalized public education funding formula and on criminal justice policy. These last two provisions are unique to Texas.

In addition to bills, members of the legislature may introduce resolutions. **Resolutions** express the opinion of the legislature on some matter or change the organizational structure of the legislature. Three types of resolutions exist. **Simple resolutions** address organizational issues like changing the number of standing committees or altering the powers of committee chairs. These resolutions may be limited to a single house of the legislature. **Concurrent resolutions** that express the opinion of the legislature require passage in both houses of the Texas Legislature. For example, the legislature may pass a resolution asking the U.S. Congress to change a policy. A resolution may also cover seemingly trivial matters like commending the University of Texas football team for winning the Cotton Bowl or the Texas A&M Women's Golf team for winning a conference championship. **Joint resolutions** are important because all amendments to the Texas Constitution are joint resolutions.

When a bill or resolution is introduced into a chamber, it is assigned a number by the secretary of the Senate or the chief clerk of the House. The number indicates

Interim committee
legislative work groups that are created during periods when the legislature is not in session to provide oversight of the executive branch and monitor public policy.

Introduce [a bill]
to officially bring a bill before a legislative chamber for the first time. Introducing a bill is the first step in the formal legislative process.

Resolutions
a legislative act expressing the opinion of the legislature on a matter or changing the organizational structure of the legislature.

Simple resolutions
address organizational issues and may be limited to a single house.

Concurrent resolutions
express an opinion of the legislature and must pass in both houses.

Joint resolution
the format for all amendments to the Texas Constitution.

Figure 3.1 How a Bill Becomes a Law in Texas

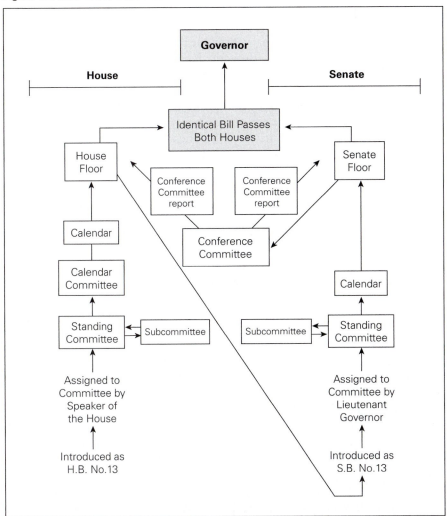

the chamber in which the legislation originated and the order that it was introduced. For example, HR 10 indicates the tenth resolution introduced in the Texas House, while SB 351 is the 351st bill introduced in the Texas Senate.

After legislation is introduced, it is assigned to a standing committee. In the Texas Senate bills are referred to committee by the president of the Senate, the lieutenant governor. Bills in the Texas House of Representatives are referred to committee by the Speaker of the House. Normally, bills are referred to the standing committee with jurisdiction over the policy area. Yet the Speaker of the House and the lieutenant governor have the power to send the bill to any standing committee in their respective chambers that they choose. In the Texas House of Representatives, if a sponsor of the bill believes the Speaker has unfairly assigned a bill to a committee to kill the bill, the sponsor may seek a "Jim Hogg Committee." Essentially, the standing committee meets in front of the entire House of Representatives to consider the bill.[49] A handful of standing committees in both chambers of the Texas Legislature contain subcommittees to aid in the legislative process. A subcommittee may conduct the detailed examination of the bill and report the bill to the whole committee before the final committee vote is taken.

After a series of public meetings, debates, mark-up sessions, and amendments, the standing committee takes a final vote on the bill. If the committee reports favorably on the bill, the bill returns to the entire membership of the chamber for consideration. In the Texas House of Representatives, the bill now goes to a special standing committee called the calendar committee. The calendar committee, not surprisingly, places each and every bill on the chamber's schedule, determining when a bill will be considered and specifying how long a bill will be debated. In the House, at least seven different calendars exist. These calendars are arranged in order of importance from most important to least important. Bills on more important calendars are considered first, with bills on less important calendars handled if time remains during the legislative session. Any bill or resolution may be shifted by the whole House of Representatives to a more important calendar by a two-thirds vote of the House.

The calendar committee is one of the key differences between the Texas Senate and the Texas House of Representatives. In the Texas Senate, there is no special calendar committee and only one calendar exists with bills listed in the order they were formally introduced. The Texas Senate almost never considers bills in the order that the bills are introduced. Instead, the Texas Senate has developed a trick to allow them to change the order. The first bill introduced each session is a **blocking bill,** a bill that is introduced not to be passed but merely to hold a place at the top of the Texas Senate calendar. This bill prevents other bills from being considered. Like the Texas House of Representatives, the Texas Senate may adjust the calendar by a two-thirds vote of the chamber. Thus, a bill scheduled for debate later in the session may be moved to the front of the calendar and before the blocking bill. Thus, senators use this technique to allow some bills to leap over other bills and to jump ahead of the blocking bill. As a result, the Texas Senate may choose which bills to consider first, second, third, and so forth.

Given that the size of the Senate is thirty-one members, the two-thirds requirement means that any eleven members can effectively prevent any bill from being moved to the floor for debate. This situation enables the minority party potentially to threaten any bill because the minority party usually holds at

Blocking bill

a bill regularly introduced in the Texas Senate to serve as a placeholder at the top of the Senate calendar.

Table 3.5 Calendars in the Texas House of Representatives (Most Important to Least Important)

CALENDAR	PURPOSE
Emergency	Emergency bills; also used for taxation and appropriation bills
Major State	Important bills with statewide impact
Constitutional Amendments	Amendments to the Texas Constitution
General State	Bills with statewide impact deemed less important than those designated "Major State"
Local, Consent, and Resolution	Bills involving activities of specific counties, cities, and other governments; non-controversial resolutions
Resolution	Votes in which the House offers an opinion on some topic but passes no bill on the topic
Congratulatory and Memorial	House resolution expressing gratitude, thanks, or recognition of some person or event but no bills passed on the matter

Source: Compiled by author from data available at www.house.state.tx.us/help/calendar.htm.

The Killer Bees

No story better reflects the eccentric politics created by the rules of the Texas Legislature than the "Killer Bees." The Bees emerged in May 1970 during a battle over whether Texas should have a separate presidential primary in 1980. One side favored a separate primary so that conservative Democrats could cast a vote in a Republican presidential primary for Ronald Reagan or former Texas governor John Connally on March 11 and then return to the Democratic Party in May to outvote the liberals in the primary for other offices. The other side wanted a single primary that would force conservative Democrats to choose a party. Lt. Gov. Bill Hobby nicknamed some of the liberal legislators who resisted his agenda "the Killer Bees" because he said he never knew where they would strike next. Opponents of the separate primary were worked into a frenzy when Hobby slipped the primary into an innocuous election bill that had already passed the Texas House and was coming before the Senate. This would have allowed him to get around the two-thirds vote required to pass most bills. With ten days left in the legislative session the Bees had grown to twelve members but knew that they lacked the majority required to block passage under the new rule. However, they also realized that the Senate would lack a quorum and couldn't pass any more bills if all twelve refused to attend.

The Killer Bees took flight and disappeared. Law enforcement was sent to round them up while the rest of the Senate found themselves unable to leave the Senate building as Hobby kept them in the Capitol. For five days the Bees evaded authorities, although nine of them were hiding in an apartment just over two miles from the Capitol. The Texas Rangers nearly caught Sen. Gene Jones after he left the Austin hideout because of claustrophobia. When lawmen arrived at Jones's new hideout, they mistakenly arrested Jones's brother when he answered the door while Senator Jones jumped the back fence.

While Texans might not have usually sided with the liberal-leaning Bees, there was little sympathy for the political interests behind the separate primary bill and Texans and the nation found themselves caught up in the spectacle of the small band of Bees eluding a statewide manhunt and foiling the powerful forces aligned against them. Eventually Hobby relented, inviting the Bees back to the Senate after abandoning his maneuvers on behalf of the bill. While the saga of the Killer Bees reads like a surreal adventure, it is evidence of a problem with the Senate's requirement of two-thirds support to pass most bills, a threshold that is high enough to allow a determined and creative minority to resist change.

least eleven seats in the Texas Senate. Thus, the majority party must regularly consider the opinion of the minority party in order to get legislation passed in the Texas Senate.

When a bill or resolution finally comes up for a debate in the chamber, the whole chamber engages in a **floor debate.** The sponsors of the bill will arrange for members to speak on behalf of the bill while opponents will recruit members to speak against the bill. The trick in both cases is gaining recognition from the presiding officer of the chamber for the purposes of addressing the chamber. Amendments to the bill are made at this time. Sometimes a **killer amendment** is introduced. Killer amendments add language to the bill often on unrelated or controversial topics in an effort to make the bill unacceptable to a majority of the legislature, who will then be more likely to vote against the bill.

Floor debate

when a bill is brought up before the entire chamber for debate for and against the measure.

Killer amendment

language added to a bill on an unrelated or controversial topic in order to make the bill unacceptable to the majority of the legislature who will then vote against the bill.

Filibuster

an effort to kill a bill by engaging in unlimited debate, refusing to yield the floor to another member and preventing a vote on the bill.

Roll call votes

votes, usually important, for which a permanent record of each member's vote is created.

Rider

an addition to a bill that deals with an unrelated subject such as changing some aspect of law or public policy or spending money or creating programs in a specific member's district.

Closed rider

a rider that is not made public until after the legislature has voted on the bill, either when the bill goes to a conference committee for reconciliation or when the governor prepares to sign the bill into law.

After the floor debate, members of the chamber vote on the various amendments and then vote on the final version of the bill. This is the "second reading" of the bill (the "first reading" occurred when the bill was introduced to the chamber). In the Texas Senate, the time of debate is unlimited, so any member may speak indefinitely on the bill. Sometimes, a member of the Senate engages in a **filibuster,** an effort to kill a bill by engaging in prolonged debate, refusing to yield the floor to another member, and therefore, preventing a vote on the bill. A filibuster is ended by a majority vote of the Texas Senate. Debate time is limited in the Texas House. The filibuster cannot occur in that chamber. A "third reading" then occurs to take the final vote on the bill. Two types of votes occur in the Texas Legislature. Votes on bills and amendments to bills may be a voice vote, in which members call out "aye" or "nay." In the Texas House, votes are recorded electronically; in the Texas Senate all votes are voice votes. Normally, however, important votes are **roll call votes.** For these votes, a permanent record of how each member voted exists. Some votes may be conducted on paper ballots.

At any time during committee action or floor debate, a member may attach a rider to an appropriations bill. A **rider** is an addition to the bill that deals with an unrelated subject, usually changing some aspect of an existing law or public policy. A rider may also spend money. Riders often spend money or create programs in a specific member's district. While riders are common in many state legislatures and the U.S. Congress, in Texas a rider may be a **closed rider,** a rider that is not made public until after the legislature has voted on the bill. Riders are revealed when a bill goes to a conference committee for reconciliation or when the governor gets ready to sign the bill into law.

Sometimes, legislators cannot be present for votes on the floor of the legislature. Casting "ghost" votes, essentially having another legislator cast a vote for the missing member, is a common practice. Although members of the legislature are supposed to be present when they cast votes, sometimes the clerk of the chamber is unaware that a specific member is not present when votes are taken. In these circumstances, legislators arrange for another member to cast votes for them. In April 2007, Rep. Mike Krusee, R-Williamson County, attended a conference in London, while also casting at least thirty votes on the floor of the House in Austin. Reportedly, Rep. Marc Veasey, D-Fort Worth, was seen punching in votes for Krusee.[50]

Once a bill has passed one chamber of the legislature, the bill goes to the other chamber for consideration. Again, bills dealing with taxation and spending must begin in the Texas House of Representatives and then go to the Texas Senate. All other bills may begin in either chamber and then go to the other chamber. As mentioned above, once both chambers have passed a bill in identical form, the bill goes to the governor for signing. If the House and Senate have passed different versions of the same bill, then the bill goes to a conference committee for reconciliation first. The conference committee may attach several amendments or may rewrite the bill. The recommendation of the conference committee is sent back to both chambers of the Texas Legislature in the form of a report. Each chamber may accept the changes to the bill, reject the changes to the bill, or send the bill back to the conference committee. If both chambers accept the changes, the bill has passed. If the bill fails to pass either chamber or the conference committee cannot reconcile the differences, then the bill dies. If a bill has not been passed by the legislature, and the session ends, then the bill dies; bills do not carry over to another legislative session. Twenty-four states, but not Texas, allow some form of carryover.[51]

After a bill is sent to the governor, he or she must sign the bill into law or veto the bill. If the governor does not sign the bill into law, after ten days, the bill automatically becomes law. While the governor posses the power to veto legislation, the power of the governor to veto bills is limited. For all bills but those dealing with spending, the governor must veto or accept the entire bill. The governor may use a **line-item veto** on spending bills only. Once a bill is vetoed by the governor, to override the veto, each house of the state legislature must vote to override the veto by a two-thirds vote. If the legislature ends its session, the governor has twenty days to veto the bill or the bill becomes law. Ninety days after the legislature ends its session, any law enacted becomes effective, unless the bill contains an **emergency clause,** which makes the bill effective immediately upon being signed into law.

Line-item veto
the ability of the executive to selectively veto only some parts of a bill; in Texas available only on spending bills.

Emergency clause
language that makes the bill effective immediately upon being signed into law, rather than being subject to the customary ninety-day waiting period.

Winners and Losers

Historically, legislative organization and process have produced clear winners and losers in the game of Texas politics. The relatively weak position of parties, coupled with the dominance of the Democratic Party, produced a system that concentrated power in the hands of the presiding officer. Thus, the two most powerful positions in Texas have been the Speaker of the House and the lieutenant governor in the Senate. The amount of power in these two offices, unchecked by an institutionally weak legislature and governor, creates the exact type of concentrated power the framers were trying to avoid. As the opening vignette about Speaker Craddick illustrates, those offices have become almost untouchable, as the Speaker of the House courts support from individual legislators and rewards supporters with favorable consideration of legislation and committee assignments.

The parties themselves became losers. Loyalty to a faction within the Democratic Party mattered more in the past. The party lacked any real ability to shape legislation or to control debate. Members of the legislature have acted as independent brokers, swapping votes and cutting deals to influence legislation. Informal networking and acting in the interest of constituents rather than the party are what matter. Only in the last two decades have the parties developed better organization to function in the Texas House of Representatives, yet, the party continues to be a relatively unimportant tool in the legislature. The special caucuses seem to perform some of the roles of parties in more organized state legislatures and the U.S. Congress: the special caucuses review legislation and provide a network of individuals, often across party lines, to support or amend legislation. Whether the emergence of the Republican majority the last few years will produce a party-centered approach to the legislature, similar to the U.S. Congress, remains to be seen. The recent revolt against Speaker Craddick may signify that the Speaker-based system is unraveling. In the Texas Senate, the relatively small chamber size, the weaker calendar committee, and the procedural motions that require super-majorities allow the minority party to exert additional influence over bills in a way that does not occur in the Texas House of Representatives.

Conclusion

ven though strides have been made to boost minority representation and even after the number of women in the legislature has increased, the legislature still does not "look like" Texas. Moreover, the legacy of Democratic Party control lingers as the two-party system emerges within the legislature itself. Presiding officers exert tremendous control over legislation and the legislative process, the parties remain weaker than might be expected, and the small Texas Senate continues to check the House by allowing the minority party greater influence over outcomes. As the two-party system develops, a greater shift toward a more party-centered model of legislative process and organization seems plausible.

Key Terms

amendment
bicameral
bills
blocking bill
citizen initiatives
citizen legislature
closed rider
committees
concurrent resolutions
conference committee
cohesion
delegate
emergency clause
filibuster
floor debate
floor whips
gerrymandering
instant run-off
interim committee
introduce [a bill]
joint committee
joint resolutions
killer amendment
Legislative Budget Board (LBB)
Legislative Redistricting Board (LRB)
lieutenant governor
line-item veto
mark-up
majority election
majority-minority districts
Multi-Member District (MMD)
nonpartisan or bipartisan independent commissions
one person, one vote
oversight
party affiliation

party caucus
party caucus chairs
party primary
plurality election
politico
president pro tempore
professional legislature
redistricting
representation
resolutions
rider
roll call votes
run-off election
simple resolutions
Speaker of the House
Speaker pro tempore
special caucuses
standing committees
structuring the vote
term limits
trustee
turnover
Voting Rights Act of 1965 (VRA)

Explore this subject further at http://college.cqpress.com/lonestarpolitics, where you'll find chapter summaries, practice quizzes, key word flash cards, and additional suggested resources.

Most politicians are not unfamiliar with a little Texas two-stepping or Houston shuffle, whether their boots are made for walking or not. At the Inaugural Black Tie and Boots Ball in Washington, D.C., George W. Bush, Texas governor Rick Perry, and Texas senators Kay Bailey Hutchison and Phil Gramm show off their fancy footwear with pride as they kick off the festivities on January 19, 2001.

CHAPTER 4

Governors and Bureaucracy in Texas

I n 2000, George Walker Bush resigned the governorship to become president and Lt. Gov. Rick Perry assumed the office. After winning two subsequent elections, Perry is now the longest running governor in the state. Perry was popular in his first term, but was barely reelected for a second term. On the other hand, Perry is now the longest sitting governor in the state's history and can use that tenure to increase his influence in the state. Nonetheless, Perry's time in office has been controversial and increasingly divisive for Republicans. As Perry's popularity has waned he has become more aggressive at confronting the legislature and attempting to get his policies passed.

In February 2007, Gov. Rick Perry issued an executive order that required all sixth-grade girls in Texas public schools to get the human papillomavirus (HPV) vaccine, designed to decrease the rates of cervical cancer. The order also provided an option for parents to opt out of the vaccine. The executive order was quickly surrounded by controversy as both Republicans and Democrats questioned the authority of the governor to issue such a far-reaching executive order. Legislators accused Perry of attempting to dictate laws while circumventing the state's legislature.

In the midst of this controversy, questions about Perry's motives for the legislation were raised. There was the issue of Perry's relationship with the drug company Merck, the manufacturer of the vaccine. Perry had received $6,000 in contributions from Merck's political action committee, including a $5,000 donation made on the day Perry's staff met to discuss the vaccine.[1] Then there was the fact that one of Merck's highest paid lobbyists is Mike Toomey, who also happens to be Perry's former chief of staff.

Texans across the state were opposed to the governor's power grab. Conservatives argued that the state should not intrude in decisions that should be made by families. Even many liberal proponents of the vaccine believed that the governor had overstepped his authority. The legislature responded first by asking the governor to repeal his executive order. When that didn't work, the legislature passed a bill that would prevent the vaccine from being required for school enrollment. The legislation passed with such large margins that if Perry chose to veto the bill, there was a good chance his veto would be overridden.[2] Perry chose not to test his veto power. While the legislature and the governor fought over executive authority, the attorney general issued an opinion stating that Perry's HPV mandate did not carry the weight of law.[3]

Interestingly, this was not the first time that Governor Perry attempted to significantly increase his formal powers through the use of executive orders. In 2005, Perry issued another executive order which would shorten the time it took coal-fired electric plants to obtain permits from one year to six months.[4] Perry argued that the state was facing a shortage of energy and needed more plants. Perry's motives were again under scrutiny when, after issuing the order, Perry received more than $100,000 from organized interests associated with coal project proposals.[5] In early 2007 a state district judge ruled that Perry lacked the authority to order shorter hearings for the permits.

These are not the only examples of Perry attempting to expand the powers of the governor's office. In several other instances, Perry issued executive orders in an attempt to pass legislation without the pesky and rather burdensome process of going through the Texas Legislature. For example, in three other executive orders, Perry ordered the Texas Education Agency to implement provisions of education legislation that had failed to pass the legislature.[6] Given the length of Perry's tenure and his apparent willingness to circumvent the legislative process, it is difficult to assess what the future Texas governor's office will look like.

In this chapter we examine the Texas governorship, including formal and informal qualifications. We then assess the powers of the Texas governor, including the extent to which the governor of Texas is a weak governorship. Finally, we explore the other members of the plural executive and the accountability of the Texas bureaucracy in general.

As you read the chapter, think about the following questions:

★ What are the formal powers of the Texas governor?
★ Is the Texas governor weak?
★ How might we change the Texas executive?
★ How is the bureaucracy held accountable in Texas?

The Office of the Governor

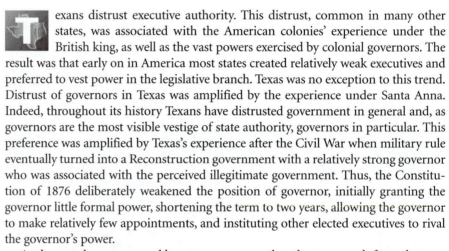

exans distrust executive authority. This distrust, common in many other states, was associated with the American colonies' experience under the British king, as well as the vast powers exercised by colonial governors. The result was that early on in America most states created relatively weak executives and preferred to vest power in the legislative branch. Texas was no exception to this trend. Distrust of governors in Texas was amplified by the experience under Santa Anna. Indeed, throughout its history Texans have distrusted government in general and, as governors are the most visible vestige of state authority, governors in particular. This preference was amplified by Texas's experience after the Civil War when military rule eventually turned into a Reconstruction government with a relatively strong governor who was associated with the perceived illegitimate government. Thus, the Constitution of 1876 deliberately weakened the position of governor, initially granting the governor little formal power, shortening the term to two years, allowing the governor to make relatively few appointments, and instituting other elected executives to rival the governor's power.

As the state has grown and become more complex, the governor's formal power has increased to some degree, but the position still has failed to keep pace with the demands of modern Texas. The legislature, for example, has granted the governor more appointment power, as it has created a growing number of minor state agencies and commissions. The governor's salary, which was notably decreased by the 1876 constitution, is now fairly competitive. And the governor's term was eventually increased from two to four years, affording governors and citizens alike a break between elections. In addition, Texas governors have needed to become increasingly astute at employing informal powers. Texas's size and geographical position create relatively unique opportunities for the state's governor. For example, Texas's international border with Mexico has allowed the state's governors to participate in national policymaking as Bush did with NAFTA and Perry with immigration policy. The national focus of the border issues have helped strengthen the Texas governorship and raise its profile. In addition, the highly visible role Texas played in Hurricanes Katrina, Rita, and, more recently, Dean, has also garnered national media attention. The power of the Texas governor has grown both formally and informally even as the preference for limited government remains entrenched in the state.

The governor of Texas tends to be a national political figure by virtue of being governor of such a large state. Although the Texas Constitution vests few formal powers in the governor, as we shall see, governors who are skilled politicians and can successfully utilize informal powers can become pivotal political figures. Often the pinnacle of a politician's career, governorships are highly visible and increasingly merely a stepping stone to other offices, including both gubernatorial and presidential appointments, and even the presidency itself. For example, former Governor Preston Smith served as chair of what is now the Higher Education Coordinating Board, after being appointed by then Governor Clements. Similarly, after his term as governor, Price Daniel was appointed by President Lyndon B. Johnson to head the Office of Emergency Preparedness, and later appointed to the Texas Supreme Court by Governor Smith. Notably Price Daniel, who had served the state in a variety of elected and appointed offices, has held more high offices than anyone else in Texas history.[7] After serving as governor of the state, John Connally, who famously survived bullet wounds in the Kennedy assassination in Dallas, became Secretary of the Treasury during Nixon's administration. Pappy O' Daniel resigned the governorship to become a U.S. senator. Most notable of course, is former governor George W. Bush, who left the governor's office to assume the presidency of the United States. Other governors, such as Bill Clements and Ann Richards, chose not to seek further elected office after vacating the governor's mansion.

Qualifications

The constitution specifies three requirements to be governor in the state. The governor has an age requirement of at least thirty years, a residency requirement of at least five years in the state of Texas, and a national citizenship requirement. In addition, the constitution stipulates that all state officeholders, including the governor, must believe in a supreme being, a term that is undefined in the constitution. The governor of the state is further restricted from holding any other job or receiving outside compensation, a restriction notably absent from the state's legislature. Specifically the Texas Constitution says:

> The Governor elected at the general election in 1974, and thereafter, shall be installed on the first Tuesday after the organization of the Legislature, or as soon thereafter as practicable, and shall hold his office for the term of four years, or until his successor shall be duly installed. He shall be at least thirty years of age, a citizen of the United States, and shall have resided in this State at least five years immediately preceding his election. (Amended Nov. 7, 1972.)[8]

Table 4.1 Texas Governors since 1876

GOVERNOR	PARTY	TERM	MILITARY EXPERIENCE	OCCUPATION	VETOES
Richard B. Hubbard	Democrat	1876–1879	Confederate Army	Lawyer	0
Oran M. Roberts	Democrat	1879–1883	Confederate Army	Lawyer/Educator	13
John Ireland	Democrat	1883–1887	Confederate Army	Lawyer	10
Lawrence Sul Ross	Democrat	1887–1891	Confederate Army	Farmer/Soldier	7
James S. Hogg	Democrat	1891–1895	None	Lawyer/Educator	21
Charles A. Culberson	Democrat	1895–1899	None	Lawyer	33
Joseph D. Sayers	Democrat	1899–1903	Confederate Army	Lawyer	41
Samuel Lanham	Democrat	1903–1907	Confederate Army	Lawyer	32
Thomas M. Campbell	Democrat	1907–1911	None	Lawyer/Railroad Exec.	32
Oscar B. Colquitt	Democrat	1911–1915	None	Lawyer/Editor	60
James E. Ferguson	Democrat	1915–1917	None	Banker/Lawyer/Farmer	29
William P. Hobby	Democrat	1917–1921	None	Editor	19
Pat M. Neff	Democrat	1921–1925	None	Lawyer/Educator	58
Miriam A. Ferguson	Democrat	1925–1927	None	Housewife	30
Dan Moody	Democrat	1927–1931	TX National Guard in WWI	Lawyer	101
Ross Sterling	Democrat	1931–1933	None	President of Mobil Oil	7
Miriam A. Ferguson	Democrat	1933–1935	None	Housewife	24
James V. Allred	Democrat	1935–1939	U.S. Navy in WWI	Lawyer	48
W. Lee O'Daniel	Democrat	1939–1941	None	Businessperson/ Salesperson	48
Coke Stevenson	Democrat	1941–1947	None	Lawyer/Banker/Rancher	56
Beauford Jester	Democrat	1947–1949	U.S. Army in WWI	Lawyer	19
Allan Shivers	Democrat	1949–1957	U.S. Army in WWII	Lawyer	76
Price Daniel	Democrat	1957–1963	U.S. Army in WWII	Lawyer/Educator/ Rancher	42
John Connally	Democrat	1963–1969	U.S. Navy Reserve in WWII	Lawyer/Rancher	103
Preston Smith	Democrat	1969–1973	None	Businessperson	92
Dolph Briscoe	Democrat	1973–1979	U.S. Army in WWII	Rancher/Banker	72
Bill Clements	Republican	1979–1983	None	Oilman	78
Mark White	Democrat	1983–1987	TX National Guard	Lawyer	95
Bill Clements	Republican	1987–1991	None	Oilman	112
Ann Richards	Democrat	1991–1995	None	Teacher/Campaigner	62
George W. Bush	Republican	1995–2000	TX Air National Guard	Oilman/Businessperson	95
Rick Perry	Republican	2000–	U.S. Air Force	Farmer/Rancher	204

Source: Compiled by author using data from University of Texas at Austin, Liberal Arts Instructional Technology Services, http://texaspolitics.laits.utexas.edu/html/exec/governors/index.html.

During the time he holds the office of Governor, he shall not hold any other office: civil, military or corporate; nor shall he practice any profession, and receive compensation, reward, fee, or the promise thereof for the same; nor receive any salary, reward or compensation or the promise thereof from any person or corporation, for any service rendered or performed during the time he is Governor, or to be thereafter rendered or performed.[9]

Beyond the constitutional requirements, Texas governors have tended to share common characteristics. Since 1876, most governors in Texas have been white, Protestant, wealthy men. The vast majority of modern governors have had some higher education, mostly in the law. Most Texas governors have also had some military experience ranging from service in the U.S. Army or Navy to the Texas National Guard or Texas Air Guard. Although the myth of the Texas rancher or Texas oilman is often used to tap into the Texas legend during gubernatorial campaigns, few modern governors actually have such experience. Notable exceptions include Dolph Briscoe who was a wealthy cattleman and horse trader and Governors Clements and Bush, who made fortunes drilling oil.

Modern governors of Texas have also, by and large, had previous political experience. Many of the state's governors have risen from the ranks of other Texas offices including the Texas Legislature, the Railroad Commission, and often the lieutenant governor's office. Others held national offices prior to becoming governors of the Lone Star State. After serving as U.S. senator, Price Daniel famously declared he would "rather be governor of Texas than the president of the United States" and returned to Texas to run for governor. Other notable examples include William Clements, who had been deputy U.S. secretary of defense, and John Connally, who ascended to the governorship after serving as the secretary of the Navy in the Kennedy administration.

On the other hand, Texas has sometimes expressed a willingness to elect governors with no political experience. Often inexperienced gubernatorial candidates can tap into the Texan's distrust of government, but a larger-than-life personality can also make up for inexperience in public service. James "Pa" Ferguson, for example, had no political experience when he was elected governor in 1914. Much of his popularity was based on his self-styled image as "Farmer Jim," representing tenant farmers and poor workers across the state. He also impressed audiences by quoting Jefferson, Hamilton, or Shakespeare whenever the occasion arose.[10]

Equally colorful, and perhaps equally ineffectual, was governor Wilbert Lee "Pappy" O'Daniel. O'Daniel worked at a flour mill, and hosted a weekly radio show where he sold his flour and expressed his opinions with his band, the Light Crust Doughboys. Despite his lack of experience, his popularity on the radio helped him win the governor's office twice and even win a congressional seat. O'Daniel was highly popular as a radio personality, but enjoyed little success as governor.

Recently George W. Bush followed in the tradition of running for governor without prior political experience. Bush enjoyed name recognition from his father's presidency and a conservative reputation in an overwhelmingly conservative state. As governor, George W. Bush was known for his ability to forge bipartisan coalitions. He successfully supported several education initiatives and state tax cuts and was a relatively popular governor.

One of the most consistent traits of Texas governors throughout the state's history is that they have tended to be conservative Democrats. Nothing was more ingrained in the Texas legend than the Democrats' hold on the state, which was nearly absolute. The state has had only three Republican governors since 1876, beginning with Bill Clements who finally broke the Democrats' winning streak in 1978. The dissolution of the Democratic Party monopoly is one of the most significant changes in the state. The change is particularly noteworthy since we have seen an almost complete reversal in party affiliation. Democratic Party dominance has given way to Republican Party control, and the recent trend of electing Republican governors will likely continue in the near future.

Ironically relatively few early Texas governors were born in the state. Since statehood, only approximately 46 percent of Texas governors, or 21 out of 46, were native born. Indeed, Texas's first native-born governor was the state's twentieth governor, James Stephen "Jim" Hogg, elected in 1890. Jim Hogg was a Democrat who nonetheless brought progressivism to the state. Texans appreciated him for protecting the interests of ordinary people rather than big business. Hogg also earned his place in Texas folklore by famously naming his only daughter Ima. The myth that he also named a second daughter, Ura Hogg, persists today, though no such person existed. Modern governors have been much more likely to be born in Texas, although Pappy O'Daniel and George W. Bush are both notable exceptions.

Although nearly all of the state's governors have been white men, Texas has also had two women governors. In 1924, Miriam A. "Ma" Ferguson was the first woman governor in Texas, and the second woman governor in the United States, since Wyoming swore in Nellie T. Ross two weeks prior to Ma Ferguson taking office. After her husband had been impeached and prevented from holding office in the state, Ma Ferguson ran as a proxy, with a campaign slogan, "two governors for the price of one." Ironically, Pa Ferguson had actively opposed women's suffrage, arguing that a woman's place was in the home. Thus, the women's suffrage movement opposed Ma Ferguson's election, though she would go on to appoint the first female secretary of state in Texas, Emma C. Meharg. Ma Ferguson's administration opposed the Ku Klux Klan (she passed an anti-mask law that the courts subsequently overturned); contested prohibition laws; and called for fiscal economy. However Ma Ferguson's administration is perhaps best known for widespread accusations of corruption, including the more than 2,000 pardons granted during her administration. Most Texans believed that pardons were for sale under the Fergusons. Ma claimed that most of the pardons were given to liquor law violators who were not really criminals, though in fact hundreds of pardons were granted to violent felons as well.[11] Ma lost her bid for reelection in the next two gubernatorial races, but was elected governor again in 1932, becoming the first governor in Texas to serve two non-consecutive terms.

Table 4.2 Terms and Qualifications of Elected Chief Executives

CONSTITUTIONAL PROVISIONS	TEXAS GOVERNOR	U.S. PRESIDENT	OTHER STATES
Age	30 years	35 years	34 states set minimum age at 30
Residence	5 years	14 years	5 years or less in 38 states
Terms	4 years	4 years (limited to 2 terms of office or 10 years)	48 states allow a four-year term, but 36 states limit number of consecutive terms

Source: Keon S. Chi, *The Book of the States: 2005 Edition*, vol. 37 (Lexington, KY: Council of State Governments, 2005).

More recently Ann Richards was elected governor of Texas in 1991. Richards had experience on the County Commissioners Court and as the Texas state treasurer. Richards represents the iconic Texas image: cowboy hat and boots, straight talk, and a reputation for being tough. A former teacher, Governor Richards decentralized education policy, encouraged economic growth, and promoted women and minorities during her administration. In contrast to Ma Ferguson, Richardson became a symbol of women's progress in the state, famously displaying a t-shirt of the state capitol with the caption "a woman's place is in the dome."

Although Hispanics have had an increasing voice in the state, and are both the largest and fastest growing minority in Texas, Texas has yet to have a Hispanic governor. In 2002, wealthy oil tycoon Tony Sanchez made an unsuccessful bid for the governor's office, spending a reported $59 million of his own money.[12] Sanchez campaigned on beefing up education in the state, including tougher discipline in public schools and increased spending on education and pay raises for teachers. He also championed affordable health care for all Texans. Many observers saw Sanchez's campaign as a test of whether the Democratic Party could tap Hispanic voters to loosen the grip of the Republican Party on the state.[13] Although Sanchez lost to Rick Perry, his campaign is an indication of the changing make-up of Texas and the critical fight among the parties to capture the Hispanic vote.

Terms

The Texas Constitution of 1876 originally established a relatively short, two-year term for the governor. Short terms, usually one or two years, were common in early American state politics, reflecting a distrust of executive power lingering after experiences with the monarch and colonial governors. Early on, most governors in Texas were elected to two terms, serving a total of four years. In 1972, however, the Texas constitution was amended increasing the governor's term to four years. Despite the fact that Texas has no term limits few governors have been elected to two terms since that time. Dolph Briscoe served six years, since he had been elected to a two-year term in 1973 before the amendment took effect and was reelected to a second term under the new rules. Governors elected after Briscoe won only a single four-year term until George W. Bush. Bush was the first governor to be elected to a second four-year term, although he resigned in 2000 to become president. Lt. Gov. Rick Perry finished Bush's term and ran successful bids for reelection in 2002 and again in 2006. Thus at the end of his current term, Governor Perry will have served ten years, making him the longest serving governor in Texas history.

Obviously, the longer a governor serves the more likely that the governor will successfully pass his or her own political agenda. That Texas has four-year terms with no term limits could be a source of power for governors who are able to obtain reelections. For instance, Perry has enjoyed the ability to appoint nearly every appointive office in the state, generating a lot of loyalty to his administration. He has also worked with the legislature long enough to cultivate strong supporters there.

Succession

If a governor is unable to fulfill his or her term, the Texas Constitution outlines an explicit line of **succession.** If the governor resigns, is impeached, or dies while in office, the lieutenant governor will succeed to the governorship. After the lieutenant governor, the line of succession goes next to the president pro tempore of the Texas Senate,

Succession
a set order, usually spelled out in the constitution, of which officeholder takes over when the sitting governor resigns, dies, or is impeached.

Ann Richards

As governor of Texas, Ann Richards reflected both new and old Texas, embracing the transformation of the state while remaining rooted in its traditions. As a woman she challenged the male dominance of the state as Texas loosened itself from the grip of generations of the male insiders frequently referred to as the "good ole boys." While changing the way things were done, Richards proved equally fluent in the language and symbols of traditional Texas.

Richards moved up quickly in the ranks of Texas politics. After teaching junior high school social studies while raising her family, Richards entered government in 1976, winning a seat on the Travis County commission. Richards fit easily into the small-town image revered in Texas, often proclaiming proudly that her father came from a town called Bugtussle and her mother from Hogjaw. By 1982 she won election as state treasurer and became the first woman elected to statewide office in Texas in fifty years by winning more votes in Texas than any other candidate that year.

Richards campaigned for the governor's office in 1990, calling for a "New Texas" that would offer opportunities to more Texans. In the end, she won a hard-fought battle, besting West Texas rancher Clayton Williams. While in office Richards worked aggressively to bring more women and minorities into state government. She made clear that women could find a place in Texas politics advising, "Let me tell you, sisters, seeing dried egg on a plate in the morning is a lot dirtier than anything I've had to deal with in politics." She appointed the first black regent to the University of Texas Board of Regents and brought more black, Hispanic, and female officers into the ranks of the legendary Texas Rangers.

Richards proved to be just as colorful as her predecessors. She once quipped, "Let me tell you that I am the only child of a very rough-talking father. So don't be embarrassed about your language. I've either heard it or I can top it." Like many of the men who came before her, Richards also had flaws, including alcoholism that ended in rehab and a strained marriage that ended in divorce.

Richards demonstrated repeatedly that women could be tough on crime, dramatically increasing the size of the Texas prison system and limiting the number of prisoners going on parole. She also championed education and environmental causes. Richards looked to modernize how departments were administered and led the state on insurance reform and ethics reform.

While her tongue was sharp, her language was folksy. Her style won her a national following when she delivered the keynote address at the 1988 Democratic National Convention. Complaining about George H. W. Bush, the Republican Party's presidential candidate, Richards suggested the Democrats would expose his shortcomings, or, "we're going to tell how the cow ate the cabbage."

Richards championed political activism, saying, "Sometimes it's serendipitous. Good things happen accidentally. But they're not going to happen unless well-meaning people give of their time and their lives to do that." One of her legacies is the Ann Richards School for young women leaders, a school focused on giving girls the education and confidence to serve as leaders in their community. She preached feminism, telling the nation, "Ginger Rogers did everything Fred Astaire did. She just did it backwards and in high heels."

Beaten by George W. Bush in her bid for reelection, Richards remained in the spotlight making frequent media appearances and working as a political consultant. Asked what she would have done if she had known she would only serve one term Richards remarked, "I would have raised more hell."

Richards died of esophageal cancer on September 13, 2006. Governor Rick Perry's eulogy summed up her already legendary status, stating that "Ann Richards was the epitome of Texas politics: a figure larger than life who had a gift for captivating the public with her great wit." Ann Richards is the embodiment of change in a state that holds fast to tradition. She embraced the traditions of the state more than many of the good ole boys, all the while challenging the state's role for women and minorities.

then the Speaker of the House, followed by the attorney general. Thus, after the 2000 presidential election, Gov. George W. Bush resigned to take the office of the presidency, Lt. Gov. Rick Perry became the governor and the Texas Senate elected Bill Ratliff as the new lieutenant governor. Ratliff became the first lieutenant governor in the history of the state to serve as lieutenant governor without winning a statewide election.

When the governor is out of the state, the lieutenant governor is acting governor for the day. Thus, when George W. Bush was running for president, Rick Perry acquired a lot of practice in the governor's office. By custom, both the governor and the lieutenant governor arrange to be out of the state at least one day during their term, allowing the president pro tempore of the Senate to act as governor for the day.

Compensation

Originally, the 1876 constitution specified the governor's salary, which meant that a pay raise would require a constitutional amendment approved by a majority of voters. In 1954, however, the constitution was amended to allow the Texas Legislature to set the governor's salary. Currently, the Texas governor is paid $115,345, which puts the state just below the average of $124,398 for all governors.[14] California has the highest paid governor, with a salary of $206,500, while Maine's governor receives the lowest salary ($70,000) in the country. Currently, there are three governors who donate their salary back to their states, including Gov. Arnold Schwarzenegger in California, Gov. Phil Bredesen of Tennessee, and Gov. Jon Corzine of New Jersey, who keeps only $1.00 of his salary each year. Ironically, governors are paid well below the average $900,000 annual salary for NCAA Division 1A head football coaches, who receive the largest salaries among state employees.[15]

In addition to salary, the governor's office includes several auxiliary means of additional compensation. For instance, Texas maintains a governor's mansion around the corner from the capitol. Most governors get free housing, although according to the Council of State Governments, Arizona, Idaho, Massachusetts, Rhode Island, and Vermont do not provide a governor's residence. The Texas governor is also allocated a travel allowance and use of a state limousine, state helicopter, and state airplane. All fifty states provide an automobile for their governor, while only forty-one states provide a state airplane. The governor also has a staff to help coordinate the governor's office. Depending on the governor, the governor's staff ranges from 200 to over 300 people.

Impeachment

The Texas Constitution vests the power of **impeachment** with the Texas Legislature. According to the constitution, the legislature can impeach the governor, the lieutenant governor, attorney general, commissioner of the General Land Office, comptroller, as well as the judges of the Supreme Court, Court of Appeals, and District Court. In order to impeach the governor, the Texas House of Representatives must approve the articles of impeachment (similar to a grand jury indictment) by a simple majority. Impeachment by the House merely suggests that there is enough evidence to proceed with a trial. Impeachments are then tried in the Texas Senate. To convict the governor requires a two-thirds vote of the Senate. While the Texas Constitution outlines a clear procedure for impeaching the governor, it is silent on what constitutes an impeachable offense.

Impeachment
formal procedures to remove an elected official from office for misdeeds; passage of the articles of impeachment by the House merely suggests that there is sufficient evidence for a trial, which is then conducted by the Senate.

Pa Ferguson remains the only governor in the state's history to be impeached and removed from office. Ferguson, whose education was limited to sixth grade, balked when the University of Texas Board of Regents refused to let him handpick university presidents or fire university professors who had opposed his governorship. When asked why he wanted to fire the professors, Governor Ferguson famously quipped, "I am governor of Texas, I don't have to give any reasons." [16] To indicate his disapproval with the Board, Ferguson vetoed the university's appropriations. Up to this point, only six American governors had been impeached and five of those were Reconstruction governors in the South. [17] Nonetheless, the Texas Legislature voted to impeach and remove the governor for misappropriation of public funds and he was barred from holding a state office again. In spite of that, Ferguson continued to exert significant influence on politics in the state. First, the day before his impeachment verdict was announced Ferguson resigned as governor. He would later claim this made the impeachment verdict obsolete. Amazingly, in 1924, despite his conviction, Ferguson would again run for governor of the state, although an appellate court upheld his prohibition from holding state office. Even this was not enough to prevent Ferguson's influence, as he subsequently convinced his wife Miriam to run for governor in his place.

Powers of the Governor

The governor of Texas is often called formally weak, and the position's strength often depends on the officeholder's ability to generate support informally for a policy agenda. In general, strong governors are often granted significant appointment power, exert considerable control over the state's budget, and exercise substantial power to veto legislation. The Texas governor's limited powers in the 1876 constitution represent a reaction to E. J. Davis's Reconstruction government, in particular the impression that that government did not represent most Texans' preferences. The formal powers in the constitution also represent a very real preference among Texans for limited government in general, a preference that continues to be prevalent today.

Executive Role

According to the Texas Constitution, the governor of the state "shall cause the laws to be faithfully executed and shall conduct, in person, or in such manner as shall be prescribed by law, all intercourse and business of the State with other States and with the United States." [18] This means the governor must work with the state bureaucracy and administer the laws passed by the state legislature. The ability of the governor to guide the bureaucracy is directly tied to his or her appointment power. A bureaucracy led by gubernatorial appointees will be much more responsive to the governor's policy goals than one which is elected independently of the governor and has its own policy agenda to pursue. In Texas, the governor's appointment powers have been traditionally limited, although they have increased in recent years. In terms of **appointment power** the Texas governor is a paradox created by continually revising an old constitution to an ever changing state. On the one hand, the governor is part of a **plural executive** sharing administrative powers with other officials that are elected independent of the governor's office. This means that often members of the plural executive are not interested in working toward the governor's goals. Since they serve based on popular election rather than gubernatorial appointment, members of the plural executive may have their own policy goals and will often work against each other. They can even be from opposing parties, making the executive more fragmented and less unified than one where the governor appoints other executive members.

On the other hand, while the governor has little influence over the most important statewide officials, Texas has gradually given the governor more control over thousands of minor appointees in the executive branch. Gubernatorial appointees usually share the governor's basic political philosophies and tend to be loyal to the governor. Governors can also make appointments based on patronage. **Patronage** occurs when individuals are rewarded for their support with public jobs such as appointments. Governor Perry has been very generous with his use of patronage to reward supporters to his campaign. According to a recent study, approximately a third of Perry's appointees made campaign donations, contributing an average of $3,769, with Perry receiving an additional 3 million dollars from his appointees' employers.[19] For instance, Governor Perry appointed Houston beer distributor John Nau to the Historical Commission in 2003, one day after Nau donated $12,500 to Perry's campaign.[20]

The governor's most significant appointment is the secretary of state, although the governor appoints other important positions, including the adjutant general, health and human services commissioner, and the state education commissioner. The governor also designates over 2,000 appointments to various boards and commissions in Texas. The governor's appointment of board members typically occurs where the legislature has specifically granted the governor that power. There are several notable boards, such as the Railroad Commission, that, though originally appointed by the governor, are today an elected body. The governor can also appoint members to fill elected positions that are vacated before the term has expired.

The governor's appointment power is limited by the terms of those serving on the board. Typically, members of Texas boards or commissions serve staggered six-year terms that overlap the governor's term. That means that the governor will not have appointed a majority of any board or commission until the end of his or her first term. On the other hand, governors who can successfully obtain a second term will eventually appoint all of the members of the boards and commissions in the state. Thus, the longer the term of the governor, the more effective the governor's appointment power will be in achieving the governor's policy goals.

The Texas Constitution mandates that all gubernatorial appointments must be approved by a two-thirds vote in the Texas Senate. Since the Texas Legislature is only in session 140 days biennially, often it is necessary to fill a position while the Senate is not in session. In such cases, the governor can make a provisional appointment, but such **recess appointments** require Senate approval within ten days of the next session. The Senate also maintains a custom called **senatorial courtesy.** Any appointees must have approval of their own state senator in order to get the support of the Senate. If the appointee's senator does not support the appointment, then the Senate will not consent to the appointment.

Governor Perry, whose long tenure has given him unprecedented control over the state's appointments, has pursued a practice designed to expand the governor's appointment power even more. During the 2007 legislative session, Perry let nearly 400 appointments expire, replacing a mere 12 percent with new appointments or reappointments.[21] If Perry lets an appointment expire, typically the old

Patronage
when individuals who supported a candidate for public office are rewarded with public jobs and appointments.

Recess appointments
gubernatorial appointments made while the Senate is not in session; these require Senate approval within ten days of the next legislative session.

Senatorial courtesy
the informal requirement that any gubernatorial appointee have approval of their own state senator in order to get support of the entire Senate.

appointee will continue to serve, thus circumventing senatorial approval. Perry merely had to wait until the legislative session ended to make his appointments to deprive the Texas Senate of their power of confirmation. One of the most controversial examples centers on Transportation Commissioner Richard R. "Ric" Williamson, whose term expired in February 2007. Williamson has taken the lead on Perry's controversial plan to expand toll roads throughout the state. By not reappointing Williamson when his term expired, Williamson continued as Transportation Commissioner while Perry avoided what would have been an ugly battle to try to get Williamson reaffirmed in the Senate. Any appointments made after the end of the 2007 session will not face Senate confirmation until the legislature reconvenes in 2009.

A final significant aspect of appointment power is the governor's **removal powers.** In terms of exerting influence over policies, boards, and agencies, a governor's appointee exerts much greater autonomy if, once appointed, the governor lacks the power to remove him or her. In Texas today, the governor can remove his or her own appointees, but is required to obtain two-thirds support of the state Senate to do so.

Removal powers

the power of the governor to remove an appointee; in Texas the governor may remove his or her own appointees, but must obtain two-thirds support of the state Senate.

In addition to appointment and removal powers, a governor's ability to influence both the legislature and the bureaucracy is significantly influenced by gubernatorial **budget power.** In a strong executive model, such as our national government, the executive exerts considerable influence on the budget by proposing the budget that the legislature will consider. However, in Texas, the governor's budgetary powers are notably weak. In 1949, the Texas Legislature created the Legislative Budget Board to seize budgetary power from the executive branch. Since then, the Legislative Budget Board, co-chaired by the lieutenant governor and the Speaker of the House, has dominated the budgeting process. The governor may still prepare his or her own budget, although recent governors have seen this as a waste of time, since the legislature favors their own budget and typically ignores the governor's version.

The governor does exert some power over the budget through the line item veto, which allows the governor to strike out particular lines in an appropriations bill without vetoing the entire bill. However, even this power is limited in Texas, where a significant portion of the budget each year is earmarked for specific purposes and therefore cannot be vetoed.

Legislative Role

In addition, the governor plays an important **legislative role** in the state. The governor can directly influence the state's legislative agenda through the **state of the state address.** According to the Texas Constitution, the governor will inform the legislature of the condition of the state at the beginning of each legislative session, as well as at the end of his or her term. Thus, at the beginning of the 80th legislative session in Texas, Perry proposed a variety of new initiatives, including a healthcare program called Healthier Texas, a mandatory HPV vaccine for sixth-grade girls, an endowed fund for public education, and an expansion of the state's pre-kindergarten program, among other things. The state of the state address can act as an important means of gubernatorial influence on the legislative agenda.

In addition, the governor is given the power to call the legislature into **special session,** "on extraordinary occasions." According to the constitution, the governor may convene the special session for thirty days and the governor determines the agenda for the session. This process stands in contrast to thirty-six states that allow the members of the legislature or the legislature and its presiding officers to call a special session. Thirty-nine states allow the legislature to determine the topic of the session, including some states that require the governor to call the legislature into session. Thirty-three states place no limit on the length of special sessions.

In Texas, governors have used these sessions to force the legislature to address the governor's legislative proposals. Thus, in 2003, Gov. Rick Perry called three special sessions when the Texas Legislature had failed to redistrict the state as directed by Perry. Texas garnered national attention when several Democrats fled the state to prevent the necessary quorum in the session. Ultimately, though, Perry was able to get most of his redistricting plan passed, which resulted in the loss of five Democratic seats in the state's congressional delegation. Obviously, this tool can be an effective source of power for a governor although not necessarily without a price. The cost of a special session is well over $1 million per thirty-day session, and governors who use this tool too often may anger voters.

One of the most important legislative tools of the governor is the **veto power.** The governor in Texas possesses a variety of tools that ensure his or her influence on legislation. Any legislation passed by the legislature can be signed or vetoed by

Budget power
the executive's ability to propose an annual budget that the legislature then considers; the Texas governor has very limited power over the budget process, since there is a Legislative Budget Board.

Legislative role
the executive's role in influencing the state's legislative agenda.

State of the state address
the requirement that the governor address the state legislature about the condition of the state; the state of the state address occurs at the beginning of each legislative session as well as at the end of the governor's term.

Special session
the ability to require the out-of-session legislature to meet; in Texas the governor can invoke this power "on extraordinary occasions" for a thirty-day period to consider an agenda the governor has predetermined.

Veto power
the formal power of the executive to reject bills that have been passed by the legislature; in Texas, a veto can be overridden only by a two-thirds vote in both houses.

the governor within ten days. If the governor does neither, the legislation will automatically become law. If the governor chooses to veto legislation, the Texas Legislature needs two-thirds vote in both houses in order to override the veto. In Texas the governor's veto power is buttressed by the short legislative session where most bills are passed at the end of the 140 days. Vetoes rarely achieve the two-thirds support necessary to be overridden. The last time the legislature successfully overrode a governor's veto was in 1979. Passing bills late in the legislative session increases the likelihood that the legislature will not still be in session once the veto occurs. After the legislative session is adjourned, the governor gets an additional twenty days to act on all bills still under consideration. **Post-adjournment vetoes,** or vetoes that occur after the legislature has adjourned, are absolute in that there is no means for the legislature to overturn the veto. Recent governors have been increasingly willing to use the veto, with current governor Rick Perry having vetoed more legislation than any previous governor, including making liberal use of the post-adjournment veto.

The veto is one of the most important sources of legislative influence for the Texas governor. Theoretically, the governor's position on any proposed legislation will be taken into account while the legislature is actually writing the bill, in order to avoid a veto. This makes the true impact of the veto power difficult to assess. On the other hand, a governor who vetoes a considerable amount of legislation may be perceived as weak, since a large number of vetoes indicates that the governor did not exert his or her influence on the proposed legislation earlier in the process.[22] A governor who successfully used the threat of a veto to gain legislative compromise without actually having to veto legislation is doubtless more powerful than the governor who has to actually resort to the veto.

Governor Perry has earned a reputation for his frequent use of the veto power. Since taking office, Perry has vetoed an average of fifty-two bills a session, considerably more than the average of thirty-one bills by both Governor Bush and Governor Richards. Moreover, on Father's Day in 2001 Perry vetoed a record eighty-three bills, more than any other governor in Texas history, in what became known as the Father's Day Massacre. Because these were post-adjournment vetoes, the legislature could not overturn the gubernatorial veto.

Judicial Roles

Framers of the Texas Constitution of 1876 sought to limit the power of the governor by making all state and county-level judges elected rather than appointed. In spite of that, the governor of Texas often makes a significant number of judicial appointments to fill vacancies in between elections, subject to senatorial approval. These judicial appointments can be a significant source of gubernatorial influence over the judiciary, since the vast majority of incumbent judges in Texas win reelection.

In addition, the Constitution of 1876 originally granted the governor the authority to "grant reprieves, commutations of punishment and pardons."[23] This power was soon curbed, particularly after claims that "Ma" and "Pa" Ferguson sold pardons. In 1936 a constitutional amendment created a Board of Pardons and Paroles authorized to grant **pardons** in the state. Today, the governor can grant clemency or mercy only with the recommendation of a majority of the Board of Pardons and Paroles. The governor exercises some influence over the Board, as members are appointed by the governor with senatorial approval. However, the governor can grant no clemency absent the Board's recommendation. The governor can grant less clemency than the

Post-adjournment vetoes
vetoes that occur after the legislature has adjourned, thus giving the legislature no way to overturn the veto.

Pardon
an executive grant of release from a sentence or punishment in a criminal case.

Board recommended, but not more. The governor can also independently grant a one-time thirty-day stay of execution in death penalty cases.

Other Roles

The Texas governor fulfills many formal and informal roles. The governor performs a variety of what might otherwise be viewed as **ceremonial duties.** However, because the governor is the state's most visible officeholder, such ceremonial roles can become important sources of power for the governor. Since the September 11, 2001, attacks, the governor's role as **crisis manager** has also become increasingly important.[24] How governors handle crises in the post–Katrina and post–War on Terror era increasingly corresponds with constituent support. For instance, most Texans viewed Rick Perry's handling of Hurricane Katrina as positive. Perry's policies were generous to evacuees (offering temporary housing and opening Texas's public schools to evacuees) and also fiercely protective of Texas (obtaining reimbursement from the federal government for the costs). Indeed, in a poll taken in the months following Hurricanes Katrina and Rita, Perry's approval rating increased by ten percentage points, and Texans polled indicated that "[t]hey felt like [Perry] was compassionate for those who were displaced and that he fought to make sure Texas did not get stuck for the cost."[25] Though these highly visible roles can be critical sources of power, particularly for the most charismatic governors, the traditional sources of power for the governor continue to revolve around his or her executive and legislative roles.

Ceremonial duties
being the most visible officeholder, the executive makes appearances at events and performs ceremonial duties; such exposure can become an important source of power.

Crisis manager
the responsibility to act as a policymaker, coordinator of resources, and point person during a variety of natural and man-made disasters that might befall the people of the state during the executive's tenure.

Military Roles

In addition, the governor of Texas is commander-in-chief of the Texas National Guard and the Texas State Guard. The governor appoints the Adjutant General to command these units. The Texas National Guard remains under the governor's control unless it is being used for national service. Many in the Texas National Guard have served in Iraq and Afghanistan recently under the direction of the president. If the Texas National Guard is unavailable, the Texas State Guard can be called into action for state emergencies, as they were recently during Hurricanes Katrina and Rita.

In 2006 the U.S. Congress restricted the governor's power over National Guard troops during natural disasters. During the chaos following Hurricane Katrina, President Bush sought federal control over guardsmen in Louisiana, but Governor Blanco refused.[26] Prior to 2006, governors had sole control of the National Guard during a crisis within the state, though the president could take command of the guard for national service and domestically in times of insurrection. After Katrina, Congress expanded the president's domestic power and now allows the president to take control of troops during "natural disaster, epidemic, or other serious public health emergency, terrorist attack or incident" if the president determines that state authorities "are incapable of maintaining public order."[27] Not surprisingly, all fifty state governors objected to this expansion of federal power.

Texas Governor: Weak?

Most analyses of Texas suggest that the governor is an institutionally weak position. Thad Beyle has created an index of institutional power based on the degree to which

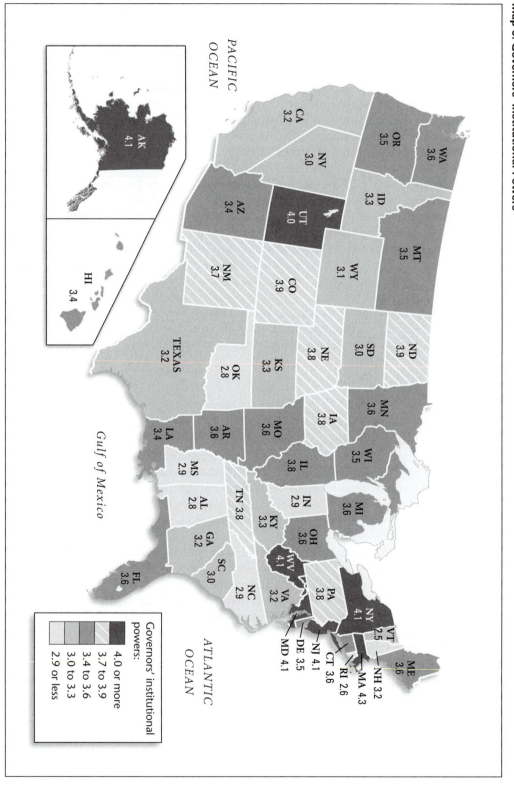

PACIFIC
OCEAN

AK
4.1

HI
3.4

CA
3.2

OR
3.5

WA
3.6

NV
3.0

AZ
3.4

UT
4.0

ID
3.3

MT
3.5

WY
3.1

CO
3.9

NM
3.7

TEXAS
3.2

OK
2.8

KS
3.3

NE
3.8

SD
3.0

ND
3.9

MN
3.6

IA
3.8

MO
3.6

AR
3.6

LA
3.4

MS
2.9

AL
2.8

TN 3.8

GA
3.2

SC
3.0

NC
2.9

FL
3.6

WI
3.5

IL
3.8

IN
2.9

KY
3.3

MI
3.6

OH
3.6

WV
4.1

VA
3.2

PA
3.8

NY
4.1

VT
2.5

ME
3.6

NH 3.2

MA 4.3

RI 2.6

CT 3.6

NJ 4.1

DE 3.5

MD 4.1

Gulf of Mexico

ATLANTIC
OCEAN

Governors' institutional
powers:

4.0 or more

3.7 to 3.9

3.4 to 3.6

3.0 to 3.3

2.9 or less

a state's executive is plural; the governor's ability to serve more terms; the level of appointment power, control of budget, and veto power the position wields; as well as whether the governor's party controls the legislature. Based on these criteria, the governorship in Texas is indeed weak compared to other states' executives. The Texas governor's institutional power score is 3.2 on a five-point scale, and thirty-five of the fifty states have governors with more institutional powers than Texas.[28] On the other hand, because Texas is such a large visible state, the governor has the potential to significantly expand his or her power through informal sources of power. Thus, in spite of the lack of vigorous institutional powers, the Texas governor has often managed through visibility, charisma, and personal power to become a presence in national politics.

Informal Powers

As we have already pointed out, the ability of the Texas governor to accomplish a legislative agenda will depend in large part on **informal powers.** Four important attributes of informal, or personal, power include a governor's electoral mandate, political ambition ladder, personal future as governor, and performance ratings.[29]

The greater the electoral victory of a governor, the more the governor can claim his or her agenda has a **popular mandate.** The legislature is less willing to challenge a popular governor. Thus, when more than two-thirds of the voters voted for George W. Bush as governor in 1998, the legislature was inclined to work with his policy proposals. During his first term, Bush earned a reputation as a bipartisan player and worked closely with the Speaker and the lieutenant governor to pass legislation regarding welfare and education reform. On the other hand, governors who win by small margins will have less political capital when dealing with the legislature and other administrators in the state than governors who can claim an overwhelming mandate. Governor Perry won a second term as governor with support from only 39 percent of voters. Since then, his relationship with the Texas Legislature has become increasingly divisive, and the governor has sought to veto or circumvent the legislature rather than working with them.

Another indicator of the governor's informal power is the governor's position on the **political ambition ladder.** A governor who has worked his or her way up to the state executive position via other state or local offices will have more allies and political savvy than an individual whose first office is the governorship, and who is learning on the job.[30] Thus, Allan Shivers, a popular Democratic governor, was elected to the Texas Senate and later elected lieutenant governor prior to becoming governor. Shivers was a successful governor, creating the Legislative Council and the Legislative Budget Board, as well as improving education and roads in the state. He is perhaps best known for supporting Texas's claims to Texas tideland, backing Republican presidential candidate Eisenhower who helped Texas maintain control of its offshore natural resources.

A third indicator of personal power is the governor's personal future as governor. Governors who have the ability to run again or are at the beginning of their terms have more ability to influence other branches and offices than those governors who are approaching the end of their gubernatorial career.[31] Absent term limits, governors in Texas have the potential to hold office for a significant period of time, amassing political allies and making all important appointments in the state.

Informal powers
attributes of personal power based on factors such as the electoral mandate, political ambition ladder, personal future as governor, and performance ratings, rather than constitutionally enumerated powers.

Popular mandate
the claim that a newly elected official's legislative agenda is the will of the people based on a high margin of victory in a general election.

Political ambition ladder
how a political figure has come up through the ranks, working through various levels of state governmental offices and positions on the way to the top position; climbing several levels on the ladder can increase a politician's contacts, allies, and political savvy.

Strong, interesting personalities have often dominated the governor's office in Texas. Sam Houston, Ma and Pa Ferguson, Pappy O'Daniel, and Ann Richards also have left their mark on Texas politics. A neighbor to the east, Louisiana, is not without its own brand of larger-than-life politics. The first governor of Louisiana, William C. C. Claiborne (1812–1816), is known for his attempts to arrest the notorious pirate Jean Lafitte, a popular figure who attained "Robin Hood" status in the state. Claiborne went so far as to offer his own money as a bounty for the capture of Lafitte, for which Lafitte allegedly then placed a bounty on the governor's head. The twentieth century abounds with larger-than-life figures who dominated the Louisiana state capitol building in Baton Rouge. Jimmy Davis ran for governor in the 1940s and again in the 1960s. He is known for taking out his guitar at campaign stops and singing the song "You Are My Sunshine," which Davis is credited with having written. Edwin Edwards, who served several terms in the 1970s through the early 1990s, is noted for various indictments in federal court on racketeering charges, some related to his frequent visits to Las Vegas and other world-famous gambling locations. Probably the best known is Huey Long, the Populist governor and "Share the Wealth" advocate who was assassinated in the state capitol building in 1935.

Lesser known both inside and outside Louisiana is Oscar K. Allen, also known as "O.K. Allen." O.K. Allen was a schoolteacher from rural Winn Parish who served in several local elected offices and the Louisiana Senate. In the Senate, Huey Long picked Allen to be the Democratic Party floor leader. Long also appointed Allen as chair of the State Highway Commission. Thus, Allen served in both the executive and legislative branches of government simultaneously. When Huey Long was elected to the U.S. Senate from Louisiana, Long hand-picked Allen to be his successor. The election of O.K. Allen as governor surprised no one in Louisiana at the time. More startling was Allen's own willingness to acknowledge the source of his power as Huey Long. Long directed Allen's agenda as governor, making almost daily telephone calls to instruct Allen on what to do.[i] Even the special session of the legislature in 1935 that Huey Long was observing when he was assassinated was formally called by Governor Allen. In fact, Huey Long had instructed Allen to call the legislature into session.

Why does Louisiana produce personality-driven politics similar to Texas? While the outcome may be the same, the sources are different. Texas's geography and weak party system contribute here. Noted scholar V. O. Key suggests that Louisiana's venture into this area is based upon the tight control of elites over the political system, which often produces populist backlash.[ii] Key suggests that Louisiana voters have long been faced with choices of "outsiders" who use charismatic appeals to the masses to court their votes and then amass political power versus "insiders," who offer a reform agenda to undo the agenda of the populists.

Thinking Critically

- Why are Texas governors often larger-than-life figures?
- Are Louisiana's governors similar? Why or why not?
- How does this type of candidate affect how you vote?
- Do you feel more connected to interesting personalities? Or more interested in campaign issues?

i. Office of the Secretary of the State, "Louisiana Governors: 1877– Present: Oscar K. Allen," www.sos.louisiana.gov/tabid/399/Default.aspx, accessed November 12, 2007.

ii. V. O. Key, *Southern Politics in State and Nation* (New York: Knopf, 1949), 156–182.

A final aspect of the governor's personal power is based on his or her performance ratings. Governors whose public approves of their performance will have greater political capital, and thus, a greater ability to influence others in the political process.[32] Since being reelected, Rick Perry's approval ratings have remained low (averaging 40 percent), indicating a limited power base.

Indeed, Beyle's 2007 rating gives the Texas governor a score of 3.8 on a five-point scale, a score that falls just below the mean of 3.9. Only fifteen state governors currently have lower personal power ratings than the Texas governor. Measures of informal power will vary over time and between governors, but it is a good indicator of the importance of informal powers for the governor of Texas.

On the other hand, personal power in Texas has always been somewhat different than in other states. As noted in Chapter 1, the size of Texas means personal politics often give way to legendary personalities. Texas governors have often been elected for their larger-than-life personalities, rather than their ability to lead.

The Texas Bureaucracy

s already noted above, the power of the governor in Texas is further limited by the creation of a plural executive. A plural executive is created by fragmenting the power of the executive branch among a number of independent offices, rather than having all executive power in the governorship.

Texas has six independently elected executive officials. Specifically, the Texas Constitution says:

> The Executive Department of the State shall consist of a Governor, who shall be the Chief Executive Officer of the State, a Lieutenant Governor, Secretary of State, Comptroller of Public Accounts, Commissioner of the General Land Office, and Attorney General.[33]

Thus, in addition to the governorship, the positions of lieutenant governor, attorney general, comptroller of public accounts, public land commissioner, and agriculture commissioner are elected to four-year terms. Because each of these individuals is elected independently of the others, they often disagree on priorities in the state, can be from different parties, and once elected possess their own independent electoral mandate for their policy agendas. A seventh major executive office, the secretary of state, is the only position in Texas's plural executive that is appointed by the governor. Although many other states elect other members of their executive, Texas is one of only eight states without a formal executive cabinet.[34]

Lieutenant Governor

The lieutenant governor is often considered the most powerful position in Texas. The lieutenant governor is elected by voters statewide every four years, with no term limits. If the position becomes vacant, the Texas Senate elects from their membership a person to serve as the lieutenant governor until the next election. The lieutenant governor is the presiding officer of the Senate, exerting great influence on both the debate and the bills that reach the floor. Although this position is mainly legislative in nature, it is also constitutionally granted some executive authority. The primary executive function of the lieutenant governor is to assume the governorship temporarily when the governor is out of the state, or permanently if the governor is impeached, resigns, or dies in office. In terms of executive powers, the lieutenant governor also exerts considerable influence on the state's budget. The lieutenant governor co-chairs the Legislative Budget Board (with the Speaker of the House) and appoints the senatorial members of that board.

The current lieutenant governor, Republican David Dewhurst, was elected in 2002 to a four-year term. Previously, Dewhurst had been the land commissioner. As lieutenant governor Dewhurst pushed through Jessica's Law, which provides tougher penalties for sexual predators, including the death penalty. Dewhurst also champi-

Table 4.3 Texas's Plural Executive

GOVERNOR OF TEXAS

- Acts as chief executive of the state; is elected by the voters every four years.
- Makes policy recommendations to state lawmakers.
- Appoints the secretary of state, members of the state bureaucracy. The governor also appoints individuals to fill vacancies in elected offices between elections.
- Exercises constitutional and statutory duties of the governor, including:
  signing or vetoing bills passed by the legislature.
  serving as commander-in-chief of the state's military forces.
  convening special sessions of the legislature.
  delivering a state of the state address.
  proposing a biennial budget.
  executing line item veto on budget approved by the legislature.
  granting reprieves and commutations of punishment and pardons upon the recommendation of the Board of Pardons and Paroles.
  declaring special elections to fill vacancies in certain elected offices.
  coordinating policy and resources during a crisis.

LIEUTENANT GOVERNOR

- Is elected by voters statewide every four years, with no term limits.
- Acts as presiding officer of the Senate.
- Acts as governor temporarily when the governor is out of the state, or assumes the governorship if the governor is impeached, resigns, or dies in office.
- Co-chairs the Legislative Budget Board (with the Speaker of the House) and appoints the senatorial members of that board.

ATTORNEY GENERAL

- Is elected by voters statewide every four years, with no term limits.
- Serves as legal representation for the state in court.
- Is charged with ensuring that corporations in Texas comply with state and federal laws.
- Collects unpaid child support and delinquent state taxes.
- Issues advisory opinions to the governor's office, the legislature, or other state agencies.

COMPTROLLER

- Is elected for four-year terms as state's accountant, auditor, and tax collector.
- Is responsible for collecting a variety of state taxes and fees.
- Manages and invests state funds.
- Estimates the amount of revenue the state will generate each year.

AGRICULTURE COMMISSIONER

- Is elected by voters statewide every four years, with no term limits.
- Heads the Texas Department of Agriculture and implements all agriculture law.
- Inspects the accuracy of market scales and gas pumps, regulates the use of pesticides, and regulates the quality of agriculture products.
- Is charged with promoting agriculture throughout the state.

Table 4.3, continued

LAND COMMISSIONER
• Is elected by voters statewide every four years, with no term limits.
• Heads the General Land Office and administers the state's public lands.
• Makes low interest loans available to veterans.
• Oversees major source of revenue for the state.

SECRETARY OF STATE
• Is appointed by the governor, with Senate confirmation, to a four-year term.
• Serves as state record keeper
• Maintains a list of lobbyist and campaign contributions, issues corporate charters, certifies notaries public, and keeps the official state seal.
• Administers elections, including conducting voter registration drives and certifying election results.
• Acts as chief administrator for the Texas Border and Mexican Affairs.
• Is designated as the chief international protocol officer who receives international delegations.

Source: Author compiled, using information from www.governor.state.tx.us/about/duties.

oned a significant property tax increase and worked to help pass "B on time" legislation which provides Texas college students zero-interest forgivable loans if they maintain a B average and graduate on time. Dewhurst has also been vocal about his desire to run for the governorship in 2010. On the other hand, Dewhurst has become an increasingly controversial leader. Dewhurst's fellow senators have complained about his leadership style, and in 2007, *Texas Monthly* magazine broke tradition by including leadership positions (including the governor, the Speaker, and Dewhurst) in their list of the top ten worst legislators.

Attorney General

The constitution requires the attorney general to "represent the State in all suits and pleas in the Supreme Court of the State in which the State may be a party."[35] This means that the main function of the attorney general is to serve as legal representation for the state in court. Texas's first constitution provided for the appointment of the attorney general, but subsequent constitutions, including the current one, stipulated that the attorney general be elected. Today the attorney general in Texas is elected in off-year elections to a four-year term, with no term limits. Like Texas, most states elect their attorney general, with twelve states continuing to appoint the office.

The attorney general's office is involved in a wide range of issues, including pursuing deadbeat dads for unpaid child support, protecting the elderly population of Texas from false consumer and insurance schemes, collecting delinquent state taxes (as it did from Enron in 2005), and recovering fraudulent Medicare and Medicaid payments, to name just a few. The attorney general is also charged with ensuring that corporations in Texas comply with state and federal laws. Thus, in 1894 the attorney general sued John D. Rockefeller's Standard Oil Company and its subsidiary Waters-Pierce for antitrust violations. The attorney general successfully made his case and these companies were barred from doing business in Texas.[36]

One of the most important roles of the attorney general is to issue advisory opinions to the governor's office, the legislature, or other state agencies. For example, in 2007 Governor Perry issued an executive order requiring that all girls get the HPV immunization before the sixth grade. State Senator Jane Nelson disagreed with the governor's mandate and met with Attorney General Greg Abbott, who ruled that the governor's HPV order was merely a suggestion and not legally binding. Once issued, the opinions of the attorney general are rarely challenged and typically carry the weight of law.

The current attorney general, Greg Abbott, was elected in 2002. Prior to becoming attorney general, Abbott had been a judge on the Texas Supreme Court. Once in office Abbott stressed family and traditional values. As attorney general, he established a Cyber Crimes Unit used to arrest Internet predators, as well as a Fugitive Unit with the aim of arresting sex offenders who violate their parole. In 2005, he also successfully defended the display of the Ten Commandments at the state capitol building before the U.S. Supreme Court.

Comptroller

Elected for four-year terms, the Texas comptroller is the state's accountant, auditor, and tax collector. The comptroller is responsible for collecting a variety of taxes including the state's sales tax (the largest source of state revenue), fuel tax, franchise tax, alcohol tax, cigarette tax, and hotel tax, to name a few. The comptroller also collects certain fees for the state, including higher education fees, vehicle registration fees, and professional fees. In addition, a 1995 constitutional amendment abolished the office of the treasurer and moved responsibility for managing and investing state funds to the comptroller's office as well.

Perhaps the most significant aspect of the comptroller's job involves the responsibility to estimate the amount of revenue the state will generate each year. The legislature is prohibited from exceeding the comptroller's estimations, unless four-fifths of both houses approve appropriations that exceed the estimates. Thus, the comptroller exercises a good deal of influence on the state's budget.

This influence can put the comptroller in an unpopular position in the state. Legislators and the governor, often motivated to spend as much money as they can get away with, prefer generous estimates. The comptroller holds the job based in part on making accurate estimates and therefore not creating debt for the state. This can be a particularly difficult job due to the biennial legislative sessions, since the state's budget is based on two-year projections. This tension was behind the 2003 battle between Comptroller Carole Keeton-Strayhorn and the Texas Legislature. Strayhorn, the state's first female comptroller, rankled the governor and the state legislature when she informed them that they faced a $9 billion budget shortfall. The feud between Strayhorn and the legislature culminated in legislation that transferred the comptroller's authority over two programs to the Legislative Budget Board.[37] Strayhorn's bitter, insult-trading public brawl with Governor Perry culminated with her run against Perry for governor in the 2006 election.

In 2006, Susan Combs, who had previously been the agriculture commissioner, was elected comptroller. As comptroller, Combs has sought to make finances in the state more transparent, by creating a Web site where citizens can look up exactly where money is spent in the state. Her office also transferred hearings on tax disputes to another office, to create a means of settling tax disputes that is independent from the comptroller's office.

Agriculture Commissioner

The agriculture commissioner is head of the Texas Department of Agriculture, which implements all agriculture laws in the state. The agriculture commissioner inspects the accuracy of market scales and gas pumps, regulates the use of pesticides, and regulates the quality of agriculture products. The office is also charged with promoting agriculture throughout the state. The commissioner oversees school nutrition and in 2003, created the Square Meals program designed to educate children about healthy eating habits. The state also began to limit access to sodas and candy in Texas schools.

The agriculture commissioner position can be an important rung on the Texas political ambition ladder. After serving three terms as a state legislator, Rick Perry was successfully elected commissioner of agriculture. Perry served two terms before running for lieutenant governor, a position he held until then Governor Bush resigned to move to the White House. When Perry vacated the office, Susan Combs became the first woman in the state to hold the position of agriculture commissioner. Combs held the position for two terms before successfully running for comptroller. The current agriculture commissioner, Todd Staples, served as a state representative and state senator prior to being elected to agriculture commissioner in 2006.

Land Commissioner

The Texas General Land Office boasts the status of being the oldest agency in the state, dating back to shortly after Texas declared its independence. The head of the General Land Office is the land commissioner, whose main job is to administer the state's public lands. The land commissioner manages just over 20 million acres of land, including supervising mineral leases and ensuring environmental protection of public lands such as the state's beaches. The general land office also makes low-interest loans available to veterans in the state as part of the Veterans Land Board (which is also chaired by the land commissioner). Since Texas boasts such abundant public lands, the land commissioner's office is a major revenue source for the state. Much of the revenue generated from public lands in Texas is allocated to the Permanent School Fund.

The General Land Office recently began harvesting another natural resource—wind. The vast plans in West Texas produce a lot of wind, and Texas has built large banks of wind turbines in the area. In 2006, Texas surpassed California to become the nation's leader in wind production.[38] In 2007 current Land Commissioner Jerry Patterson added off-shore wind leases to Texas's already profitable off-shore oil industry. Texas has begun leasing wind rights in the Gulf Coast, generating millions of dollars for the state over the life of the leases. Reflecting the Land Office's traditional role as income generator for the state, Patterson boasted that "[t]he future of offshore wind power in the [United States] is right here in Texas, and the Land Office is open for business."[39]

Secretary of State

The Texas Constitution mandates the office of secretary of state, which is appointed by the governor with Senate confirmation to a four-year term. The traditional function of the secretary of state is that of state record keeper. The office is responsible for keeping records concerning banking and other business activities. The secretary maintains a list of lobbyist and campaign contributions, issues corporate charters, certifies notaries public, and keeps the official state seal. The *Texas Register,* a list of all rules and regulations for the state's bureaucracy, is also published in the secretary of state's office.

An increasingly important role, however, is the secretary of state's role in state elections. The office administers elections, including conducting voter registration drives and certifying election results. The importance of this function was evident in the 2000 election when the Florida secretary of state certified Florida's electoral results for George W. Bush. The Texas secretary of state also oversees Project V.O.T.E. (Voters of Tomorrow through Education), which is designed to teach school aged children about the process and importance of voting.

Through executive orders, recent governors have expanded the job of the secretary of state, adding two roles to the office. First, the secretary of state is now the chief administrator for the Texas Border and Mexican Affairs, charged with overseeing border issues and Mexican-Texas relations. The secretary has also been designated the chief international protocol officer, who receives international delegations.

The secretary of state is one of the oldest and most honored offices in the state. Texas's first secretary of state was Stephen F. Austin, who, along with Sam Houston, is often referred to as the father of Texas. This office was also one of the first to have a woman in a highly visible state position after Ma Ferguson appointed Emma C. Meharg to be the first female secretary of state. The current secretary of state, Phil Wilson, was appointed by Governor Perry in 2007.

Boards and Commissions

The Texas bureaucracy is a complex system of elected and appointed officials, along with a wide range of boards and agencies. There are close to 300 boards and commissions in the state, some specified in the constitution, although most have been created by the legislature. Depending on the political mood and particular needs when a board or commission was created, the membership, size, and autonomy may vary greatly. Some boards are elected, giving them a good deal of autonomy, while others are appointed, and therefore, more obliged to the governor or the legislative leadership that appoints them. Three of the most important state agencies are the Texas Railroad Commission, the State Board of Education, and the Public Utilities Commission.

Texas Railroad Commission

The Texas Railroad Commission was created by Governor Hogg to regulate the railroads, decrease corruption, and protect the state's large agrarian population from crooked railroad practices. The Texas Railroad Commission was the first regulatory agency in the state, and one of the most important commissions in the state's history. The Texas Railroad Commission is comprised of three members each independently elected in a statewide election. The members serve overlapping six-year terms, with one member being reelected every two years. By custom, the chair rotates every two years, and is the member who is in the last two years of his or her term. Originally created to regulate railroads, this commission's mandate has expanded over time to include regulation of the oil and gas industry, protection of the environment, and

Texas Railroad Commission

One of the legends of Texas government is the Texas Railroad Commission. While the commission is the oldest regulatory agency in Texas and one of the few elected regulatory agencies in the nation, today the commission fails to live up to its name. In November 1890 Texas voters approved an amendment to the Texas Constitution that empowered the legislature to create an agency to regulate railroads. While the state had initially encouraged the railroads, by the 1890s many Texans, especially farmers, had grown to resent the railroads. The "Texas Traffic Association," an organization made up of the major railroads, set the rates, and with poor roads and unnavigable rivers, Texas farmers had no real alternatives for shipping goods. In 1891 the legislature followed up by establishing the Texas Railroad Commission. Initially, commissioners were appointed by the governor. However, in 1894 voters approved an amendment making the commissioners officials who were elected to six-year terms. Since that time the Texas Railroad Commission has had the unique designation of a regulatory agency headed by elected officials.

Attorney General James Stephen Hogg had made the call for creation of a railroad commission the centerpiece of his campaign for governor. The railroads labeled Hogg "communistic," but his reforms proved popular and his election represented the first stirrings of a populist reform movement in Texas. The creation of the Texas Railroad Commission was proclaimed a way of producing fair com-

petition, but in its actual workings, the commission was used more to restrict out-of-state railroads and protect Texas-based businesses from international competitors.

In the 1920s the Railroad Commission was given responsibility for regulating motor carriers, in addition to railroads. However, responsibility for motor carriers ended in 1994 when trucking was deregulated and responsibility for trucking safety moved to the Texas Department of Transportation (TxDOT).

Today the Railroad Commission oversees oil and natural gas exploration and production, natural gas and hazardous liquids pipeline operations, natural gas utilities, LP gas service, and coal and uranium mining, with about three-quarters of the commission's efforts focused on regulating oil and natural gas exploration and production.

In 2005 the commission's responsibility for rail safety was transferred to the TxDOT, the last step in removing the railroads from the responsibility of the Railroad Commission. While the commission retains the distinction of the state's oldest regulatory agency, nothing remains of its original mission and the Texas Railroad Commission no longer regulates railroads.

promotion of alternative energy sources. There have long been charges that oil and gas interest groups exert too much influence over these commissioners. The commission has had the reputation of emphasizing protection of the oil and gas industry at the expense of environmental protection.

State Board of Education

The State Board of Education is another example of an elected board. This board is composed of fifteen members each elected from single member districts. The state board's main jobs include approving state-curriculum and textbooks, determining passing scores for state educational testing, and managing the Permanent School Fund.

Additionally, the commissioner of education is appointed by the governor with senate approval from a list of candidates supplied by the board. The commissioner administers the Texas Education Agency, which develops curriculum standards, administers state testing requirements, and accredits and rates schools in the state.

Public Utilities Commission

The Public Utilities Commission (PUC) is an example of an appointed regulatory commission in Texas. The commission is made up of three members, each appointed by the governor with Senate approval for six-year overlapping terms. Traditionally, the PUC was charged with regulating phone and energy companies in the state. The commission, with a mission to protect consumers from unfair rates and practices, set rates that phone companies and energy companies could charge. The role of the commission has changed over time. In 2002, for example, Texas legislators voted to deregulate energy. Since that time, energy prices have fluctuated. The commission continues to be charged with protecting consumers. For instance, in 2001, the Texas Legislature authorized the PUC to create a Texas no-call list.

Bureaucratic Accountability

s we have seen, the bureaucracy of Texas is a complex and diverse array of agency heads, board members, and commissioners who may be elected or appointed to their post. Executive control of the bureaucracy is tenuous at best. Thus several tools have developed in Texas to exert control over the bureaucracy.

Texas has a series of **sunshine laws,** or laws designed to make government transparent and accessible to the people. One such law, the Texas Public Information Act, allows citizens to have access to government records in the state. Similarly the Texas Open Meetings Act generally requires governmental bodies to notify the public of the time, date, and nature of scheduled meetings and to open those meetings to the public. Sunshine laws received a significant boost in November 2007, when Texas voters overwhelmingly passed an amendment that requires both houses of the Texas Legislature to record a final vote on bills and make that vote available on the Internet.

In addition, the state enacted a **sunset review process** to assess all of the statutory boards and commissions in the state. The Sunset Advisory Commission was created by the Texas Legislature in 1977 to review the effectiveness of agencies. The commission is made up of twelve members; five members are from the Texas House, appointed by the Speaker of the House, and five members are from the Texas Senate, appointed by the lieutenant governor. The other two members are public members, one appointed by the Speaker and one by the lieutenant governor.

The sunset review process requires most governmental commissions or agencies to be reviewed every twelve years. The commission reviews a Self-Evaluation Report (SER) submitted by the agency under review, as well as developing its own reports and holding a public hearing. The commission can then recommend that an agency be continued, reorganized, or merged with another agency. If the commission takes no action, the sun automatically sets on that agency. According to the Sunset Advisory Commission's estimates, since it began fifty-two agencies have been abolished and twelve have been consolidated. Estimates from the period between 1982 and 2005 suggest that the commission has saved the state $784 million in that twenty-three-year period.[40]

Sunshine laws
laws designed to make government transparent and accessible.

Sunset review process
a formal assessment of the effectiveness of all statutory boards, commissions, and state agencies.

Figure 4.1 Sunset Review Process

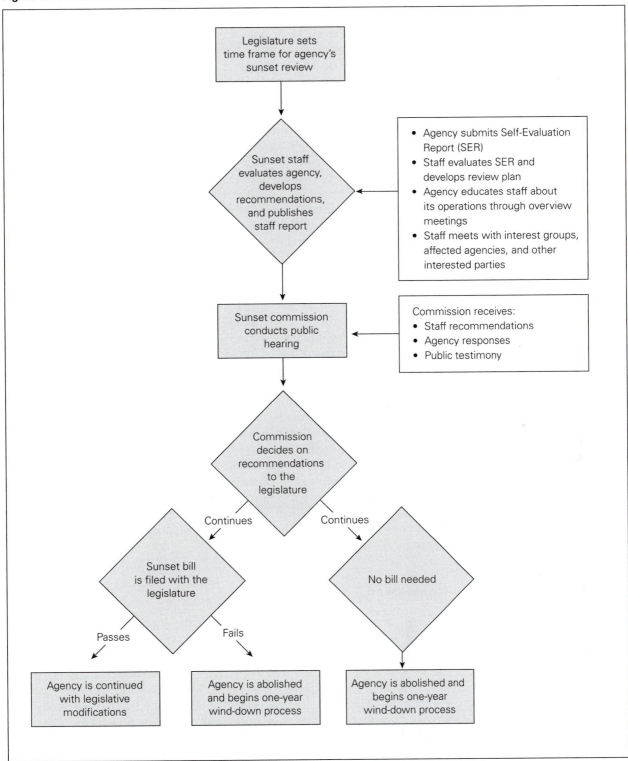

Source: Sunset Advisory Commission, *Guide to the Texas Sunset Process* (January 2006).

Winners and Losers

Creating an executive vigorous enough to lead the state and act as a check on the legislature, while not so powerful as to allow tyrannical tendencies, is difficult. The political culture in Texas continues to support the idea that executive power should be relatively limited. However, the potential cost of a weakened executive branch is not creating an energetic check on the legislative branch. Texans have a weak governor at the cost of having few checks on the legislative branch. By not making the governor responsible for the budget, Texans lose direct accountability. By denying the governor significant appointment power Texans also deny the governor the mechanisms to coordinate policy and ensure that laws are executed. In general, by fragmenting the executive, the resulting government often works at cross purposes, while the citizens in Texas pick up the tab. The cost is not only taxes for inefficiency in government, but also the loss of an accountability mechanism, as few Texans know who is in control of any particular process.

On the other hand, a governor who lacks formal power has often become a governor attempting to gain power by other means. When there is a vacuum created by a lack of executive authority and a part-time legislature, a crafty politician can successfully step in. As Governor Perry's influence began to wane he launched an all-out strategy designed to increase the governor's power. Perry's refusal to make most appointments while the legislature is in session denies the Texas Senate their check on gubernatorial appointments. Perry's use of executive orders also indicates a desire to pass preferred policies while circumventing the legislative process. His extensive use of post-adjournment vetoes, often without attempting to inform the legislature that he opposes a bill until he actually vetoes it, subverts the traditional negotiation process between the legislature and the executive.

When the formal structure lags too far behind the needs of the state, enterprising politicians will step in, allowing constraints on power to be left to day-to-day partisan politics rather than to a clear system of checks and balances. The ambiguities of the current system leave politicians scrambling to grab power and make deals. In Texas the people have continued to resist an overall change in the formal powers granted to the governor even as the state has continued to change and face increasingly complex problems. Texans remain content to allow their political institutions to evolve, rather than address a wholesale change in their institutional design.

Conclusion

The current structure of the Texas executive was created over 100 years ago out of a political preference for a weak executive, during the unpopular Reconstruction in the South, and in a state that was far less complex than the Texas of today. Texas voters have often favored personality over skill and governors have often adopted some version of the legendary Texan with cowboy boots and straight talk, an image that remains popular in the state today. Although the governor's powers remain institutionally weak, the strong personalities and clever use of informal powers have created governors who can often foil the legislature.

Rather than creating an institutional structure in which an energetic legislature and an energetic executive each possesses enough power to check the other, the Texas system creates an institutional arrangement designed to keep the executive weak.

Within that system, especially in recent years, the governor has attempted to increase his power informally and, more importantly, undermine the current institutional distribution of power.

Key Terms

appointment power
budget power
ceremonial duties
crisis manager
impeachment
informal powers
legislative role
line item veto
pardon
patronage
plural executive
political ambition ladder
popular mandate
post-adjournment vetoes
recess appointments
removal powers
senatorial courtesy
special session
state of the state address
succession
sunset review process
sunshine laws
veto power

Explore this subject further at http://college.cqpress.com/lonestarpolitics, where you'll find chapter summaries, practice quizzes, key word flash cards, and additional suggested resources.

The county courthouse in Atascosa County reflects the style common to Spanish missions. Courthouses throughout Texas sit in the center of a town's square and continue to epitomize the state's respect for tradition.

CHAPTER 5

Texas Judicial System

On September 25, 2007, the U.S. Supreme Court issued the surprise announcement that it would consider the appeal of two Kentucky men on death row. The appeal argued that the drug cocktail used to kill death row inmates violates the Eighth Amendment's prohibition against cruel and unusual punishment, because the lethal agent in the drug cocktail can produce unnecessary pain, while the sedative prevents the inmate from moving. The current execution procedure used by Texas involves three drugs, one to sedate, one to relax, and one to kill. Of the states with the death penalty, almost all use lethal injection (Nebraska still uses the electric chair). A few hours after the Supreme Court announced it would review the death penalty, lawyers for Michael Richard scrambled to put together a request to stop his execution until the U.S. Supreme Court ruled on the constitutionality of lethal injection. Richard was scheduled to be executed in Texas that day.

Richard's attorneys were putting their appeal together when their printer malfunctioned. The attorneys called the Texas Court of Criminal Appeals, the highest criminal court in the state, and requested that the court stay open an extra twenty minutes, so they could file the appeal. Although courts have stayed open in the past to hear last-minute appeals, Sharon Keller, the presiding judge, refused the request. Keller did not consult Judge Cheryl Johnson who later told the *Austin American-Statesman* that she would have accepted a last-minute filing, nor did Keller consult with the three other judges on the Texas Court of Criminal Appeals who stayed late that night anticipating a last-minute filing based on the U.S. Supreme Court's announcement.[1] Governor Perry, who could have issued a thirty-day reprieve, has said that this was a matter for the courts to resolve. Unfortunately, as Judge Keller explained, the Texas Court of Criminal Appeals "close[d] at 5:00."

Richard was executed that night. Since Richard's execution, Judge Keller has faced national criticism, including the voices of a growing number of lawyers in the state and several justices from the Texas Court of Criminal Appeals. While other states were staying executions until the Supreme Court could rule on the constitutionality of lethal injection, Texas proceeded with its next case. Carlton Turner was scheduled to be executed in late September, but his execution was halted at the last minute by the U.S. Supreme Court. Even after the Supreme Court stepped in, Texas has remained committed to the death penalty. A spokesman for Attorney General Greg Abbott explained that "The Supreme Court's decision to stay convicted murderer Carlton Turner's execution will not necessarily result in an abrupt halt to Texas executions. . . . State and federal courts will continue to address each scheduled execution on a case-by-case basis."[2] By early October 2007, however, the Texas Court of Criminal Appeals had changed its tone, indicating it would suspend executions until the Supreme Court rules on the Kentucky case. By November, the Texas Court of Criminal Appeals ruled that it would now allow e-mail appeals to be filed in death penalty cases, instead of requiring paper filings.

In order to explore the nature of justice in Texas, this chapter begins by outlining the structure of the Texas judiciary. The structure of the judiciary is central to a consideration of justice in Texas, as the system reflects ad hoc changes rather than a cohesive system of justice. Next we examine the role of judges in the state and explore questions regarding the current method of electing judges, as well as other possible methods of judicial selection. Finally we explore justice issues, especially the controversial issue of capital punishment.

As you read the chapter, think about the following questions:

★ What contributes to the lack of a cohesive court structure in the state?
★ Should Texas retain its current system of selecting judges?
★ How might Texas decrease its incarceration rate?
★ Why are Texans so committed to the death penalty?

Texas Courts

 he Texas court system is part of the larger American system. The American court system is based on **judicial federalism,** where judicial authority is shared between levels of government. The U.S. Constitution has created a national system of courts including trial courts, appellate courts, and a Supreme Court to hear questions of national or constitutional law. At the same time, the states create the court system for their respective state and local levels of government. Questions of local or state law, as well as questions regarding the state's constitution, are heard at the appropriate local- or state-level court. As we shall see, in Texas determining which court will hear which case is far from straightforward. The state's constitution says this:

> The judicial power of this State shall be vested in one Supreme Court, in one Court of Criminal Appeals, in Courts of Appeals, in District Courts, in County Courts, in Commissioners Courts, in Courts of Justices of the Peace, and in such other courts as may be provided by law.
>
> The Legislature may establish such other courts as it may deem necessary and prescribe the jurisdiction and organization thereof, and may conform the jurisdiction of the district and other inferior courts thereto.[3]

The court system in Texas is a highly complex, confusing, and muddled judicial system. Courts in Texas are divided by their jurisdiction, their origin, and their geographical coverage. A court's **jurisdiction** refers to the court's sphere of authority. One issue of authority is whether a case is at the original or appellate stage. Courts with **original jurisdiction** hear the initial cases. Typically, courts of original jurisdiction hear evidence and establish the record of the case. Courts with **appellate jurisdiction,** on the other hand, hear appeals of cases where a decision has previously been rendered by a lower court. Rather than hearing new evidence, appellate courts are restricted to reviewing the court record from the original trial and determining whether specific points of law or procedure were applied correctly. This distinction becomes blurred in the Texas judiciary, where lower level courts often do not keep official records. In addi-

Judicial federalism
a system in which judicial authority is shared between levels of government.

Jurisdiction
the court's sphere of authority.

Original jurisdiction
courts with the authority to hear the initial case; this is where the evidence and the case record are established.

Appellate jurisdiction
the authority to hear the appeal from a lower court, which has already rendered a decision; appellate courts review the court record from the original trial and do not hear new evidence.

tion, courts are sometimes given **exclusive jurisdiction,** meaning a particular level of court has the sole right to hear a specific type of case. Conversely, in Texas courts often have overlapping original jurisdiction, called **concurrent jurisdiction.** The result is a judicial system with an ill-defined and confusing structure.

A second issue of jurisdiction distinguishes whether a case is a criminal case or a civil case. In **criminal cases,** an individual is charged by the state with violating the law, and the state brings the suit. In **civil cases,** an aggrieved party sues for damages based on claims that he or she has been wronged by another individual. In Texas, the lower level courts (the municipal courts, justice of the peace courts, and county courts) are limited to the least serious criminal and civil cases. By contrast, the most serious criminal charges, called felonies, and civil suits over a certain dollar amount, are heard in district courts.

A third important question of jurisdiction has to do with geographical coverage. Jurisdiction in the Texas lower courts is based on the geographical municipality, precinct, or county where the court is located. There are 437 district courts in the state, 97 of which overlap with more than one county. The geographic jurisdiction of district courts therefore often overlaps with county courts. Conversely, in larger counties such as Harris and Dallas County, there may be more than one district court. The state is also divided into fourteen appellate districts. The two highest courts, the State Supreme Court and the State Court of Criminal Appeals, serve the entire state of Texas. This distinction often becomes confused since, depending on the population of a city or county, courts have evolved to serve different functions and often have overlapping jurisdiction.

Courts in Texas are further distinguished by their origin. The Texas Constitution specifically provides for justice of the peace courts, county courts, district courts, and appellate courts, including the two highest courts. The legislature is left to determine the exact number of these courts. In addition, the legislature can create other levels of courts. Thus the legislature creates all municipal courts, statutory county courts, and probate courts.

Local Trial Courts

 t the local level there are two types of trial courts, each with limited jurisdiction: the municipal courts and justice of the peace courts.

Municipal Courts

Municipal courts are courts created by the state legislature for cities in Texas. There are currently 915 municipal courts in the state, with larger cities often having more than one municipal court. Municipal courts have original and exclusive jurisdiction over violations of municipal ordinances, those that typically deal with zoning requirements, fire safety, litter laws, or dog regulations. Municipal courts can impose fines of up to $2,000 for violations of municipal ordinances. In addition, municipal courts have jurisdiction over class C misdemeanors (criminal matters punishable by a fine of $500 or less, with no possible jail time). Because justice of the peace courts also have jurisdiction over class C misdemeanors, this is an example of concurrent jurisdiction. Typically, if an officer of the city issues the citation, then the case is heard in municipal court, whereas citations issued by county officers (such as sheriffs) are heard in the justice of the peace court. By custom, the municipal courts also

Exclusive jurisdiction
a particular level of court with the sole right to hear a specific type of case.

Concurrent jurisdiction
a system where different levels of courts have overlapping jurisdiction, often resulting in a confusing and ill-defined system.

Criminal cases
cases in which an individual is charged by the state with violating the laws and the state brings the suit.

Civil cases
cases in which an aggrieved party sues for damages claiming that he or she has been wronged by another individual.

Figure 5.1 Court Structure of Texas as of March 1, 2007

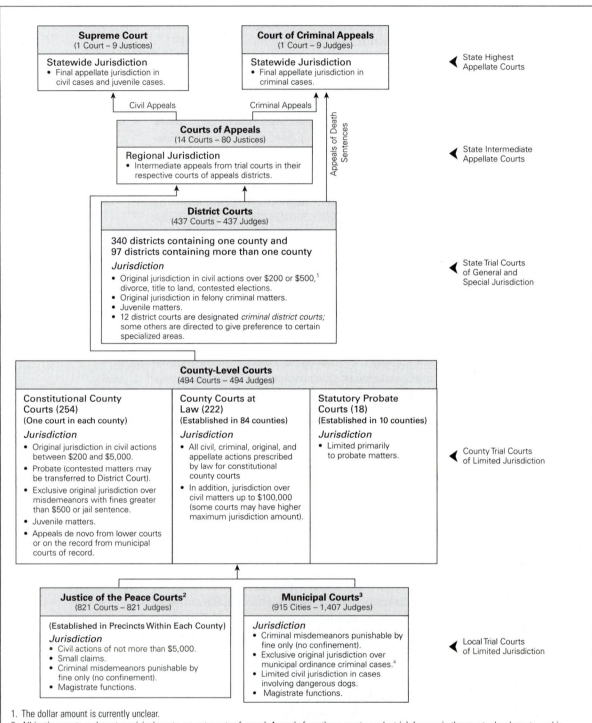

1. The dollar amount is currently unclear.
2. All justice courts and most municipal courts are not courts of record. Appeals from these courts are by trial de novo in the country-level courts, and in some instances in the district courts.
3. Some municipal courts are courts of record—appeals from those courts are taken on the record to the county-level courts.
4. An offense that arises under a municipal ordinance is punishable by a fine not to exceed: (1) $2,000 for ordinances that govern fire safety, zoning, and public health or (2) $500 for all others.

Source: www.courts.state.tx.us/pubs/2007_Judicial_Directory/Court_Structure_Chart_2007.pdf.

perform **magistrate functions.** As magistrates, municipal courts can issue search and arrest warrants, conduct preliminary hearings, and set bail for more serious crimes. The magistrate functions allow municipal courts to help decrease the workload of higher level courts. Today, the vast majority of the cases heard in municipal courts, approximately 83 percent, deal with traffic or parking violations.[4]

Appeals from municipal courts are typically heard in county-level courts. If the municipal court is a court of record, then the county-level court exercises appellate jurisdiction. However, most municipal courts are not courts of record, meaning no official transcript is recorded of the cases that are brought before the court. Absent an official record, appeals from municipal courts are heard *de novo,* or with a new trial, in county-level courts.

Municipal judges are typically appointed by city councils to two-year terms. The city council also determines the salary for municipal judges, which varies substantially throughout the state. When the state legislature passes statutes creating municipal courts of record, they require the judges to be licensed attorneys in the state of Texas. Since most municipal courts are not courts of record, most municipal judges are not required to be attorneys. Even in the absence of the licensed attorney requirement, nearly half of all municipal judges are licensed attorneys.[5]

Justice of the Peace Courts

The constitution provides that each county have between one and eight justice of the peace courts:

> Justice of the peace courts shall have original jurisdiction in criminal matters of misdemeanor cases punishable by fine only, exclusive jurisdiction in civil matters where the amount in controversy is two hundred dollars or less, and such other jurisdiction as may be provided by law. Justices of the peace shall be ex officio notaries public.[6]

Justice of the peace courts, or JP courts, are precinct-level courts. The number of judicial precincts in a county depends on that county's population size. Currently there are 821 JP courts. Like municipal courts, JP courts are courts of original jurisdiction only. Civil jurisdiction of JP courts extends to cases which involve $5,000 or less. This jurisdiction is concurrent with county and district courts in cases involving amounts of $200 to $500. The JP has nearly exclusive jurisdiction in civil cases involving less than $200. The criminal jurisdiction extends to misdemeanor cases with fines up to $500 and no jail time, concurrent with municipal courts. Approximately 91 percent of all JP cases are criminal cases, and 79 percent of these cases are traffic cases.[7]

The presiding officials of JP courts perform marriages, act as notaries public, and serve as magistrates for higher courts. JPs also serve as small claims courts. One of the more interesting responsibilities of the JP is to act as coroner in counties without medical examiners. The job of the coroner is to determine cause of death, even though JPs do not generally have any medical training. JP courts are not courts of record, so any appeals are heard *de novo* in the county courts.

JPs, like other state judges, are elected in partisan elections to four-year terms. Lack of educational requirements is one of the most consistent criticisms of JP courts. There are no formal qualifications for JP judges. In 2006, the Annual Statistical Report for the Texas Judiciary reported that 92 percent of JP judges graduated high school, 32 percent graduated from college, and a mere 7 percent graduated from law school.[8] Salaries vary significantly by county and are set by the County Commissioners Court.

Magistrate functions
the authority to conduct the preliminary procedures in criminal cases, such as issuing search and arrest warrants, conducting preliminary hearings, and setting bail for more serious crimes.

De novo
to hear an appeal with a new trial, most commonly taken in the absence of an official case record.

County-Level Trial Courts

 t the county level there are three types of trial courts: constitutional county courts, county courts at law, and statutory probate courts.

Constitutional County Courts

The constitution mandates a county-level court in each of the 254 counties in the state; these courts are sometimes referred to as constitutional county courts.

> There shall be established in each county in this State a County Court, which shall be a court of record; and there shall be elected in each county, by the qualified voters, a County Judge, who shall be well informed in the law of the State; shall be a conservator of the peace, and shall hold his office for four years, and until his successor shall be elected and qualified.[9]

Constitutional county courts exercise exclusive and original jurisdiction over misdemeanors where fines can exceed $500 and jail time can be imposed (class A and class B misdemeanors). Original civil jurisdiction extends to cases involving amounts from $200 to $5,000, and is concurrent with JP courts. These courts can also exercise probate jurisdiction, including cases involving guardianship, uncontested wills, and determination of mental competency. Constitutional county courts also possess appellate jurisdiction over cases from both the JP and municipal courts. Appeals from these courts are by and large *de novo,* which increases the workload of the court. Since the workload of JP and municipal courts is by and large traffic-related and county-level courts tend to be overworked, appeals of traffic offenses are a common strategy to attempt to get these cases dismissed. Often traffic appeals are not a priority in an overworked county-level court. Constitutional county courts are required to be courts of record.

The constitution requires county judges to be "well informed of the law," which has been interpreted to mean that they do not have to have law degrees. In 2007, the office of court administration reported that 64 percent of county judges had graduated from college and 14 percent had graduated from law school.[10] In larger counties, the county judge often works exclusively on administrative duties and is a judge in name only. County judges are elected in partisan elections to four-year terms. Their salaries vary by county, and are set by the county commissioners. In addition to judicial responsibilities, the county judge exercises administrative duties over the county government. In counties with larger populations, the state legislature has created statutory county courts to help with the case load. Thus, Harris County has twenty-three statutory courts, while Dallas County has twenty-one and Tarrant County has fifteen.

County Courts at Law and Statutory Probate Courts

Statutory courts, also called county courts at law, are so called because they are created by legislative statute, rather than required by the constitution. Jurisdiction of these courts varies greatly, according to the statute, but is generally consistent with part or all of the constitutional county courts. Thus, statutory courts may be conferred civil, criminal, or probate jurisdiction, or all of these, for the county. Like constitutional county courts, statutory courts are courts of record. In addition, the legislature can also create courts that specialize in probate. The statutory judges are elected in partisan elections to four-year terms. They are required to be trained in the law, and nearly all of these judges have law degrees.[11]

Judge Roy Bean

Roy Bean, a legend of the Texas judiciary, reflects the lax nature of frontier justice in Texas and the state's fondness for amateur justice. Born in Kentucky in 1825, Bean had no formal education that prepared him for service as a judge. However, Pecos County needed a judge that would allow the Texas Rangers to clean up the area without having to make a 400-mile round trip to the nearest courthouse and jail. Thus, for lack of a better choice, Roy Bean became a Texas judge on August 2, 1882.

Prior to serving as a judge, Bean's legal experience had been on the other side of the bench and cell door. After fleeing legal trouble in several states, Bean settled briefly in San Diego, California, where his brother was mayor. In 1852 Bean was arrested and charged with assault with intent to murder for participating in a duel over a woman. He eventually escaped from jail, allegedly using a knife smuggled inside some tamales to dig himself out. After relocating to San Gabriel, California, Bean would become involved in another duel in 1854, killing his romantic rival. This time, Bean didn't appear before a court, and instead was almost lynched by his victim's friends.

Bean supplemented his judicial earnings by running a bar called Jersey Lilly, named for Lillie Langtry, a British actress that Bean was obsessed with. (Contrary to rumor, Langtry, Texas, was not named after her. The city, originally named Eagle Nest, was renamed in honor of George Langtry, an area railroad engineer.)

While occasionally voted out of office, Bean mostly held onto that position of judge until his retirement in 1902. Despite the lack of training and possession of only one law book, Bean's justice was creative. Because he lacked a jail, most sentences set fines rather than jail time. Horse thieves were generally released with a fine if the horses were returned. When a man died after falling off a bridge, Bean discovered that the man had been carrying forty dollars and a concealed pistol. Bean fined the man forty dollars for carrying a concealed weapon and used the money to pay for his funeral expenses.

Bean's legal and bartending careers complimented each other nicely as Bean required that jurors buy drinks at his saloon during every judicial recess. Bean's most famous venture came in 1896 when he organized a world championship boxing title match. Since boxing matches were illegal in Texas, Judge Bean arranged for Bob Fitzsimmons and Peter Maher to box on an island in the Rio Grande. While the fight lasted less than two minutes, word of the match and its promoter spread throughout the United States.

Portraying himself as the "Law West of the Pecos" Judge Roy Bean epitomized Texas justice in its infancy. Bean died in 1903, but his legacy continues to shape the town of Langtry. In 1939 the State of Texas purchased Bean's "Jersey Lilly," making it the centerpiece of Langtry's Old West tourism, with over one million visitors to date.

District Courts (State-Level Trial Courts)

State-level trial courts in Texas are called district courts. Every county in the state is served by at least one district court, while more populated areas often have several. According to the Texas Constitution, district court jurisdiction is:

exclusive, appellate, and original jurisdiction of all actions, proceedings, and remedies, except in cases where exclusive, appellate, or original jurisdiction may be conferred by this Constitution or other law on some other court, tribunal, or administrative body.[12]

Thus, the jurisdiction of district courts can vary according to the jurisdiction of other courts in a particular area. In some areas of the state, there are family district courts, criminal district courts, or civil district courts. Generally, though, district courts are granted civil jurisdiction in cases involving $200 or more (concurrent with JP and county courts). District courts exercise original jurisdiction over contested probate issues, divorce, land title claims, slander, child custody, and contested elections. Their original criminal jurisdiction includes all felony cases. They also have jurisdiction over misdemeanors when the case involves a government official. In larger areas, these courts often specialize in one of these areas. Appeals from district courts are heard at the courts of appeals, with the exception of death penalty cases, which go directly to the Texas Court of Criminal Appeals.

Judges in district courts must be at least twenty-five years old, a resident of Texas, and a U.S. citizen. In addition, they must be a licensed attorney with at least four years experience as either an attorney or a judge. District judges are elected in partisan elections to four-year terms.

Appellate Courts

The Texas judiciary has two levels of appellate courts. Initial appeals are heard at the court of appeals. After the initial appeal, cases can be appealed to one of the state's two highest courts. Texas is one of only two states with two high courts (the other being Oklahoma). The Texas Supreme Court hears final appeals in civil cases and the Texas Court of Criminal Appeals hears ultimate appeals in criminal cases. Appellate judges must be at least thirty-five years old, a resident of the state, and a U.S. citizen. Appellate judges are also required to have at least ten years' experience as a lawyer or a judge and be a licensed attorney. Judges are elected in partisan elections for six-year terms.

Courts of Appeals (Intermediate Appellate Courts)

There are fourteen courts of appeals in Texas. Each court has between three and thirteen judges, including one chief justice. With the exception of death penalty cases, all civil and criminal appeals from the county and district courts are initially heard in the courts of appeals. Appellate courts hear no new evidence or new witnesses. Instead, judges make their decisions based on a review of the written record from the trial, as well as written briefs and oral arguments by attorneys arguing legal or procedural points. Typically an appeal is heard by a panel of three judges, although they can be heard *en banc,* or by the entire court. Panels of judges, rather than single judges, are traditionally used in appeals courts since there are no juries. Including more than one judge provides some limits on the power of individual judges. The case is decided by a majority vote of the judges. The court can affirm, reverse, or modify a lower courts decision, or can remand the case to the trial court for reconsideration. Civil cases heard by the court of appeals can be appealed to the Texas Supreme Court, while criminal cases can be appealed to the Texas Court of Criminal Appeals.

En banc

an appeal that is heard by the entire court of appeals, rather than by a select panel of judges.

State Highest Appellate Courts

exas has two courts to hear appeals that are brought to the highest level in the state: the Supreme Court, for appeals from civil cases, and the Court of Criminal Appeals, for appeals from criminal cases including death penalty appeals.

Texas Court of Criminal Appeals

The Texas Court of Criminal Appeals is the state's highest court for criminal appeals. Like other appellate courts, the Texas Court of Criminal Appeals reviews the trial record and hears no new evidence. The court consists of nine judges, including a presiding judge. The court can hear appeals in panels of three judges, though most cases involve the entire court. Cases are decided by majority vote. The most important job of the Texas Court of Criminal Appeals is to hear automatic appeals in death penalty cases. The court typically considers death penalty cases *en banc*. In 2006, the court heard twenty-six death penalty cases. It upheld twenty-four convictions and reversed two cases. The court is the final court of appeals for questions of state law and the state constitution. However, cases involving questions of federal law or the U.S. Constitution can ultimately be appealed to the U.S. Supreme Court.

Supreme Court

The Texas Supreme Court is the highest court in Texas for civil cases in the state. The Supreme Court consists of eight justices, plus one chief justice, and cases are decided by majority vote. The Supreme Court also makes procedural rules for lower courts, approves law schools in the state, and appoints members of the Board of Legal Examiners. Like the Court of Criminal Appeals, the cases from the Texas Supreme Court can be appealed to the U.S. Supreme Court if they concern issues of federal law or the U.S. Constitution.

Texas Judges

istorically the Texas judiciary, like other elected positions, was dominated by Democrats. Since the late 1980s, however, Republicans have dominated the judiciary, holding almost all appellate posts. In addition, judges in Texas today come largely from upper middle-class families. Recall that microcosm theory (introduced in chapter 3) suggests that representation occurs when the institution mirrors society at large. Although women make up about half of the population, the vast majority of judges in the state are men. In terms of lower courts, female judges constitute 24 percent of municipal judges, 33 percent of JP judges, 12 percent of constitutional county court judges, and 31 percent of statutory court judges. Females do not fare much better at state-level courts, composing 29 percent of district judges and 40 percent of appellate judges. At the state's highest courts, females currently comprise 11 percent of the Texas Supreme Court and 44 percent of the Texas Court of Criminal Appeals.

The racial distribution of the courts is even more troublesome, particularly given the overwhelmingly low representation of both Hispanics and African Americans in the judicial system. Although African Americans comprise about 12 percent of the state's population, African American judges remain relatively rare in lower-level courts in the state, ranging from 1 percent of Constitutional County Court Judges to 5 percent of municipal judges. African American representation on state-level courts is uneven, comprising a mere 3 percent of district or appellate judges and but 22 percent of the Texas Supreme Court judges. Hispanics make up approximately 35 percent of the state, but their representation in the Texas judiciary remains well below this average. Hispanic representation on lower level courts ranges from a paltry 8 percent on constitutional county courts to 19 percent on JP or statutory county courts. Hispanics make up 14 percent of the judges at the district or appellate level, but only 11 percent of the Supreme Court justices. The Texas Court of Criminal Appeals, the court responsible for all death penalty appeals, has no racial minorities at this time.

Issues of minority representation in Texas remain a major concern. The selection process of the judges is tied to issues of minority representation. Some minorities charge that partisan elections and the dominance of the Republican Party in Texas make it difficult for minorities to get elected. According to this perspective, merely removing party labels from the ballot will increase the likelihood of a minority candidate being elected to the judiciary.

The nature of judicial districts may also prove an important impediment to minority representation in the state. Large counties in particular often treat the county as one district and then elect quite a few judges from that district as a whole. Minorities contend that using **at-large elections** to select district and county judges makes it less likely that minorities will win. (See Chapter 3 for more information on at-large elections.)

Some minorities increasingly contend that **cumulative voting** would benefit minority candidates. Cumulative voting lets voters take the total number of positions in a district and divide those among one or a few candidates. Thus in a district with fifty-nine judges, such as Harris County, a voter could vote for fifty-nine candidates, or vote fifty-nine times for one candidate. This system allows voters to concentrate all of their votes in a district on one or two candidates, making it more likely that a minority candidate will be elected. (See Chapter 6 for a discussion of cumulative voting.)

At-large elections

elections where a county is treated as a single district and candidates are elected from the entire district as a whole.

Cumulative voting

a system that allows voters to take the total number of positions to be selected in a district and divide the votes among one or a few candidates.

Figure 5.2 Racial Representation of Justices and Judges in Texas

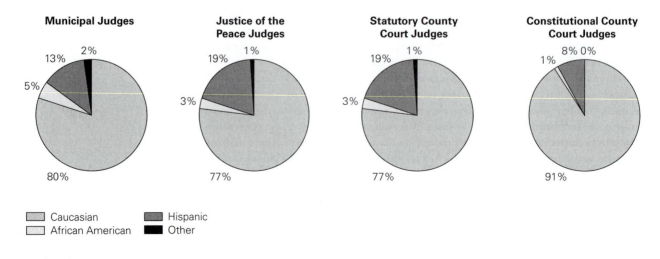

Municipal Judges	Justice of the Peace Judges	Statutory County Court Judges	Constitutional County Court Judges
2%	1%	1%	8% 0%
13%	19%	19%	1%
5%	3%	3%	
80%	77%	77%	91%

Caucasian   Hispanic
African American   Other

Judicial Selection

One of the more controversial aspects of the Texas judicial system is the selection process for judges. With the exception of municipal judges, judges in Texas are elected in partisan contests. In order to become a judge, candidates have to raise enough money to win the election. Once on the bench, judges need to constantly raise money for their reelection. Texas is one of nine states who elect their Supreme Court justices in partisan elections. Another thirteen states elect their judges in non-partisan elections, a system which decreases the likelihood that votes will be based solely on partisan labels.

The argument for electing judges is rooted in democracy. The people are theoretically retaining political influence, since it is the people who choose the judges. Unfortunately, there are several impediments to the actual popular influence of judicial elections. Most importantly, Texans are faced with a long ballot almost every major office in the state. In addition to choosing the country's president and the state's national congressional delegation, Texans elect members of the plural executive and other bureaucratic offices, members of the state legislature, and a wide range of judicial offices in the state. The democratic charge for the average Texan is literally overwhelming and the issues in judicial selection are often relatively subtle. The result is that most Texans simply do not pay much attention to judicial campaigns. Rather than voting based on judicial competency, voting in judicial elections often amounts to little more than voting for partisan labels or image and name recognition.

One of the most important outcomes of requiring Texans to elect so many positions in the state is the tendency for many to vote along party lines or even **straight ticket voting.** Texas is one of sixteen states that allow straight ticket voting in electing state officers. The problem is that party labels are less meaningful when in judicial races than other political contests. Party labels in judicial campaigns can have substantively different meanings than party labels in other political campaigns. For instance, Republicans have tended to favor big business and defendants in civil trials, whereas Democrats are more likely to side with plaintiffs. A watch group called Court Watch estimates that the 2005–2006 Republican dominated Supreme Court

Straight ticket voting
allowing a voter to select all of the candidates running under a party label by simply checking off a box with the party label.

Figure 5.2, continued

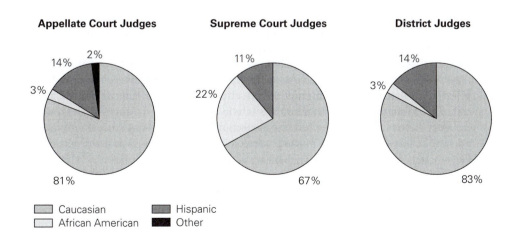

Appellate Court Judges — 2%, 14%, 3%, 81%

Supreme Court Judges — 11%, 22%, 67%

District Judges — 14%, 3%, 83%

Caucasian
African American
Hispanic
Other

ruled in favor of big business, insurance companies, medical practitioners, or government agencies 84 percent of the time.[13] Moreover, the Supreme Court has become progressively more anti-consumer in recent years, overturning 81 percent of the cases decided by juries in lower level courts.[14] Thus Republican dominance of the state judiciary in recent decades has had significant impacts on the rights of individuals in the state, a right most Texans still vigorously seek to protect.

Name recognition

making a voting choice based on familiarity with or previous recognition of a candidate's name.

In addition, **name recognition** provides a common method of voting in Texas, where knowledge of judicial credentials is limited. In one study, for example, Dallas County voters repeatedly recognized the name of only one in eight district judges.[15] Texans often vote on names that they recognize or even names that sound respectable. This tendency has produced some particularly peculiar effects in a state where most judicial candidates are unknown to the voters. One of the most visible examples of the power of names in judicial campaigns is that of Don Yarbrough. Yarbrough successfully ran for the Texas Supreme Court in 1976, claiming God wanted him to run. Yarbrough ran against a well respected judge who was endorsed by the Texas State Bar. Yarbrough was elected in spite of the fact he had a number of suits pending (including charges of business fraud) and was facing disbarment proceedings by the Texas State Bar Association. Most agree that Yarbrough was elected largely because voters confused him with another Don Yarborough who had several unsuccessful bids for governor in the state. Others may have confused him with progressive Ralph Yarborough, who had served in the U.S. Senate. Eventually, after being indicted for a felony and facing impeachment proceeding, Yarbrough resigned and fled the country.

The long campaign season exacerbates the tendency for judicial candidates to run unopposed. According to retired Supreme Court chief justice Thomas Phillips, the "filing deadline is a year before you take office if you win, and so a lot of lawyers feel like they really don't want to be running against the judge—it's not going to be the best way to attract business for a year. So most of our rural judges, literally a majority, have never been opposed."[16] The tendency for candidates to run unopposed means the perception of democratic control on the judiciary remains largely a myth. Moreover, **incumbency advantage** in Texas is especially robust. In fact most incumbents run unopposed, since incumbents by-and-large tend to win reelection. This tendency undermines the effectiveness of popular control on the judiciary.

Incumbency advantage

advantages enjoyed by the incumbent candidate, or current officeholder, in elections. Incumbency advantages are based on greater visibility, proven record of public service, and often better access to resources.

Judicial Appointment

Although judicial selection in Texas technically occurs with partisan elections, the vast majority of judges originally reach the bench through appointment. The constitution provides that the governor can appoint judges to fill vacancies on district and appellate-level courts. These gubernatorial appointments must be confirmed by the Texas Senate. In 2007, 40 percent of district or appellate judges originally assumed office by gubernatorial appointment. The fact that the governor ends up making judicial appointments in a system that purports to leave the choice of judges up to the voters is an important aspect of the judicial election system in Texas, since a significant number of the judges chosen by the governor will run unopposed in future elections where voters will be essentially rubberstamping the governor's choice.

Judicial Removal

There are three primary means of removing judges in Texas. The most common means of removing a judge is for the voters not to reelect him or her in the next election. In addition, the constitution grants the Texas Supreme Court the power to remove district judges for incompetence, official misconduct, or negligence. Judges can also be impeached by the Texas House and tried in the Texas Senate, with a two-thirds vote necessary in each house.

Moreover, a 1965 amendment to the constitution provides for a Commission on Judicial Conduct. The thirteen-member commission investigates allegations of judicial misconduct. According to the Texas Constitution, judicial misconduct includes

> willful or persistent violation of rules promulgated by the Supreme Court of Texas, incompetence in performing the duties of the office, willful violation of the Code of Judicial Conduct, or willful or persistent conduct that is clearly inconsistent with the proper performance of his duties or casts public discredit upon the judiciary or administration of justice.[17]

If the commission finds the judge guilty of misconduct, it can issue a public or private censure or warning, issue an official reprimand, order additional education, or make a recommendation that the judge be removed from office.

Of the 985 cases disposed of by the Commission on Judicial Conduct in 2006, 58 percent alleged no judicial misconduct. In the cases that did allege judicial misconduct, two of the most common forms of misconduct reported in 2006 involved a lack of professional competence and inappropriate or demeaning conduct in the courtroom.[18] Some level of discipline, ranging from public sanction to suspension, was ordered in forty-two of the cases. In three cases the judges agreed to voluntarily resign to avoid disciplinary action.

Problems with the Texas Judiciary

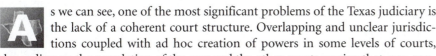

s we can see, one of the most significant problems of the Texas judiciary is the lack of a coherent court structure. Overlapping and unclear jurisdictions coupled with ad hoc creation of powers in some levels of courts, depending on the population of the area and the other courts serving that area, produces one of the most cumbersome legal systems in the country. Thus, in 1991 the Texas Research League, a nonprofit group, concluded that the "Texas court system really is not a system at all. Indeed, Texas's courts are fragmented without a central focus and are going along in their own discretion and at their own pace."[19] Two years later a commission established by the Texas Supreme Court concluded that "The Texas trial court system, complex from its inception, has become ever more confusing as ad hoc responses are devised to meet the needs of an urban, industrialized society. No one person understands or can hope to understand all the nuances and intricacies of Texas's thousands of trial courts."[20] The lack of a clear system is exacerbated by problems of lower courts without court reporters creating the need to hear appellate cases *de novo.*

In addition, a significant number of judges in the state have no legal training. The lack of training of judges at the city and county level creates real questions of justice throughout the state. Texas judges are infamous in the nation for sleeping during hearings, making inappropriate comments, and in at least one case, using sock puppets to communicate to the court. Moreover, in rural areas where there is no medical examiner, the use of JP judges, most of whom have no medical training, to determine cause of death undermines the validity of death certificates. More generally, when judges perform duties absent professional training or expertise it serves to further undermine the credibility of the entire judicial system to the people of Texas. Mistrust of the judicial system is aggravated in a state known for selling justice.

Perhaps even more detrimental, however, is the need for judicial candidates to raise campaign funds to compete for judicial positions. The need to raise funds opens the Texas judiciary up to potential influence by campaign donors. Since average Texans don't pay attention to judicial races, special interests, big business, and attorneys are the main contributors to judicial contests. This influence is likely to be the greatest in Supreme Court races, where campaign costs can exceed one million dollars. In 2006 Texans for Public Justice reported that a little over half (51 percent) of the contributions to the candidates for the 2006 Texas Supreme Court race were donated by attorneys and law firms. According to their report, "Leading contributors to high-court candidates include some of the court's busiest litigators, including Vinson & Elkins ($95,000) and Fulbright & Jaworski ($50,412)."[21] In addition to attorneys, big business in Texas actively supports judicial candidates. In the 2006 Supreme Court race, the largest donors after law firms were "Texans for Lawsuit Reform PAC ($75,000), HillCo PAC ($40,000), and the Texas Medical Association ($26,037) . . . [who] have a vested interest in the court interpreting tort, labor, and environmental laws in favor of business—even when such rulings come at the expense of consumers, workers, or communities."[22] The need to raise substantial sums of money to compete in a judicial race in the state opens judges up to undue influence, or at the very least the potential for influence. The result is a perception, even if not the reality, that the judicial system in Texas protects business at the expense of the individual.

One of the most visible recent cases of influence is that of Supreme Court Justice Nathan Hecht. Hecht incurred extensive legal fees when he appealed a public reprimand from the State Commission on Judicial Conduct. In order to pay his legal debt, he received "late-train" donations, or donations given after the election, from several law firms and business groups. Texas Watch, a non-partisan group, reported that seventeen parties, who had each contributed at least $5,000 to Hecht, subsequently had cases before the Texas Supreme Court. Hecht's vote on the court sided with his donors 89 percent of the time.[23]

The perception of justice for sale in Texas remains strong throughout the United States. National media often cover the explicit appearance of injustice in the state, including most notably a segment produced by the investigative television news program *60 Minutes* in the late 1980s and again in the late 1990s and more recently in a PBS *Frontline* Special Report. Still there has been little momentum within the state to change the selection process of judges. One notable exception is the 1995 Judicial Campaign Fairness Act. The purpose of the act is to limit contributions of individual donors to no more than $5,000 per election for statewide judicial campaigns. The primary election and general election are treated as separate elections, meaning that an individual can contribute to a candidate in each election. PAC (the fundraising arms for interest groups) contributions (including contributions from law firms) are limited to $30,000 per election for judicial candidates. Additionally, candidates are prevented from receiving more than $300,000 total from PACs. However, a candidate's participation in the limits set by the Judicial Campaign Fairness Act is voluntary. Any candidate who consents to these voluntary limits can affirm their compliance in their campaign material and television ads.

Alternative Systems of Judicial Selection

 here are other systems of judicial selection which have been adopted at the state and federal levels.

Appointment

At the national level, undue influence of the federal judiciary is stymied by lifetime appointment of judges. The advantage of appointing judges rather than electing them is that the judiciary can remain independent of undue political pressure. Three states use this model, allowing the governor to appoint their state judges. Another two states allow the state legislature to appoint judges to their appellate-level courts, including the state's Supreme Court.

Merit System

One alternative to electing judges in partisan elections is using a merit system to select judges, sometimes referred to as the Missouri Plan. The merit system relies on a panel of experts in an attempt to balance the need for judicial independence with the accountability associated with electing judges. The panel of experts typically includes judges, lawyers, legal scholars, and sometimes citizens, who review potential candidates and develop a list of potential judicial nominees. The governor then nominates judicial candidates from the list. Once on the bench, the judges will face periodic retention elections. Judges would keep their job so long as a majority of voters approved. A retention election allows voters to vote to retain or remove a judge without the competition that would make campaigning necessary.

Although America has long embraced the necessity of an independent judiciary, and many Texans have supported changing the current process in Texas, the businesses and professions who are benefiting from this system have strongly opposed change. Moreover, although "it has passed the State Senate four times . . . it's never been allowed to have a vote in committee much less on the floor of the House of Representatives, and that's due to the power of political parties."[24] Thus, so far, there appears to be sufficient political opposition to thwart the adoption of a merit-based judicial selection system.

Winners and Losers

 he Texas judiciary is fraught with impediments to justice for the average Texan. The system is overly complex and unnecessarily confusing, making it difficult for most Texans to understand. In addition, the large number of judges elected in the state creates an excessive democratic cost. Thus, it is not surprising that democratic mechanisms to protect individuals in the state provide little protection. Ironically, Texans resist change in the judiciary largely because they want to guard their individual rights, such as the right to choose judges. But that right is, more often than not, overwhelmed by the complexity of the system and the number of judicial campaigns in the state. Texans who are fiercely protective of their independence and their influence on government in the end yield judicial selection to big donors in judicial campaigns. Business and law firms that donate significant sums of money to judicial campaigns continue to dominate the Texas judiciary. These groups protect their interests, often at the expense of individual rights. In the end, individuals lose in Texas.

Minorities also lose. Minorities hold few judicial posts in a state that is tough on crime, has one of the largest prison populations in the country, and is rarely sympathetic to appeals. The judicial system in Texas remains dominated by middle- and upper-middle-class white males, even though the state's demographic make-up continues to become more diverse. The current system of electing judges, particularly in a Republican-dominated state, ensures that minorities will continue to be underrepresented in Texas. Overall, the perception that the Texas judicial system is unjust continues to prevail and harms all Texans. With a judicial system that its citizens don't have faith in, every Texan loses.

Justice in Texas

Criminal cases deal with individuals charged with violating criminal laws or committing crimes that, although there may be a victim, are technically crimes against the state. The **prosecutor** in a criminal case is the lawyer who represents the government. The **defendant** is the person charged with committing a crime. Criminal law ranges from traffic violations to robbery, sexual assault, or murder. Lower-level criminal violations, such as public intoxication or resisting arrest, are referred to as misdemeanors. Misdemeanors typically involve fines or prison sentences of less than a year. Felonies are more severe criminal offenses, such as sexual assault or murder, and involve harsher punishments. In criminal cases, a twelve-member **grand jury** determines whether there is enough evidence to warrant a trial. If nine of the twelve jurors on the grand jury agree that a trial is warranted, the grand jury issues an **indictment,** a document formally charging an individual with a crime, indicating that there is enough evi-

Prosecutor

a lawyer who represents the government and brings a case in criminal trials.

(Criminal) defendant

a person charged with committing a crime.

Grand jury

a panel of twelve that reviews evidence, determines whether there is sufficient evidence to bring a trial, and issues an indictment.

Indictment

a document that formally charges a defendant with committing a crime.

Death row was located in Huntsville, Texas, from 1923 until 1999, when it was relocated to a few miles outside the community. Today Huntsville remains the center for death penalty protests in the state.

dence to warrant a trial. The trial jury or **petit jury** determines whether or not an individual is guilty. Petit juries are guaranteed in criminal cases and may also be used in civil cases. The accused is presumed innocent and the state must prove that the individual is guilty. In order to determine guilt, the burden of proof in a criminal trial is based on whether the state has submitted sufficient evidence to prove the guilt of the accused **beyond a reasonable doubt.** Texas requires a unanimous verdict in criminal cases. If an individual is found guilty in a criminal case, the punishment can include fines paid to the government, imprisonment, or in certain cases, the death penalty.

Civil cases, by contrast, involve disputes between individuals. The **plaintiff** in a civil case claims to have been wronged by another party, the **defendant.** Civil law cases often involve breach of contract and other contractual disputes, but also include family law issues such as divorce, neglect, custody, or probate questions regarding wills. Civil cases also include tort cases, claiming personal injury or property damage. Civil cases can be tried by a jury or, if both parties agree, can simply be decided by the judge. In civil cases, the burden of proof is based on a much lower standard than criminal cases. To win the civil case a plaintiff merely has to show through a **preponderance of evidence** that the defendant is likely to have been guilty. Whereas criminal cases may result in jail time, plaintiffs in civil cases may ask the court to redress the grievance, or award monetary damages. **Compensatory damages** are monetary awards designed to compensate the injured party, for instance for medical bills incurred or lost income due to missed work. If the court wants to send a message, it may also award **punitive damages,** which are typically larger monetary awards intended to punish the defendant.

Incarceration in Texas

Everything is bigger in Texas, including the prison system. Several things contribute to the Texas-sized prison system. First, the culture in the United States supports higher incarceration rates than other countries. According to the U.S. Justice Department, the United States currently has the highest incarceration rate in the world.[25] Currently, Texas has the second highest incarceration rate in the country. As of 2006, the Texas prison incarceration rate was 687 inmates per 100,000, significantly higher than the U.S. incarceration rate of 497 inmates per 100,000. Not only is Texas a world leader in imprisonment, but that number is projected to increase significantly in the next decade.[26] Texas political culture continues to fiercely prefer politicians and policies that are "tough on crime." That means policies in Texas tend to criminalize more behavior and favor tougher sentences than other states. In addition, in the last two decades the Texas population has increased, while stiffer immigration and drug laws have produced a glut of potential prisoners in the state.

Given its high levels of imprisonment, it is not surprising that Texas jails continue to struggle with overcrowding, and legislators predict this problem will only worsen. At the same time, many of the current jails are getting old and often maintenance is not kept up. Thus, in 2007 the Texas Commission on Jail Standards found that one-third of the jails in Texas failed to meet state standards. Inspections revealed buildings with structural problems and mold, and prisons that were overcrowded and understaffed. In addition, substandard or scarce medical care has often contributed to death or injury of inmates.[27] As Texas's existing prisons have deteriorated and its prison population has increased, Texas, more than any other state, has embraced private prisons.

Petit jury
a trial jury, which attends a trial, listens to evidence, and determines whether a defendant is innocent or guilty.

Beyond a reasonable doubt
in a system where the defendant is presumed innocent, this is the standard for the burden of proof of a defendant's guilt in criminal trials.

Plaintiff
the party claiming to have been wronged and bringing the suit.

Defendant (civil)
the party alleged to have committed the wrong at issue in the suit.

Preponderance of evidence
the burden of proof in a civil case, which is lower than that in a criminal case; the plaintiff must show merely that the defendant is likely to have committed the wrong.

Compensatory damages
monetary damages designed to compensate the injured party.

Punitive damages
larger monetary awards designed to punish the defendant and, perhaps, send a message to the larger society.

In 1940, Missouri took the radical step of moving from partisan elections for state judges to the Nonpartisan Retention Plan, often called the "Missouri Plan." Under the Missouri Plan, an independent commission nominates three candidates to fill a vacancy on a court. The governor chooses one of the three candidates to serve on the court. After one year on the court, the judge faces a retention election in which voters decide if the judge remains on the court or must step down. After the initial retention election, the judge faces another retention election every four, eight, or twelve years depending on the court. All judges must retire at the age of seventy.

Missouri uses this system for state courts of appeals and the Missouri Supreme Court. Courts in Clay, Jackson, St. Louis, and Platte counties, as well as courts in the city of St. Louis, use the retention election system. Many other local courts in Missouri use partisan elections for selecting judges. Twelve states have adopted the "Missouri Plan," and a few other states, like Florida, use a modified version of the plan. Texas uses partisan elections for staffing all state and local courts.

Proponents of the "Missouri Plan" point toward the use of independent commissions to nominate judges as shifting the focus of judicial selection to finding better-quality judges. The use of a retention election allows the public to have periodic say on whether a judge remains in office, providing a degree of democratic accountability.

Opponents of the system point toward the fact that most judges are retained election after election, in effect, creating a lifetime appointment. No Missouri Supreme Court or appeals court judge has ever lost a retention election and been voted out of office. One study found that over a thirty-year period, only 1.3 percent of judges lost a retention election.[i] Based on these results, critics question the point of the retention elections.

Thinking Critically

- Do you think the "Missouri Plan" offers advantages that the partisan system of electing judges used in Texas lacks?
- Does the low rate of rejecting judges in Missouri undermine the "Missouri Plan"?
- How do you think a plan similar to the "Missouri Plan" would affect the Texas court system and Texas politics?
- Would you favor adopting such a plan?

i. Larry Aspin, William Hall, Jean Bax, and Celeste Montoya, "Thirty Years of Judicial Retention Elections: An Update," *Social Science Journal,* vol. 37, no. 1 (2000): 1–17.

Privatization of Prisons

Private prisons

private, for-profit prison corporations that staff and run the prison facilities in a state.

One way Texas has tried to deal with its increasing prison population is to use **private prisons.** Texas embraced the privatization craze, and currently leads the country in this trend, housing about 18,000 of its 154,000 prison beds in private facilities.[28] In addition private prisons based in Texas often have contracts with other states, meaning violent criminals from other states are transferred into Texas. Defenders of privately owned prisons argue the costs for the state are significantly lower than state or locally run facilities. They often point to jobs created by private prisons that are built in rural areas of the state. Opponents point to the poor conditions, underpaid and poorly trained guards, and high-profile scandals involving the largest private prison corporations. Because the prisons are motivated to make a profit, providing adequate facilities and services often take a back seat to the bottom line. Moreover, research suggests that the few jobs created by the prison facility are outweighed by negative job growth, as private prisons have actually impeded economic growth overall.[29] In addition, critics contend that inmates moved to private facilities from other states, faced with poor conditions, often are more likely to be clinically depressed and less likely to have access to family or other visitors, making rehabilitation more difficult. The state's choice to allow so-called private prisons to be built means Texas is increasingly choosing to take on other states' and the national government's prisoners.

Several high-profile scandals have drawn attention to these facilities. For example, in 2007 a GEO Group, Inc. prison company was fired by the Texas Youth Commission (TYC) for squalid conditions after one prisoner (transferred from Idaho) committed suicide.[30] Shortly after the suicide, Idaho corrections officials visited the facility and concluded it "was the worst correctional facility" and was "beyond repair or correction." In spite of chronic questions regarding the conditions in these private jails, a *Dallas Morning News* study found "only a few instances of TYC not renewing contracts because of poor performance" and no cases where the TYC has fined for-profit contractors for problems, though it has the authority to assess such fines.[31]

While Texas has a proclivity for being tough on crime, recently legislators have turned their attention to rehabilitation and reducing **recidivism** (or the return to crime after being released from prison). Rather than focus on building new prisons, the 80th legislature expanded state rehabilitation facilities, including mental health and substance abuse facilities, as well as increasing the number of halfway houses and drug treatment programs in state prisons. The action of the 80th legislature amounts to a significant shift in policy specifically designed to deal with the considerably higher incarceration rates in the state.

Recidivism
a former inmate's return to crime after being released from prison.

Capital Punishment

In 1923, Texas officially adopted the electric chair (referred to as "Old Sparky") as the official state method for capital punishment. Prior to the 1920s, hanging was the preferred method of state execution. In 1972, the Supreme Court ruled that the imposition of capital punishment amounted to "cruel and unusual punishment," since its selective application violated due process. Up to that point, Texas had electrocuted 361 people. A few years later, states, including Texas, changed their procedures to be less arbitrary, including a two-stage process, first deciding guilt and then punishment. By the time Texas reinstated the new process for imposing the death penalty, Texas had adopted lethal injection as its official means of execution. Between 1982 and 2007, Texas executed over 400 individuals with lethal injection. Most executions in the United States occur in the South, accounting for approximately 82 percent of all U.S. executions since 1976. Texas executes far more people than any other state in the United States and has carried out almost 40 percent of all executions in the country since 1976. Internationally, the death penalty has become increasingly unpopular. Currently, 130 countries ban the death penalty, including all western industrialized countries except the United States. Texas not only leads the nation, but also consistently ranks among the top few countries in conducting executions worldwide. According to the Death Penalty Information Center, six countries accounted for approximately 91 percent of all known state executions in 2006. That same year, Texas executed twenty-four people.

Why do Texans execute significantly more people than other states? Texans have a strong sense of right and wrong and are deeply attached to the idea of the death penalty as a deserved punishment. Whereas other states that use the death penalty may see it as a necessary evil, Texas culture embraces the state's right to execute citizens for violating certain laws. Frontier Texans were often left to secure their own towns and preferred little governmental interference. That attitude still prevails in

Table 5.1 Countries with the Highest Number of Confirmed Executions in 2006

1. China (1,010)
2. Iran (177)
3. Pakistan (82)
4. Iraq (65)
5. Sudan (65)
6. United States (53)

Source: Death Penalty Information Center, www.deathpenaltyinfo.org/article.php?did=127&scid=30#interexec.

The Texas Rangers

The Texas Rangers are a vivid example of the transformation of the state and its legends. The Texas Rangers have become icons of law enforcement, originally galloping through serials like *The Lone Ranger* featured on the radio and television, and in the movies played by western stars like Roy Rogers, Gene Autry, and Tex Ritter. Long after the early western stars left their horses behind, the Texas Rangers continue to capture viewer's imaginations on shows like *Walker, Texas Ranger* and movies like *Man of the House,* starring Chuck Norris and Tommy Lee Jones.

The Rangers can trace their origins back to Stephen F. Austin, who first referred to the citizens asked to protect his settlements as "rangers" because they had to range over the countryside. The Rangers became official extensions of the temporary government of Texas in 1835, when they were called upon to protect the frontier during the Texas Revolution.

While generally revered, the Rangers' image has suffered from time to time. When Sam Houston wanted to move the state's capital out of Austin, the two Rangers who went to Austin to retrieve the archives met resistance from the local citizens and returned with their horses' manes and tails shaved. In 1918 Governor William P. Hobby allegedly used the Rangers to suppress turnout for James Ferguson in South Texas during that year's Democratic primary. During the 1932 election the Texas Rangers made the mistake of backing Governor Sterling. When Ma Ferguson won office she retaliated by firing the entire force of 48 Rangers and replacing them with 2,300 "special" Rangers, many of them criminals. When the legislature responded by authorizing the hiring of only thirty-two Rangers, the state was under-protected as Bonnie Parker and Clyde Barrow (the infamous Bonnie and Clyde) roamed the state robbing banks. The Rangers' image was further tainted by accusations of being instruments of discrimination and intimidation against Tejanos. Captain Leander McNelly, whose tactics included piling the bodies of dead Mexican rustlers in the Brownsville town square, made the Rangers unpopular among many Tejanos in the 1870s.

The Rangers' image combines the independence of the state with that of law and order. While the details of the story vary, a common tale of the Rangers' ability involves citizens of a town calling for a company of Rangers to stop a prize fight. When the local people arrive at the train station to greet the twenty Rangers they need to quell the expected riot, they are disappointed to see only one Ranger get off the train: Legendary Ranger Captain Bill McDonald, who answered the citizens' disappointment over the arrival of only a single Ranger by saying, "Hell! Ain't I enough? There's only one prize-fight!" Since that time, "One riot, one Ranger" has been a common slogan associated with the Rangers. [i]

Today, the Texas Rangers are a highly professional and modern law enforcement organization that has been part of the Department of Public Safety since 1935. Perhaps less colorful than many of their predecessors and their television and cinema image, today's Rangers are designed to meet the demands of a high-tech state. Today, the Rangers include 118 commissioned officers, three crime analysts, a forensic artist, and a fiscal analyst. These Rangers assist local law enforcement with criminal investigations, help with the suppression of major disturbances, and conduct special investigations. While today's Texas Ranger may look little like their predecessors, they still abide by the creed set down by Captain McDonald: "No man in the wrong can stand up against a fellow that's in the right and keeps on a-comin."

i. Quotations from Captain McDonald taken from Texas Department of Public Safety, www.txdps.state.tx.us.

most of the state, where Texans' attachment to the death penalty is as strong as their attachment to guns. That attitude prevails among Texans sitting on juries, but also among members of the Texas Court of Criminal Appeals, as well as the Texas Board of Pardons and Paroles. As a former Smith County district attorney put it, "the death penalty in Texas is primarily a function of the fact that it is in our law. We have conservative jurors and district attorneys run for election and so it's very important that DAs . . . [who come up for reelections] make decisions on cases that are consistent with the feelings of their constituents." [32]

Support for the death penalty in the state remains strong, as recent polls suggest that while 58 percent of Americans support a moratorium on the death penalty, 70 percent of Texans continue to support the death penalty.[33] As the introductory story indicates, Texans' preference for the death penalty remains so strong that often the actions of Texas courts seem downright odd to the rest of the country. In fact, in one now infamous case, a panel of three judges from the Fifth Circuit Court of Appeals upheld a death penalty sentence, even though the defendant's attorney had slept through portions of the trial. The panel ruled that since they could not determine whether the attorney had slept through critical parts of the trial, there was no basis to overturn the conviction. Although the full Fifth Circuit Court later overturned this ruling, the initial ruling is indicative of prevalent attitudes toward justice in Texas.

In Texas, you can face the death penalty if you are found guilty of murder of a public safety officer, firefighter, correctional employee, child under the age of six, or multiple murders. In addition, murder during a kidnapping, burglary, robbery, sexual assault, arson, prison escape, or murder for payment are all crimes eligible for the death penalty. You can also face the death penalty if you murder a prison inmate serving a life sentence for murder, kidnapping, aggravated sexual assault, or robbery. In 2007, the Texas Legislature expanded the death penalty to include repeat sexual offenders. **Jessica's Law** provides that sexual predators whose victims are under the age of fourteen can now face the death penalty. In 2007, the Texas Department of Criminal Justice reported that of the 370 inmates on death row, 41 percent were African American, 30 percent were white, and another 28 percent were Hispanic. Critics of the death penalty continue to be concerned that minorities are more likely to be given the death penalty. On the other hand, women make up approximately 3 percent of death row inmates.

Jessica's Law
a law, adopted in several states, that provides for the death penalty or life imprisonment without parole for repeat sexual predators whose victims are underage, in Texas, defined as under the age of fourteen.

In addition to a long-held cultural preference for the death penalty, proponents in Texas and elsewhere also argue that it acts as a deterrent on crime. This argument is consistent with the preference for politicians and courts in Texas to be tough on crime. However, opponents of the death penalty point out that states without the death penalty have lower murder rates than states that use the death penalty. One study by the *New York Times* concludes that ten of the twelve states without the death penalty have murder rates that are lower than the national average whereas half the states with the death penalty have murder rates higher than the average.[34]

Moreover, opponents point out the added expense of death penalty cases, which involve automatic appeals to the state's high court among other things. The average time spent on death row is slightly over ten years, although one person in the state spent twenty-four years on death row. In 1992, a *Dallas Morning News* study estimated that taxpayers pay $2.3 million for the average death penalty case in Texas, compared to $750,000 to imprison someone in a single cell at the highest level of security for forty years.[35] The cost of the death penalty, coupled with the comparatively large number of executions in the state each year, places a significant burden on taxpayers in the state.

The U.S. Supreme Court has recently recognized some significant limits on the death penalty. In 2002, the Supreme Court ruled that it is unconstitutional for the state to execute defendants that are mentally retarded (see *Atkins v. Virginia*).[36] A few years later the Supreme Court ruled that juveniles could no longer be given the death penalty, in *Roper v. Simmons*.[37] As mentioned in the introductory story, the U.S. Supreme Court has recently agreed to hear a new challenge on the constitutionality of lethal injection as a method of execution. The case will probably be heard early in 2008. This is the first time since 1878, when the U.S. Supreme Court upheld the use of a firing squad, that the top court in the United States has considered the constitutionality of a *method* of capital punishment. Even if the U.S. Supreme Court rules that the current cocktail used for lethal injection amounts to cruel and unusual punishment, that by no means suggests that the Court will rule that the death penalty itself is unconstitutional.

Winners and Losers

n many ways, Texans' preference for a tough approach to crime, love of justice, and ardent support for the death penalty sets them apart from the rest of the country. However, those political preferences have produced a high cost to the average Texan. Money spent on imprisonment rather than rehabilitation means that Texas's high imprisonment rates entail a high cost in taxes. Embracing the privatization of prisons also entails significant costs. Often these for-profit centers have had high-profile breakouts, where local and state law officials have picked up the tab for the statewide searches of the escaped convicts. Although these prisons are often cited for poor conditions, Texas has yet to impose fines on these facilities. Texans are also willingly taking on other states' criminal populations, as Texas leads the way in building private prisons and other states send their prisoners to the state. On the other hand, recent trends by the Texas Legislature may help the state become a real winner as rehabilitation rather than punishment becomes a major thrust of the Texas justice system.

Texans win and lose with the death penalty. Although increasingly unpopular nationwide, in Texas the death penalty remains revered. So Texans have continued to win as they lead the country in executions, a clear reflection of their policy preference. On the other hand, Texans pay the high costs necessary to ensure that potential death penalty cases follow due process, a cost that is significantly higher than life imprisonment. While executions in the state are temporarily suspended, there is little doubt that, if necessary, Texas will quickly develop a new means of execution and reinstate the death penalty.

Conclusion

ustice in Texas is a complicated affair. The judicial system is complex and confusing. There is a widespread perception among Texans that justice is for sale. Many outside the state view the justice system as medieval and unyielding. Texans' strong affinity for the death penalty and its frequent use makes the state unique among other states. Texans have a strong desire for justice that the Texas judicial system rarely satisfies. In order to get a more responsive judicial system, Texans may need to reevaluate how their preferences are represented in the current system.

For instance, the preference for voters to retain control of judicial selection on the ballot entails a high cost and, given the overwhelming job of selecting nearly all of the judges in the state, provides very little payoff. More generally, Texans' resistance to change means the Texas judiciary, like other institutions in the state, is only corrected piecemeal over time. The result is a system that in many ways no longer makes sense for the state, while its citizens continue to cling to the myth that the system is working for them.

Key Terms

appellate jurisdiction
at-large elections
beyond a reasonable doubt
civil cases
compensatory damages
concurrent jurisdiction
criminal cases
cumulative voting
defendant
de novo
en banc
exclusive jurisdiction
grand jury
incumbency advantage
indictment
Jessica's Law
judicial federalism
jurisdiction
magistrate functions
name recognition
original jurisdiction
petit jury
plaintiff
preponderance of evidence
private prisons
prosecutor
punitive damages
recidivism
straight ticket voting

Explore this subject further at http://college.cqpress.com/lonestarpolitics, where you'll find chapter summaries, practice quizzes, key word flash cards, and additional suggested resources.

Efforts to increase or maintain economic development are a priority for local governments like cities and counties. The construction of the new stadium for the Dallas Cowboys, a Texas legend in professional football, is just one example. At one point, Arlington almost lost the stadium project to the City of Dallas. Attempts to replace the existing stadium culminated in an agreement between the City of Arlington and the Dallas Cowboys organization in which the City of Arlington would provide $325 million in financing for the new $1 billion stadium. Voters in Arlington approved tax increases related to the stadium project in November of 2004.

CHAPTER 6

Local Government in Texas

Founded in the 1850s, Buffalo Gap in Taylor County was promoted as "The Athens of the West."[1] The town flourished as a center of higher education, commerce, and buffalo hunting. Sitting along the old Center Line Trail, which ran from Texarkana to El Paso, Buffalo Gap became a natural choice for the seat of Taylor County when the county was organized in 1878. Two other major trade routes ran through Buffalo Gap at the time. At its peak, 1,200 people called Buffalo Gap home. Four grocery stores, a jail, a big hotel, a drugstore, and other businesses operated in the town. In short, Buffalo Gap was a thriving, prosperous community poised for additional growth.

However, economic development soon left Buffalo Gap behind. In 1883, ranchers north of Buffalo Gap heard about the plans for the Texas and Pacific Railroad to move west. The ranchers met with officials from the railroad, offering part of their land for the railroad and bypassing Buffalo Gap. The Texas and Pacific Railroad moved its headquarters to the newly established town of Abilene. Within two years, Abilene had surpassed Buffalo Gap in population and had become the county seat of Taylor County. Although Buffalo Gap eventually attracted the Santa Fe Railroad in 1895, Abilene continued to thrive, while Buffalo Gap declined. Within a few years, Buffalo Gap had half the population of its peak.[2] At the same time, Abilene saw its role as a transportation center attract more businesses to the city. The advent of the automobile, and the creation of federal highway systems, enhanced Abilene's stature as U.S. Highways 83, 84, and 277 passed through Abilene. Later, Interstate 20 was routed through Abilene, while Buffalo Gap sat several miles from any of these major routes. Two Texas Farm roads intersect in Buffalo Gap.

Abilene is now the home to over 110,000 residents. The railroad and commercial economy diversified with the rise of the oil industry in Texas and with the establishment of a U.S. Air Force base after World War II. Fifteen miles to the south, Buffalo Gap remains a quaint community of about 450. Ironically, the city's major attraction is the Buffalo Gap Historical Village, a recreation of life in the late 1880s.

This "tale of two towns" from the Texas frontier illustrates the contrast between Texas of the Old West and the more modern, economically viable Texas. Cities and towns shape their futures by enacting policies to promote particular values: economic growth versus traditional ways of life, modern conveniences versus rustic preservation, jobs and job creation versus protection of local businesses. At the heart of all of this is local government. The choice of strategy determines the direction that a community takes, either future-oriented and prosperous or status quo-oriented and stagnant.

In this chapter, we review the basic foundations of local government in Texas, discussing the creation, powers, and organization of county government. Then, we review city government, focusing on the differences between general law and home rule cities. We also examine the functions of city governments and elections to city government. The chapter concludes with a review of other forms of local government, including public education and special districts.

> **As you read the chapter, think about the following questions:**
> ★ To what extent does the structure of Texas counties limit large counties such as Harris County or small counties such as Loving County?
> ★ How do the functions of county government differ from the functions of city government?
> ★ What are the different types of city government?
> ★ What are the issues with funding local government?

Local Government: The Basics

 ocal government involves a wide range of entities. Most often, local government refers to cities and counties. In Texas, that list also includes school districts, community college districts, municipal utility districts (MUDs), water conservation districts, and airport districts, among others.

Texas has the third highest number of local governments of any state in the United States. Adjusting for the size of population, smaller population states like North and South Dakota possess more governments per person than Texas. In fact, Texas does not even rank in the top half of states ranked according to governments per person, coming in at thirty-third. Thus, although Texas and other large-population states seem to have a lot of local governments, compared to population size, they do not.

The common characteristic of all of these local governments is that they exist as an arm of the state government. Regardless of the type of local government, all local governments are creatures of the state government, a concept known as **Dillon's Rule.** In a case before the Iowa Supreme Court, Justice John Forrest Dillon affirmed the principal that local governments have only those powers specifically granted to them by the states.[3] The U.S. Supreme Court later echoed this sentiment. The high court ruled that states may change the powers of their cities, even if the residents living in the city do not approve.[4] By extension, this concept applied to all forms of local government within a state, including counties and special districts.

In other words, the powers, duties, and very existence of each and every local government are determined by the state government. This legal status is true of the relationship between local governments and their respective state government in every state of the United States. In Texas, the Texas Constitution provides a basic framework to define the types, powers, and responsibilities of local governments in Texas. Statutory laws like the Texas Local Government Code, Texas Education Code, and Texas Utilities Code supplement the framework found in the Texas Constitution. For example, the Texas Constitution specifically grants to the Texas Legislature "the power to create counties for the convenience of the people."[5] These constitutional provisions and statutory laws go so far as to specify how local governments elect officials, which administrative offices must exist, and what types of taxes local governments may use to fund their activities.

Dillon's Rule

the principle that regardless of the type of local government, all local governments are creatures of the state government and have only those powers specifically granted to them by the state.

Table 6.1 Units of Local Government Compared to State Population (2002)

NUMBER OF LOCAL GOVERNMENTS		LOCAL GOVERNMENTS PER 10,000 PEOPLE		
STATE	**NUMBER**	**STATE**	**GOVERNMENTS PER 10,000**	**RANK**
Top Five		*Top Five*		
Illinois	6,904	North Dakota	43.2	1
Pennsylvania	5,032	South Dakota	24.6	2
Texas	4,785	Nebraska	16.2	3
California	4,410	Wyoming	14.5	4
Kansas	3,888	Kansas	14.3	5
50 State Average	1,751	*50 State Average*	3.0	
Bottom Five		*Bottom Five*		
Maryland	266	Nevada	1.0	46
Nevada	211	Virginia	0.7	47
Alaska	176	Florida	0.7	48
Rhode Island	119	Maryland	0.5	49
Hawaii	20	Hawaii	0.2	50
Texas	**4,785**	**Texas**	**2.2**	**33**
States Bordering Texas		*States Bordering Texas*		
Oklahoma	1,799	Arkansas	5.9	13
Arkansas	1,589	Oklahoma	5.2	16
New Mexico	859	New Mexico	4.6	18
Louisiana	474	Louisiana	1.1	45

Source: Kendra A. Hovey and Harold A. Hovey, *CQ's State Fact Finder* (Washington, D.C.: CQ Press, 2007), 105.

Because there are fifty states in the United States, essentially fifty different systems of local government have developed. States diverge tremendously in the structure and functions of local governments. As examples, Connecticut and Rhode Island lack county government in the sense that Texas and other states use county government. In Connecticut, counties serve primarily as a method of reporting population for the U.S. Census. Most functions that Texans associate with county government are performed in Connecticut by township governments. Other states, like Georgia, maintain countywide school districts. Arkansas allows school district boundaries to cross county lines.

Because local governments of all types are extensions of a state government, a second relationship exists: the relationship between local governments and the national government in Washington, D.C. This relationship is more complex. Officially, the U.S. Constitution mentions only state governments and the national government. As a result, on a legal and technical level, local governments do not exist in the eyes of the U.S. Constitution. In reality, because state governments and state constitutions create local governments, the national government recognizes that other governments exist within states, but holds the state governments responsible for the policies and procedures of local government. For example, if local school districts are unable or unwilling to comply with a federal law or federal court decision, the U.S. government ultimately requires the state government to solve the problem. A dramatic example involved the failure in the 1970s and 1980s of the Kansas City, Missouri, public school system to integrate their schools. The federal courts went so far as to hold the Missouri state government responsible for the problem and to require the use of statewide taxes to pay for integrating the Kansas City schools. [6]

A federal system of government, as described in Chapter 2, occurs when the powers of government are divided between the national government and state governments, with each level of government having an independent base of power. This arrangement contrasts with a unitary system of government in which all power is centralized and other levels of government are given their powers by the central government. The exact division of powers in a federal system could be dual federalism, in which each level has distinct and separate powers, or cooperative federalism, in which the state governments and the national government jointly carry out some tasks.

Two other arrangements within federal systems are fiscal federalism and **administrative federalism.** Under fiscal federalism, the U.S. government sets goals and objectives or develops new programs, then the national government provides financial incentives for the state governments to participate in the program. As a result, states begin to develop new programs or change policies to match what the national government wants. In exchange, states receive money from the national government to cover some of the costs of the program. For example, suppose the U.S. Congress and the president believe that providing computers and Internet access to students in elementary, middle, and high schools is essential to learning in the twenty-first century. Then, a program is created to provide money to states to buy new computers and equip new and existing schools with Internet access. The national money is matched with contributions from the state government and then given to schools. There are many examples of these types of programs, including health care for the disabled, immunization programs for poor children, road construction, and draining and sewer systems improvements, among others.

Administrative federalism works in a similar manner in that the national government sets up guidelines for policy, then expects the state government to pay for the programs without additional national money. The best current example of administrative federalism is probably "No Child Left Behind" (NCLB). NCLB sets a broad set of objectives for states to follow regarding the performance of elementary and secondary schools. These objectives include rates of high school dropouts and student truancy. Methods of assessing whether students are learning essential knowledge are also included. However, the national government does not provide money to states to implement NCLB. States must pay for NCLB themselves.

What is the connection to local government? In fiscal federalism, a key method of the national government to provide money is grants, sums of money given to the state or local government to fund a program or policy. Usually, states allow local governments to apply to the state for a share of the money, often through a competitive process. Thus, local governments must develop the skills and staffs to write the applications, provide evidence of the need for the funds, and develop budgets. In addition, once a local government receives a grant, it must report back in detail to the state government how the money was used. Local governments become the key agencies for implementing programs. For administrative federalism, the decision of the state government on how to follow the federal government's objectives are often outlined and then handed to the local government to carry out. Again, using NCLB as an illustration, the Texas Education Agency (TEA) developed a set of guidelines to meet the objectives of NCLB, using the Texas Assessment of Knowledge and Skills (TAKS) test. However, the TEA does not give the test to school students. Instead, the TEA gives the tests to each Independent School District (ISD), which then gives the TAKS test. If a specific school does not perform well, the local ISD then develops a plan to bring up the test scores.

Administrative federalism
the national government sets up guidelines for policy, then expects the state government to pay for the programs without additional money.

County Government: Texas Style

ounty government is a product of the historical development of the state and the constitutional provisions regarding the function of county government. Texas counties vary tremendously in population, natural resources, and land areas. However, all Texas counties are structurally governed the same. As a result, Texas county government is a one-size-fits-all approach. The lack of variation in government structure makes Texas unusual compared to some other states.

History and Function of Counties in Texas

Local government in Texas is rooted in the old municipality system of the Mexican Republic. Under Mexican rule, Texas contained four municipalities, large areas containing a town and surrounding rural areas. Initially, the four municipalities were San Antonio, Bahia (Goliad), Nacogdoches, and Rio Grande Valley. The number of these governments increased as the population and settlements grew. When the Republic of Texas was established, twenty-three counties were created based upon these Mexican municipalities, including Nacogdoches, Bexar, and Brazos. At statehood in 1845, the county system was retained. The Confederate Constitution of 1861 created 122 counties, and the number of counties continued to increase under subsequent state constitutions. In 1931, Loving County became the last county to be established. Interestingly, the organization of Loving County began its second era of existence. The first Loving County had originally been formed in 1893 from Reeves County as part of a scheme to defraud landowners and the state of Texas by the organizers of the county. Loving County was abolished by the Texas Legislature in 1897. The arrival of the oil industry to western Texas led to the reestablishment of the county.[7]

Texas has 254 counties, more than any other state. Georgia is the next closest with 159 counties. Hawaii and Delaware have the fewest, with three counties each. In Texas, counties are created by laws passed by the state legislature, subject to a few limitations from the Texas Constitution. New counties may not be smaller than 700 square miles. Existing counties from which the new county is created cannot be reduced to less than 700 square miles.[8] Historically, county boundaries were drawn so that the citizens could travel to the county courthouse and return home in the same day.[9] A few interesting facts about counties in Texas include the fact that by population, Harris County is the largest, with over 3.4 million people. Only two counties in the entire United States are larger in population than Harris County: Cook County, Illinois, and Los Angeles County, California. The smallest county in Texas by population is Loving County with sixty people. Loving County also holds the distinction of being the smallest county in terms of population in the entire United States. In terms of geographic area, Brewster County is the largest in Texas at 6,204 square miles, larger than the combined size of the states of Connecticut and Rhode Island. Rockwall County, near Dallas, is the smallest at 129 square miles.[10]

County names in Texas reflect a variety of historical and cultural forces at work in Texas. Twelve counties are named for defenders of the Alamo, including Bowie, Fannin, and Taylor Counties. Several reflect geographic features like rivers, streams, and landforms, such as Pecos and Sabine Counties. Some are named for governors and other figures in Texas politics, like Coke County or Lamar County. Panola County is named for the Native American word for "cotton," while Lampasas County comes from the Spanish word for "lilies." Freestone County is named for a variety of peach.

County government is essential in Texas because counties carry out many duties for the state government. The role and function of counties is especially important in rural areas of the state, where cities and towns are few and far between. In the days before well-maintained roads and highways, the state government in Austin was largely inaccessible to many Texans. County government was designed to bring state government closer to the people. County government is also essential to the function of both administrative and fiscal federalism because counties are often the front line for the delivery of a variety of policies for the state.

Texas's counties perform at least six key functions for the state government. Counties operate courts for the state, including justice of the peace, county, and district courts. Counties make available public health clinics, conduct immunization programs, enforce state health regulations, and inspect restaurants. Counties also maintain vital records for the state like marriage licenses, death certificates, birth certificates, and property deeds. Another function of counties is to collect some forms of taxes for the state government. Property taxes, license plate fees, and motor vehicle title fees are collected by counties. Counties also conduct elections for the state, including the maintenance of election equipment, the registration of voters, and the operation of polling places. Finally, counties jointly carry out other functions with the state government. For example, counties help with law enforcement by maintaining sheriff or constable offices and operating county jails. Counties build roads and bridges that connect to the state's network of roads and highways.

In a strange twist on Texas politics, the Texas Constitution contains a strong provision against imprisonment for debt. However, the Texas Constitution also allows each county to provide a "Manual Labor Poor House and Farm, for taking care of, managing, employing, and supplying the wants of its indigent and poor inhabitants."[11] Apparently, being in debt is not grounds for state judicial action, but being poor is.

The state permits counties to carry out certain activities that may also be provided by other forms of local government, including cities and special districts. Counties sometimes operate parks, run libraries, own airports, and manage hospitals. Services such as water, sewer, and garbage collection may also be provided by a county.

Governing Texas Counties

All Texas counties are governed the same way. By law, all counties are general law counties. This means that counties are controlled directly by state laws. Thus, all 254 counties in Texas have the same form of government. Every county government is led by a **commissioners court.** The commissioners court is made up of four elected commissioners and the county judge from the county constitutional court. The elections for the commissioners and the county judge are **partisan elections** in which candidates normally compete for office with both the candidates' names and party affiliations listed on the ballot. The elections for the four commissioners in every county are by Single-Member District Plurality (SMDP) elections. This election system is discussed in Chapter 3 regarding the state legislature, and again later in this chapter, in reference to city council elections. The county judge is elected at large by voters across the county. The members of the court,

Commissioners court

the governing body for Texas counties, consisting of four elected commissioners and the judge from the county constitutional court.

Partisan elections

elections in which candidates compete for office, with both candidates' names and party affiliations appearing on the ballot.

Figure 6.1 The Structure of County Government in Texas

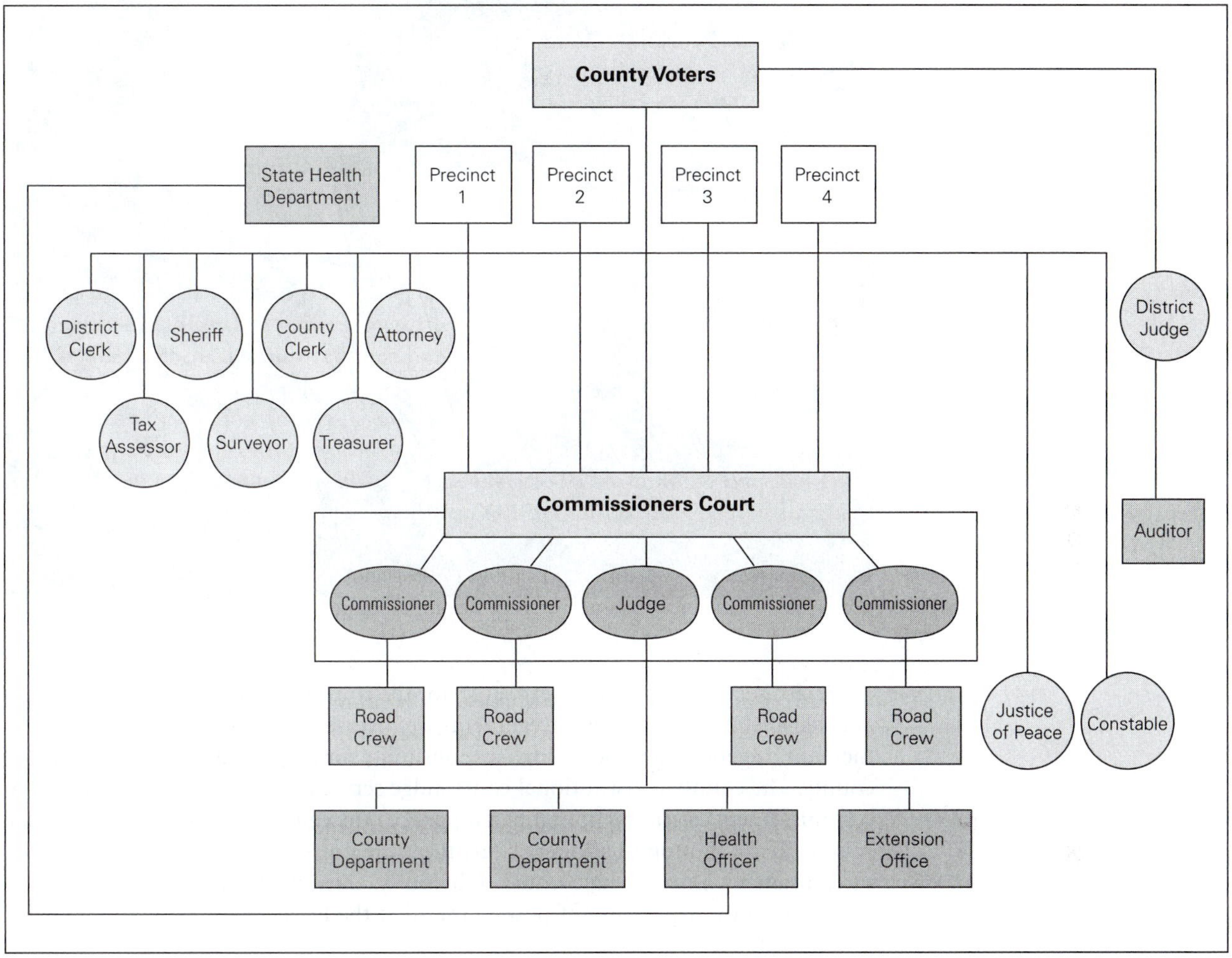

Source: John A. Gilmartin and Joe M. Rothe, *County Government in Texas,* issue 2, V. G. Young Institute of County Government, Texas Agricultural Extension Service, Texas A&M University.

including the county judge, are elected for four-year terms. Commissioners are elected to staggered terms of office.

Each commissioner is responsible for running the county government in his or her own district. One of the primary responsibilities of a commissioner is the maintenance of roads and bridges in the district. The commissioners determine which roads are paved and repaved, when bridges are repaired, and which company receives the contract to perform road projects in the district. In some counties, the commissioners agree to pool resources and make these decisions about roads and bridges collectively in the interest of the whole county.

Students of Texas politics are often confused by the term commissioners court, which implies a judicial function. This confusion is increased by the presence of the county constitutional court judge as part of the commissioners court. In reality, the commissioners court serves as a legislative body for the county. The commissioners court passes laws that govern the county, determines types and rates of taxes to fund the county government, and passes the annual county budget. The commissioners

Law enforcement in Texas is a function of city, county, and state government. While cities like Tyler have police departments, county governments use sheriffs, justices of the peace, and constables to enforce the law. At the state level, the Texas Rangers and Texas Highway Patrol serve as law enforcement agencies.

court also serves as a collective executive for the county. The court administers state and federal funds for local government use, oversees the various county departments and agencies, and holds final responsibility for the conduct of elections in the county. The county constitutional court judge serves as the presiding officer of the commissioners court and appoints temporary replacements when a commissioner resigns. Thus, the commissioners court fuses the power of the legislative and executive branches into a single entity. Obviously, this arrangement differs tremendously from the separation of powers found at the levels of the state and national governments.

The county constitutional court judge, of course, also serves as the justice for the county court. Thus, the role of the county judge crosses all three branches of government. The county constitutional court judge is in charge of the county budget, an executive function; serves on the commissioners court, a legislative function; and hears cases before the county court, a judicial function.

To assist the commissioners court, the voters elect a variety of other county officers. Typically, these officers are elected for four-year terms. Voters elect a county **sheriff** to oversee law enforcement in the county. The sheriff appoints deputy sheriffs and operates the county jail. The **county clerk** is responsible for maintaining county records including births, deaths, and marriage licenses. In some counties the county clerk also serves as the county elections officer. The **county attorney** serves as the chief prosecuting attorney for misdemeanors in local courts, represents the county in legal activities, and offers legal advice to the county government. The county **tax assessor** collects property taxes, license plate fees, title certificates for cars and trucks, and, in a handful of counties, acts as the registrar of voters. Since 1978, many counties have created a unified tax assessor district, which provides property tax assessment and collection for the county, cities, and school districts in the county. In the case of voter registration, this function is a holdover from the days of the

Sheriff
the elected county official who oversees county law enforcement.

County clerk
the elected county official who maintains county records and in some counties oversees elections.

County attorney
the county official who represents the county in legal activities and offers legal advice to the county government.

Tax assessor
the elected county officer who collects county taxes and user fees.

poll tax discussed in Chapter 7. The **justices of the peace and constables** serve as judicial officers for minor criminal and civil cases. Normally each of the four districts of the county has a justice of the peace and a constable.

Several other officers may be elected or appointed. A district clerk maintains court records for county and district courts. For larger counties, an **auditor** is appointed by the district judge, who serves the state's district court in the county, to oversee county finances; a county public health officer directs local public health clinics; and a county agricultural agent assists in rural counties with the needs of the farming community. Some counties have a county elections officer.

These officials are assisted by a host of employees that work for the various departments of the county government. From receptionists and administrative assistants to county land surveyors, counties employ thousands of Texans to perform the day-to-day operations of county government. In all but a handful of Texas counties, these jobs are essentially patronage. In a patronage system, elected officials give out government jobs to whomever the elected official wishes to have the job, often a loyal supporter. A person hired for a government job then serves at the wishes of the elected official and may be fired at will for any reason. Historically under patronage, government jobs were handed out as political favors by the person winning an election. In some cases, the person who got a job in government service lacked any qualifications for the position. Of course, many of the men and women who work for county governments throughout Texas are competent, qualified people. But, the fact remains that these people hold jobs without the protections of a **merit system** or **civil service system.** In a merit system, people receive government jobs based upon a formalized system of qualifications, usually holding formal training for the position including college degrees or vocational certification. Often, merit systems require an applicant to take a test or examination to determine if the applicant is qualified. Individuals receive promotions and salary increases based upon a standard scale or series of performance goals. A patronage system may mimic the merit system by writing qualifications for offices or setting minimal standards for getting a job, yet the fact remains that these standards are not mandated by anything other than the decisions of county commissioners.

The Texas Local Government Code allows counties with 200,000 or more people to create a merit system or civil service system. Counties with less than 200,000 retain a patronage system. The creation of the merit system may be by a vote of the county's commissioners court or by the county's voters.[12] In counties with over 500,000 people, a civil service system may be limited to the county's sheriff's department. As a result of the 2000 census, twenty counties in Texas qualified for a civil service system; only eight had created a countywide civil service system. Harris County, the most populous county, lacks a civil service system for county employees. Among the seven counties with populations large enough to establish a civil service system for the sheriff's department, all seven had done so. Thus, in Harris County, sheriff's department employees were subject to a civil service system, but the rest of the county's employees were not.[13]

A civil service system for a county is administered by a **county civil service commission.** The commission is appointed by the commissioners court for terms of two years. The civil service commission develops job definitions, qualification processes, classification of employees, requirements for promotion and tenure, disciplinary procedures, and grievance processes.

Justices of the peace and constables
elected county officers who act as judicial officers for minor criminal and civil cases.

Auditor
the county officer appointed by the district judge, who oversees county finances.

Merit or civil service system
a system in which people receive government jobs based upon a set of qualifications and formal training; job promotion and pay raises are based upon job performance.

County civil service commission
the agency administering the county's civil service system, by developing job definitions, qualification processes, employee classifications, and other aspects of the system.

County Finances and Operations

To provide for day-to-day operations, counties in Texas rely on property taxes as their primary source of income. Other sources of revenue are motor vehicle license fees, service fees, and federal aid. Service fees include the costs of obtaining official documents such as marriage licenses and birth certificates, as well as court fees to file a case with the county court.[14] In counties without incorporated cities or transportation districts, the county may also use sales taxes to finance the county government. While county governments face an upper limit on the rate that may be assessed for property tax rates, voters may agree to additional property tax rates to fund roads and bridges in the county. Services beyond those financed by the county budget may be funded by creating special districts to fund hospitals, libraries, ports, airports, etc. Some counties have created special districts, called Municipal Utility Districts (MUDs) to provide basic utilities like water, sewers, and electrical delivery. These special districts are discussed later. In some counties, the county government contracts with private businesses to provide the basic services counties once provided. This process involves either **privatization** or **contract outsourcing** of government services. A new trend is building toll roads. In some counties, a private company is contracted to build and maintain a highway for the county or state. Individuals who use the highway pay a fee to drive on the road. This fee helps to repay the private company for the cost of building the road and for routine repairs to the highway. Harris, Dallas, Tarrant, Bexar, Travis, and Smith counties now have toll roads.

Property taxes provide the primary source of funding for county governments in Texas. However, rates of property taxes vary tremendously in Texas. In 2005, Sutton County represented the low end of property tax rates in Texas, with rates at $0.18 per $100 of the assessed value of the property, while Duvall County maintains the highest rate at $1.03 per $100. In Duvall County $1.03 per $100 includes $0.30 in special taxes to fund roads and bridges, including maintenance on the county's farm roads. The average for counties in Texas is $0.51 per $100 of the assessed value of property. In Texas, real estate is the only property that is routinely taxed for the purposes of funding local governments. Other states assess personal property taxes as well. Personal property may include recreational vehicles, furniture, electronic appliances, and animals. Some states include the cars and trucks that a family or business owns in their personal property tax assessments as well. In states like Missouri and Kansas, the tax on cars and trucks can be quite substantial. For example, Greene County, Missouri, assesses cars at 33.3 percent of the assessed value of the vehicle per $100 times the local tax rate. So, a person with a $20,000 car in Greene County follows this formula to determine the tax. $20,000 (the value of the car) divided by 100, multiplied by 0.333, then multiplied by 4.26 (the property tax rate). The tax in 2006 on the car, not counting other forms of property, was approximately $280.[15]

The use of property taxes as the primary source of funding for county government is not without controversy. For counties with high property values, the use of property taxes provides ample revenue to fund county services. The reliance on property taxes stems in part from the inability of many counties to levy sales taxes to fund local government. In addition, property taxes permit the state of Texas to avoid the imposition of income taxes, common in many states. However, property values vary tremendously across counties in Texas; in many rural areas without significant natural resources or economic development, lower property values might mean an

Privatization

when a government entity sells off assets or services to a private company, such as a school district selling its buses to a private company and allowing the private company to provide transportation to school.

Contract outsourcing

when a government entity contracts with a private company to perform a service that governments traditionally provide, such as a contract to collect trash and garbage.

Table 6.2 Property Tax Rates in Texas

COUNTY	TAX RATE PER $100	GENERAL FUND	OTHER
Five Highest Rates			
Duval	1.03	0.70	0.33
Jim Hogg	0.99	0.73	0.26
Throckmorton	0.99	0.82	0.17
Fisher	0.95	0.80	0.15
Froad	0.94	0.79	0.15
Five Lowest Rates			
Midland	0.25	0.25	0.00
Collin	0.25	0.25	0.00
Denton	0.23	0.23	0.00
Dallas	0.21	0.21	0.00
Sutton	0.18	0.15	0.03

Source: Texas Association of Counties, "Texas Total Property Tax Rates 1991–2006," www.county.org/resources/ countydata/products/TaxRates/index.html, accessed November 17, 2007.

inability to raise adequate revenue. In some instances, property tax rates are substantially higher in these counties to compensate for the relatively lower value of property in the county.

The structure of county government in Texas reflects the continuity and tradition of Texas. While counties have changed in the number of counties and the population of counties, the Texas Constitution and statutory law prevent variation in the structure of the commissioners court and its powers. As a result, Harris County and Loving County essentially share the same system of government, despite the tremendous difference in population and demand for government action. Clearly, the ability of Harris County Commissioners Court to govern a county of 3.4 million people is less effective. County governments cannot adapt to the realities of their situation or the changes that occur over time.

Cities

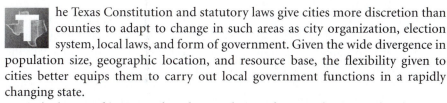he Texas Constitution and statutory laws give cities more discretion than counties to adapt to change in such areas as city organization, election system, local laws, and form of government. Given the wide divergence in population size, geographic location, and resource base, the flexibility given to cities better equips them to carry out local government functions in a rapidly changing state.

A city is created in Texas when the population of an area that is not already incorporated as a city reaches at least 200 people. To form a city, the residents must also define the exact boundaries of the city and negotiate with the county regarding the services that the city will provide versus those the county provides to the residents. At this point, residents may gather signatures of those living in the area that support the creation of a city. After gathering the required number of signatures, up to 10 percent of the registered voters of the proposed city, the petition is given to the county constitutional court judge, who places the issue on the ballot at the next county election. A city may also be created when residents living within an existing city receive permission to leave the existing city and form a new city. Once a city is created, it continues to exist even if the population drops below 200 people. Only a majority vote by the registered voters living in the city dissolves a city.

The Texas Constitution provides for two categories of status for cities: general law and home rule. A city is normally a **general law city.** In other words, the default status of cities is general law. The Texas Local Government Code specifies the exact forms of government, ordinance powers, and other aspects of city government. However, general law cities often find that this arrangement is too rigid to adapt to the demands of population growth, demographic change, or economic development.

Actually, three types of general law cities exist in Texas. These types are referred to as General Law Type A, General Law Type B, and General Law Type C cities. General Law Type A cities are typically larger cities, which contain at least 600 residents. Type A cities must have the strong mayor form of city government.[16] Type A cities may choose between Single-Member District Plurality and At-Large election systems. These cities are required to have a wider range of city officials, either appointed or elected, than other types. For example, Type A cities must have a tax assessor, a treasurer, a city secretary, and a city attorney. In contrast, General Law Type B cities contain between 201 and 9,999 residents. These cities may choose between the strong mayor and weak mayor forms of government. Normally, Type B cities with the strong mayor form of government have six members elected using an At-Large system. The city council may create city offices as they so choose. State law does not mandate specific offices that must exist.[17] General Law Type C cities have between 201 and 4,999 residents. These cities are required, unless otherwise approved by the state government, to have a weak mayor system of government.[18] The mayor and commission normally serve two-year terms in office.

Almost a century ago, a 1912 amendment to the Texas Constitution began to give cities more flexibility by allowing some cities to become home rule cities. A **home rule city** is a city that has been granted greater freedom in the organization and function of city government. A general law city with 5,000 or more people is permitted to shift to home rule. The advantage to being a home rule city is the ability to adopt any of the three forms of city government, to change the administrative structure by creating or abolishing departments, and to alter systems of electing city officials without seeking the permission of the state. Home rule cities also have the ability to establish a **city charter** for approval by the voters in the proposed city.[19] A city charter is a plan of government that details the structure and function of the city government. The city charter also discusses land usage within the city limits, specifies the election system for elected city officials, and details the types of ordinances the city may enact. (An **ordinance** is a law passed by a city government.) A city charter is like a constitution for a city. Note that general law cities of all types lack a city charter and are governed directly by state law and city ordinances. Home rule cities have more freedom to pass ordinances and have some influence over land usage just outside the city boundaries. The land usage power varies from half a mile for cities over 1,500 people to five miles for cities over 25,000. Home rule cities have greater powers of **annexation,** the addition of areas adjacent to the city into the city limits. Once a city becomes a home rule city, it retains this status even if the population falls below 5,000.

The overwhelming majority (71.9 percent) of Texas cities are general law cities. This figure includes many cities with populations of more than 5,000. The residents of these cities choose to leave the city government as a general law city. Note

General law city
the default organization for Texas cities, with the exact forms of government, ordinance powers, and other aspects of city government specified in the Texas Local Government Code.

Home rule city
a city that has been granted greater freedom in the organization and functioning of city government, and can make changes without seeking permission from the state.

City charter
in home rule cities, a plan of government that details the structure and function of the city government, similar to a constitution.

Ordinance
a law enacted by a city government.

Annexation
adding areas adjacent to a city into the city limits.

that a very small fraction of Texas cities, less than one-half of one percent, are classified as "other." These cities have exemptions from the general law–home rule dichotomy. Only two cities fall into this category: Josephine in Collin County and Latexo in Houston County.

Forms of City Government

There are three basic forms of city government in Texas: the strong mayor-council system, the weak mayor-council system, and the council-manager system. The strong mayor-council system occurs when the voters of the city elect a mayor as the chief executive and a city council to serve as the city's legislature. Together, the mayor and city council make policy for the city, pass ordinances for law-making, and oversee the city's various departments.

The mayor develops the city budget, appoints the heads of the departments of city government, sets the agenda for the council, and serves as chief administrator of the city's departments. The mayor also serves as a representative of the citizens of the city: opening businesses, speaking on behalf of the citizens, attending conferences with other mayors, and negotiating on behalf of the city. In many cities, the mayor may veto ordinances passed by the city council. The city council passes ordinances, and in some cities, may override a veto by the mayor. In addition, the council approves the city budget. In small cities, the mayor and council members may be part-time positions. In large cities both positions may be well compensated because serving as mayor or sitting on the council are full-time jobs. In Texas, the strong mayor system is sometimes called the mayor-council, mayor-commission, or mayor-alderman forms of government.

The advantage to the strong mayor system is the concentration of power in the hands of the mayor. The mayor provides leadership on issues of the day and on the priorities of the city. The mayor's control over the city budget and over the city's departments allows for greater harmony and efficiency in policy implementation. In addition, the strong mayor system mirrors the separation of powers between the executive and legislative branches of government found in the national government. However, the concentration of power in the hands of the mayor may lead to personality-driven politics to the detriment of current issues. The power of the mayor also reduces the influence of the city council, which is designed to be the representative branch of city government.

In contrast, the weak mayor-council system contains a directly elected mayor whose powers are much more diluted relative to the city council. The mayor and city council share power over the creation and adoption of the city budget. Ordinances are jointly determined by the mayor and council together. Collectively, the mayor and city council choose the heads of the various city departments and jointly oversee the city bureaucracy. In some systems, voters directly elect the heads of the various city departments, like the chief of police and city attorney. In Texas, the weak mayor system is often referred to generically as the "council" form of government or the "commission" form of government.

By dispersing the powers of city government and balancing the powers of the mayor and council, the weak mayor-council system attempts to avoid the problems of the strong mayor system. Essentially, the mayor becomes just another member of the city council. On the other hand, the weakened position of the mayor means

Figure 6.2 Texas Cities by Statutory Type

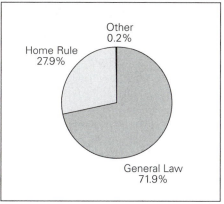

Source: Texas Municipal Association, "Annual Survey of Members" (Denton, Tex.: Texas Municipal Association, Inc., 2007).

Chicago is the third largest city in the United States, ranking just one place above Houston. Like the Texas Constitution, the Illinois Constitution sets out the specific duties and responsibilities of city governments. Illinois also allows home rule for its cities and counties, but cities are automatically granted home rule status when their population reaches 25,000 residents.[i]

The City of Chicago and the City of Houston both are home rule cities. Both cities are also strong mayor-council systems of government. In Chicago, the city council consists of fifty aldermen elected from Single-Member Districts or wards. The council divides itself into nineteen standing committees to assist in the process of developing and reviewing new ordinances. In this sense, the city council operates similar to a state legislature. Voters in Chicago directly elect the mayor, treasurer, and city clerk. To organize the city's bureaucracy, over forty city departments and agencies exist. In Houston, voters elect the mayor and city comptroller directly. The Houston City Council is chosen by a combination of Single-Member Districts and At-Large seats. Houston's city government consists of over twenty different departments and agencies. Some of these agencies correspond to departments in the city of Chicago. For example, both cities have fire, police, library, and aviation departments. However, many aspects of city government differ. Chicago's city government contains a Board of Ethics, the Chicago Film Office, the Environment Department, and the Cultural Affairs Office. Some agencies and departments in Houston, like parks and recreation, have counterparts that are not controlled directly by the city of Chicago. In Chicago, parks are controlled by a related but independent government agency.

City Government in Chicago and Houston

FACTOR	CHICAGO	HOUSTON
Population	2.8 million	2.1 million[a]
Elected executive offices	3	2
Size of city council	50	14
Members of council per person	56,000	150,000
Number of city departments and agencies	40+	20+
City employees (full-time)	40,100	22,100
City expenditures	$7.0 billion	$3.1 billion[b]
Spending per person	$2,536	$1,476

a. U.S. Census Bureau, "Annual Estimates of the Population for Incorporated Places Over 100,000," www.census.gov/popest/cities/tables/SUB-EST2006-01.xls, accessed November 17, 2007.

b. U.S. Census Bureau, "The 2007 Statistical Abstract of the United States." Figures for city employees are from 2004, while city expenditures are from 2003.

Thinking Critically

- How do Houston and Chicago compare in the size of their city councils?
- Are these cities similar in the election systems for their councils?
- How do the cities compare in the size of city government in terms of number of departments and city employees?
- How do you think these differences and similarities affect each city's citizens and local politics?

i. Illinois Constitution (1970), art. 7, sec. 6.

that the city government may be less able to act quickly, since in essence, the city is governed by a committee.

According to a survey by the Texas Municipal League, the strong mayor-council system is more common than the weak mayor-council system in Texas. Only a handful of cities used the latter system, while nearly 40 percent of cities are strong mayor systems. The most common system, however, is the council-manager system, accounting for 58 percent of cities in Texas. [20]

A council-manager system occurs when voters in a city elect a city council that then hires a manager to run the day-to-day administrative functions of the city. The manager proposes new ordinances for the city council to consider and develops the city budget. The city manager also hires the heads of the city departments and oversees the city departments. The city manager is essentially a chief executive officer (CEO) for the city, similar to a business. Usually, the city manager is hired based upon professional qualifications, including prior experience in city government and academic background in public administration. Confusion arises when sometimes a council-manager system includes an elected mayor who serves merely as a spokesperson and representative for the city. In this situation, the mayor is merely a figurehead and holds no significant power beyond that of a member of the city council. In other cities, the role of mayor as spokesperson for the city is performed by a member of the city council. Council-manager systems, sometimes called the commission-manager systems, are most common among home rule cities in Texas.

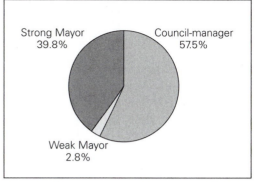

Figure 6.3 Forms of City Government in Texas

Source: Texas Municipal Association, "Annual Survey of Members" (Denton, Tex.: Texas Municipal Association, Inc., 2007).

The advantage of the council-manager system is the removal of day-to-day administration of the city from politics. Routine decisions can be made outside partisan politics or personality politics of an elected city council and mayor. The resulting management of city government is assumed to be more professional and efficient than other forms of government. Yet, because city managers are involved in formulating policies for the city and are charged with initiating the city budget, city managers are inevitably involved in politics.

City Elections

The Texas state government distinguishes between general law and home rule cities with respect to the type of election system that a city uses. Home rule cities are permitted to choose among four different election systems for elections to the city council. These cities may choose At-Large, At-Large by Place, Single-Member District, or Cumulative Voting systems. Some cities also employ a combination of Single-Member District and At-Large systems.

The Single-Member District system, discussed extensively in Chapter 3, occurs when the city is divided into several election districts. The number of districts equals the number of seats on the city council. Each district elects one member of the city council, so that if there are seven seats on the city council, then there are seven districts. Voters in each district cast a single vote for their most preferred candidate. Typically, in a Single-Member District Plurality system, the candidate with the most votes in the district wins the seat on the city council. Some cities require that the winning candidate win a majority of the votes, or 50 percent of the vote plus one additional vote.

In an At-Large system, candidates compete for seats on the city council without reference to specific districts or seats on the council. Instead, voters are allowed to vote for as many candidates as there are seats on the council. For example, if there are seven seats on the city council and eighteen candidates running for office, each voter will vote for up to seven of the eighteen candidates. The candidates with the most votes, up to the total number of seats on the city council, win election to the city council. If there are seven seats on the council, the seven candidates with the most votes of the eighteen are elected to the city council.

A variation of the At-Large system is the At-Large by Place system. In this system, candidates declare that they are running for particular positions or seats on the

Figure 6.4 Mayor-Council Form of City Government with a Weak Mayor

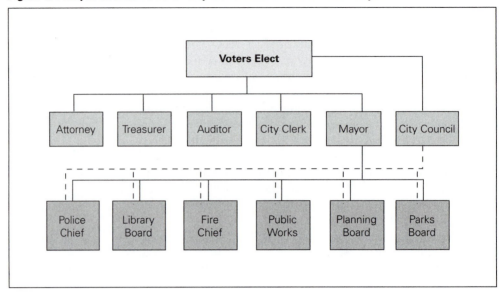

Figure 6.5 Mayor-Council Form of City Government with a Strong Mayor

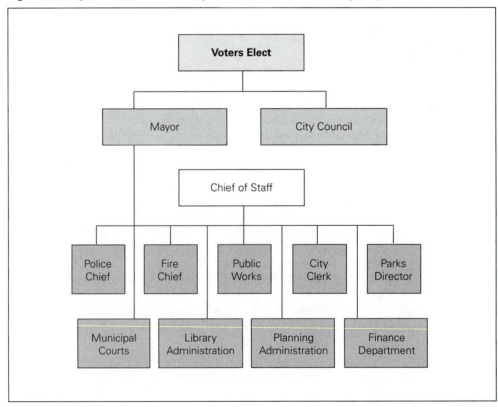

Figure 6.6 Council-Manager Form of City Government

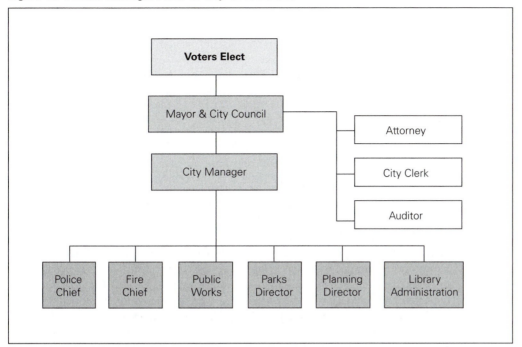

city council. The candidate for each seat that receives the most votes wins the seat. Thus, if there are seven seats on the city council, a candidate decides for which seat he or she is running. At the election, a voter has seven votes, and chooses one candidate running for each of the seven seats. The key difference between the At-Large and the At-Large by Place system is the fact that in the At-Large by Place system, candidates are grouped into seats reflected as different "places" on the ballot. In contrast to the Single-Member District system, the seats or places for which candidates compete lack any connection to specific geographic areas or neighborhoods in the city.

The final system is the Cumulative Voting system. Like an At-Large election, all candidates compete for seats on the city council without reference to specific seats or districts. Voters possess a number of votes equal to the number of seats on the council. However, voters may choose to give all of their votes for the same candidate or may spread their votes among several candidates. Thus, if the city council contains seven seats, a voter may give all seven votes to the same candidate or may give three votes to one candidate and four votes to another candidate. The voter may spread the votes among as many or few candidates as the voter desires, so long as the voter casts no more votes than there are seats on the council. The candidates with the most votes, up to the number of seats on the council, win election to the city council. Again, if there are seven seats, the top seven candidates win.

Advocates of the Single-Member District system suggest that the direct connection between a member of the city council and the voters is an advantage. Each voter knows that a specific member of the council represents the voter's area of the city. If a problem occurs, the voter knows exactly whom to approach. Thus, government should be more responsive to citizens. Another advantage appears to be that Single-Member District city elections provide more racial and ethnic diversity among the candidates that are elected to the city council. This prospect for minority representation is an outgrowth of the Voting Rights Act of 1965, discussed in Chapters 3 and 7. Since the 1970s, many cities in Texas have moved from At-Large systems to Single-Member District systems, including El Paso, Fort Worth, and San Antonio. However, district systems suffer from the same issues of partisan gerrymandering that occur for the state legislature and U.S. House of Representatives. In the late 1800s and early 1900s, the Single-Member District system became associated with city-based **machine politics,** in which political organizations headed by a local party boss controlled specific seats on the city council by using city jobs, government contracts, and other techniques. The party boss ran the city for personal power and gain.

The advantage of the At-Large system is the ability of the city council to act on behalf of the entire city and to consider ordinances and policies from the perspective of the whole city, not the particularistic views of an area or neighborhood in the city. Citywide campaigns may also produce better-qualified candidates with broad-based, citywide appeal. At-Large systems were also offered in the past as a method of solving the machine politics problem associated with Single-Member District systems. However, At-Large systems were used in Texas to suppress minority votes, especially those of African American and Hispanic voters. Very simply, the Caucasian majority historically voted exclusively for the white candidates and overwhelmed minority voters and candidates. Some cities have seen that members of the council consistently come from wealthy areas in town and less well-off and minority voters have found themselves governed by officials who see or understand little about where minority voters live.

Cumulative Voting advocates point to the ability of voters to express intensity of preference among the candidates running for the city council. By giving three or four votes to the same candidate, a voter indicates a greater preference for that candidate than if the voter gives only one or two votes for a candidate. Another advantage is the ability to enhance minority voting by concentrating votes. If minorities concentrate their votes among one or two candidates while whites disperse votes among several candidates, the likelihood of minority candidates winning is increased. Recent evidence from school board elections in Texas suggests that minority representation is enhanced under Cumulative Voting.[21] However, so few local governments use this system, whether or not minority representation is actually increased remains uncertain. Also, the issue of concentrating or dispersing votes creates a greater possibility of spoiled ballots.

Some cities attempt to keep the best of both worlds by creating a hybrid of Single-Member District systems and At-Large systems. Houston is an example of this hybrid approach. The fourteen-member city council in Houston consists of nine members elected from Single-Member Districts and five members elected at large. A candidate chooses either to run in the district in which he or she lives or may choose to conduct a citywide campaign for an at-large seat.

Election systems in city politics remain an area of change and transition in Texas. Cities, especially those with home rule, have city election systems to produce more representative outcomes, such as more minorities getting elected to the city council. The shift away from At-Large and At-Large by Place systems to Single-Member Districts is indicative of this change. In some cities, experiments with hybrid systems containing both At-Large and Single-Member District seats also demonstrate the adaptability of Texas cities. Whether cities will make additional changes to election systems based upon the recent success of Cumula-

The Galveston Hurricane

By the start of the twentieth century, Galveston had become the state's leading port and one of its largest cities. By 1900 about 37,000 people lived in Galveston and the city was often referred to as the "Queen City of the Gulf." The prosperous city enjoyed gas streetlights and theaters, funded by the commerce from one of the nation's leading ports and investment flowing through twenty-three stock companies. Until a few years earlier, it had the largest population in the state, briefly edging out San Antonio. Galveston reflected the optimism of the time. It had been hit by hurricanes in 1867 and 1875, but continued to rebuild and thrive despite dire warnings about future storms.

The storm that hit on September 8, 1900, proved to be more powerful than any before, producing 120-mile-per-hour winds and a 15-foot storm surge on an island whose highest point was only nine feet above sea level. The storm killed about 6,000 people and destroyed 3,600 buildings—more than half the buildings in the city.

After the devastation of the hurricane residents feared that Galveston would suffer the same fate as Indianola, which went from being the second largest port in the state to obscurity after being hit by storms in 1875 and 1886. In response to the crisis, the citizens created a new system of government designed to facilitate the rebuilding. Under the "Galveston Plan" the city was initially governed by five commissioners that were partly elected and partly appointed by the governor, although later the legislature modified the system requiring citywide election of all commissioners. Commissioners were chosen citywide to promote cooperation across parts of the city and minimize the corruption brought by localized "bosses," who might dispense jobs in return for political support. Collectively, the commission wrote the basic policies of the city as did other city councils. However, in addition to these general duties, each commissioner administered a specific portion of the city's functions, like safety or public works.

The city's recovery under the Galveston Plan was considered remarkable. The city constructed a seawall seven miles long and seventeen feet high. Thirty million cubic yards of sand were pumped from the Gulf of Mexico to raise the ground level of the city by seventeen feet and the houses that survived the storm were raised and placed on new higher foundations. These preparations would help the city survive hurricanes in 1909 and 1915.

The Galveston Plan would become one of the most widely adopted reforms of the Progressive era. Houston would adopt the system in 1905, and by 1917, about seventy-five Texas cities and 500 cities nationwide were using the commission form, which was embraced by reformers, including Presidents Theodore Roosevelt and Woodrow Wilson.

Ironically, the Galveston Plan can no longer be found in Galveston or anywhere in Texas. The city, like many others, has adopted the council-manager form. Economically, Galveston lost much of its luster as Houston succeeded in dredging a ship channel that would allow it to create a port that brought railroads and ships together in a safer inland location. While Galveston's charming historic residences and buildings remain a popular tourist destination, it is no longer a major commercial center. In addition, Galveston is once again facing a challenge as recent surveys have indicated that the island is gradually sinking, meaning that the city will once again have to band together to hold off the sea.

tive Voting in producing more diverse city councils and school boards remains uncertain.

Issues in City Government

Because cities are most often the level of government closest to the people, citizens face a number of issues that require attention from the city government. Most of the streets within a city's boundaries are maintained by the city government. Cities often provide a variety of services to residents, including libraries, museums, and parks. Cities offer public health and safety services like police protection, fire protection, restaurant inspections, and child-care facility inspections. Many cities also engage in policies to attract new businesses to the community for the purposes of economic development.

Zoning and planning policies are among the most controversial issues that cities confront. Given the average Texan's attitudes toward land, including a commitment to the idea that individuals retain maximum rights to use their property as they see fit, conflicts between individual property owners and the broader needs of the city are inevitable. This desire to allow individual owners to maintain absolute control over their property is a key reason why the city of Houston, despite being among the largest in the United States, has largely avoided the issue of zoning. In **zoning policy,** the city restricts what property owners may do with their property. Most often, zoning involves designating parts of a city for residential use, commercial use, and industrial use. Within these, residential use may vary from restricting use to only single-family housing, to limiting the number of houses built per acre, to permitting apartments and condominiums only in certain areas. Commercial zoning may vary from where large-scale shopping centers and shopping malls are built, to limits on the number of entrances or exits to the businesses' parking lots, to restricting the location of establishments that serve alcoholic beverages. Industrial zoning varies by identifying where large factories, industrial plants, and high technology firms may build their facilities. Other issues in zoning policy range from the size of signage that the business may erect to the regulations on how residential homes are built.

Zoning and planning often pits those seeking to develop property, build new shopping centers, and construct more houses against established neighborhoods. These battles are usually played out in local politics. Recently, the state legislature, often a target of campaign spending by major property development companies in Texas, attempted to enter into the issue of zoning. A bill introduced into the Texas Legislature in 2007 tried to restrict the ability of cities to designate certain parts of the city as historic areas. Often historic districts require that changes to buildings in the area be approved by a review board as conforming to the historic look of the area.[22] In some instances, local zoning laws in historic areas prevented developers from buying older homes, tearing down the homes, and building new ones.

Related to zoning and planning is the issue of annexation. When a city attempts to expand its borders, the expansion occurs for several reasons. The residents of the area that the city plans to expand to may want to be annexed. The residents may see benefits to being within the city limits including access to services the city provides. Perhaps the city has a good police department or excellent fire protection or maybe the city's water system is superior to that of the county.

Economic development may be spurred by annexation. So economic development is a reason for annexation. The city adds new territory to the city in order to

Zoning policy

policy in which the city restricts what individuals and entities may do with their property, usually by designating certain areas of the city for industrial, commercial, and residential uses.

entice new businesses to locate in the area. Similarly, cities seek to expand to prevent themselves from becoming hemmed in, surrounded by other cities. Once a city is surrounded on all sides by other cities, the city is trapped. Population growth and economic development occur only within the existing city's land capacity. Cities may also annex areas to increase revenue to the city. Newly annexed areas are new sources of property and sales taxes. Cities especially desire to annex areas that are economically and financially wealthier. In addition, the annexation of new areas allows cities to receive more money from the state and national government. Often funding formulas for grants are tied to the size of the city. Politically, larger cities receive more seats in the state legislature as well. State law permits cities to annex up to 10 percent of its land area each year. If a city annexes less than 10 percent, then the difference may be carried over to another year. However, a city may not annex more than 30 percent of its land area in any year.[23]

Beyond annexation, cities are interested in economic development for other reasons. As illustrated at the beginning of this chapter, attracting the right businesses into a community produces rewards of population and economic growth. These results may lead to the ability to attract even more businesses to the community. As businesses locate in a community, new jobs are generated. The new businesses and their employees pay taxes, giving city governments more reason to welcome newcomers. To attract businesses, cities often provide incentives like rebates on city sales tax and reductions on property tax rates. Cities often build infrastructure for businesses as well: access roads to the business, water lines to the property, and other essentials that the business may require. On the down side, more development means more traffic to channel, more children to educate, more garbage to collect, and more services of every kind.

City budgets are often a source of conflict. Budgets for the city are produced from a variety of sources. Cities levy property taxes just like counties do. Cities may collect franchise fees, for example, fees paid by cable television, electrical power, and natural gas providers operating within the city limits. Cities also raise revenue from hotel and motel occupancy taxes and from fines from traffic tickets issued by police. Cities may also raise money by levying sales taxes on purchases made within the city limits. To fund special projects, like acquiring land for parks, building city courthouses, or establishing a city museum, cities may issue **municipal bonds,** which are certificates of indebtedness. With a municipal bond, the city pledges to pay back a loan over time with interest. Regardless of the sources of revenue, the city must prioritize how to spend the revenue it raises. Because revenues are limited, emphasizing the expansion of the city park system or the building of new sidewalks inevitably means less money for other projects like public health initiatives or erecting new streetlights.

Cities are allowed some flexibility in the form of government and election system. Thus, cities are allowed a degree of transition and change to adapt to new circumstances that counties are not afforded in Texas. As Texas continues to experience high population growth rates in the early twenty-first century, the demands of citizens for more services, better services, and faster services requires flexibility. The concentration of Texas's population in metropolitan areas, including the development of massive suburbs and bedroom communities in former pine forests, farms, and ranches, is creating a profound challenge to city and county governments. Although this flexibility is found primarily among home rule cities, General Law Type B cities also possess a degree of freedom as well. Cities also win because they are able to collect revenue from a wider variety

Municipal bonds
certificates of indebtedness, in which there is a pledge to pay back the loan over time with interest, issued by cities to raise money for services and infrastructure.

of sources than counties. Cities can also exert influence on the zoning and use of land just outside their boundaries. Counties lack this ability. In fact, this ability infringes on the rights of property owners outside the city limits and on the ability of counties to regulate land use within unincorporated areas of the county near the city's boundaries. Larger cities, with home rule status, also win by becoming freer of state control over their plan of government, the content of city ordinances, and the process of changing these arrangements.

Other Forms of Local Government

n addition to counties and cities, Texas contains a variety of other forms of local government. Here we discuss two of these types of local governments. Public education, through the independent school district systems, is examined. We also look briefly at some special districts, such as community college districts.

Public Education as Local Government

An important function of state government is the education of its citizens. The state constitution makes specific references to education, including public schools, universities, and community colleges.[24] Texas, like other states, uses several forms of government to provide for the education of its citizens: universities, community colleges, state technical schools, elementary schools, middle schools, and high schools.

Among the local governments that are most familiar to Texans is the local school district. In most instances these are referred to as independent school districts (ISDs). Basic elementary and secondary education is the responsibility of the local board of education. These boards exist at the discretion of the Texas Legislature and operate under the authority of the Texas Constitution. The Texas Education Code, a statutory law passed by the legislature and signed by the governor, provides additional guidelines for K–12 education. Most students enrolled in K–12 education in Texas attend a school that falls under the jurisdiction of one of the more than 1,000 separate independent school districts. However, a handful of public schools continue to operate from the pre-ISD system. Under the Texas Education Code, pre-existing school systems like common schools, county schools, and municipal schools may still exist.[25] County and city governments, and the voters in these counties and cities, determine if the pre-existing schools continue to survive or if the schools are converted into an ISD.

The term "independent school district" refers to the fact that the local school district is governed separately from, or independent of, any other form of local government or state government control. Previously, county schools and municipal schools were funded and operated by county or city governments. Under the ISD system, each local school district is governed by a board of trustees who are elected by the voters living within the boundaries of the school district. The board is elected by At-Large, At-Large by Place, or Cumulative Voting systems.[26] Members of the board serve four-year terms in office, with staggered elections so that half the board is elected every two years. The board of trustees of an ISD consists of three to seven members. To be a trustee, a candidate must reside within the school district and must be registered to vote. County and municipal school districts may have an elected board of education or may have a board chosen by the county or city gov-

Texas versus Louisiana

In terms of local organization, Louisiana provides elementary and secondary education in a very different manner from Texas. There are only sixty-eight school districts in the entire state of Louisiana, compared with over 1,200 in Texas. One of the key differences in Louisiana is the use of parish-wide (county-wide) school districts. Of the sixty-eight Louisiana school districts, sixty-four are parish-wide. The exceptions to the parish-wide rule include a handful of cities that operate school systems independent of the surrounding parish system. These include the cities of Monroe, Bogalusa, Baker, Central, and Zachary.

The last three exceptions are all located within East Baton Rouge Parish. Prior to 2001, the parish contained a single, parish-wide school system. In Texas, statutory law and voter input created the independent school district (ISD) system. Louisiana's school districts are defined by the Louisiana Constitution. Creating new school districts in Louisiana first requires that both houses of the state legislature pass a bill to authorize the creation of the district through an amendment to the state constitution. Then, a majority of voters must approve the amendment to the state constitution in a statewide referendum.

The three new districts in East Baton Rouge Parish are rooted in disputes over the problems of racial segregation and integration in the East Baton Rouge Parish school system. Beginning in 1981, students throughout the parish were bussed to create a racial balance of whites and African Americans in individual schools. Following a decade of trying, voters across the state of Louisiana in 1995 approved the separation of schools in the City of Baker from the parish school system. Baker schools mirrored the racial makeup of the parishwide school system. The City of Zachary then wanted to leave the parish school system in part because the removal of Baker schools left Zachary largely isolated from the rest of the school system. Voters statewide amended the Louisiana Constitution to create a separate school system in Zachary in 1999.

The final exception has proven to be the most unusual. Residents of the Central community, in the northeast part of the parish, worked with members of the state legislature from the area to create a separate school system. However, efforts were blocked in the state legislature for two reasons. All previous exceptions to the parish-wide school system rule were actual cities or towns. Central was an unorganized community. Also, the proposed boundaries of the Central Community School District were drawn so that over 85 percent of the students were white, affecting the racial balance of the remaining East Baton Rouge school system. In the end, residents of Central first created an incorporated city and then petitioned the state legislature to create a new school district. In 2006, voters in Louisiana overwhelmingly voted to allow Central to create a school system.

Thinking Critically

- What advantages do you think exist with the county-wide school system approach used in Louisiana?
- What advantages do you think exist with the ISD system of Texas?
- Does the creation of the Central Community School District in Louisiana raise questions about how district lines were drawn in Texas?

ernment. The boundaries of an ISD may be contained within a county, may include parts of two or more counties, and may include a city or parts of a city.

The ISD system is not unique in the United States, although the term to describe the system is. Several states like Arkansas have school districts that are independent of local governments. In Arkansas, school district lines may cross county lines or may be contained within a single county. District lines may also be limited to a single city or include several cities. Even in Louisiana where, with a handful of exceptions, parish-wide (county-wide) school systems exist, local school boards are elected separately from parish and city governments. The parish school boards make decisions independent of the parish government.

The board of trustees of an ISD oversees the schools of the district by authorizing construction of schools, selling bonds to finance projects, collecting property taxes to fund operations, and providing guidelines for schools. These guidelines include such subjects as hiring of teachers and administrators, curriculum decisions, discipline policies, and budget decisions.[27] In effect, the board of trustees runs the schools in the district.

Although the ISD system attempts to give citizens local control over their schools, outside control by the State of Texas exists in several areas. The state uses its power over the creation, existence, and support of school districts to force statewide policies. These policies include the classes that students must take, the textbook that students use, and the structure of district budget.[28] To this end, the Texas Constitution provides for a State Board of Education.[29] The State Board of Education consists of fifteen members elected from Single-Member Districts across the state. The structure, function, and policy implications of the State Board of Education are discussed in Chapter 9.

Special Districts

Special districts are created when the residents within the proposed boundary of the district petition to create the district. Examples of special districts are airport authorities, library districts, municipal utility districts, and community college districts. The process is similar to the process of creating a city. In contrast to a city or county, a special district provides a single service or a limited number of services to the residents of the district. However, the process is a bit more complicated, depending on the type of district. Hospital districts are created by first passing an amendment to the Texas Constitution, then by the approval of voters in the proposed district. Community college districts are first authorized by the Texas Legislature. The Texas Commission on Environmental Quality approves the creation of Municipal Utility Districts. Special districts have even been created to build and to manage sports stadiums for professional sports teams in Texas.

Normally, special districts are created when a county or city government is unable or unwilling to provide a service itself or if the existing local government prefers to allow a special district to provide the service. Because counties face limits on the amount of property tax they levy, special districts allow counties to overcome this limit by essentially "farming out" new services to a special district. In some instances, residents of a county may choose to join a special district that exists in another county. Special districts are funded primarily by property taxes that residents agree to pay to provide for the services. If the district crosses county lines, then arrangements are made for the tax assessors in each of the counties to collect the taxes and transfer funds to the district. Thus, special districts often can overcome the problems of coordinating services across multiple cities and counties. This approach is very useful in major metropolitan areas like the Dallas-Fort Worth Metroplex for example. Some special districts are authorized by voters to issue municipal bonds, while others charge user fees for the services.

Special districts are governed by a board, usually five members. The board is often elected by voters in the district. In some instances, the board is appointed, usually by the mayors, city councils, and commissioners courts operating within the district. The board oversees the regular operation of the special district, hires necessary staff and professionals, and makes policies regarding the provision of services. For example, the board of trustees of a community college hires the chan-

Texas versus Iraq

Austin, the capital of Texas, is like most major cities in the United States. The city contains an integrated 911 system to speed responses of city police, fire, and emergency medical services when an accident or disaster occurs. At times, a coordinated reaction by all three groups is needed. It is common to see police cars, fire trucks, and ambulances arrive on the scene.

As part of the transition from the authoritarian system of Saddam Hussein to a democratic system, the U.S. government has involved Iraqi local governments in a series of conferences and training programs to equip the local government. In October of 2007, representatives from the Austin police, fire, and emergency services department met with officials from the Baghdad city government. Currently, public service officials in Baghdad and throughout Iraq do not work jointly to coordinate responses to a situation. At the request of the U.S. Defense Department, the Austin delegation began the process of introducing the city of Baghdad to an integrated response to disasters and accidents. The goal is to create the first 911 emergency system in Iraq.

A new Department of Public Safety will be organized in Baghdad to assist in this effort. According to George Bratmore of the Austin Fire Department, "The way the Iraqi public services are run today can't be changed overnight. This is going to take time, and it's up to the Iraqi government to recognize whether or not this kind of system will work for them."[i]

Thinking Critically

- Why does Baghdad need assistance from Austin in setting up 911 services?
- Do you think that Baghdad's situation is unique to Iraq?
- Do you think rivalries exist between agencies of city government in the United States?

i. Jason Dangel, "Austin Police, Fire Officials Help Iraqis Aim for Better Public Services," *Multi-National Force–Iraq,* October 24, 2007, www.mnf-iraq.com/index2.php, accessed October 29, 2007.

---

cellor or president of the college. The board decides, within state guidelines, the degrees that will be offered and the coursework that is required. The board also establishes pay scales for faculty and staff, qualifications to be on faculty, and rates of tuition and fees for students. Currently, fifty separate college districts exist in Texas. Community colleges educate over 550,000 Texans.

The advantage of a special district is the ability to provide services that ordinarily might not be provided. In addition, the services may be provided to promote economic development. In the case of **municipal utility districts,** which provide water, sewer, and similar services to individuals and businesses outside city limits, these services may entice new businesses to relocate to the area or developers to construct new homes. Again, in some instances, the special district may be able to overcome disputes between cities or counties over the provision of services. However, like other local government elections, special election district elections are low turnout elections, thus the decisions by voters may only reflect the wishes of the few. Also, the proliferation of special districts in an area creates confusion among residents, who may not know who is responsible for what. Special districts also encourage conflict among local governments as multiple districts compete for property tax resources and pursue contradictory goals.

Municipal utility districts
special districts that provide water, sewer, and similar services to individuals and businesses outside city limits.

Winners and Losers

s we've seen in previous chapters, choices about the structure of government, the distribution of powers within government and between levels of government, and how that government is selected, directly impacts the citizens. In Texas, various levels of local government provide different services and create additional tax burdens on its citizens. To the extent that local government in Texas creates flexibility, citizens win. To the extent that each level of local government creates additional obscure taxes, citizens lose.

The winners in education and special district local governments are often the residents of the districts. In the case of the ISDs, residents benefit by having local school boards that govern smaller areas than might otherwise occur under a countywide system. School boards should be more responsive to voters and parents, especially in smaller enrollment school districts. Schools are also more likely to be community-based. This arrangement reinforces the small-town and rural bias common in Texas political history. Regarding the special districts, residents are winners if they are willing to create the district and are willing to see their property taxes rise to cover the additional services that the special district provides. In addition, residents within a city or in part of a county may elect to create the district to provide selected services to a particular area even if the majority of residents in the entire city or county do not want the services. Thus, the creation of special districts gives Texans the freedom to choose whether to accept certain services and the corresponding taxes or not. However, this buffet style approach produces significant variation in the services that residents receive and results in divergent rates of property taxes within cities and counties. In fact, the heavy use of property taxes to fund all of these services may depress property values in some parts of the state.

On the other hand, the funding of local government through a variety of property taxes and fees often creates a significant and obscure tax burden on citizens throughout the state. The reliance on property taxes, discussed here and returned to in Chapter 9, overburdens citizens who live in larger metropolitan areas, where the property values are significantly higher than in rural Texas. The property tax is a distinct burden on retirees, whose spending and income often decrease (triggering a decrease in the associated taxes) at the same time their property value continues to increase. As noted above, the property tax burden is also not evenly shared in local government, as individuals who do not own property continue to utilize basic services such as emergency care or education. In addition, as local governments have faced additional strains on their resources, the current trend toward toll roads creates an additional tax on citizens. To the extent that the tax burden for Texans is complex, in which citizens pay city sales and property taxes, county property taxes, special district property taxes, as well as indirectly paying the interest on municipal bonds, government ends up becoming unnecessarily complex and perhaps costly.

Conclusion

ocal government in Texas is a diverse set of governments: ultimately, all local governments are dominated by the state government, which determines the powers of local governments and the organizational structure of local governments. Local government in the form of cities, counties, and special districts exist to aid the state of Texas in carrying out public policies like transportation, education, and public health. Citizens also create local governments, with the permission of the state, to provide specific services that the citizens want. Texas provides little flexibility to its local governments, although cities are afforded more freedom under home rule provisions than other forms of local government. However, residents of cities must still choose to grant their city home rule status. In the end, Texans are confronted with a set of overlapping jurisdictions providing a variety of public services and overseeing a plethora of public policies.

Key Terms

administrative federalism
annexation
auditor
city charter
civil service system
commissioners court
constables
contract outsourcing
county attorney
county civil service commission
county clerk
Dillon's Rule
fiscal federalism
general law city
home rule city
justices of the peace
machine politics
merit system
municipal bonds
municipal utility district
ordinance
partisan elections
privatization
sheriff
spoils systems
tax assessor
zoning policy

Explore this subject further at http://college.cqpress.com/lonestarpolitics, where you'll find chapter summaries, practice quizzes, key word flash cards, and additional suggested resources.

Dressed to display the legendary pride of Texas and its cowboy legacy, the Texas delegation to the Republican National Convention participated in the re-nomination of native son George W. Bush for U.S. President. These delegates were selected to attend the convention as part of the indirect primary elections used in Texas for presidential primaries.

CHAPTER 7

Elections: Texas Style

In 2006, Texans experienced a larger-than-life, chapter-for-the-history-books election for governor. The incumbent governor, Rick Perry, a Republican, easily won the Republican primary. In an increasingly Republican state, in which all major executive offices were held by Republicans and in which Republicans were expected to maintain control over both houses of the state legislature, Perry might be expected to coast to victory. However, Perry faced some major challenges and some minor challenges. Perry's proposals to develop the Trans-Texas Corridor, a superhighway and rail system running from the Mexico border in the south to the Oklahoma border in the north, aroused anger from several groups. Farmers and ranchers objected to the amount of land being acquired for the project. Opposition also came from landowner rights advocates who were angered about the potential taking of property by the government, especially when it was to be given to foreign firms that would profit from managing the Trans-Texas Corridor. A statewide poll conducted by the *Dallas Morning News* just a month before the election found that only 48 percent of likely voters approved of the governor's performance while 42 percent disapproved.[1] This same poll indicated that only 38 percent of likely voters intended to vote for the governor.

The Democratic Party primary gave the party's nomination to Christopher Bell, a former member of the Houston City Council and the U.S. House of Representatives. Bell lacked statewide exposure and two-thirds of Texans indicated that they did not know enough about Bell to have an opinion about him. Only 15 percent of likely voters said they planned to vote for Bell a month before the election.

While the Perry campaign might have rejoiced that the candidate from the opposition party seemed to be in worse shape than the governor, two "wild cards" appeared in the deck. Carole Strayhorn, the two-term comptroller of Public Accounts, a statewide elected office, entered the race for governor. A Republican, Strayhorn decided to avoid facing Perry in the Republican primary and instead declared herself an independent candidate. Her campaign styled her "One Tough Grandma," to convince voters that her term as comptroller gave her credentials as a fiscal conservative who had stood up to loose spending by the legislature and governor. Strayhorn targeted her campaign at disaffected Republican and independent voters, and her strong stand against the Trans-Texas Corridor encouraged support from farmers and ranchers in the state.

The most unusual candidate in the 2006 race was author, humorist, and self-styled "Jewish Cowboy" Richard S. "Kinky" Friedman. While Strayhorn's credentials as an "independent" were obviously suspect, Friedman was clearly an independent who bashed both major political parties. His straightforward, everyday-language approach appealed to many Texans. His style also attracted those alienated from traditional politics, in part by presenting himself as different from "politics as usual." Friedman himself stated, "Musicians can run this state better than politicians. We won't get a lot done in the mornings, but we'll work late and be honest."[2] His cowboy hat and swirls of cigar smoke, present even during the televised governor's debate, complemented his style of speech and enhanced his image as a new, different alternative.

The presence of two independent candidates, as well as a relatively unknown Democratic candidate, aided Governor Perry's reelection. Perry won with only 39.0 percent of the vote. Bell finished second with 29.8 percent of the vote, with Strayhorn (18.1 percent) and Friedman (12.4 percent) coming in much further behind. In comparison, Perry had won the governor's race in 2002 with 51.8 percent of the vote, and the opponent Perry defeated in 2002 won more votes than Perry did in 2006.

In this chapter, we explore the nature of elections in Texas. We begin by considering the issue of who is eligible to vote in Texas. The struggle for the right to vote among African Americans, Hispanics, and women is examined. Then, we look at the issue of ballot access. A discussion of the various types of elections follows, including general elections and primaries. Next, we discuss voter turnout in Texas elections. We review electoral competition between the major parties with a focus on the changes in competition over the past few decades. Finally, the chapter concludes with a consideration of the campaign finance system.

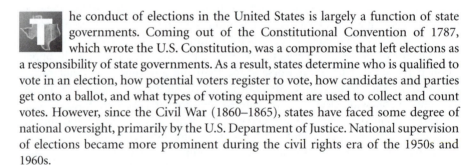

As you read the chapter, think about the following questions:

★ What obstacles to voting were faced by groups in Texas?
★ To what extent is low voter turnout impeding democracy?
★ How might Texas make participation in voting more likely today?
★ Should Texas adopt stricter campaign finance restrictions?

Background to Elections in Texas

The conduct of elections in the United States is largely a function of state governments. Coming out of the Constitutional Convention of 1787, which wrote the U.S. Constitution, was a compromise that left elections as a responsibility of state governments. As a result, states determine who is qualified to vote in an election, how potential voters register to vote, how candidates and parties get onto a ballot, and what types of voting equipment are used to collect and count votes. However, since the Civil War (1860–1865), states have faced some degree of national oversight, primarily by the U.S. Department of Justice. National supervision of elections became more prominent during the civil rights era of the 1950s and 1960s.

Voting Qualifications

Access to the voting booth is a vital issue in a democracy. The rules of who may vote, how they vote, and under what conditions they vote significantly impact the legitimacy of the government and its responsiveness to the people. Thus, voting rights and qualifications are essential to determining who gets what, when, and how. For example, if voting rights are denied to a group of people based upon their race, candidates running for office might ignore the issues and concerns of people of that race. Prior to the civil rights era of the 1950s and 1960s, the state of Texas through a variety of laws and practices attempted to deny African Americans the right to vote. Candidates often ignored issues of concern to African Americans, like the condition of their schools and crime in their neighborhoods. As a result, government policy made upgrading schools in white communities or addressing crime problems in white areas the priority.

Because state governments in the United States are responsible for voter registration, there are fifty different sets of voter registration processes, procedures, and qualifications. For example, North Dakota lacks any formal voter registration process. On Election Day, voters simply show a driver's license or state identification card indicating that he or she lives in the state and community in order to vote. Minnesota allows same-day voter registration, meaning that a person may register to vote and vote in the election on the same day.

Voter registration in Texas is a bit more complicated. To register to vote, a person must be a citizen of the United States, have attained at least eighteen years of age, and must have resided in Texas for at least thirty days. To vote in a county or other local government election, the thirty-day residency requirement applies, even if a voter is already a resident of Texas. So, a voter who moves from San Antonio to Amarillo must live in Amarillo at least thirty days before voting in an Amarillo city election. If a voter owns property in several locations within Texas, the voter chooses which address serves as his or her primary residence for the purpose of voting.[3]

To register to vote, a voter registration form must be completed and submitted to the county elections office. The form is available from county elections offices or online from the Texas Secretary of State. Since 1993, residents of Texas may register to vote when applying for a driver's license or when renewing a license. This development occurred when the U.S. Congress passed the National Voter Registration Act, sometimes called the **Motor Voter Act.** As an election nears, local civic organizations like the League of Women Voters or a university's student government association often hold voter registration drives to get more people registered to vote. In these situations, those wanting to register to vote fill out the form and return it by mail, or the civic organization returns all of the cards to the county elections office. Some public libraries and schools have voter registration forms available. Regardless of how a person registers to vote, the form must be submitted to the county elections office no later than thirty days before an election.

Since 1972, Texas has maintained a permanent list of voters. The maintenance of the voter registration list is the responsibility of county governments. In most of Texas's counties, the responsibility falls to the county clerk, a county official who also maintains birth records and other vital statistics. In fact, 186 counties rely on this method. Seven counties make elections a responsibility of the county tax assessor. The remaining 61 counties have a separate office for elections. Although larger population counties tend to have separate elections offices, this is not always true.

Texas maintains two other qualifications. Individuals judged to be mentally incompetent are ineligible to vote. Interestingly, the Texas Election Code seems to leave the issue of determining mental competence solely in the hands of the clerk of the court in each county. Likewise convicted felons over the age of eighteen are stripped of the right to vote until they have completed their sentence, including parole or probation.[4] This reflects the traditionalistic politi-

Motor Voter Act
the National Voter Registration Act that allows citizens to register to vote when applying for or renewing their driver's license.

cal culture of Texas, which emphasizes the need to punish criminals and the idea that the rights of citizenship are not automatic.

Texas is one of thirteen states to require registration at least thirty days before an election. Only Georgia and Nevada are more restrictive, at thirty-five days. On the other hand, several states allow registration on Election Day or on the day before the election, including Minnesota, New Hampshire, and Wyoming. North Dakota has no registration process.

Voting Rights in Texas

Suffrage
the legal right to vote.

With respect to the right to vote in Texas elections, the Republic of Texas Constitution allowed whites and Hispanic males to vote in elections. However, Native Americans and African Americans were denied **suffrage,** the legal right to vote. Upon joining the United States, the Texas Constitution of 1845 continued to deny access to voting to both groups. As mentioned above, the U.S. Civil War resulted in an increased role for the national government in state election processes. The process of expanding the role of the national government continued into the twentieth century.

Legal Barriers to Voting in Post–Reconstruction Texas

After the U.S. Civil War, the U.S. Constitution was amended to include the Thirteenth, Fourteenth, and Fifteenth Amendments. The Fifteenth Amendment specifically requires that state governments ensure the right to vote regardless of race or prior status as a slave. With the end of military occupation of the southern states and the end of Reconstruction in 1876, states like Texas officially maintained the right of African Americans to vote, while imposing a series of barriers to former slaves actually voting. For example, Texas, like other southern states, used the **grandfather clause** to prohibit African Americans from voting while allowing whites in a similar situation to vote. Essentially, the grandfather clause restricted the right to vote to those whose grandfathers had the right to vote. Given that most African Americans in Texas at the time had been slaves, the right to vote for African Americans was greatly restricted. Another technique to discourage African Americans from exercising their right to vote was the **literacy test,** a test of the prospective voter's ability to read and to understand aspects of American government. When registering to vote, the potential voter had to answer a series of questions, to read one or more paragraphs, and to explain the material. The poor state of public education within African American communities throughout the South from the end of Reconstruction into the 1950s ensured that many African Americans were denied the right to vote. In some communities, African Americans were given different, harder tests than whites. In Texas, the use of the literacy test was rare. Texas favored other techniques to exclude African Americans.

Another legal barrier instituted to prevent African Americans from voting was the **poll tax,** an annual tax paid before one was allowed to vote. In 1902, an amendment to the Texas Constitution allowed poll taxes to be used by the state, county, and local governments in Texas.[5] The state imposed a rate of $1.50 per voter annually, while counties could impose a tax of up to $0.25 on each voter. Since most African Americans in Texas earned relatively lower incomes compared to whites, African Americans faced the choice between purchasing basic necessities versus participating in politics.

Grandfather clause
the granting of voting rights only to those citizens whose grandfathers had the right to vote; used to bar African Americans from voting in the South after the end of Reconstruction.

Literacy test
a test of a prospective voter's ability to read and understand aspects of American government; used to bar African Americans from voting in many parts of the post–Reconstruction South, but not widely used in Texas.

Poll tax
an annual tax paid before one was allowed to vote; allowed by a 1902 amendment to the Texas Constitution and used to legally bar African Americans from voting.

The poll tax was used to deny the right to vote to many African Americans in Texas. This actual poll tax receipt from Navarro County in 1943 shows that the poll tax had been paid in full, thereby allowing the individual to vote in upcoming elections.

The poll tax prevented many poor whites from voting as well. In addition, disenfranchising poor, rural white voters served another purpose—diluting the strength of the Populist Party. The Democratic Party feared the growing challenge of the Populist Party, which was based in farmer and labor movements throughout the United States and directly challenged wealthy interests in Texas politics. Populists attempted to focus on the economic plight of poor, small- and medium-sized family farms and to shift the race-based politics of the Civil War, Reconstruction, and Post–Reconstruction eras to a class-based politics of the lower and middle classes versus the upper classes. Thus, the poll tax served several purposes for the Democratic Party: African Americans were eliminated from voting, potential Populist voters were similarly disenfranchised, and, consistent with Texas's traditional political culture, only the "better" elements of society were given the right to rule. As a result, the Democratic Party, by staving off a potential challenging party, was able to remain the majority party for decades. Racial appeals by traditional Democrats continued into the 1950s and 1960s. For example, Governor Shivers complained of "creeping socialism" by the national Democratic Party leadership and the need for "moral regeneration" or a "spiritual awakening" to prevent integration of the races.[6]

A final technique for disenfranchising African American voters in southern states was the **white primary.** Essentially, participation in primary elections to nominate candidates for office was restricted to members of the party only, and membership in the party was limited to white voters. Because the primary election determined the Democratic Party nominee for the general election and because the primary was restricted to white voters, the "white primary" guaranteed that parties and candidates responded only to issues of concern in the white population. Texas was unusual in that the white primary as a practice occurred as a result of state law. All other states implementing the white primary did so as a matter of party rules or custom rather than law.[7]

White primary
the attempt by the Democratic Party in Texas to limit the voting in party primaries only to party members.

Eliminating Barriers to Voting for African Americans

Removing these barriers gave the national government greater control over state voter registration processes, thereby taking power away from the state governments. For example, the grandfather clause was eliminated when the U.S. Supreme Court issued its ruling in *Guinn v. United States* (1919). In this case, the U.S. Supreme Court

Equal Protection Clause

this clause of the Fourteenth
Amendment to the U.S. Constitution
requires that state laws and state
constitutions treat all citizens the same.

Voting Rights Act of 1965 (VRA)

a federal statute that eliminated
literacy tests as a qualification to vote,
greatly increasing African Americans'
access to the ballot box.

declared that the grandfather clause clearly violated the Fifteenth Amendment of the U.S. Constitution. In doing so, the U.S. Supreme Court relied on the **Equal Protection Clause** of the Fourteenth Amendment to the U.S. Constitution. The Equal Protection Clause requires that state laws and state constitutions treat all citizens the same. Because the grandfather clause treated African Americans, whose grandfathers clearly did not have the right to vote, differently from whites, the grandfather clause violated the idea that the law treat all citizens the same.[8]

Another attempt to remove the barriers to voting came in 1965. The U.S. Congress passed the **Voting Rights Act of 1965 (VRA),** which among other things, eliminated the literacy test as a qualification to vote among those with at least a sixth-grade education. The removal of the literacy test greatly increased African Americans' access to the ballot box. This provision applied to all elections conducted by the states.

Eliminating the poll tax proved to be more complicated. The poll tax in national elections was eliminated by the Twenty-fourth Amendment to the U.S. Constitution in 1964. However, states assumed that state and local elections, which clearly did not involve the national government, remained solely the domain of state law. Poll taxes continued for state and local elections for another year. In *Harper v. Virginia Board of Elections* (1966) the U.S. Supreme Court struck down the poll tax in Virginia state and local elections as a violation of the Equal Protection Clause of the Fourteenth Amendment to the U.S. Constitution.[9]

Challenging the white primary also proved difficult, especially in Texas. In the Texas-based case *Nixon v. Herndon* (1924),[10] the U.S. Supreme Court invalidated the white primary when required or sanctioned by state law. In reaction, the Texas Democratic Party, with the support of Texas's key political leaders, declared itself a "private organization." Ultimately, in *Smith v. Allwright* (1944),[11] the U.S. Supreme Court threw out the white primary by declaring that the vital function of nominating candidates for office meant that political parties were public organizations. Not accepting of this decision, the Democratic Party in Fort Bend County attempted a "Jaybird" pre-primary in which only whites cast informal votes to consolidate support behind a single candidate, allowing all white voters to back that candidate in the official primary. Seeing through this attempt at coordination and control, the U.S. Supreme Court outlawed the practice in *Terry v. Adams* (1953).[12] One estimate suggests that removing the barriers to voting had the immediate impact of allowing as many as 200,000 African Americans in Texas to vote.[13]

Hispanics and Voting Rights

The struggle for voting rights among Hispanics presents a more complex story. In the days of the Texas Republic and early statehood, some discrimination against Hispanics existed, but the extent to which barriers to voting were enacted seemed to be less than those faced by African Americans.[14] For example, the literacy test used widely throughout the South did not exist in Texas. Hispanics who tried to register did not have to interpret the state constitution or answer questions about the federal government. Also, Hispanics were often allowed to vote in the white primary and formed an important base of support for the Democratic Party in southern parts of Texas, but some scholars assert that the white primary did prohibit Hispanic voters.[15] Along the Mexican border, many local elected officials were Hispanic,[16] so at the local level at least, the primary system did not prohibit Hispanic candidates from getting elected. In contrast, the poll tax disenfranchised many Hispanics, as well as poor whites and African Americans.[17] Therefore, the removal of the poll tax in federal and state elections provided an opportunity for more Hispanics to register to vote.

Although the VRA originally applied only to attempts to disenfranchise African American voters, the renewal of the act in 1975 led to the extension of the VRA to Hispanic voters. After 1975, the VRA applied to states or counties with a history of low levels of voting, where elections were conducted only in English, and more than 5 percent of the voting-age population was part of a language minority.[18] As a result, states like Texas and California were required to provide bilingual ballots to allow Hispanic voters who are citizens to participate in elections. This provision has also been applied to Native Americans in Alaska, California, Oklahoma, New Mexico, and South Dakota. Asian Americans also are covered by this provision in selected counties across the United States.

The key source of disenfranchisement among Hispanics appears to have been economic harassment. Whites boycotted Hispanic businesses, linked bank loans to support for white candidates in the election, and fired Hispanics who engaged in political campaigns. In addressing discrimination against Hispanics voting in Bexar County, the Supreme Court identified the sources of discrimination to be primarily economic, educational, and linguistic rather than legal barriers.[19] Although significant in Bexar County, the use of economic and other tools to disenfranchise Hispanics varied by county.[20] Thus, rather than the formal and legal barriers that African Americans faced, the primary barriers to voting for Hispanics were intimidation tactics.

Voting Rights for Women and Younger Voters

Texas proved slightly more progressive on the extension of voting rights to women. As early as 1915, the Texas legislature considered women's suffrage, and by 1918 allowed women, or at least white women, to vote in primary elections, two years before the Nineteenth Amendment to the U.S. Constitution gave women the right to vote in federal elections as well. Texas also proved somewhat forward-thinking by being the first state in the "Old South" to ratify the Nineteenth Amendment. A further extension of voting rights concerned the voting rights of young adults. The right to vote was associated with being an adult, historically defined as having attained the age of twenty-one. In 1971 the Twenty-sixth Amendment to the U.S. Constitution lowered the minimum voting age to eighteen in federal elections. States followed quickly to lower the minimum voting age to eighteen in state and local elections. This extension of voting rights to those between age eighteen and twenty-one occurred in part because many youth of this era were fighting for their country in the Vietnam War but were unable to vote in national or state elections. The discrepancy between being able to die for one's country and not being able to participate in the selection of one's political leaders seemed somehow un-American. An unusual quirk of the Texas Constitution is that with the exceptions of treason, felony, or disturbing the peace, voters are exempt from arrest while going to and returning from voting.[21]

The history of voting rights in Texas appears to be periodic attempts to restrict the right to vote to only the "right" kinds of voters: white and, at times, Hispanic voters with better education and more money. The Democratic Party of the post–Reconstruction era sought to maintain this power base by writing the "rules of the game" to exclude African Americans and to prevent the state government from responding to the demands of all citizens. As a result, state politics and policy reflected primarily the wishes of those able to vote, not all of the citizens of Texas. Only after the civil rights era of the 1950s and 1960s did significant numbers of poorer whites and African Americans attain access to the ballot box. More recently, attempts to include Hispanics more completely as voters, candidates, and elected officials in Texas politics have occurred.

The expansion of voting rights is a clear example of transition in Texas elections. The right to vote has grown to encompass more fully both Hispanic and African American voters. However, the white establishment continued to attempt to prevent both disenfranchised groups from voting to maintain the tradition of white dominance in Texas politics. It was largely through the actions of the federal government that Texas was forced to change election rules and practices to be more inclusive. In addition, the right to vote expanded to include women and young adults.

Getting on the Ballot in Texas

An important element of elections is whose name appears on the ballot. Everyone running for office in the state of Texas must be a resident of Texas and of the relevant election district. A candidate must also be registered to vote. Beyond these requirements, getting on the ballot as a candidate is a result of one of two processes: either nomination by a political party or qualifying as an independent candidate.

For candidates running with a party nomination, the candidate gets on the ballot either by competing in and winning a primary election or being selected from a party convention. For political parties with 20 percent or more of the vote in the last governor's election, the party must hold primary elections. To qualify for the primary election, a candidate pays a filing fee. The filing fee varies from $5,000 for a candidate for U.S. senator to $300 for candidates for the state board of education. In lieu of paying the filing fee, candidates may qualify for a party primary by filing a petition with a set number of signatures from registered voters, varying from 5,000 to 2 percent of the vote in the governor's election in the state, county, or election district. If a party receives 5 percent or more of the vote, but less than 20 percent, the party may use a primary election or nominating convention to place candidates on the general election ballot. However, provisions regarding the filing fee remain in place. Parties with less than 5 percent of the vote in the most recent governor's election must first register with the Secretary of State's office by collecting signatures of registered voters who support the party. A party must secure enough signatures to equal 1 percent of the total votes for all candidates for governor at the last election. For 2008, parties will need 43,992 signatures.

Independent candidate

a candidate running for office without a political party affiliation.

An **independent candidate,** a candidate running for office without a political party affiliation or nomination, must submit an application for a place on the general election ballot. In addition, the candidate must gather signatures of registered voters willing to sign a petition that the candidate's name should appear on the ballot. The number of signatures needed varies from 1 percent to 5 percent of the total votes for all candidates for governor at the last election. If the independent candidate is running for a countywide office, the candidate needs to collect 1 percent to 5 percent of the total votes for governor in that county. Because they lack party affiliation, independent candidates do not compete in primary elections in Texas. In fact, independent candidates cannot declare their intention to run for office until after the primary elections are over and cannot have voters who participated in the primary elections sign the petition form to get on the ballot. Write-in candidates qualify by either paying a filing fee or completing a nomination petition like independent can-

Landslide Lyndon

Today, visitors to the Lyndon B. Johnson Presidential Museum in Austin can watch a mechanical figure of the former president lean on a split-rail fence and spin yarns about Texas. Johnson occupies a unique position in that he has both starred in and recounted many Texas legends.

The career of Lyndon Baines Johnson saw his rise from teacher in a poor school in Pearsall, Texas, to president of the United States. When "Pappy" O'Daniel, in what one newspaper called the "most constructive act" of his career, retired from the U.S. Senate, the battle to succeed O'Daniel pitted Johnson against former governor Coke Robert Stevenson. Stevenson was considered unbeatable by some but Johnson won the endorsement of many of the state's newspapers and "Ma" Ferguson, who remembered that Johnson attended the funeral of her husband while Stevenson skipped the service. Johnson concentrated on the large urban areas and zipped around the state by campaigning with a helicopter while Stevenson was content to drive around in an old Plymouth.

Stevenson finished first in the primary, easily besting Johnson by a vote of 477,077 to 405,617. However, lacking the majority needed to win the nomination, the two candidates faced off in a runoff election. Official returns from the runoff took three days to compile, before the Texas Election Board announced that Stevenson had won by 362 votes. However, "late returns" were still coming in, including what would become the legendary Box 13 from Alice, Texas, which belatedly revealed 203 uncounted ballots, 202 of them for Johnson. Upon further examination, the poll lists showed that Box 13's voters had signed in and voted in alphabetical order and in identical hand-

writing. Amended returns gave Johnson an 87-vote margin statewide and the nickname of "Landslide Lyndon."

The State Democratic Executive Committee had the final word on the primary returns and voted 29 to 28 to certify the Johnson victory. While some of Johnson's critics have pointed to evidence of voter fraud in Alice, others point out that there was evidence of similar vote fraud on behalf of Stevenson in East Texas. As T. R. Fehrenbach concluded in his classic history of Texas, "Johnson's men had not defrauded Stevenson, but successfully outfrauded him." [i]

While Johnson's leadership of the nation as it tackled landmark civil rights legislation including the Civil Rights Act of 1964 and the Voting Rights Act of 1965 have given him a well-deserved place in history, it's worth remembering that Johnson, like many other leaders of his time, came to power under the wing of powerful party bosses and sometimes won high office by taking the low road.

i. T. R. Fehrenbach, *Lone Star: A History of Texas and the Texans,* updated ed., (Cambridge, Mass.: Da Capo Press, 2000), 659

didates. Once a candidate decides to run for a party nomination either by party primary or party convention, he or she cannot be an independent candidate in the general election.

The tradition of Texas ballot access includes the ability of parties, independent candidates, and write-in candidates to appear on the ballot. Yet another tradition in Texas is the use of rules and procedures to make access for minor parties challenging. By requiring minor parties to constantly reapply to have their party name and label on the ballot based upon statewide totals in the governor's election, the rules favor the established Democratic and Republican parties.

Electronic Voting in Texas

n the wake of the 2000 presidential election, including a large number of irregularities in the state of Florida, Congress acted to create a single national standard for election procedures for presidential and congressional elections by passing the **Help America Vote Act (HAVA)** in 2002. Ultimately, many states and local governments began adapting procedures for non-federal elections to comply with HAVA simply because state and local elections are often held simultaneously with federal elections. Therefore, HAVA has the effect of giving the national government more control over elections.

HAVA mandates that every polling station possess electronic voting equipment, and at least one voting booth that is also accessible for those with a disability. HAVA also requires that state and local voting officials conduct educational activities and equipment demonstrations to allow voters to become familiar with the new equipment. While HAVA does not specify the exact equipment to be used, standards are set for the equipment. Congress, recognizing the expense of purchasing new equipment, provided limited funds to states and local governments to implement HAVA. In Texas, the Secretary of State's Elections Division certified several types of equipment, including optical scanners, touch-screen voting, and dial-controlled computer voting (E-slates). County governments may select from one of four companies to supply the equipment.

The shift to electronic voting is meant to overcome the perceived problems of other forms of balloting. Traditional paper ballots are subject to ballot-box stuffing, in which additional paper ballots are placed in the box to ensure a particular candidate wins. When questions arise about the final vote totals, paper ballots are recounted by hand, a process that is not the most reliable. Lever-operated voting machines if not maintained properly can cause errors in tabulating vote results, and these machines do not have a paper record of the vote to compare the results with the actual choice of individual voters. Punch card ballots, a primary cause of the difficulties in the 2000 presidential election in Florida, are among the least reliable, with high error rates in counting the ballots and determining the actual choice of the voter.[22] However, electronic voting methods, like touch screens and E-slates, are not without problems, including the possibility of software tampering, the lack of a paper ballot to verify the results,[23] errors in saving votes to a database, and voter distrust in computer-based voting.[24]

At the time that Congress passed HAVA in 2002, about a third of Texas's counties still used paper ballots for voting. Fourteen counties had punch-card systems, and three counties used lever machines. All of these counties were required to replace all of their voting processes with electronic systems. In 2000, the majority of counties employed optical scanners. With optical scanners, a voter marks a ballot, the ballot is scanned, and the results are added by the scanner's software to the database. Although optical scanners were allowed to continue under HAVA, counties using optical scanners were still mandated to have at least one E-slate or touch-screen system available at each polling place for those with disabilities. As a result, almost all of Texas's 254 counties needed to upgrade equipment, with a substantial portion needing to entirely replace their equipment.[25]

The cost of these upgrades is often costly. Estimates from the Texas Secretary of State's office suggest that more than $170 million was needed to comply with HAVA.[26] Funds were made available to counties from the state based upon a formula that included the number of voting precincts and voting-age-eligible population.

Loving County, the smallest in population, with only fifty-four age-eligible voters, received $27,000 in 2003 and $40,000 in 2004. Implementation of HAVA in Harris County, with almost 2.5 million voters cost over $6 million in 2003 and $12 million in 2004. In the trade-off between ensuring the accuracy of the vote and need to fund elections, Congress chose to pass most of the cost onto states and local governments. Again, the role of the national government in promoting change in Texas elections becomes evident. The transition to electronic voting resulted from laws passed by the U.S. Congress.

Texas Pioneers: Early Voting

National elections are required by the federal law to be held on the first Tuesday following the first Monday in November. State and local elections in Texas are also typically held on a Tuesday and polls are open from 7:00 a.m. to 7:00 p.m. While these hours might seem extensive, given that many people work from 8:00 a.m. until 5:00 p.m., with commute times to and from work, these hours are not convenient to everyone. To help Texans vote, Texas began in 1988 to experiment with **advanced or early voting,** which allows a voter to cast a ballot before an election without giving a specific reason. Historically, to cast a ballot before Election Day, a voter had to qualify for an absentee ballot, documenting a specific reason for being absent on Election Day: being on vacation, being on a business trip, or being a student away at college. In early voting, the local voter registration opens the polling to voters during specified times and days in the weeks leading up to the election. In Texas, early voting days include weekends. Voting essentially becomes "easier" and at the leisure of the voter, rather than occurring during a hectic workday when voting booths are open primarily during the time most people are at work. As shown in Figure 7.1, early voting has become quite popular in Texas, especially in presidential election years.

Advanced or early voting
a voting system that allows a voter to cast a ballot before an election without giving a specific reason, thus making voting more convenient for the voter.

Figure 7.1 Early Voting in Texas

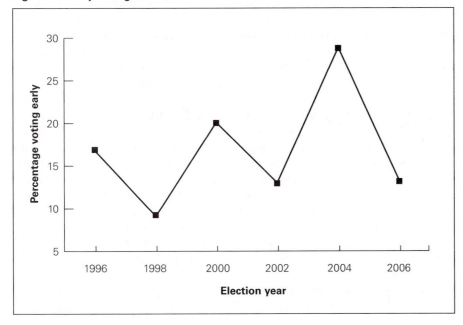

Types of Elections in Texas

Primary elections
intraparty elections in which candidates compete to determine who will win the party's nomination in the general election.

Direct primary
an election in which the winning candidate directly receives the party nomination.

Indirect primary
a primary in which voters elect delegates to a party convention; delegates are pledged to support a specific candidate seeking the party nomination.

Preference primary
a primary in which voters indicate their choice to hold office, but the actual selection is left to the political party elites.

General election
the interparty election in which candidates from two or more political parties compete for actual political office.

Closed primary
an electoral contest restricted to party loyalists and excluding supporters of other political parties and independent voters.

Open primary
an electoral contest in which voters do not have to declare a party affiliation to participate, but must request a specific party's ballot at the primary, and are then barred from participating in the other party's primary.

everal types of elections exist. **Primary elections** are essentially intra-party elections. In these elections, candidates compete to represent the political party in a general election. Thus, the winner of a primary "wins" the party's nomination and a place on the ballot in the general election. Primary elections may be **direct primaries,** in which the winning candidate automatically receives the party nomination. In some situations, the primary election may be an **indirect primary** or **preference primary.** In an indirect primary, voters elect delegates to a party convention. Delegates are pledged to support a specific candidate seeking the party nomination. At the convention, the delegates vote among the various candidates. The winner receives the party nomination. In a preference primary, voters indicate their choice to hold office, but the actual selection is left to the political party elites.

Primary Elections versus General Elections

After the primary, the winner of a political party's primary moves onto a **general election,** in which candidates from two or more political parties compete for elected office. These elections are inter-party elections in which voters choose among several candidates representing different political parties and independent candidates. The winner of the general election is rewarded by becoming an actual officeholder such as the governor, a member of the state legislature, or a judge.

In Texas, primary elections, in most instances, are direct primaries. Direct primaries are used for parties to nominate candidates for all state offices, plus the U.S. House of Representatives, and the U.S. Senate. In the presidential primaries, Texas and many other states use an indirect primary to nominate candidates for president. Alternatives to the indirect primary to select delegates to attend a national party convention include caucuses and preference primaries. In some states, parties are allowed to pick how their delegates are selected. In Texas, the two major parties must use a primary election.

Three types of primaries exist: closed primaries, open primaries, and blanket or wide-open primaries. A **closed primary** restricts the voters who participate in the primary to party loyalists. Typically prior to the primary, often when registering to vote, each individual voter must declare a party affiliation. At the primary, when a voter shows up to cast a ballot, the voter's name is checked against a list of registered party supporters. Obviously, this approach limits the number of voters in the primary to those voters willing to specify a party affiliation. A positive aspect of the closed primary is the fact that candidates who win the party nomination more closely reflect the beliefs and ideas of the party faithful. On the negative side, candidates may not reflect the beliefs of the entire electorate because independent voters and supporters of other political parties are excluded from voting. A closed, enforced primary ensures that only the registered party supporters vote in the primary. However, some states and localities use a closed, unenforced primary. In this case, although voters register with a specific party affiliation, at the actual primary election, a voter's name is not checked against a list of registered party supporters. A voter may therefore be registered with the Democratic Party but vote in the Republican Party primary, or vice-versa. In states with closed primaries, political parties may hold their primaries on different days.

In an **open primary** system a voter does not have to declare a party affiliation. At the primary, the voter requests a specific party's ballot. However, the ballot con-

Texas versus Oregon

While Texas serves as a pioneer in early voting, Oregon decided to follow a different path by allowing "vote by mail." In the vote-by-mail system, the state of Oregon mails a ballot to every registered voter about two weeks before the election. At their leisure, a voter marks the ballot and mails the ballot back in a special envelope. A voter may also hand-deliver the ballot to designated locations throughout the state.

Historically, states have allowed voters to receive a ballot early and mail it back only for absentee voting. Absentee voting required that the voter provide a legitimate reason for not being in the community on Election Day in order to cast an early ballot. In 1981, Oregon allowed limited experiments with mail-in ballots for all voters in local elections. In December 1995, Oregon extended the process to party primaries. By 1998, all elections in Oregon included the vote-by-mail system. One review of the research on the impact of voting by mail suggests that voter turnout increases between 5 to 10 percent over traditional in-person voting.[i]

Here are some statistics regarding turnout in Oregon elections since it became a statewide process in 1998.

Voter Turnout in Oregon and Texas

ELECTION	OREGON TURNOUT	TEXAS TURNOUT
2000 Presidential Election	79%	44%
2002 November General Election	69%	29%
2004 Presidential Election	86%	46%
2006 November General Election	70%	26%

Thinking Critically

- What is vote by mail?
- How is the vote-by-mail system similar to early voting in Texas?
- Do you think a vote-by-mail system would help boost voter turnout in Texas?
- Have you ever voted with early voting in Texas?
- Would you be more likely to vote if you could vote by mail?

i. Paul Gronke and Peter Miller, "Voting by Mail and Turnout: A Replication and Extension," paper presented at the Annual Meeting of the American Political Science Association, Chicago, Illinois, August 20, 2007.

tains only those candidates from the party that the voter requested. Once a voter participates in a specific party's primary, he or she is prohibited, usually by law, from participating in another party's primary. In some states, the parties may hold their primaries on different days. Independent voters often prefer the open primary because they are allowed to participate in at least one party's primary. Moreover, cross-party voting often occurs because Republicans may vote in the Democratic Party primary, and vice-versa. Of course, if a Republican chooses to vote in the Democratic primary, the voter is then barred from participating in the Republican primary. On the down side, the open primary is more exposed to manipulation from the outside. For example, if a Democratic Party candidate is running unopposed in the Democratic primary, party officials may encourage Democratic voters to show up for the Republican primary and help the most extreme or easiest-to-defeat candidate win the Republican nomination. Republicans may easily engage in the same behavior in a Democratic primary.

Until recently, a few states used the **blanket or wide-open primary.** In this system, voters do not register a party affiliation. At the primary, voters receive ballot papers containing the names of all candidates from all political parties running for office. Voters still may choose only one candidate per office, not one candidate per political party. In the partisan blanket primary, the Democratic Party candidate with the most votes moves onto the general election as the Democratic nominee, and the Republi-

Blanket or wide-open primary
a primary in which voters do not register party affiliations and receive ballot papers containing the names of all candidates from all political parties running for office; usually voters may choose only one candidate per office, rather than one candidate per political party.

SAMPLE BALLOT
INSTRUCTIONS FOR VOTING

Machine Certified for Use in This State and
Official Ballot Prepared and Certified by

Secretary of State

1. Press the white square ☐ to the right of the candidate of your choice; a green ☒ will appear indicating your selection.
2. To change a selection, press the white square ☐ again. The green ☒ will disappear and you may make a new selection.
3. Make **ALL** selections, then press the ☐ button located in the lower right corner. This electronically records all of your votes.
4. Part the curtains and exit the voting booth.

Wds./Dists./Pcts. 801, 804, 808, 815

39 ST. TAMMANY

Governor		Secretary of State		State Senator		SPECIAL ELECTION	
(Vote for ONE)		(Vote for ONE)		1st Senatorial District		Justice(s) of the Peace	
				(Vote for ONE)		Justice of the Peace Ward 8	
B. Alexandrenko	1	"Jay" Dardenne *Republican*	19	A. G. Crowe *Republican*	47	(Vote for ONE)	
Walter J. Boasso *Democrat*	2	Scott Lewis *No Party*	20	"Joey" Di Fatta *Republican*	48	Sandra Johnson *Republican*	82
Foster Campbell *Democrat*	3	"R" Wooley *Democrat*	21	Kenneth L. Odinet, Sr. *Democrat*	49	Tracey Turgeau Powell *Republican*	83
Vincent Mark Castillo *No Party*	4	**Attorney General**		**State Representative**		Floyd Trascher *Republican*	84
Sheldon Forest *No Party*	5			76th Representative District			
Anthony "Tony G" Gentile	6	(Vote for ONE)		(Vote for ONE)			
John Georges *No Party*	7	Royal Alexander *Republican*	22	Lee Balinas *Republican*	53		
T. Lee Horne, III *Libertarian*	8	James D. "Buddy" Caldwell *Democrat*	23	"Ray" Canada *Republican*	54		
"Bobby" Jindal *Republican*	9	Charles C. Foti, Jr. *Democrat*	24	Kevin Pearson *Republican*	55		
M. V. "Vinny" Mendoza *Democrat*	10	**Commissioner of Agriculture and Forestry**		Mark Sigur *Republican*	56		
Arthur D. "Jim" Nichols *No Party*	11	(Vote for ONE)		**Parish President**			
Hardy Parkerson	12	Wayne Carter *Republican*	25	(Vote for ONE)			
Mary Volentine Smith *Democrat*	13	Don Johnson *Republican*	26	Freddie Boothe, III	61		
Lieutenant Governor		"Bob" Odom *Democrat*	27	Kevin C. Davis *Republican*	62		
(Vote for ONE)		Mike Strain *Republican*	28	"Greg" Sharp *Democrat*	63		
Gary J. Beard *Republican*	14	**Commissioner of Insurance**		**Council Member**			
Norris "Spanky" Gros, Jr. *No Party*	15	(Vote for ONE)		District 5			
Thomas D. Kates *No Party*	16	James "Jim" Crowley *Democrat*	29	(Vote for ONE)			
"Sammy" Kershaw *Republican*	17	"Jim" Donelon *Republican*	30	"Gene" Bellisaro *Republican*	72		
"Mitch" Landrieu *Democrat*	18	Robert Lansden *Republican*	31	"Randy" Caire *Republican*	73		
		Jerilyn Schneider-Kneale *Republican*	33	Donna Holmes Faucheux *Republican*	74		
				"Bill" McCormick *Republican*	75		

Above is a sample ballot for the nonpartisan blanket primary system used in Louisiana. Note the listing of candidates from various political parties on the ballot. Independent candidates are listed as "No Party." As instructed on the ballot, a voter may pick only one candidate per office.

Cross filing

a system that allows a candidate to run simultaneously as a Democratic and a Republican candidate, essentially competing in both parties' primaries.

can candidate with the most votes competes in the general election as the Republican nominee. The same results hold true for any and all other parties holding primary elections. The states of Washington, Alaska, and California required the partisan blanket primary until the U.S. Supreme Court in *California Democratic Party v. Jones* (2000) upheld the right of political parties to choose their own primary system as a First Amendment right to association.[27]

As a result, only Louisiana is left with a blanket-primary system for state and local races. Louisiana's nonpartisan blanket primary system is a bit different from other blanket primary systems. In Louisiana, the top two candidates regardless of party affiliation move on to the general election. In the 1970s and 1980s, a common outcome of the primary resulted in two Democrats competing in the general election, with no Republicans on the general election ballot. Another unusual aspect of Louisiana's system is the fact that if a candidate wins a majority of the vote in the primary election, the candidate wins the office and no general election occurs. In effect, the primary becomes a general election.

Texas's primary system is technically a closed system, as required by state law. In practice however, Texas's system is considered semi-open.[28] The designation of semi-open is more appropriate because, like an open primary, voters in Texas do not have to declare a party affiliation when registering to vote. However, the system becomes functionally closed at the primary election. Upon requesting a specific party's ballot at the primary, this information is recorded. For the next year, the voters cannot change party affiliations. Since multiple primaries may be held in a given year, the voters become locked into voting in the same primary for twelve months. At the next primary, voters are automatically given the party ballot of their previously recorded party.

The history of primaries in Texas is riddled with political manipulation to produce certain outcomes. To stave off possible defections to the Republican Party as national Democratic Party leaders began to emphasize civil rights legislation in the 1950s, the election reforms of 1951–1952 allowed **cross filing.** In cross filing, a candidate may run simultaneously as a Democratic candidate and a Republican, essentially competing in both parties' primaries.[29] This tactic allowed Democrats to control the Republican Party as Republicans held their first presidential primary election in Texas. Democratic voters were able to cross over to support Republican candidate Dwight Eisenhower for U.S. president yet ensure that state and local candidates who won the Republican primary were also loyal Democrats. Republicans named such Democratic voters "One-Day Republicans."[30] This practice seems unusual, but Texas Republicans, as recently as 1948, approached several prominent Democrats to run as Republicans, including candidates for governor.[31] Note that some states today allow a related practice called electoral fusion, in which more than one party nominates the same candidate in the general election, and the candidate carries both party labels on the election ballot.

Direct Democracy Elections

A final type of election is the direct democracy election. At the state level, three of the Progressive Party's ideas associated with direct democracy and voter input into the decision-making process have been enacted: the referendum, the initiative, and the recall. These three types of direct democracy elections are broader in scope than the amendment processes for state constitutions discussed in Chapter 2.

In a referendum, the state legislature proposes a new law and places the proposed law on an election ballot. At the next election, a statewide vote of citizens determines whether the new law is adopted or rejected. Twenty-two states use the referendum for approving new laws. Texas lacks the referendum in this sense although the Texas legislature must submit amendments to the state's constitution to the voters for approval. However, the referendum process is used in most states.

In comparison, an initiative occurs when citizens propose a new law by collecting the signatures of registered voters on an initiative petition form. When a set number of registered votes, which varies by state, have signed the form, the form is submitted to the state's chief elections officer for certification. Once certified, the proposed law is placed on an election ballot for voters statewide to accept or reject. Sometimes the initiative mechanism is called the initiative petition or just proposition. Twenty-four states allow some form of the initiative petition, either for new laws or amendments to state constitutions.[32] The Texas Constitution does not permit the initiative petition.

The recall petition is a method of removing a sitting elected official before he or she completes the term of office. The recall operates similar to a petition in that signatures are collected on a petition, in this case a petition to remove an official from office early. Once a predetermined number of signatures are gathered, the petition is submitted to the state's chief elections officer for certification. Following the certification, voters at the next election determine if the official remains in office. Eighteen states allow the recall petition for elected officials. Texas lacks this type of direct democracy election for state officials. However, local officials in Texas may be recalled in some counties and cities depending on their local plan of government.

Too Much Democracy?

 n Texas's general elections, voters confront the long ballot, a Progressive era reform, which made as many state and local offices as possible directly elected by the voters. The long ballot is so-called simply because each Texas voter is asked to choose six statewide executive offices: the governor, the lieutenant governor, the comptroller of Public Accounts, the commissioner of the General Land Office, the commissioner of Agriculture, and the attorney general. At the same time a voter is often asked to choose a state senator, a state representative, a member of the U.S. House of Representatives, a U.S. Senator, members of the Texas Railroad Commission, members of the Texas Board of Education, a justice of the peace, county commissioners, county tax assessors, a mayor, members of the city council, as well as local, county, and state court judges. In the case of state courts, voters elect judges for district courts, appeals courts, as well as the Supreme Court of Texas and Texas Court of Criminal Appeals.

The sheer number of elected offices and candidates running for office means that voters are often overwhelmed at the polling place. One result is that voters tend to vote for the offices that appear higher on the ballot, while ignoring and leaving blank offices that are farther down. Typically, this corresponds to voting for the most "important" offices like the U.S. president, governor, or U.S. senator and leaving "lesser" offices at the county and local level blank. This phenomenon is called **roll off**.[33] For example, in 2006, the total number of votes cast for the statewide race for governor totaled almost 80,000 more than the total number of votes cast for lieutenant governor, a difference of 1.8 percent. More dramatic was the difference between votes cast for governor and railroad commissioner. There were 198,000 fewer votes or 4.5 percent fewer votes for railroad commissioner in 2006. Another result of the long ballot is **party-line voting or straight-ticket voting.** Party-line voting occurs when a voter selects candidates simply by their party affiliation, recording a vote for all Democratic candidates or all Republican candidates. In this way, the voter avoids tough decisions of going office-by-office and candidate-by-candidate to mark the ballot.

The advantage of the long ballot is, of course, greater accountability of elected officials to the voters in the state, county, city, or other agency of state government. However, the long ballot, if used as intended by the Progressives, requires that voters ignore partisanship as a guide to selecting a candidate in the election. Instead, voters are expected to be well informed about all candidates and issues in the election, selecting wisely the most qualified candidate or the candidate with the closest views to the voter's. Such expectations may be unrealistic given the sheer number of races to be decided on a lengthy ballot. Again, voters may tend to rely on heuristics or "short cuts" to decide for which candidate to vote.[34] Short cuts include party labels, as suggested above,[35] name recognition, and ideology. Overall, the increase in the number of elected offices contributes to voter fatigue and raises the costs of voting, and has the unintended effect of fewer voters turning out on Election Day.

Roll off

occurs when a voter marks off only the "more important" offices on a lengthy ballot—usually the national or statewide offices—and leaves the county or local office choices blank.

Party-line or straight-ticket voting

when voters select candidates by their party affiliation.

Voter Registration and Turnout

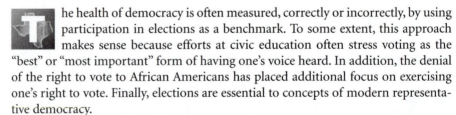

The health of democracy is often measured, correctly or incorrectly, by using participation in elections as a benchmark. To some extent, this approach makes sense because efforts at civic education often stress voting as the "best" or "most important" form of having one's voice heard. In addition, the denial of the right to vote to African Americans has placed additional focus on exercising one's right to vote. Finally, elections are essential to concepts of modern representative democracy.

Figure 7.2 gives the rate of voter registration among the adult age-eligible population in the state of Texas. Beginning in 1974 and continuing into the 1990s, the rate of registration remains relatively stable, hovering in the low- to mid-60-percent range for most of the period. Registration peaks during presidential elections. From the high of 71.2 percent in the wake of the Watergate scandal in 1976, it trends downward and doesn't reach 70 percent until 1984. In 1994, the trend is toward higher rates of voter registration, leveling off in the low 80-percent range by the mid-2000s. Why did voter registration spike in the mid- to late-1990s? One important explana-

Figure 7.2 Rate of Voter Registration (1976–2006)

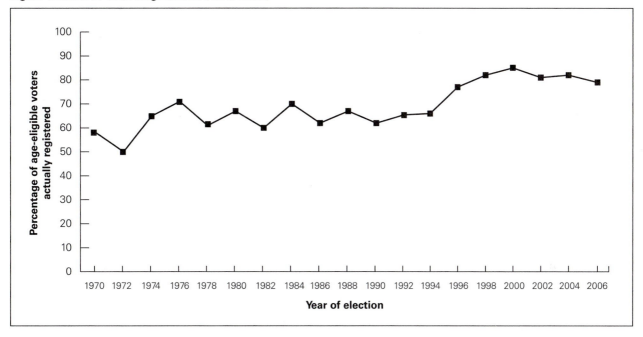

tion is the impact of the 1993 "Motor Voter Act." In addition, the implementation of online voter registration forms made access to registration easier for many potential new voters, leading to potentially higher registration rates. The advent of new technologies like computerized databases and better training of local election officials influences the rates of voter registration as well.

You'll often hear about voter turnout. In Texas, **voter turnout,** that is the number of people casting ballots in an election, resembles the trends from across the United States. Voter turnout tends to be higher in presidential election years than in off-year, mid-term elections. Moreover, special elections and local elections tend to have very low levels of voter turnout.

Voter turnout is calculated two ways, as the percentage of ballots cast in the election based upon the total number of registered voters or the total population over age eighteen (or voting age eligible population). Often government officials like to report turnout based on the first method, in part, because rates of turnout are inflated with the first measure. Obviously, the total number of registered voters is normally lower than the total number of people who are of eligible voting age.

This issue of using registered voters or age-eligible population is important when comparing voter turnout rates over time or across states. States sometimes change the eligibility requirements, for example southern states like Texas have clearly manipulated registration requirements to exclude African Americans, as discussed earlier. Also, registration processes and voter eligibility varies from state to state. North Dakota, as mentioned earlier, lacks any form of registration, so that anyone showing up on Election Day with a valid state driver's license or other proof of residency is allowed to vote. In neighboring Minnesota, voters are allowed to register to vote up to and including Election Day. These differences produce variations in the percentage of the age-eligible population that is registered to vote.

Voter turnout

the number of people casting ballots in a given election.

Table 7.1 Percentage of Eligible Voters Registered, November 2006 (selected states)

STATE	PERCENTAGE REGISTERED	RANK
Top Five States		
Alaska	100.0%	1
Michigan	97.4%	2
Oregon	96.5%	3
South Dakota	95.7%	4
Iowa	94.0%	5
Texas	**89.3%**	**14**
U.S. Average	85.5%	n/a
States Bordering Texas		
Louisiana	86.0%	25
New Mexico	79.9%	37
Arkansas	78.8%	39
Oklahoma	78.8%	40
Bottom Five States		
California	75.1%	43
Idaho	74.6%	44
Hawaii	74.3%	45
Alabama	70.8%	46
Wyoming	67.6%	47

Source: Kendra A. Hovey and Harold A. Hovey, *CQ's State Fact Finder* (Washington, D.C.: CQ Press, 2007), 118. Note that Maine, North Dakota, and Wisconsin are unranked because these states conduct election-day registration.

Thus, the more accurate figure, especially for comparison purposes, is to use the total population over age eighteen (or voting age eligible population). In general, voter turnout among the age-eligible population hovers in the 40 to 50 percentage range for presidential elections but declines to the high 20 or low 30-percentage range for mid-term, off-year elections. Interestingly, the gap between turnout among the age-eligible population and actual registered voters has narrowed since the election of 1992. According to the 2006 estimates, almost 90 percent of Texas's age-eligible population was registered to vote, placing Texas in fourteenth place in the United States. This narrowing of the gap reflects the trend toward more of the population registering to vote, whether as a result of the Motor Voter Act, on-line registration, improvements in database management, or some other cause.

What about special elections? Figure 7.3 shows the trends in voter turnout in special elections in Texas since 1977. With the exceptions of the May and June elections of 1993, all other special statewide elections since 1977 concerned amendments to the Texas Constitution. In general, voter turnout in special elections is quite low, never reaching higher than 35 percent of registered voters or 20 percent of age-eligible voters. Two of the three most recent special elections, 2003 and 2005, saw slight increases in the rate of turnout compared to earlier elections. The rate of voter turnout fell, however, in 2007.

The 2005 special election involved a series of constitutional amendments, including a controversial proposal involving the definition of marriage as between a man and a woman. This amendment energized social conservatives who supported the

Figure 7.3 Turnout in Texas Special Elections

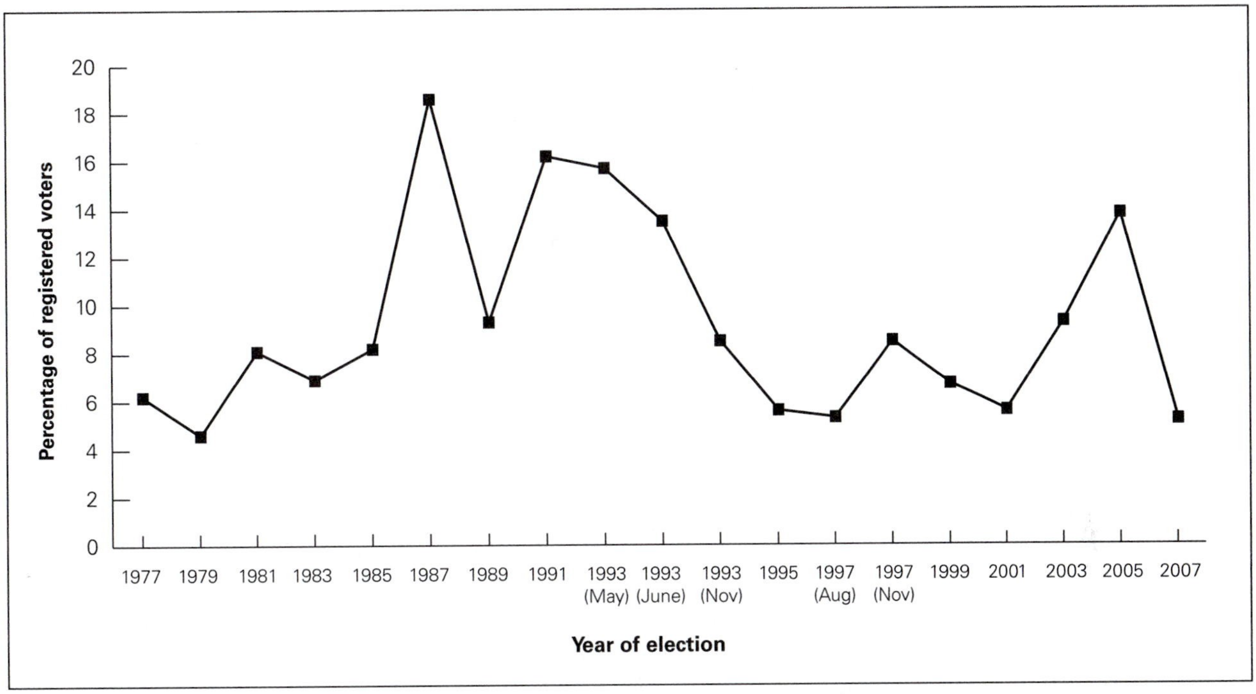

Y-axis: Percentage of registered voters (0 to 20)

X-axis (Year of election): 1977, 1979, 1981, 1983, 1985, 1987, 1989, 1991, 1993 (May), 1993 (June), 1993 (Nov), 1995, 1997 (Aug), 1997 (Nov), 1999, 2001, 2003, 2005, 2007

Source: Compiled by author from data available from the Texas Secretary of State, www.sos.state.tx.us/elections/historical/index.shtml, accessed May 14, 2007.

language of the amendment that limited marriage to a union between a man and a woman. However, many opponents, including gay and lesbian organizations, were also mobilized to vote to prevent the amendment from passing. Their efforts were unsuccessful because the amendment passed 76.3 percent to 23.7 percent. The May 2007 amendment concerned a much less controversial topic: property tax rates paid by senior citizens. This relatively uncontroversial issue produced extremely low voter turnout (5.2 percent).

So, why is voter turnout typically higher for presidential elections than in mid-term elections for governor, members of the U.S. House of Representatives, and the state legislature, and why do mid-term elections have higher voter turnouts than special elections? One answer lies in what scholars who compare elections across different countries refer to as **second order elections**.[36] Second order elections are elections for offices other than the national executive in presidential systems like the United States or the national legislature in parliamentary systems like Great Britain. The term second order refers to the fact that these elections are simply less important in scope and impact on the country as a whole, with less ability to shift the direction of the entire political system. Because the stakes are less, voters see fewer benefits from voting and see the act of voting in these elections as less important. Another explanation is the issue of mobilization. Presidential elections in the United States are simply more likely to be discussed in the media, often more intensely advertised, and more importantly, the political parties and candidate campaigns are more active in contacting potential voters to vote.

Voting behavior in Texas is in a state of transition. More and more Texans are now on the voter registration list, but this upward trend in registration is not reversing the general trend in low voter turnout. Voter turnout remains alarmingly low in

Second order elections

elections for offices below the national executive level in countries with presidential systems like the United States or the national legislature level in parliamentary countries like Great Britain; generally seen as less important in scope and impact on a country.

special elections. Congressional and statewide elections not held in conjunction with presidential elections tend to have lower voter turnout as well.

Who Votes?

In general, Texas is characterized by low rates of voter turnout, compared to other states. Texas typically ranks near the bottom in voter turnout. Low voter turnout is a result of several factors such as the relative difficulty in accessing the ballot and the focus on charismatic candidates and "personality" approaches to campaigns. Lower turnout is also a result of the traditionalistic political culture of many Texans, which contains negative views of politics and political life, as well as the strain of extreme individualism in the culture, where voting is seen as a duty or chore. Finally, the relatively weak organizational nature of Texas's political parties limits their ability to mobilize voters to vote in an election. We return to this theme in Chapter 8.

The rate of turnout in Texas is not stable across demographic groupings such as race/ethnicity, gender, and age. To illustrate these differences, the 2004 presidential elections provide an example of the patterns of turnout in an election in Texas. Table 7.2 provides comparisons between Texas, the U.S. average, Minnesota, and Hawaii. Minnesota had the highest turnout in 2004, while Hawaii had the lowest.

Note the differences in the rate of voter turnout between various demographic groups. For example, women are less likely to vote than men. Non-Hispanic whites voted more than other ethnic groups. These trends are consistent with national trends on turnout by gender and ethnic group.

Throughout the United States and in Texas, voter turnout varies considerably by age group. The youngest voters, ages 18–24, consistently vote at levels much below the national or state average. While some improvement occurs in the 25–44 age bracket, the highest rates of voting seem to occur among those over the age of 45, especially among those in the 65–74 age bracket. As a result, candidates and parties often address the concerns of older voters, not those of younger voters. Compared

Table 7.2 Voter Turnout Rates across Various Demographic Groups in the 2004 Elections

CHARACTERISTIC	TEXAS	UNITED STATES	MINNESOTA	HAWAII
Sex				
Men	48.1%	56.3%	74.0%	43.7%
Women	52.4%	60.1%	79.3%	48.4%
Race/Ethnicity				
White, non-Hispanic	63.4%	65.8%	79.7%	65.2%
African American	55.8%	56.3%	64.7%	N/A
Asian	29.9%	29.8%	41.1%	42.0%
Hispanic	29.3%	28.0%	45.6%	N/A
Age				
18–24	33.5%	41.8%	65.8%	N/A
25–44	43.6%	52.2%	75.5%	37.9%
45–64	60.7%	66.6%	81.2%	56.0%
65–74	65.6%	70.8%	82.5%	N/A
75+	61.1%	66.7%	78.0%	47.9%

N/A = Not Available

Source: U.S. Census Bureau, *Current Population Survey,* November 2004.

Campaigning in Texas

Election campaigns in Texas have regularly been the stuff of legends, starting in the era of the Republic of Texas. Running for his second term as president of Texas, Sam Houston was attacked by Vice President David Burnet, who described Houston as a drunken coward who failed to fight the Mexican Army before San Jacinto, and possessed "beastly intemperance and other vices degrading to humanity." Houston responded by calling Burnet a hog thief. When Burnet became enraged and challenged Houston to a duel, Houston laughed off the challenge, in part, because he "never fought down hill." i

After statehood, this trend continued. In his 1857 run for the governorship, Houston gave speeches sometimes with an antislavery message that ranged from two to four hours. When pro-secession candidates attacked him, Houston responded by telling this audience that one candidate had left a political career in Arkansas because of a banking fraud scandal and that the other had killed two men in South Carolina before coming to Texas.

Race played an issue in many Texas campaigns. However, the races under attack have not always been the same ones. Playing off the distrust of Germans resulting from World War I, opponents of James Ferguson claimed that the improper loans that had led to Ferguson's impeachment were from the Kaiser of Germany. Ferguson retorted that Hobby, his opponent, had put "full-blooded Germans" in key government positions.

The U.S. Civil War as an issue still lingered as late as 1912, as Governor Colquitt struggled in his reelection bid because he had criticized the state textbook board after they rejected a history book because it contained a photograph of Abraham Lincoln. Many Texans also flocked to see Colquitt's opponent William Ramsay, who played upon southern sentiments in his speeches and had bands play "Dixie" during campaign events.

Radio and then television played a role in Texas as they have in other states. Wilbert Lee "Pappy" O'Daniel used his radio show to launch his campaign for governor. The years since have seen the broadcast media of radio and television become the central tool of candidate's campaigns. While candidates still travel the state and personally interact with voters, the battles of advertising and efforts to get covered by news organizations have become the primary concern of campaigns.

Today's campaigns are modern, with high-tech use of the Internet and Photoshop. In the 2006 election, candidate Kinky Friedman used the Internet to show Texans his "Kinkytoons," commercials that showed what the defenders of the Alamo would have done if led by today's parties. While not as colorful as Kinky Friedman (pictured), the other independent candidate, Carole Strayhorn, took to the television airwaves to paint herself as "one tough grandma." Trying to live up to the larger-than-life legacy of earlier Texas politicians, Democrat Chris Bell appeared in an ad as a giant figure looming over Texas landmarks like the Capitol Building and the Alamo. The larger-than-life Texas campaign is alive and well.

In general, campaigns in Texas are very much like those in the rest of the nation. The state's large size does require that candidates come up with a little more cash and produce a little more style. Texas voters also remain connected to their legends of Texas history, meaning that candidates will continue to use Texas icons like the Alamo and the cowboy heritage. Ironically, campaigns embrace the larger changes in the state by adopting new technologies like the Internet to transmit these time-tested messages of traditional Texas mythology.

i. Randolph B. Campbell, *Gone to Texas* (New York: Oxford University Press—USA, 2004), 175.

with the 2000 election, the 2004 presidential elections saw gains among the 18–24 voters, increasing by 11 percent.[37]

Low voter turnout may have consequences for Texas politics. Assuming there are differences in the policy preferences, party identifications and other characteristics of voting behavior between the various ethnic groups, low voter turnout among African American and Hispanic voters in Texas means that fewer government decisions reflect these groups' beliefs than might otherwise occur. Similarly, government decision makers are less responsive to the concerns of younger voters because they, as a group, tend to vote less. In addition, lower turnout among various ethnic groups reduces the likelihood that minority candidates are elected to office. As a result, the system is less representative of the population as a whole.

Electoral Competition in Texas Elections

Merely holding an election to fill an office does not equal democratic, representative government. Iraq under the rule of former president Saddam Hussein held regular elections for the presidency. In the Iraqi case, voters simply voted whether Hussein should remain as president. Does Texas meet the American standard of democratic elections and what can be done to create a competitive Texas democracy? Truly democratic elections require some degree of choice. A ballot with only one candidate hardly seems to be a choice. More importantly the choice must be between viable alternatives. In other words, elections imply that the choices are not just A versus B, but that A and B have some possibility of actually winning the race.[38] Also, this concept of two or more choices each with some possibility of winning, or electoral competition, is important for another reason. Electoral competition has been linked to higher rates of voter turnout.[39]

In Texas, the dominance of the Democratic Party from the end of Reconstruction in 1876 until the civil rights era of the 1950s and 1960s challenged the democratic and representative nature of Texas politics. Disenfranchising African American and other voters certainly brings into question the representative nature of the system. However, the Democratic Party's attempts to limit the access of Republicans to the ballot process and to prevent competition from non-Democratic candidates also raises concerns about the nature of elections in Texas, and throughout the South. This era of the "Yellow Dog" Democrat began to end as the national Democratic Party in the 1950s and 1960s embraced civil rights, and Texans dissatisfied with this shift looked toward the Republican party as an alternative.

To some extent, the Republican Party has become more competitive in Texas elections since the 1960s, in terms of getting more votes in an election at the state and national levels. The number of Republicans getting elected to state and national office has also increased. Perhaps the first cracks in Texas's association with the Democratic Party began in 1952 when Texas voters flocked to Republican candidate and popular war hero Dwight D. Eisenhower in the presidential election. The real breakthrough occurred in 1961, when a little-known Republican professor of government at Midwestern State University in Wichita Falls, John Tower, won the U.S. Senate race and become the first Republican in Congress from the South since the late 1800s. In 1978, William Clement won the governorship and became the first Republican governor since Reconstruction. Since then, Republicans have regularly won statewide elected offices and seats in the U.S. House of Representatives from Texas. Currently, both U.S. senators from Texas, Kay Bailey Hutchison and John Cornyn, are both Republicans. The Texas delegation to the U.S. House of Representatives is currently nineteen Republicans and thirteen Democrats. In 1996, Republicans won control over the Texas State Senate, and in 2002, Republicans won control of both houses of the Texas state legislature for the first time since 1876.

The trend toward Republicans getting more votes, holding more offices, and ending the "Yellow Dog" Democratic dominance over Texas politics suggests that Texas politics has transitioned away from the traditional one-party system of the past. Transitions similar to that in Texas also appear among Republican parties throughout the South, but the trend really began with Texas. Texas is often considered the least "southern" of the southern states[40] and, thus, a trend leader in southern development. The "Texafication" of American politics includes an emphasis on low taxes, high-tech industry, and limited spending on social welfare.[41] Republicans throughout the region, and nation, have capitalized in part on the success of Texas Republicans.

However, the rise of the Republicans does not mean that Texas is a two-party state. In fact, evidence suggests that recent Texas elections are becoming less competitive. Republicans may simply be winning elections in which Democratic candidates are no longer competing.

For example, in 2006, sixteen seats in the Texas State Senate were up for election. Of these seats, seven were contested by Republicans without a Democratic challenger, while two were contested by Democratic candidates without a Republican challenger. This means that only seven seats were competitive in the sense of being contested by both Democratic and Republican candidates. Over half of the seats lacked a choice between the two major parties.

In general, the two major parties in Texas run candidates for all six statewide elected offices in every election. Likewise, a Democratic and a Republican candidate appears on the ballot for elections to the U.S. Senate. As illustrated in Table 7.3, most elections since 1992 for Texas's seats in the U.S. House of Representatives are contested by Democratic and Republican candidates. In fact, in five of the elections since 1992, both major parties have contested at least 75 percent of seats. Although the low point occurred in 1998, with 60 percent of seats contested, the redistricting battles of 2002 and 2004 have led to a slight increase in the number of districts with both Democratic and Republican candidates. Thus, at the level of statewide elected office and U.S. congressional elections, the Republican and Democratic parties appear to be competitive.

In contrast to elections for national and major statewide offices, state legislative elections paint a somewhat different picture of electoral competition. Elections to the state legislature are much less likely to be contested by candidates from both major parties. In the Texas State Senate elections, rarely are more than half of the seats competitive in this sense. In fact, since 1992 the general trend line has been one of decline until the election of 2006.

Texas House of Representatives elections also tend to be one-party races. Since 1992, only between 26.7 percent and 46.7 percent of the 150 seats have been contested by both parties in an election. Again, while the general trend in the 1990s was toward less competitive elections, since 2000, both parties have contested at least 40 percent of the seats. The trend toward more Republicans running in uncontested seats appeared to be offset in the 2006 election.

Another method of assessing party competition in states is to develop a measure that takes into account the patterns of competition across gubernatorial elections, percentages of state legislature seats won by parties, the length of time the governor-

Table 7.3 Party Competition in Texas Elections

ELECTION / YEAR	SEATS CONTESTED BY REPUBLICANS ONLY		SEATS CONTESTED BY DEMOCRATS ONLY		SEATS CONTESTED BY BOTH PARTIES	
	NUMBER	PERCENTAGE	NUMBER	PERCENTAGE	NUMBER	PERCENTAGE
U.S. House of Representatives Texas						
1992	2	6.7%	3	10.0%	25	83.3%
1994	5	16.7%	0	0.0%	25	83.3%
1996	2	6.7%	0	0.0%	28	93.3%
1998	5	16.7%	7	23.3%	18	60.0%
2000	3	10.0%	6	20.0%	21	70.0%
2002	4	12.5%	5	15.6%	23	71.9%
2004	4	12.5%	3	9.4%	25	78.0%
2006	1	3.1%	5	15.6%	26	81.3%
Texas State Senate						
1992	4	12.9%	9	29.0%	18	58.1%
1994	6	19.4%	9	29.0%	16	51.6%
1996	5	33.3%	3	20.0%	7	46.7%
1998	5	31.3%	4	25.0%	7	43.8%
2000	6	40.0%	4	26.7%	5	33.3%
2002	10	32.3%	9	29.3%	12	38.7%
2004	6	40.0%	5	33.3%	4	26.7%
2006	7	43.8%	2	12.5%	7	43.8%
Texas State House of Representatives						
1992	36	24.0%	61	40.7%	53	35.3%
1994	37	24.7%	62	41.3%	51	34.0%
1996	49	32.6%	43	28.7%	58	38.7%
1998	53	35.3%	44	29.3%	53	35.3%
2000	53	35.3%	57	38.0%	40	26.7%
2002	48	32.0%	35	23.3%	67	44.7%
2004	51	34.0%	39	26.0%	60	40.0%
2006	37	24.7%	43	28.6%	70	46.7%

Source: Compiled by author from data available from the Texas Secretary of State, www.sos.state.tx.us/elections/historical/index.shtml, accessed May 14, 2007.

ship and legislature are controlled by each party, and the proportion of time the parties divide control over state government. This method is called the Ranney Index. Calculated for 1999–2003, the Ranney Index places Texas in the range of two-party competition, but leaning toward one-party Republican control. In fact, Texas scores closer to traditional Republican states like Nebraska and North Dakota than "Solid South" Democratic-controlled states like Mississippi.[42] Moreover, Texas looks nothing like all four of its neighboring states. Arkansas, Louisiana, New Mexico, and Oklahoma lean much more toward the Democratic Party.

Thus, while the Democratic and Republican parties contest elections throughout Texas, the patterns of party competition suggest that Republicans have emerged as a major competitor to the Democratic Party in recent years. The days of Democratic Party dominance of Texas politics in the late nineteenth and early twentieth centuries are gone. Republicans now compete effectively to win statewide offices, and in fact, Republicans now dominate these offices. At the federal level, Republican and Democratic candidates usually face each other for seats in the U.S. House of Representatives. At the level of state legislature, the Texas State Senate is somewhat competitive. The Texas House of Representatives features a high number of non-competitive races with many districts dominated exclusively by one major party or the other. Thus, transition has come to electoral competition in Texas.

Table 7.4 Party Competition in U.S. States

STATE	RANNEY INDEX	RANK (most Democratic to most Republican)
Top Five Democratic States		
Hawaii	0.735	1
Mississippi	0.716	2
Maryland	0.707	3
Rhode Island	0.700	4
Massachusetts	0.694	5
Texas	**0.378**	**36**
50 State Average	0.483	n/a
States Bordering Texas		
Arkansas	0.657	9
New Mexico	0.617	12
Louisiana	0.577	15
Oklahoma	0.570	17
Top Five Republican States		
Wyoming	0.284	46
Kansas	0.284	46
Utah	0.249	48
South Dakota	0.247	49
Idaho	0.167	50

Source: Kendra A. Hovey and Harold A. Hovey, *CQ's State Fact Finder* (Washington, D.C.: CQ Press, 2007), 118.
Note: The Ranney Index runs from 0 to 1, with 0 indicating complete domination of the state governorship and legislature by Republicans and 1 indicating complete control by Democrats.

In most elections where an **incumbent** is running, the incumbent possesses significant advantages over his or her challenger. The incumbent, by virtue of already holding office, is well known to voters. The advantage of having the voters familiar with the identity of a candidate is called name recognition. Name recognition is also enhanced by media coverage of the incumbent's activities, speeches, and public appearances before and during the election campaign as the incumbent carries out the duties of the office in which he or she serves. Of course, challengers with previous office-holding experience in other elected positions also have a degree of name recognition, as do celebrities and sports figures.

Incumbents are also favored by having an existing record of positions on issues from previous elections and in the context of decisions made while in office, an advantage known as **position taking.** For the executive branch offices, this advantage includes a record of accomplishments, including programs created or abolished, new initiatives created, and the like. In the legislature, incumbents are advantaged by having a record of votes on specific bills and resolutions. The legislator's position is therefore known based upon the voting record in the legislature. Presumably the incumbent has attractive positions to some of the voters, otherwise the incumbent would not likely have been elected in the first place.

Another positive aspect of incumbency is the ability to engage in **credit claiming.** Credit claiming occurs when an incumbent points out positive outcomes for which the incumbent is responsible. Credit claiming could include obtaining state funding for new buildings at a local community college or state university, sponsoring a bill

Incumbent
the candidate already holding office.

Position taking
an incumbent's advantage in having an existing record of positions on issues from previous elections and in the context of decisions made while in office.

Credit claiming
the advantage derived from incumbents' ability to point out positive outcomes for which they are responsible.

that changed the penalties for underage consumption of alcoholic beverages, or taking a stand against perceived runaway spending by the legislature.

In elections to a legislature like the Texas Legislature or U.S. Congress, incumbents are also favored by **casework,** solving problems for the people back home. However, the most important advantage of incumbency may be the advantage that an incumbent possesses in raising money for an election campaign. Incumbents typically raise much more money than non-incumbents during an election cycle. Organized interests, knowing the advantages that the incumbent has, contribute willingly to the incumbent's reelection campaign to remain in good standing with the incumbent or court new relationships with the incumbent.

Campaign Finance in Texas

nevitably, the discussion of elections turns to the issue of money in elections. Campaign finance is important, because without money, candidates and political parties have trouble getting out their message and voters have a difficult time gathering information and making decisions about which candidate they will vote for. Money also provides essentials for election campaigns like television and radio advertising, and travel throughout the state or election district. Also important is paying for office space, telephones, Web sites, public-opinion polls, and campaign staff.

The issue of campaign finance is also important to a discussion of the health of American democracy, voter participation, and outcomes of elections. In a large, diverse state like Texas, a well-funded campaign is often viewed as crucial. However, the source of financing is often linked to concern about who is giving money to candidates and what candidates may be doing in return. For example, a group will give campaign contributions with the expectation that the candidate will at least listen to the group's concerns and issues. The issue of campaign finance also raises the issue of whether organized interests "buy" favorable legislation, court rulings, and executive decisions.

Because money matters, the issue of free speech comes into question. On the one hand, campaign contributions are a form of political speech, because by giving a contribution to get a candidate elected, an individual citizen or an interest group indicates their political position. In contrast, the cost of modern campaigns suggests that perhaps those with more money to contribute are "heard" more often, regardless of the opinions of the entire electorate or even a majority of voters. In 1976, the Supreme Court examined this issue, ruling that campaign contributions were a form of speech and that limits on contributions limited freedom of speech.[43] According to the Court, limits on what an individual contributed to his or her own campaign violate the First Amendment of the U.S. Constitution. Likewise what an individual or organized interest spends on their own, independent of candidate campaign funds, cannot be limited. In 2005, the Supreme Court revisited this issue, allowing more limits to be placed upon independent spending by individuals and interest groups,[44] only to reverse itself again in 2007.[45]

Some countries, like Germany, have addressed this issue by providing **public financing** of elections. Essentially, the government covers the costs of an election by providing subsidies to parties and candidates or by providing a reimbursement for campaign costs. Thus, parties and candidates do not have to raise money for the campaign from private citizens or organized interests like labor unions, special

Casework
solving problems for constituents.

Public financing
a system of campaign financing in which the government covers the cost of elections for political parties or candidates.

Texas versus Georgia

Although incumbency and significant levels of campaign finance are important factors in winning an election, both of these are not always enough to guarantee the outcome of an election. In 2002, Texans and Georgians went to the polls on Election Day in November to elect the governors of their respective states. In Texas, the incumbent was Rick Perry, the former lieutenant governor who became governor after Gov. George W. Bush became president of the United States. In Georgia, Roy Barnes was the incumbent Democrat running for reelection.

Barnes's campaign was well financed, raising almost $17 million in funds from a variety of sources. Lawyers and lobbyists alone raised over $3 million to support Barnes's reelection. His challenger, "Sonny" Perdue, had served in the Georgia Senate for two terms. Little known outside his home district in Houston County (pronounced "Hows-ton" in Georgia), Perdue was underfunded compared to Barnes. The Perdue campaign war chest totaled less than $5 million. The largest single contribution, $50,000, came from Perdue's own pocketbook.[i] When the election was over, Perdue won with over 51 percent of the vote.

Why did a well-financed incumbent with much better name recognition lose the governor's election in Georgia? Two issues changed the dynamics of the election campaign. As governor, Roy Barnes launched an overhaul of the state's education system, focusing on the issue of teacher certification and recertification. In doing so, he alienated an important and organized interest group. The second issue was the decision by Barnes to change the Georgia flag to eliminate the Confederate Battle Flag from the design. While updating Georgia's image was supported by civil rights groups and business interests in Atlanta, in many other parts of the state the decision to change the flag proved unpopular. Among other things, Perdue promised to hold a popular vote on the flag design.

Thinking Critically

- Why do you think incumbency is an advantage?
- What are the limits of incumbency in an election?
- In what ways might Governor Perry's incumbency affect his reelection?

i. www.followthemoney.org/database/StateGlance, accessed November 12, 2007.

---

interests, and corporations. A public finance system is in contrast to the reliance on **private financing.** Private financing occurs when individual citizens, interest groups, labor unions, and corporations make donations to candidates and political parties to cover the cost of an election.

The United States possesses a mixture of systems, with most elections being privately financed. The exception is the U.S. presidential election, which features some public financing. In addition, the United States tends to emphasize reporting the sources of campaign finance, the size of donations, and the patterns of candidate spending rather than limiting campaign spending. Campaigns for federal offices, including U.S. presidential, U.S. Senate, and U.S. House of Representatives elections are governed by federal laws like the Federal Election Campaign Act of 1974 and the Bipartisan Campaign Reform Act of 2002. The Supreme Court has also been active in this area, as mentioned above.

State and local elections are governed by state campaign finance laws and rulings by state courts. All state and local elections in Texas are privately financed. In Texas, the emphasis is placed upon **disclosure.** Disclosure is the idea that each candidate reports who contributes money to the campaign and how much is contributed by an individual or group. Texas does not place limits on how much an individual, interest group, labor union, or corporation may contribute. The logic here is that merely providing this information allows voters to become informed about who is supporting

Private financing
occurs when citizens, interest groups, labor unions, and corporations make donations to candidates and political parties to cover the cost of an election.

Disclosure
the reporting of who contributes money to the campaign and how much is contributed by an individual or corporation.

the candidates or constitutional referendums in an election. However, political organizations outside the state are limited to $500 or less.

Texas campaign finance laws apply to both primary elections and general elections. The responsibility for collecting this information and for providing the information to the public is given to the Texas Ethics Commission. Candidates are required to file reports with the Texas Ethics Commission every month once a candidate begins to campaign. After an election, a final report must be filed within three months of the election. The Texas Ethics Commission maintains a searchable database for citizens on its Web site, www.ethics.state.tx.us.

Because state and local judges are elected in Texas, judicial elections are also covered by campaign finance laws. To prevent fears of justice being "bought" through campaign contributions, an additional set of regulations limit the size of all contributions made to a candidate's campaign to get elected as a judge. The limits on individual donors depend on the size of the judicial district, with limits ranging from $1,000 for judicial districts with a population of 250,000 or less, to $5,000 for judicial districts of one million or more people, as well as statewide judicial offices. Law firms may contribute up to six times the individual limits before individual members of the law firm are limited to $50 contributions. Similarly, statewide candidates may accept only $300,000 from political action committees (PACs). Judicial candidates may also opt to accept voluntary spending limits. Like contribution limits, the voluntary limit for a judicial office is based on the size of the judicial district. For example, the limit begins at $100,000 for districts that have less than 250,000 people and eventually rises to $500,000 for districts with more than one million people. The limit for statewide office is $2 million. Candidates accepting these limits enjoy an unusual reward—if their opponent exceeds the expenditure limits the candidate is no longer subject to limits on contributions and expenditures.

The 2006 elections illustrate the role of money in Texas elections. Across all state government elections, $179.3 million was contributed to candidates running for executive, legislative, and judicial elections.[46] This figure includes races for Texas Railroad Commission and State Board of Education. The race for governor accounted for over $49.2 million collected by the four major candidates in the primaries and general elections. The candidates spent over $52.7 million on the election.[47] Table 7.5 gives the amounts raised and spent for the four candidates seeking the governorship in the 2006 election. The table also calculates the spending per vote received.

The race for Lieutenant Governor proved more interesting as David Dewhurst, the Republican, raised $10.2 million for his reelection, while his Democratic opponent, Maria Alvarado raised only $50,991. As might be expected, Dewhurst received 58 percent of the vote, compared with Alvarado's showing of 37 percent. This situation suggests that a link exists between campaign finance and electoral competition. Running a well-financed campaign in a geographically large state like Texas is often a precondition to being a viable, competitive candidate in the election. Similar disparities in financing occurred in 2006, including for other statewide offices like Texas agriculture commissioner, comptroller of Public Accounts, and attorney general. Candidates for the Texas Senate pulled together over $28.5 million, averaging $433,885 per candidate. Comparable figures for all candidates running for the 150 seats in the Texas House of Representatives were $65.4 million or $148,657 per candidate.

The sources of contributions provide interesting insight into present day Texas politics. As might be expected, the oil and gas industry contributed large sums of money. Across all races and candidates, oil and gas companies gave over $7.9 million. However, this level of giving placed the industry in third place behind real estate

Table 7.5 Campaign Spending for Candidates in the 2006 Texas Gubernatorial Election

CANDIDATE (party affiliation)	AMOUNT RAISED	AMOUNT SPENT	VOTES RECEIVED	MONEY SPENT PER VOTE
Rick Perry (Republican)	$20,199,539	$26,723,217	1,716,792	$15.57
Chris Bell (Democratic)	$7,359,018	$6,440,256	1,310,337	$ 4.91
Carole Strayhorn (Independent)	$9,084,635	$14,349,456	796,851	$18.01
Kinky Friedman (Independent)	$6,288,113	$5,246,550	547,674	$ 9.58

Source: Texas Ethics Commission and author's own calculations.

($8.9 million in contributions), and lawyers/lobbyists ($25.6 million in contributions). A list of the top individual or group contributors reveals that Bob J. Perry, the owner of a large home construction firm, contributed almost $3.8 million to various candidates for office, followed by Texans for Lawsuit Reform, a lawyer/lobbyist organization at $3.4 million. David Dewhurst gave $2.7 million of his personal money to his own campaign for lieutenant governor, while Chris Bell's unsuccessful attempt to win the governorship included $1.7 million of his own personal fortune. Interestingly, the San Antonio-based H-E-B grocery store chain appeared in the list of top twenty contributors, only to announce a series of store closings not six months later in an effort to control costs and maintain profitability.

Winners and Losers

Politics involves decisions about who gets what, and thus it is not surprising that those groups that participate in politics are more likely to be the winners in a state's distribution of resources. In theory, the strength of democracies lies in the ability of average citizens to exert pressure on the political system. When democracies are working, policy represents compromise, but must take into account the needs of all groups in society. Historically differences in participation were created by institutional barriers to voting, ranging from outright denial of suffrage to certain groups to obstacles such as white primaries and poll taxes designed to stifle a particular group's participation. Removing these barriers to voting has occurred slowly and often as a result of federal imposition of election standards.

Unfortunately, in spite of the enfranchisement of minority groups in the state, minority voting remains significantly lower than white participation. Asian and Hispanic groups in particular exhibit extremely low levels of voting participation. Minorities will continue to struggle to have their preferences represented in the state as long as they participate in voting at lower levels. Texas is one of the most diverse states in America, but this is not reflected in the voting patterns.

Voter turnout is also significantly lower among certain age groups. College-age voters, in particular, are the least likely to show up to the polls and, therefore, the least likely to be represented by state policies. Thus, policies in Texas often ignore the needs of college-age voters and, in times of budget crisis, college students are often the first group that legislators target. Thus, the deregulation of tuition at state universities and Governor Perry's veto of appropriations for state community colleges provide two recent examples of such targeting. Groups in the state who remain apathetic will continue to be the first groups sacrificed in times of budget cuts.

Finally, the long ballot in Texas exerts a palpable cost, by increasing voter apathy throughout the state. Ironically, Texans resist changing a system where we elect most important public offices because Texans distrust government. Our political culture creates a preference to keep the option of electing officials in the hands of the people, even when, in any given election, most Texans are not exercising that option. The result is that average Texans are becoming increasingly disconnected from the political process.

Conclusion

Texas elections, like all election systems, are designed to produce certain types of outcomes. Historically, the election rules and voting rights were designed to disenfranchise African American voters, and to a lesser extent, poor rural white voters. The rules historically were also designed to allow the Democratic Party to maintain control over the election system. Thus until the 1960s, white elites and the Democratic Party were clearly the winners of the electoral game. The transition of Texas politics toward inclusion of minorities and women occurred in large part through the national government's actions to secure voting rights, especially for African Americans and Hispanics. By increasing the national government's role, a second transition developed: Congress and the U.S. Court moved into the area of elections by establishing over time a set of standards that states must follow in the conduct of national, state, and local elections. The movement toward electronic voting equipment is the latest example.

Since the 1960s, the emergence of the Republican Party has altered Texas politics by developing greater electoral competition. While this transition may be true at the level of statewide elected offices, and to a lesser extent, the races for Texas's seats in the U.S. House of Representatives and Senate, this emergence of the Republican Party has not necessarily produced more electoral competition at the level of the state legislature. The absence of electoral competition in some elections, combined with voter apathy and disengagement by certain demographic groups, means that the real outcome may be greater empowerment of those who contribute money to finance the election campaigns. The candidates who are well financed do quite well. The organized interests who donate to campaigns expect some form of return for their efforts to fund the winner's campaign. The influence of organized interests and the role of the political parties in this financing system are explored more thoroughly in the next chapter.

Key Terms

advanced or early voting
blanket or wide-open primary
casework
closed primary
credit claiming

cross filing
direct democracy election
direct primaries
disclosure
Equal Protection Clause
general election
grandfather clause
Help America Vote Act (HAVA)
incumbent
independent candidate
indirect primary
literacy test
Motor Voter Act
open primary
party-line or straight-ticket voting
poll tax
position taking
public financing
preference primary
primary elections
private financing
roll off
second order elections
suffrage
voter turnout
Voting Rights Act of 1965 (VRA)
white primary

Explore this subject further at http://college.cqpress.com/lonestarpolitics, where you'll find chapter summaries, practice quizzes, key word flash cards, and additional suggested resources.

The oil tanker *Tugela* floats below the Harbor Bridge on its way to port in Corpus Christi, Texas. Oil interests represent just one of the many organized groups exerting influence on politics in the Lone Star state.

CHAPTER **8**

Parties and Organized Interests

I n 1996 an apparently unlikely battle was being played out at the Texas Republican Convention. Kay Bailey Hutchison, elected to the U.S. Senate two years earlier by the largest statewide margin ever enjoyed by a Texas Republican, saw herself facing a challenge from within her own party as she attempted to become one of the state's 123 delegates to the Republican National Convention. While members of Congress and other elected officials routinely serve as delegates at their party's convention, Senator Hutchison saw her seat at the convention challenged by pro-life Republicans because she favored allowing abortion in certain circumstances. She and some other Republicans had refused to sign a pledge vowing to oppose any changes in the party platform's call for a constitutional amendment that would define a fetus as a human life with rights.

Senator Hutchison enjoyed the support of prominent conservatives, including Gov. George W. Bush, and Bob Dole, the party's presidential candidate in that election. Phil Gramm, the state's other U.S. senator and a well-established champion of conservative causes, called those behind the effort to oust Hutchison "bullies," and said that if Hutchison was not sent to the national convention he would not go either. Despite the strong endorsement of some conservatives, the convention was closely divided on the vote for the state's delegates. After an extended battle at the convention State Party Chairman Tom Pawkin proclaimed the slate containing Hutchison elected on a voice vote and dismissed the pro-life delegates' demand for a roll-call vote. While Senator Hutchison survived the challenge and made it to the national convention, two of the party's members of the U.S. House, Henry Bonilla and Mack Thornberry, were denied positions as delegates, as was Dole's campaign vice chair Dick Collins and Fred Meyer, a former chairman of the Texas Republican Party.

While such an open rebellion is somewhat rare, the 1996 Texas Republican convention dramatically reflects the everyday reality of politics as an arena in which parties and organized interests must sometimes work together, but must also resolve differences as they work to influence government according to sometimes different agendas. Parties are driven by the need to win elections in order to succeed and must struggle to hold together the broad coalitions of voters needed to win elections. In contrast, organized interests need to remain committed to the core issues and must labor to advance a more narrow policy agenda.

In this chapter we'll look at the impact that organized interests and political parties have on the practice of democracy in Texas. Lurking in the shadows of the three branches of Texas government, political parties and organized interests remain unpopular but important partners in Texas politics. While organized interests and political parties can foster citizen participation, we'll see that they often fail to represent the citizens of the state and have become hindrances to the state's ability to keep pace with today's rapid changes.

> **As you read the chapter, think about the following questions:**
>
> ★ How have political parties changed in Texas?
> ★ What are the main functions of political parties?
> ★ To what extent do parties and organized interests represent citizens of the state?
> ★ In what ways does Texas attempt to regulate interest group influence?

The Development of Political Parties in Texas

While the battle between political parties has often served as the premier forum for competition in U.S. politics, Texans have rarely enjoyed the benefits of a truly competitive party system. Early Texans were not strangers to political parties, but initially shunned them. Sam Houston had been a close political ally of Andrew Jackson, whose patronage system did much to build the early Democratic Party in the United States. Despite his Democratic roots, Houston generally avoided party labels in his Texas campaigns and the state's earliest elections were dominated by personalities as Houston and his enemies battled for control.

Ironically, just as political parties were taking root in Texas, the national Whig party collapsed in the mid-1850s and their replacement, the Republicans, held antislavery positions that ensured they would find little support in the state. The American or "Know-Nothing" party, an anti-immigration party, aggressively cultivated Texans, forcing the Democratic Party to become fully organized in Texas for the first time in 1854.[1] Then, just as the Democratic Party was beginning to take hold in the state, the coming Civil War divided Texans between pro-union and secessionist factions and blotted out any chance of Republicans winning statewide office. The bitterness that followed Reconstruction was directed toward the Republican Party, allowing the Democratic Party to dominate the state for decades. The biggest challenges to the Democrats came from the Greenback Party in the 1870s and 1880s, and then the Populists or "People's Party" in the 1880s and 1890s.

The Populist Party, backed largely by small farmers looking to democratize the economic system, favored programs like a graduated income tax, an eight-hour workday, and government control of railroads. The Populists made the greatest gains in the American Midwest, but the party shared a common cause with the Farmer's Alliance (itself an outgrowth of the Grange Movement) that had organized in Lampasas, Texas, in the mid-1870s.[2] Texas's Populist Party built on the foundation of the fundamentalist churches, an especially important social network in early Texas, one of the few that brought farm families together. Farmers thus often linked religious themes with their desire for relief from economic dilemmas.[3] Before fading from the Texas scene, the Populists won 44 percent of the vote for J. C. Kearby, their candidate in the 1896 election running with the support of the Republicans who had not fielded their own candidate that year. However, the Populists' call for government ownership of the railroads and limits on land ownership by corporations made them a poor match for the more business-minded Republicans. Eventually, the partnerships with the Republicans and other groups took their toll on the Populists as these undermined the consistency of the Populist ideological foundations. Meanwhile, some of their more popular ideas were appropriated by Democratic politicians like Gov. Jim Hogg, who won the favor of many Texas farmers by taking on the railroads.

The next challenge to the Texas Democratic Party emerged from the Progressives. While a formidable force for reform in much of the country, Texas's Progressives lacked the corrupt, big-city party machines as targets for reform or the economic issues that energized the party nationally, and instead turned to more cultural issues like alcohol prohibition.[4]

Texas had a few local party machines where local party officials used patronage, offering government jobs, contracts, and other favors to party loyalists, to perpetuate their power. George Parr's political machine ran Duvall County in South Texas for thirty years after Parr inherited it from his father, Archer. By working closely with them and getting to know them Parr earned the loyalty of poor Hispanics, whose votes Parr could then deliver. He built a political and economic empire founded on money taken from businesses and government accounts. Parr's ability to deliver votes to friendly candidates made him kingmaker in Texas, with Lyndon Johnson being his most famous product.

George Parr wasn't the first Texas official involved in creative ballot counting. In 1869, citizens in Navarro County were unable to cast their votes after the county's registrar absconded with the registration lists before the election. In the same year, Milam County ballots were never counted and in Hill County an official took the ballots to another jurisdiction to count, with results that surprised many Hill County voters.[5]

In general, the Progressives found themselves caught up in the prohibition movement because promoting political reform and banishing alcohol were seen as tools for building a better society. As with the Populists, churches played an important role and evangelicals and women's groups were drawn to the Progressive cause.[6] And, as with the Populists, the Progressives saw much of their agenda absorbed by the Democrats.

The Republican Party in Texas slowly developed in the early twentieth century, only to suffer a major setback during the Great Depression, a disaster that many Texans blamed on President Herbert Hoover and the Republican Party. While the Depression and World War II hurt Republicans seeking statewide office, Texans were beginning to show more and more interest in Republican presidential candidates. In 1952 the Texas Democratic Party officially supported Republican candidate Dwight D. Eisenhower, and for the first time in Texas's history, a Republican presidential candidate carried the state. Texas Democrats avoided the Republican tide across the state in 1952 though, when every Democratic nominee for statewide office, except one, cross-filed for positions on the ballot as both Democrats and Republicans under the provisions of a 1951 law.

While the Democratic Party would eventually lead the nation in civil rights, from Reconstruction until the 1960s it often supported segregation and racism in Texas and elsewhere in the South. African Americans were barred from participating in the Democratic primaries and the party created special white primaries as a matter of law in Texas and as a matter of practice in other southern states. Since the Democratic Party enjoyed a virtual monopoly in statewide general elections, African Americans were effectively shut out of any meaningful role in elections. Democratic governor James "Pa" Ferguson would proclaim, "A negro has no business whatever taking part in the political affairs of the Democratic party, the white man's party."[7]

In November of 2006, voters in Texas and in New York participated in elections for one of their U.S. senators. Texas voters selected from three candidates: a Republican, a Democratic, and a Libertarian. In New York, voters selected from among candidates from nine different political parties. One key difference between the two elections is the fact that in New York three political parties selected and listed the same candidate for U.S. senator–Hillary Clinton. She was the candidate for the Democratic Party, the Independence Party, and the Working Families Party. Her primary opponent, John Spencer, ran as the Republican Party candidate and as the Conservative Party candidate. In New York, the ballot is laid out so every party and candidate appears separately. As a result, Hillary Clinton's name appeared on the ballot three times and John Spencer's name appeared twice.

The practice of two or more parties legally running the same candidate for office is called electoral fusion. Electoral fusion is allowed in a handful of states, including New York. While electoral fusion was once practiced in Texas as a means of protecting Democratic dominance, it is now illegal.

The practice of electoral fusion allowed voters to support Hillary Clinton or John Spencer without voting for either of the two major parties. In addition, during the campaign both Clinton and Spencer had to address issues of concern not only for their respective party's base of voters but also for the additional parties that gave them a nomination.

U.S. Senate Election in New York, 2006

CANDIDATE	PERCENTAGE OF VOTES	PARTY
Hillary Rodham Clinton	60.1%	Democratic
John Spencer	27.0%	Republican
John Spencer	4.0%	Conservative
Hillary Rodham Clinton	3.6%	Independence
Hillary Rodham Clinton	3.3%	Working Families
Howie Hawkins	1.2%	Green
Jeffrey T. Russell	0.4%	Libertarian
Roger Calero	0.2%	Socialist Workers
William Van Auken	0.1%	Socialist Equity

Thinking Critically

- What is electoral fusion?
- How does electoral fusion allow third parties to participate in an election?
- How does electoral fusion legitimize voting for third parties?
- Why did Texas Democrats support electoral fusion in the past?
- Why did the practice become illegal in Texas?

Eventually, the civil rights issue split the Democratic Party of Texas, a breakup common throughout the Southern states.

In the latter part of the twentieth century Texas starred in the transition that would see the South turn from heavily Democratic to heavily Republican. The Republicans finally broke the Democratic dominance in 1961 and won statewide office for the first time since Reconstruction, when Republican John Tower won the U.S. Senate seat vacated by the election of Democrat Lyndon Johnson to the vice presidency. The Republicans did not win the governorship until 1978 when William Clements won a surprise victory. By 2000 Democrats were unable to effectively challenge Republicans for any statewide office. Thus, in less than forty years Texas went from domination by the Democratic Party to domination by the Republicans. Exit polls from the 2006 election for governor revealed that 40 percent of Texas voters identified themselves as Republicans, while 31 percent called themselves Democrats and 29 declared themselves independents.

The domination by one party is not the norm in American politics. After the 2006 election half of the states had some divided government, with a governor facing at least one house of their state legislature in the hands of the opposition party. Of the other half, fifteen states have their legislatures and governors' mansions in the hands of Democrats while the other ten are in the hands of Republicans.

The dominance of one party does not necessarily mean that there is no competition. It has often been said that Texas only has one party but has enough conflict for six. For much of the state's history the political battles of the state were waged in the process of nominating Democratic candidates. With Republicans unable to mount a serious challenge, Texas politicians realized that the winner of the Democratic nominating primary was effectively the election winner. The battles to win the primary were often as hotly contested as any general election contest for office.

While the Republican Party does dominate statewide elections and appears strong, citizens' participation in the parties has weakened, and today, few voters take part in the primaries of the two parties. For example, turnout for the primaries leading up to the 2006 election totaled only seven percent of the state's voting age population with 3.1 percent of Texans voting in the Democratic primary and 3.9 percent voting in the Republican primary. In contrast, turnout for the Democratic primary during the 1970s when the Democratic Party dominated was generally between 15 percent and 19 percent. As Table 8.1 shows, in the 1970s less than 5 percent of Texans took part in the Republican primaries, a matter of little consequence since Republican gubernatorial candidates were seen as having little chance of winning office. However, since that time the stature of the Republican Party has changed dramatically, even while its participation rates in the primary have not increased. It appears that the GOP hasn't grown into its new boots and the Democrats have unfortunately joined them in the race to narrow participation. With 3.9 percent of eligible citizens selecting the Republican nominees that are almost certain to win statewide office it appears that the parties are not creating the broad participation and healthy competition that the state needs to help it respond to changes.

Table 8.1 Turnout as Percentage of Voting Age Population in Primaries

YEAR	DEMOCRATIC PRIMARY TURNOUT	REPUBLICAN PRIMARY TURNOUT
1970	14.1%	1.5%
1972	28.4%	1.5%
1974	18.4%	0.8%
1976	17.3%	4.0%
1978	19.3%	1.7%
1980	13.8%	5.3%
1982	12.3%	2.5%
1984	12.9%	3.0%
1986	9.3%	4.6%
1988	14.4%	8.3%
1990	11.9%	6.8%
1992	11.5%	6.2%
1994	7.9%	4.3%
1996	6.7%	7.4%
1998	4.7%	4.2%
2000	5.4%	7.8%
2002	6.5%	4.0%
2004	5.2%	4.3%
2006	3.1%	3.9%

Source: Texas Secretary of State's Office, www.sos.state.tx.us.

Political Parties in Texas

 exas history has often strained traditional definitions of political parties. One classic definition of a political party comes from eighteenth-century British political philosopher Edmund Burke, who described a party as people "united for promoting their joint endeavors the national interest, upon some particular principle in which they are all agreed."[8] As we've seen, Texas has experienced as much fighting within its parties as between them, straining the application of the traditional definition of parties to Texas politics. For example, while today's Republican Party can be labeled a "conservative" party, Republicans often clash on the meaning of conservatism as conflict over issues like immigration and abortion divide Texans who claim the conservative label. Further complicating matters, as we will see later, the Texas Republican Party disagrees with the national Republican Party, and even Texan George W. Bush, on several issues.

The realities of political parties in Texas are best captured by Leon Epstein's definition of a **party** as "any group, however loosely organized, seeking to elect governmental office-holders under a given label."[9] While this definition does not meet everyone's hopes for the function of party, it does match the realities of Texas's parties historically and distinguishes parties from interest groups, in that parties nominate candidates for office under their label while interest groups do not.

Texas provides an interesting case to examine the role that many political scientists want parties to play. Some scholars want politics to meet the standards of the **responsible party model** of politics in which each party holds firmly to a consistent, coherent set of policies with a consistent ideology that is distinct from the other parties. The virtue of responsible parties is that they provide voters with clear choices and firm positions the parties are pledged to honor if elected. In contrast, political scientist Anthony Downs has described an **electoral competition model** in which parties move to the center of the political spectrum as they attempt to win votes, sacrificing the more purely ideological positions preferred by the proponents of the responsible party model. In this view, the political parties are more pragmatic than ideological and are ready to shift their issue stands from year to year in order to win office. Like American political parties in general, parties in Texas do not match either model perfectly.

Functions of Parties

State and local parties have a variety of important roles in a democracy. One of the most obvious is nomination of party candidates. Since the distinguishing characteristic of a party is electing candidates under their label, selecting the nominees is a central function of the state and local parties. Slating, or putting together a list of candidates for all positions is often seen as an important role of state and local parties as they assemble teams of candidates ready to bring their party's ideas into a variety of offices.

Related to getting candidates on the ballot and elected is the need to seek out the right candidates. Thus, one of the most important functions of state and local parties is recruitment. As each party attempts to build a winning team they will seek out the most politically talented individuals for the next generation of politics. Precinct and county party leaders must be alert to the presence of individuals with the talent to take themselves and their party to victory in an election. Before he was president of the United States, George W. Bush was a governor of Texas who was urged by Texas Republicans (and some Democrats) to run for president. Before that, he was a businessman urged into politics by local Republican leaders.

The next step is the function of supporting candidates. Both state parties provide logistical support and campaign staff training for party candidates. Some of the support is financial, with parties providing cash contributions as well as advertising

Party

any group, however loosely organized, seeking to elect governmental office-holders under a given label.

Responsible party model

the theoretical view that each party should hold firmly to a clear and consistent set of policies with a coherent ideology distinct from that of other parties to present voters with clear choices.

Electoral competition model

the view that parties make a pragmatic move to the center of the political spectrum as they attempt to win votes, sacrificing the more purely ideological positions.

and similar support. The parties also provide training for candidates and their campaign staffs.

One function is rapidly expanding and may define modern parties: fundraising. Headlines about presidential involvement in fundraising in the 1990s clouded the fact that much of the fundraising being done was actually for state parties. Fundraising and spending in campaigns has shifted to the states because federal laws restrict how much individuals can give to the national parties. State parties in general faced few such restrictions and thus found themselves the recipients of the big checks their national parties could not legally accept. While fundraising remains an area of controversy, the parties must raise funds to promote their agendas or help their candidates, and the parties thus remain locked in a money competition in which they try to raise more money than the other.

Another function that parties must spend money on is mobilizing voters. Through phone banks, door-to-door canvassing, mailings, and advertising the parties reach out to voters and encourage them to vote. Of course, a party is most likely to reach out to those voters that will support the party's candidates. However, democracy in general can benefit from a healthy competition if both parties reach out to voters and increase turnout in general.

Parties can also be an important tool for representation. The one-party nature of Texas has often meant our general elections were not competitive and the redistricting process described in chapter 3 has even further divided the state by creating districts that are heavily either Republican or Democratic. This means that many Texans live in districts in which it is unlikely that their party will be able to effectively compete. As a consequence, some citizens will see themselves as part of a **chronic minority,** a group destined to rarely win an election or achieve majority status. Such citizens will see few reasons to become actively engaged in politics and have little hope that their views will be reflected by their representatives in Austin. Parties can offer some hope that such views will be heard even if these views are transmitted by an elected official from another area of the state. For example, the Democrats in areas that find themselves represented by Republicans in the Texas House and Senate may hope that Democrats from other parts of the state will give voice to their concerns and advance their cause.

In some ways the ultimate function of political parties is controlling government since the point of winning elections is getting party candidates into office. In some ways this function of political parties goes against the constitutional order because our system of checks and balances and separation of powers are intended to keep any one faction from having too much influence. However, parties are elected so they will have influence and get things done and their ability to coordinate the efforts of officials across the branches of government can be an important tool in creating the kind of leadership a state in transition needs.

Chronic minority

a group that rarely wins elections or achieves majority status, and thus sees few reasons to become actively engaged in politics.

The Consequences of Weak Parties

The scholar V. O. Key observed that Texas's geographic size made it hard for well-formed political networks to function. Without closely-knit political networks, it has been harder for parties to maintain enduring political organizations across the broad geographic expanse of Texas. Those parties that were able to build personal followings did so through dramatic appeals to the public that were generally short-lived and created a political following based more on personality than policy goals. For example, it was his skills as a flour salesman rather than dependence on a well-

Pappy O'Daniel

As we've noted, Texas's size has given an advantage to characters flamboyant enough to grab the voters' attention across the state. One of Texas's legendary governors, "Pass the Biscuits, Pappy" O'Daniel (pictured, sitting, with Harry Akin) is a fine example of the ability of a colorful outsider to push aside established party leaders and land on the top of the state's power structure.

Wilbert Lee O'Daniel was born in Ohio but moved to Texas in 1925. As sales manager for a flour mill, O'Daniel would become well known as the host of a radio show featuring music from Bob Wills' and Milton Brown's band, The Light Crust Doughboys. The show opened with someone saying, "Pass the Biscuits, Pappy," and the show mixed inspirational stories with music, including songs that O'Daniel penned, with titles like "The Boy Who Never Got Too Big to Comb His Mother's Hair." In 1938, purportedly spurred by listener letters urging him to run for governor (although others suggest that wealthy business interests and a public relations expert had done the real urging), O'Daniel declared his candidacy, proclaiming the Ten Commandments as his platform and the Golden Rule as his motto. O'Daniel won the Democratic nomination without a runoff and, facing no real opposition, won the general election with 97 percent of the vote.

An estimated 100,000 people packed into Memorial Stadium in Austin to witness his inauguration, but O'Daniel quickly exhibited his lack of political skill by proposing a thinly-disguised sales tax, making numerous questionable appointments, and forgetting his only specific campaign promise—a $30 a month pension for every Texan over 65. By the time of his reelection campaign, he was opposed by almost every newspaper in the state, with the *Dallas Morning News* proclaiming, "The highest office in the state has been the laughing-stock of the United States for a year and a half."[i] Voters returned the eighty-six-year-old O'Daniel to office, but he accomplished little in his second term beyond positioning himself for a move to the U.S. Senate by appointing Andrew Jackson Houston, Sam Houston's only surviving son, to fill a vacancy left after Sen. Morris Sheppard died in April 1941. Houston, the oldest man to serve in the U.S. Senate to that point, died the next year, leaving O'Daniel without an incumbent to worry about in the special election. O'Daniel's only serious primary challenger was a young ex-congressman named Lyndon Baines Johnson. Johnson led through much of the ballot counting, but late returns from rural districts gave O'Daniel a victory, leaving Johnson to await another day.

Johnson's years of service to the party would not pay off immediately as he found himself swept aside by the colorful character of O'Daniel in this particular race. However, the down-home, colorful stylings of O'Daniel won him few victories in Washington, D.C. O'Daniel's public appeal made him a legend in Texas, but his leadership did little to leave any real legacy of accomplishments either in Austin or Washington, D.C.

i. Randolph B. Campbell, *Gone to Texas* (New York: Oxford University Press—USA, 2004), 394.

ordered political machine that brought Pappy O'Daniel into the governorship. In contrast, other southern states saw the rise of personal political machines, some like that of the Longs in Louisiana, which spanned several generations.

With no well-organized party organization to provide resistance, political outsiders have often found their way into the Texas governor's mansion. In the absence of a well-established political order, working through the system has less value and a political newcomer's dramatic appeal can more easily win the election. While the early twentieth century saw some lively outsiders like "Pa" Ferguson and "Pappy"

O'Daniel, more recent elections have seen the rise of political newcomers like William Clements and George W. Bush leading the Republican revival in the state.

Party Organizations

ecause of the role they play in the practice of democracy in the state, the organization and functioning of the political parties is subject to some regulation by the state. The U.S. Supreme Court has ruled that state law can regulate the internal affairs of political parties only if it is "necessary to ensure that elections are orderly, fair, and honest." [10] Texas state law still places restrictions on the selection, composition, rules, and meeting dates of the state and local political party committees. In fact, Texas is rated as a "Heavy Regulator," with some of the most extensive laws governing the state's parties. [11]

Political parties in the United States are composed of both temporary and permanent organizations. The **temporary party organizations** are gatherings of ordinary party members through primaries and in the meetings known as caucuses and conventions. The **permanent party organizations** are those party officials selected by the temporary organizations to conduct the business of the party in between primaries, caucuses, and conventions.

While the temporary nature of party conventions may make them seem less important, like any democratic organization, America's political parties draw their legitimacy from the participation of citizens. As such, political parties are **grassroots organizations,** or groups where power and decision making reside with average citizens. This relationship makes these gatherings of party members the foundation to the party's claim to legitimacy.

Citizens' participation in Texas's two major parties begins at the local level through primaries, elections in which ordinary citizens vote to choose the candidates that will represent a party on the ballot in the general election. In Texas, the parties may also use primary elections to have party members vote on resolutions that voice demands for specific legislation or any other matter. Primaries have been part of Texas elections since the Terrell Election Law in 1905 mandated that major political parties use primaries to select their nominees. Prior to that, parties were free to make their nominations however they pleased, with nominees usually being chosen by nominating conventions composed of party leaders without input from average citizens. Progressives promoted primaries as a means to take the choice of candidates away from political bosses meeting behind the scenes and expand participation to ordinary citizens.

Current Texas law requires that the major parties (those that received 20 percent or more of the vote for governor in the last election) use primaries to choose their candidates for office. Parties whose candidate for governor received between 2 percent and 20 percent of the vote in the last election have a choice between nominating candidates by convention or by primary. Parties whose gubernatorial candidates received less than 2 percent of the vote must use conventions because of the costs involved in holding primaries. Primaries require separate voting booths for each party in every precinct in the state.

As noted in chapter 7, Texas party primaries are technically closed primaries with only party members allowed to vote. In practice Texas primaries are much more accessible and function as semi-open primaries in which any voter may participate without having previously registered a party affiliation. When Texans vote in a party's primary their voter registration cards are stamped with the name of that

Temporary party organizations gatherings, such as primaries, caucuses, and conventions, at which ordinary party members meet.

Permanent party organizations the party officials selected by the temporary organizations to conduct party business between the primaries, caucuses, and conventions.

Grassroots organizations groups in which power and decision making reside with average citizens; average citizen participation is the foundation of these groups' legitimacy.

Figure 8.1 Texas Party Organization

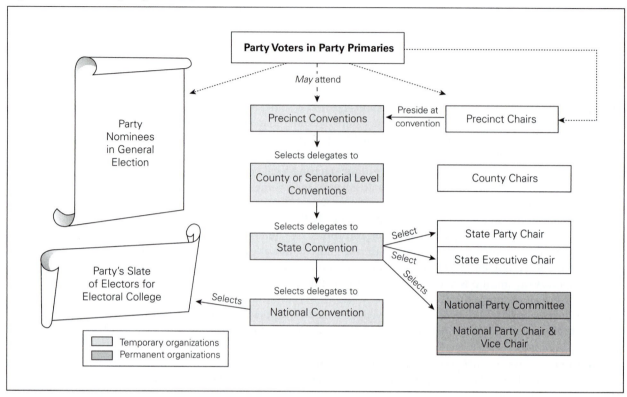

party. Under state law this "affiliates" citizens with a party for an entire year and thus makes them eligible to participate in that party's primary. While this affiliation does make them a member of the party for that year in some sense of the word, this affiliation does not obligate them to contribute to, vote for, or support in any way that party's candidates. By law, a party affiliation expires at the end of each voting year and before the primaries in the next set of elections two years later; all voters will receive a brand new registration card with no party affiliation stamped on it, leaving them free to vote in whichever primary they choose. The impact of affiliating with a party by voting in its primary is that the citizen is excluded from participating in the nominating process of other parties or independent candidates. In addition, Texas's "sore loser law" prohibits someone from voting or running in the primary of one party and later running for office under the label of another party in the same year.

In some states with more restrictive closed primaries citizens have a deadline for declaring their party affiliation as many as eleven months before the primary if they wish to participate. One advantage of such strict rules is that they ensure that the people who vote in the primaries are "real" party members. A disadvantage is that voters who are excluded from the party's primary by such rules may feel less inclined to get behind the party's candidates.

The flexibility of Texas's primary voting system can create its own set of problems. For generations, many conservative Texans continued to vote in the Democratic primary since they could often nominate like-minded conservatives as Democrats and see them elected in November. Meanwhile, other conservatives preferred attempting to make the Republican Party more viable. Today, Democrats face a similar dilemma. Many vote in the Republican primary hoping to make that party's nominee as moderate as possible. Others will seek out the nominee that will most embarrass their opposition party.

Under state law a political party's nominee must receive a majority of the total number of votes in the primary. Races that generate competition from three or more candidates raise the possibility that no nominee will get the required majority, necessitating a **runoff primary** in which the top two finishers from the first primary face off.

Local parties

Party primaries also elect local party officers. In Texas, party members in each voting precinct elect by a majority vote a **precinct chair** and countywide voting selects each party's **county chairs.** These officers are responsible for managing the local affairs of their party for the next two years. To be eligible to be a county or precinct chair of a political party, a person must only be a qualified voter and not hold or be a candidate for any elective federal, state, or county office. And, to make participation as easy as possible, state law provides that a candidate for county chair or precinct chair may not be required to pay a fee in order to get on the primary ballot.

At the county level each party has a County Executive Committee composed of a county chair and the precinct chair from each precinct in the county. This committee is the permanent committee that oversees the party's organization, fundraising, and campaigning within the county. There is often little competition for these positions, and they sometimes go vacant. However, in some areas conservative Christian groups have aggressively sought to win those positions in the Republican Party as a means of exerting more influence over party affairs, a strategy that has contributed to their success in gaining control of the Republican Party statewide. The success of conservative Christian political forces in Texas illustrates that big political victories are often built upon many small efforts.

While these local offices still have some influence, their role has been diminished over the last century. The power of local party officials to select political candidates and select delegates to state and national conventions was lost as the parties became more democratic through the introduction of primaries. Also, when campaigns relied on the labors of individuals communicating one-on-one, the local party was one of the few organizations positioned to mobilize the necessary human resources. Today, campaigns are increasingly coming into the hands of media-savvy campaign specialists and they require less human effort and more cash to pay for advertising on television and radio and technical know-how to establish a presence on the Internet.

On the same day as the primary voting the parties hold precinct-level meetings or **conventions** (although much of the nation calls these meetings **caucuses** when conducted at the local level) in which party members meet to conduct a range of party business. Primary conventions are temporary organizations in the party structure that convene on primary election day between 7:00 and 9:00 p.m., usually in the same location as the primary election. Sometimes, Republicans and Democrats hold their precinct conventions in different rooms in the same building, often the same school, church, fire station, or other building that hosted voting earlier that day. State law requires that a written notice at the polling place provide to primary voters the date, hour, and place for convening the precinct convention.

While these meetings are open only to party members, recall that party affiliation in Texas requires only showing up for the primary and requesting the party ballot.

Runoff primary
primary that occurs if no nominee receives the required majority of the votes in the primary; the top two finishers face off in a second primary to determine the nominee for the general election.

Precinct and county chairs
precinct chairs are selected by party members in each voting precinct by majority vote; county chairs are selected by countywide voting. These party officials are responsible for managing the local affairs of their party for the next two years.

Conventions (caucuses)
meetings at which party members participate in a range of party business that usually occur on the same day as primary election day.

While most states require parties to hold primaries to nominate candidates for the general election, Iowa uses a system of caucuses. The word "caucus" allegedly comes from a Native American word for a meeting between tribal leaders.[i] The Iowa caucus system developed in the late 1800s within political parties as a method of selecting delegates to political party conventions. The Iowa Caucuses operate similarly to a closed primary in that the participants must be registered with a political party. This process effectively limits the Republican caucuses only to Republicans and the Democratic caucuses only to Democrats.

On the night of the Iowa Caucuses, participants gather in over 2,000 local, precinct-level meetings. Historically, these meetings occurred in the homes of local party activists, creating a feeling of neighborliness among participants. In recent years, the meetings have occurred at a local school, library, church, or similar place. To some extent, the caucuses still take on the flavor of a giant precinct party.

The two major parties have slightly different rules concerning how the caucus proceeds. For the Republican Party, the caucus consists of participants dropping the name of a candidate in a hat. Results are then tabulated. At a separate meeting, participants choose delegates to attend a state convention, where the official nomination of party candidates for the general election takes place. At the Democratic caucus, participants break into groups based upon which candidate they support. If any group consists of less than 15 percent of the total number of participants, then the group members must realign with another group. Participants then lobby and persuade members of the group or groups with less than 15 percent to change their preference. When all remaining groups supporting a candidate are above 15 percent of the total participants at that location, delegates to the party county convention are allocated based upon the size of the groups. Note that "Undecided" is an acceptable grouping. Here is a comparison of the results of the party caucuses since 1972, when the Iowa Caucuses gained national attention by candidates running for president.

By tradition, the Iowa Caucuses are the first caucuses held in the United States. Because winning, or at least doing well, in the Iowa Caucuses creates momentum for a candidate's campaign and encourages financial support by donors, the Iowa Caucuses are very important to candidates running for U.S. President. As a result, critics suggest that Iowa carries too much weight in presidential elections, especially considering the relatively small and homogenous population.

While turnout for Texas primaries is quite low, and falling over the last two decades, the turnout rates for Iowa Caucuses appear to be increasing. However,

Minor parties that do not use primaries to nominate candidates obviously cannot require that citizens vote in their primary to participate in the party's convention. In these cases a citizen wishing to participate in the convention of a party that has not held a primary may affiliate with that party simply by taking an oath prescribed by law: "I swear that I have not voted in a primary election or participated in a convention of another party during this voting year. I hereby affiliate myself with the _____ Party."

Precinct conventions are used primarily to elect **delegates** (and alternates) who will attend the party's conventions held at the county level or Texas senatorial district level. A precinct's number of delegates is based on how many members of the party voted in that precinct in that election. While selecting those party members to represent the precinct at future conventions is the primary function of the precinct conventions, attendees may also vote on resolutions related to political issues, especially those that citizens want their party to take an official stand on.

On the third Saturday after the primary election the major parties hold their

Delegates

party members elected to attend their party's conventions held at the county level or the Texas senatorial district level.

turnout for the Iowa Caucuses is harder to determine simply because no official counts occur, and in contrast to closed primaries, lists of registered Democratic or Republican voters do not exist. Estimates of participation in the Democratic caucuses indicate that the percentage of the population that participates in the caucuses is increasing over time.[ii]

Thinking Critically

- Have you ever voted in a primary in Texas? Why or why not?

- Would you be more likely to participate in the Texas presidential primaries if they occurred earlier in the nomination process or if the candidates campaigned more actively in the state?
- What do you think the advantages or disadvantages of a system like the Iowa Caucuses would be if Texas changed to that system?

i. "Frequently Asked Caucus Questions," *Des Moines Register,* www.desmoines-register.com, accessed November 5, 2007.
ii. Ibid.

Results of the Iowa Caucuses since 1972

YEAR	DEMOCRATIC PARTY IOWA CAUCUS WINNER	NATIONAL PARTY NOMINEE	REPUBLICAN PARTY IOWA CAUCUS WINNER	NATIONAL PARTY NOMINEE
2004	John Kerry	John Kerry	George Bush	George Bush
2000	Al Gore	Al Gore	George Bush	George Bush
1996	Bill Clinton	Bill Clinton	Bob Dole	Bob Dole
1992	Tom Harkin	Bill Clinton	George H.W. Bush	George H.W. Bush
1988	Richard Gephardt	Michael Dukakis	Bob Dole	George H.W. Bush
1984	Walter Mondale	Walter Mondale	Ronald Reagan	Ronald Reagan
1980	Jimmy Carter	Jimmy Carter	George H.W. Bush	Ronald Reagan
1976	Uncommitted	Jimmy Carter	Gerald Ford	Gerald Ford
1972	Edward Muskie	George McGovern	Richard Nixon	Richard Nixon

county or senatorial district conventions. A county convention is held in a county if the county is not situated in more than one state senatorial district. If a county is in more than one state senatorial district a senatorial district convention is held in each part of the county that is in a different senatorial district. These conventions will select delegates to the statewide convention and deal with other party business.

County or senatorial district conventions

held on the third Saturday after the primary election, these conventions select delegates to the statewide convention.

State Parties

The political parties hold their state conventions biennially in June. The convention includes delegates selected by the county or senatorial district conventions, although nominees for or holders of state or national government offices are entitled to attend a state convention of their party, but they may not vote in the convention unless they have been selected to serve as delegates by their county or senatorial district through the usual process.

While the state conventions are temporary party organizations, meeting on a few days every two years, they are important events because state parties really only take form when the parties' members gather every two years in state conventions. For example, state law requires that party rules must be approved by the party's state convention. While gathered, each state convention writes and approves their **party platform** (the individual issue positions of which are often referred to as **planks**), the document that officially spells out the issue stands of the party.

Each party's state convention also selects a **state party chair** and **executive committee** to carry on the activities of the party between state conventions. By law, each party's state executive committee consists of one man and one woman from each state senatorial district. In addition, the state committees' chair and a vice chair must include a man and a woman. Texas's state party executive committee is typical of state party committees, if there is such a thing as a typical state party committee. As one text points out, "So great are the differences between these committees from state to state—in membership selection, size, and function—that it is difficult to generalize about them." [12] Texas's parties, like most of those in the South, are relatively weak. For example, Texas's party leaders do not make pre-primary endorsements, a practice more common in the Northeast and Midwest. The permanent officers of the parties do hold some authority, yet they are often rivaled by elected officials from their party. While the head of the Republican Party is selected by the state Republican Convention, Governor Perry can rightfully claim that he reflects the wishes of the Republican voters statewide. Thus, the label of "party leader" is much more subjective than the official party organization charts would suggest.

Nominating Presidential Candidates

In addition to conducting the business of the state parties, the state party conventions in presidential election years must also select the party's delegates to the national party convention, representatives to the party's national committee, as well as the slate of electors who will be available to serve in the Electoral College.

Today, state law requires that major parties in Texas hold presidential "preference primaries" in presidential election years, in conjunction with their regular primaries. Texans may use this primary to express their preference for one of the candidates on the ballot or vote "uncommitted," if the rules of their party allow such a vote. While holding these primaries at the same time as the nominating primaries for other offices makes some sense by consolidating voting dates, it presents a dilemma in national politics as many states attempt to move their primaries earlier in the year to garner as much attention as possible from presidential candidates. Texas, which held its primaries in June for many years, moved its primary date up to early March in 1988 and joined the ranks of "Super Tuesday" primaries, so named because many of the large states held their party primaries on that Tuesday. In 2007, in light of other states moving their primaries earlier, the Texas Legislature considered moving its primary to February to avoid being left to vote on presidential nominations after a candidate had already won enough votes to lock up the nomination. Texas Republicans and Democrats cast their votes on March 4, 2008, by which date about two-thirds of the states will have cast their votes and the presidential nominees of the parties might already be determined.

The problem for Texas is many citizens prefer to nominate their candidates a little closer to Election Day. Moving up the nominating process would only extend an already long campaign season. Some states hold separate presidential primaries at

Table 8.2 Comparison of Texas Party Platforms

ISSUE	2006 TEXAS REPUBLICAN PARTY PLATFORM	2006 TEXAS DEMOCRATIC PARTY PLATFORM
Abortion	"We affirm our support for a human life amendment to the Constitution and we endorse making clear that the Fourteenth Amendment's protection applies to unborn children."	"Texas Democrats trust the women of Texas to make personal and responsible decisions about when and whether to bear children, in consultation with their family, their physician, and their God, rather than having these personal decisions made by politicians."
Homosexuality	"We believe that the practice of sodomy tears at the fabric of society, contributes to the breakdown of the family unit, and leads to the spread of dangerous, communicable diseases."	[No stated position appears in 2006 platform.]
Capital punishment	"We believe that properly applied capital punishment is legitimate, is an effective deterrent, and should be swift and unencumbered. When applied to the crime of murder, it raises the value of human life."	"The current system cannot ensure that innocent or undeserving defendants are not sentenced to death."
Immigration	"No amnesty! No how. No way. With growing impatience, the American people in overwhelming numbers have asked our government to secure our borders. They now demand it and we as a party agree with the American people. Illegal aliens have, by definition, committed a criminal act. We oppose illegal immigration, amnesty in any form, or legal status for illegal immigrants. The American people remember the broken promises of 1986 and will not be misled again."	"We support the creation of a policy that would establish a path to citizenship for the majority of those currently here, without undue financial burden, and with priority for those who have lived or worked here the longest, provided they qualify and seek to become part of our national community. We strongly oppose Republican proposals that they should be charged with a felony simply because they are undocumented."
The federal role in education	"We call for the abolition of the U.S. Department of Education and the prohibition of the transfer of any of its functions to any other federal agency."	Requires the federal government to fully fund all federally mandated education programs, including those required by the No Child Left Behind Act, and special education requirements such as assistive technologies.
Kindergarten	"We believe that parents are best suited to train their children in their early development years (ages 0 through 5) and oppose mandatory pre-school and kindergarten. We urge Congress to repeal government-sponsored programs that deal with early childhood development, and phase them out as soon as possible."	We should "[e]nsure universal access to pre-kindergarten and kindergarten."
Bilingual education	"We demand the abolition of bilingual education as it currently exists in Texas."	"We [s]upport multi-language instruction to make all children fluent in English and at least one other language and reject efforts to destroy bilingual education."
Evolution versus intelligent design	"We support the objective teaching and equal treatment of scientific strengths and weaknesses of scientific theories, including Intelligent Design. We believe theories of life origins and environmental theories should be taught as scientific theory not scientific law; that social studies and other curriculum should not be based on any one theory."	[No stated position appears in 2006 platform.]

Table 8.2 Comparison of Texas Party Platforms, continued

ISSUE	2006 TEXAS REPUBLICAN PARTY PLATFORM	2006 TEXAS DEMOCRATIC PARTY PLATFORM
Minimum wage	"We believe the Minimum Wage Law should be repealed and that wages should be determined by the free market conditions prevalent in each individual market."	"To improve wages and working conditions, we believe the minimum wage must be increased meaningfully to make up for lost purchasing power and must be indexed from now on to keep it from eroding again; and workers should be paid a living wage with provisions for health care benefits for their families, as well as their future retirement."
Iraq	"We commend President George W. Bush, his administration, and the U.S. Armed Forces in their strategy and execution of the War in Iraq. We support the establishment of a representative form of government for the people of Iraq to protect them from the tyranny of dictatorial regimes and as a stabilizing force in the Middle East in the greater war against terrorism. We support the continuation of economic and security assistance to Iraq as it rebuilds its country, establishes its government, secures its country from terrorism, and solidifies its newfound economic and individual freedoms."	"All Americans recognize that Saddam Hussein was an odious dictator, and none mourn his defeat. But the Bush administration's case for going to war was built on false pretenses and those deceptions have been exposed. Weapons of mass destruction have not been found in Iraq. The administration's claim of links between Al Qaeda and Saddam Hussein was rejected by the bipartisan '9-11' Commission. Global U.S. security interests have been badly served by the Bush administration's excessive investment of resources in Iraq."
United Nations	"We believe it is in the best interest of the citizens of the United States that we immediately rescind our membership in, as well as all financial and military contributions to, the United Nations."	Urges the president to "convene an emergency meeting of Iraq's leadership, Iraq's neighbors, our allies and the United Nations to create an international peace-keeping force in Iraq and to replace U.S. troops with Iraqi police and Iraq National Guard forces."
Eminent domain	"We support limiting the definition of eminent domain to exclude seizing private property for public or private economic development or for increased tax revenues."	"We . . . oppose the use of eminent domain to deprive any property owner of the possession, use, or the ability to control the use of their property, for the pure purpose of economic development; without just compensation; in the absence of an obvious and compelling public need."
School choice	"We encourage the governor and the Texas Legislature to enact child-centered school funding options—which fund the student, not schools or districts—to allow maximum freedom of choice in public, private or parochial education for all children. This measure could only be considered upon passage of a state constitutional amendment that prohibits imposition of state regulations on private and parochial schools."	"The Texas Constitution provides for free public schools budgeted with public tax dollars, yet many Republicans seek to siphon off public education funds for inequitable, unaccountable voucher and privatization schemes that interfere with that constitutional mandate."

Sources: 2006 Texas Democratic Party Platform, Texas Democratic Party, www.txdemocrats.org/issues/party_platform; 2006 Republican Party of Texas Platform, The Republican Party of Texas, http://www.texasgop.org.

different times from the primaries used to select other offices. Other states, like Kansas, have opted not to hold a presidential primary in their state.

Texas's presidential primary has not always been binding. While voters filed through the voting booths during the day to vote in the primary, the number of delegates that their favorite candidate received was decided in the precinct conventions that evening or at other conventions later in the spring. Today, while the party conventions select which individuals will be sent to the party's national convention as delegates, the allocation of these delegates between the competing candidates for president is determined by party rules which use voting in the presidential preference primary to allocate candidates on a district-wide or statewide basis. Currently, state law requires that at least 75 percent of delegates representing the state at the party's national convention be allocated based on the votes in the presidential primaries. However, the law does not dictate exactly how the parties use the results of primary voting in allocating delegates. For example, the Republicans have an elaborate system of allocating delegates using the vote counts at the congressional district and statewide level. A candidate that receives more than 50 percent of the votes within a congressional district is entitled to all of the delegates to the Republican convention from that district. When no candidate gets 50 percent, the delegates are divided between those candidates that received more than 20 percent of the vote.

The lack of precise national party rules for counting delegates reflects the independence of the state parties and the nature of American political parties. In 2007 many states rebelled, moving their presidential primaries to dates earlier than those allowed by national party rules. The national parties responded by threatening to reduce the number of delegates of states that violated party rules.

The State Parties and the National Parties

Although citizens generally consider parties to be consistent across all levels of government, there are actually significant differences between the expressed opinions of the parties. Because American parties are grassroots organizations in which the power flows from the bottom up, the national parties are not able to impose their views on the state parties. Texas political parties vividly illustrate the inability of the national parties to control party members. For example, for years the national Democratic Party championed civil rights while the conservative Democrats who controlled the Texas Democratic Party often vigorously opposed these laws. More recently, the 2006 Texas Republican party platform has "demanded" the elimination of presidential authority to issue executive orders and the repeal of all previous executive orders, despite the fact that the executive order has become a common tool of President Bush and other Republican presidents.

While the Texas Republican Party's attempt to oust Kay Bailey Hutchison and the 2006 party platform's independence from President Bush illustrate the potential autonomy of the state parties, such rebellion remains rare because the national party conventions have come to be dominated by the campaign organization of the presidential candidates rather than by the state parties. Because delegates to the national convention are selected based on attachment to national presidential candidates rather than service in the local party, the local party's role is diminished. This undermines some of the representational role of parties as local concerns disappear behind national politics.

State and local parties in the United States remain in a precarious position. While local party leaders remain important actors in recruiting party candidates and building the parties at the local level, the rise of mass media and the candidate-centered campaigns have taken away some of the local parties' most important functions as vehicles for getting candidates' messages out. Some have called state and local parties "Mom-and-Pop Shops in the Information Age,"[13] and as citizens make more use of television and the Internet to learn about candidates, local parties may find less to do. This represents one way in which changes in the state may permanently transform the way the parties operate and who in the parties holds significant power.

Winners and Losers

lthough the primaries and conventions may technically be open to any eligible voters willing to declare themselves members of the party, Texans seem increasingly uninterested in participating in the business of parties. V. O. Key argued, "over the long run, the have-nots lose in a disorganized politics."[14] According to Key, when there are no strong parties, no one has the incentive and ability to mobilize disorganized interests. Without well-organized parties, some citizens will remain disorganized and their interests diffuse. Organization is especially important to anyone wishing to promote serious reform, since reform efforts require battling an entrenched status quo.

Domination by one party complicates matters. Without groups to mobilize the masses, there is no policy debate, leaving voters less informed and the meaning of election victories less clear. Without an ongoing agenda, party labels are much less meaningful and differences between parties are more difficult for voters to discern. This means that new Texans looking to take their place in politics and old Texans interested in reforming the system to create a new Texas will both need to be well organized as they promote change. This lesson has applied to Hispanics as they have increasingly attempted to exert influence in Texas politics and Republicans as they have attempted to remove institutional barriers to their political rise.

Organized Interests in Texas Politics

rganized interests step into some of the vacuum left by the lack of party competition. With Republicans now winning statewide elections, as Democrats did a few decades earlier, some of the competition has moved from between the parties to between interest groups. Some organized interests have done well working with members of both parties while others have worked consistently with one party.

This text will use the term *organized interest* for what most textbooks, journalists, and citizens label as "special interests" or "interest groups." We prefer the label organized interest because the political science literature points out that many, if not most, of the forces tugging at the political system are not the large membership organizations that we generally think of as interest *groups*.[15] Many of the important players in politics are individual citizens or businesses, not groups. Nowhere is this more evident than in Texas, where many individual businesses like AT&T and TXU Energy spend millions of dollars lobbying the Texas Legislature without benefit of joining a group, and where individuals like James Leininger pour millions of dollars into campaigns to advance issues like public school vouchers.

Our definition of **organized interest** is any organization that attempts to influence public policy decisions. "Organization" in this sense does not mean a collection

Organized interest
an individual, group of people, or group of businesses that organizes its efforts to influence public policy.

of individuals.[16] Instead, organization reflects the direction of systematic efforts aimed at influencing the political process. Thus, organized interest sometimes refers to the systematic efforts of an individual. In addition, it should be clear that many of the organizations in politics are groups of corporations, not individuals. For example, the Chamber of Commerce, a very important group at the state and federal level, is a collection of businesses, not individual citizens.

Our definition is also better suited for some of the key issues in this chapter because, as we will see, many interests in the state may be special, but they are not organized and will not have a meaningful impact on the state's politics. In fact, one of our key arguments is that the failure of some interests to organize is fundamental to understanding who wins and who loses in Texas politics.

Interest groups in Texas benefit from the part-time nature of Texas government. Legislators meeting during the frantic 140-day legislative session find themselves moving through legislation quickly and needing help to sort out the issues. With little professional staff available, lawmakers are more reliant on the kind of information and assistance lobbyists dish out. The part-time commissioners who head bureaucratic agencies provide another entry point for interests' influence in the state. As governors look for citizens to occupy the boards that oversee so much of the Texas bureaucracy, they are likely to turn to wealthy donors—especially those with a connection to the policy area being regulated.

Interest Group Formation

A variety of factors play into Texans' decisions to join interest groups. Some of Texas's early organized interests were held together by the provision of **solidarity benefits,** social interactions that individuals enjoy from joining a group and from working together for a common cause. Texas's size shaped its politics from its earliest days as the Patrons of Husbandry, more commonly known as "the Grange," was formed in 1867 largely to escape rural isolation and address the educational and social needs of the farmers who found themselves widely dispersed on the Texas plains. Over time, the Grange became more engaged in economic matters and farmer protests. By 1875 the Grange would have more than 1,000 lodges in Texas, claiming over 40,000 members in a state with about 250,000 voters.[17] Even when the Grange faded it was replaced by the Farmers' Alliance that had started in 1877 as an attempt to let farmers sell their goods without intermediaries. While modern Texans may not be as isolated as their ancestors who labored on widely dispersed farms, Texans still join a group to make new friends, spawn new romances, or simply enjoy working alongside others with similar interests.

Solidarity benefits
the social interactions that individuals enjoy from joining a group and from working together for a common cause.

The advantage of organizing political interests upon pre-existing social networks continues today. In modern Texas the role of churches remains strong, in part because churches are already bringing Texans together for religious communion and this expedites mobilizing them for political action. While the impact of conservative Christians is large, that impact is the result of many groups, including the Texas Christian Coalition, the Texas Restoration Project, Texas Eagle Forum, and the American Family Association of Texas, that tap into the social networks already in place in churches.

Another motivation for group membership is the **expressive benefits** citizens enjoy from taking action to express their views. Many individuals and groups protest even in the face of widespread antipathy or rejection. While this behavior may seem irrational at some level, so is yelling at the television during sporting events—a behavior that is not limited to Texans.

Expressive benefits
benefits that arise from taking action to express one's views; serve as another motivation for group membership.

Another theory of group formation is **disturbance theory.** According to disturbance theory organized interests have become more numerous as society has changed. As society and the economy develop, becoming more complex and diverse, new interests will emerge to voice their concerns. This will lead established interests to mobilize in order to protect themselves from these new, emerging interests.[18] This would explain the rising number of organized interests evident in politics that seem to be in response to the ongoing transformation of the state.

The **free-rider problem** arises in that some citizens will not contribute to the efforts of a group, even though they enjoy the results of the group's efforts. The problem is that groups labor for **collective goods,** benefits that once provided go to everyone and cannot be effectively denied to others, even those who did not contribute to the effort. Those who do not organize to advance their interest still enjoy as many benefits as those that do. The dilemma of the free-rider problem is that citizens will see little point in making an individual contribution to political efforts since their individual contribution is small and the work will go on without them. For example, all students may enjoy lower tuition, better facilities, and similar benefits from group action even if they do not belong to any student-oriented group or contribute to student organizations in any way.

The free-rider problem is actually a common problem in politics, as well as the rest of life. Government itself is a partial solution to the free-rider problem, as it creates rules and compels citizens to share the burden of the advancement of a common good. Government partially solves the free-rider problem by jailing citizens that refuse to pay taxes or abide by common rules. College students sometimes become familiar with their own free-rider problem in the form of roommates who eat groceries that another roommate paid for or don't do their share of cleaning chores.

Several things can happen when some Texans do not organize and leave politics to others. One result is that things don't get done. When only a few people who take an interest in an issue become active, their impact will be minimal. Another problem is that when only a narrow slice of interested citizens becomes involved, the few that do take action may poorly reflect the views of others. In a process known as *unraveling,* a relatively small number of people may take over an organization and define its goals in a way that drives away more moderate members. As moderate members are driven away, the group may become even more radical, creating an even more radical approach that drives away even more moderates.

Given these problems, what keeps like-minded Texans working together? One common solution to the free-rider problem is providing **selective incentives.** These are benefits that can be given to members but effectively excluded from nonmembers. For example, the Texas State Teachers Association proudly proclaims it is "Fighting for Public Schools." However, new members are drawn into the organization with the promise of savings on services ranging from shopping to snowboarding. Current members are encouraged to log in for updates by monthly drawings for "free stuff." Because these benefits go only to members, they can help organizations build membership. However, many observers may worry about the moral authority of groups built on free tote bags and discounted travel.

The dynamics of interest group organization is that often the citizens with the greatest needs often face the greatest barriers to getting organized. Lacking the resources to organize members and pour money into political campaigns and professional lobbyists, some Texas citizens are at a disadvantage. For example, college students are impacted tremendously as the Texas Legislature, Higher Education Coordinating Board, and other officials grapple with the costs of higher education in

Texas. Administrators and regents of the schools are well represented, while students have few opportunities to express their own concerns, therefore it is easy for legislators to overlook the views of students who are apathetic and less organized than other players in the higher education system. Thus, in 2003, when Texas faced a budget crunch it was easy for the Texas Legislature to respond by passing a law that allowed state schools to raise their tuition at will.

Types of Interests in Texas

Probably the most visible organized interests in Texas are economic interests. These are organizations that attempt to produce economic benefits for group members. These might be corporations working individually or collectively to lower taxes, reduce regulation, or alter some other business policy to help their bottom line. As Table 8.3 indicates, many of Texas's businesses hire lobbyists to represent them in Austin. The large dollar amounts reflected in the table often conceal the full effort of these businesses, since some business leaders will lobby on behalf of their businesses without additional compensation.

Economic interests also include **labor unions,** which seek better pay or working conditions for their membership. For example, the Texas AFL-CIO spent most of 2007 lobbying for bread-and-butter issues such as raising the minimum wage and improving the quality of schools. In a similar fashion, **professional associations** like the Texas State Teachers Association and the Texas Medical Association represent the needs of professionals that are not represented by unions. Some businesses work together in **trade associations,** organizations of similar businesses working together to advance shared goals. The Texas Hospitality Association is a coalition of restaurants and bars that lobbies on state laws related to how the food and beverage service sector does business. For example, the THA's mission calls for repealing the state law that requires distilled spirits to be purchased only from a retail store.

In contrast, **public-interest groups** pursue non-economic policies on behalf of the general public (even if not all members of the general public agree on the issues, policies, or solutions). For example, Texans for Public Justice attempts to promote better government by scrutinizing campaign finance and lobbying, while Texans for Lawsuit Reform seeks to reduce the abuse of the legal system. Some **single-interest groups** might also be considered public interest groups since their issue is one that impacts the public in general. For example, the Texas Right to Life Committee and the Texas Abortion and Reproductive Rights Action League focus their efforts primarily on the issue of abortion, while the Texas State Rifle Association and Texans for Gun Safety square off over gun rights.

Another type of interest is other governments, often referred to as the **intergovernmental lobby,** in which different levels of government lobby each other. As a state, Texas sits in the middle of the intergovernmental lobby, lobbying the national government and being lobbied by cities, counties, and school districts. For example, the cities of Austin and Houston spent more over one million dollars each on lobbying in 2005 while the Metropolitan Transportation Authority of Harris County spent about $845,000 on its own lobbying effort. In addition, the state is lobbied on behalf of state institutions like universities. While some of this lobbying is done on a contract basis with professional lobbyists, many institutions like universities rely on their upper administration to represent them in Austin.

Texas state government works closely with members of the U.S. Congress from Texas to maximize federal grants coming into the state. In 2006 questions were

Labor unions
organizations that represent the interests of working people seeking better pay and better working conditions.

Professional associations
organizations that represent the needs of professionals not represented by unions.

Trade associations
organizations of similar businesses, which work together to advance shared goals.

Public-interest groups
organizations that pursue noneconomic policies on behalf of the general public, even if all members of the general public do not agree on these issues or policies.

Single-interest groups
groups usually organized around one side of a single issue, such as pro-choice or anti-abortion groups.

Intergovernmental lobby
the lobbying that occurs between different levels of government, such as between the state and national government or between local governments and the state government.

Table 8.3 The Top Lobbyists in Texas (2005)
(sample ranked by estimated maximum value of 2005 lobbying contracts)

LOBBYING CLIENT	INTEREST TYPE	CONTRACT VALUES
SBC Corp. (now AT&T)	Individual business	$ 7,010,000
TXU Corp.	Individual business	$3,200,000
Texas Medical Association	Professional association	$2,135,000
Verizon	Individual business	$2,035,000
Linebarger Heard Goggan	Lawyers/Lobbyists	$1,965,000
Assoc. of Electric Companies of Texas	Trade association	$1,560,000
CenterPoint Energy	Individual business	$1,470,000
City of Austin	Intergovernmental	$1,455,000
Big City Capital LLC	Individual business	$1,375,000
Texas Association of Realtors	Professional association	$1,325,001
City of Houston	Intergovernmental	$1,320,000
Texas Municipal League	Intergovernmental	$1,285,000
Texas Trial Lawyers Association	Professional association	$1,250,001
American Cancer Society	Public interest	$1,150,000
AT&T	Individual business	$1,105,000
Entergy/Gulf States, Inc.	Individual business	$1,090,000
Affiliated Computer Services	Individual business	$1,080,000
Wholesale Beer Distributors	Professional association	$930,000
Edwards Aquifer Authority	Intergovernmental	$850,000
Texas Hospital Association	Trade association	$875,000
Metro. Transit Authority of Harris County	Intergovernmental	$845,000
Texas Civil Justice League	Public interest	$730,000

Source: Texans for Public Justice, "Austin's Oldest Profession: Texas's Top Lobby Clients and Those Who Service Them," August 2006, www.tpj.org/reports/austinsoldest06/austinsoldest20063.pdf.

raised about $1.2 million that had been paid for lobbying contracts spanning the period between 2003 and 2007. The Office of State-Federal Relations had hired outside lobbyists, including Washington, D.C., lobbyists with connections to the Jack Abramoff lobbying scandal. An article in the *Austin-American Statesman* indicated that the contract was awarded to the lobbying firm of Cassidy & Associates despite the fact that the company's bid was higher than some of the other bidders and it was initially given lower scores based on the criteria of the contract.[19] The defense that the firm rose in the rating after its "references" were checked did little to reduce fears that favors were being traded. Some members of the Texas Legislature objected to paying professional lobbyists to work with Congress when members of Congress from Texas carried influence in Washington and there was a Texan in the White House.

While the idea of governments lobbying each other may sound odd and the prospect of Texas paying millions of dollars for representation in Washington may seem wasteful, Texas receives over one-third of its budget—almost $24 billion in 2007—from the national government. If paying lobbyists a million dollars a year to represent the state's interests would increase federal grants by only 1 percent, this outcome would represent a roughly twenty-fold return on lobbying dollars.

Contributions of Organized Interests

Organized interests in Texas play the same kind of roles that they do in other states and countries. However, given the condition of Texas's parties, some of these functions are especially important in Texas.

One of the primary functions of organized interests is to provide representation for groups to complement the geographic representation provided by elected officials. In an essentially one-party state like Texas, group representation is especially important since many Texans live in an area in which no one from their party/ideology holds office. Beyond that, Texans have interests that may be best represented based on something other than geography. For example, Texas's teachers come together through groups such the Texas State Teachers Association to work on educational issues. Public school teachers, while a small part of any one community, comprise a huge bloc of voters across the state.

The role of education is also very important since many of the issues that impact Texans' lives lie beyond their everyday experiences and knowledge. Organized interests in Texas help bring attention to issues and educate citizens. For example, environmental groups draw citizens' attention to environmental issues and help them understand the scientific and technical aspects of these issues.

Similarly, Texans may benefit from program monitoring as organized interest groups invest their effort in monitoring the many large bureaucratic agencies and small boards that do much of the work of governing in the state. The average citizen has little time to do this and may lack the expertise to track levels of pollution or budget implementation issues. Organized interests serving as watchdogs may help uncover bureaucratic misbehavior in some cases and deter it in others.

Organized interests can also play an important role by providing program alternatives. In education, for example, teacher groups and other organized interests have put forward alternative reforms to public schools in Texas and helped give citizens alternatives that might never emerge from the education bureaucracy. Organized interests may not seem the best source of reform, however they may prove more supportive of reform and innovation than bureaucrats and elected officials.

What Texas Organized Interests Do

Organized interest groups have several strategies for influencing policy: electioneering, litigation, and lobbying. With **electioneering,** interests try to shape public policy by influencing who is elected to office. Seeking a statewide office like governor requires reaching into every corner of the state, which requires lots of advertising dollars. Most candidates find that they cannot raise enough money for such a campaign from small individual donors, therefore large donors like organized interest groups become especially important in deciding which campaigns get off the ground.

Organized interests influence elections in a variety of ways. The most visible and perhaps the most important is through spending. People like James Leininger or Bob Perry have the resources to make large donations as individuals and can have a major impact. However, other people contribute to campaigns as part of a group in order to bring together enough money to also have an impact on the candidates. These contributions pass through interest groups in the form of **political action committees (PACs)**. PACs are essentially the fundraising arms of interest groups organized in order to meet the requirements of state and federal campaign finance laws. During the 2005–2006 election cycle 1,132 general-purpose PACs reported expenditures of over $99 million. Over 57 percent of that amount was spent by

Electioneering
method used by organized interests to try to shape public policy by influencing who is elected to office, especially by serving as sources of campaign funding.

Political action committees (PACs)
the fund-raising arms of interest groups that have been organized to meet the requirements of state and federal campaign finance laws.

business PACs. Ideological PACs, including single-issue PACs and PACs associated with political parties, totaled about 37 percent, while labor PACs accounted for just over 5 percent of PAC dollars.

Currently, the biggest spending PAC in Texas is Texans for Lawsuit Reform. In 2006 Texans for Lawsuit Reform spent about $4.2 million in an effort to elect legislators and judges supportive of their desire to reduce the cost of non-meritorious lawsuits. Another PAC, Annie's List (named in honor of Anne Webb Blanton, the first woman to win statewide office in Texas), spent just over $1 million helping Democratic women candidates in an attempt to increase their representation in office.

Organized interests often supplement the money they give to candidates by spending money on their own advertising or providing materials that others may distribute. The Christian Coalition, for example, produces "voter guides," brochures that list the candidates' positions on issues important to the group that members can print and distribute at their own expense. Organized interests may also provide other kinds of assistance to candidates. Labor unions and other groups with large memberships may provide volunteers to help staff phone banks, campaign door-to-door, stuff envelopes, or provide other kinds of help with campaigns. This is one area in which student groups hold an advantage. While they may lack the financial resources to make large cash contributions, student groups can provide much-needed volunteers to campaigns.

Access can be promoted in a number of ways beyond traditional campaign contributions. House Speaker Tom Craddick was criticized for raising over a million dollars for renovation and upkeep on the Speaker's apartment in the Texas Capitol after AT&T and Dallas oilman T. Boone Pickens led the list of donors, each chipping in $250,000 for the apartment. While the money is controlled by the State Preservation Board, many people are concerned by the presence of gambling and other special interests behind the money used for the Speaker's living quarters.

Sometimes organized interests turn to the courts for assistance and use litigation to advance their causes. For example, as mentioned in Chapter 3, the League of United Latin American Citizens (LULAC) filed a lawsuit challenging the Texas Legislature's redistricting plan on the grounds that it violated the voting rights of the Latino community in Texas according to the 1965 Voting Rights Act. The resulted in the 2006 U.S. Supreme Court decision *LULAC v. Perry* (2006) that the redistricting plan diluted representation in violation of the Voting Rights Act.[20]

In Texas law, **lobbying** is defined as contact by telephone, telegraph, or letter with members of the legislative or executive branch to influence legislation or administrative action. "Lobbying" embraces a wide range of efforts. For example, in early 2007 Texans for Lawsuit Reform offered massages, manicures, and pedicures on top of the usual food and drink to the "ladies of the Legislature" at their annual "Girls Night Out" event at the Four Seasons Hotel in Austin. While the legislators and staffers in attendance were not offered money, sixteen of the roughly eighteen legislators who attended won $1,000 scholarships to be donated to the school of their choice.[21]

One technique is not entirely new, but has been facilitated by advances in mass communication. Through **grassroots lobbying** groups will attempt to influence legislators through public opinion. Grassroots lobbying is a legitimate extension of democratic principles where groups of citizens spontaneously mobilize to build support for a cause. However, the misuse of public opinion has stirred concerns, as some groups have used negative or misleading information to advance their cause. One variation of grassroots lobbying, not surprisingly, is known as **astroturf lobbying.** As

Lobbying
direct contact with members of the legislative or executive branch to influence legislation or administrative action.

Grassroots lobbying
attempts by organized interests to influence legislators through public opinion; extension of democratic principles in which groups of citizens spontaneously mobilize to build support for a cause.

Astroturf lobbying
a simulation of grassroots support, usually conducted by specialized lobbying firms and involving spending large sums of money to generate the appearance of public support to advance a group's agenda.

the name implies, astroturf lobbying is simulating grassroots support in an attempt to influence legislators. Often done by specialized lobbying firms, astroturf lobbying involves political elites spending large amounts of money to create public opinion designed to advance a group's agenda. Sometimes this involves large donors using phone banks to urge citizens to contact legislators based on misleading or incomplete information.

One less democratic version of grassroots lobbying is **grasstop lobbying,** attempting to influence legislators through key constituents or friends of legislators. Rather than calling upon thousands of citizens to contact their elected officials, grasstop lobbying efforts rely on the influence of a few key citizens to sway elected officials.

Grasstop lobbying
the attempt to influence legislators through key constituents or friends.

Lobby Regulation

For most of its history, Texas has had little meaningful regulation of lobbying activity, reflected in legends such as those about poultry magnate Lonnie "Bo" Pilgrim passing out $10,000 checks on the floor of the Texas Senate in 1989. In 1957 the Lobby Registration Act required that lobbyists disclose certain activities and began the process of reform. Today, Texas law prohibits contributions from thirty days before the start of a legislative session to twenty days after the session ends.

With millions of dollars at stake, it should be little surprise that lobbying is a well-developed industry in Austin. Texas law defines lobbying as communicating directly with a government official for the purpose of influencing legislation or administrative action. The law requires that a person attempting to influence policy this way register as a lobbyist if they expend more than $500 or receive more than $1,000 in compensation in a three-month period. Lobbyists in Texas must file reports that disclose the range of lobbyists' salaries and their clients.

Overseeing lobbying in Texas is the Texas Ethics Commission (TEC), created by a constitutional amendment approved by Texas voters in 1991. The commission is composed of eight members, with no more than four members from the same party. Four of the commissioners are appointed by the governor, two by the lieutenant governor, and two by the Speaker of the Texas House.

The Texas Constitution provides the TEC with the authority to recommend the salary and per-diem payments of members of the legislature, the lieutenant governor, and the Speaker of the House of Representatives, subject to approval by the voters. The commission is also charged with administering laws related to political contributions to candidates, the election of the Speaker of the House, as well as regulation of lobbyists, personal financial disclosure of state officials, and other matters related to integrity in state government. The commissioners meet roughly every two months with an executive director selected by the commission to manage the commission staff and the daily work of the commission.

Today Texas Ethics Commission rules prohibit officeholders from accepting certain gifts and track what government officials receive. Officeholders are prohibited from accepting anything in consideration of an official act and are not allowed to accept honoraria or other compensation for speaking if the invitation is related to their status as an officeholder. While travel expenses to a speech can be accepted, the officeholder may not accept any pleasure travel from a group. Lobbyists may pay for food for officeholders when they dine together without limits.

The Center for Public Integrity, a national organization interested in government reform, estimated that in 2004 just over $162 million was spent on lobbying in the

Table 8.4 Companies or Groups Spending more than One Million Dollars on Lobbying in Texas in 2005

CLIENT	CONTRACT VALUES
SBC Corp. (now AT&T)	$7,010,000
TXU Corp.	$3,200,000
Tex. Medical Assoc.	$2,135,000
Verizon	$2,035,000
Linebarger Heard Goggan	$1,965,000
Assoc. of Electric Co.'s of TX	$1,560,000
CenterPoint Energy	$1,470,000
City of Austin	$1,455,000
Big City Capital LLC	$1,375,000
Tex. Association of Realtors	$1,325,001
City of Houston	$1,320,000
Tex. Municipal League	$1,285,000
Tex. Trial Lawyers Association	$1,250,001
AT&T	$1,105,000
Entergy/Gulf States, Inc.	$1,090,000
Affiliated Computer Services	$1,080,000

Source: Texans for Public Justice, http://www.tpj.org.

Revolving door

the phenomenon of legislators and members of the executive branch moving easily from government office to lucrative positions with lobbying firms.

state, placing Texas second to California. While Texas's large size and population make it a logical state for large amounts of lobbyist spending, the dollar amounts are dramatic when you consider that the Texas Legislature meets every other year.

The amounts spent by some companies and groups illustrate the level of interest in Texas policy. Communications giant SBC, recently changed to AT&T, spent just over $7 million lobbying in Texas in 2005, leading the pack of sixteen companies or groups spending over one million dollars on lobbying that year.

While there is considerable debate about how much influence these large lobbying contracts actually have, there is no doubt that they have some impact. These large companies did not become large by making unprofitable investments. Clearly, these organizations have reaped some reward in keeping their perspective before the legislature.

Lobbying has long been a concern in Texas. However, there has often been disagreement about the proper relationship between lobbyists and legislators. For example, at one time it was considered acceptable for large companies to keep legislators who were also lawyers "on retainer." In this arrangement, members of the Texas Legislature would accept payments from companies even as they deliberated over legislation impacting that company.

The fluid movement of people between public service and lobbying concerns many Texans. The **revolving door** that sees legislators and members of the executive branch moving easily from government office to lobbying firms raises concerns because former officials are using the access they have developed over their years in public service for private gain. According to the Center for Public Integrity, between the close of the 2005 legislative session and the start of the 2007 session, eight former legislators became lobbyists, helping Texas lead the nation in lawmakers turned lobbyists with seventy having made the transition.[22] In 2007, renewed concern developed after Governor Perry issued an executive order calling for all sixth-grade girls to get mandatory vaccines designed to protect them from cervical cancer. While many citizens applauded the Governor's enthusiasm for combating cancer, others questioned the need for mandatory vaccines, particularly after it became public knowledge that Perry's former chief of staff was now a lobbyist for the vaccine's manufacturer. Stopping the revolving door, or even slowing it down, is politically difficult because it asks the state legislators to support laws limiting their future careers. Also, limits on what officials do after their years of public service are limits on their First Amendment rights and may keep some from lobbying for causes they truly believe in or that their constituents would favor.

Many family members of legislative leaders have found jobs as well-paid lobbyists, suggesting that interest groups are buying influence through family members. One study found that at least six well-paid lobbyists had members of their family serving in high-level positions in Texas government.[23] One member of the legislature, Jim Pitts, had a twin brother, John, who worked as a lobbyist. While the two claim to avoid discussing issues during the legislative session, the close connection illustrates the concern of many. Although an interest in politics is often shared in families, and it would not be unusual to find several members of a family ending up in different areas of politics, these close relationships and the size of the lobbying contracts raise concerns.

Texas versus Washington

The State of Washington tackles the issue of lobbying very differently than Texas. In 2007, one ranking of attempts to regulate lobbyists and their activities placed Washington as first in the nation, while Texas ranked twelfth.[i] Among the points of comparison was the fact that, in 2005, lobbyists spent over $173 million dollars lobbying in Texas and only $37 million in Washington. In Texas, there are nine registered lobbyists with the state government for every member of the state legislature. In Washington, the ratio is six lobbyists per member of the state legislature. More telling is the fact that seventy of the lobbyists in Texas were former members of the legislature now hired to lobby their former colleagues. In Washington, only fifteen former members of the state legislature work as lobbyists.

Regarding the issues of defining and registering lobbyists and their activities, the two states differ in a number of areas.

As the table comparing Texas with Washington shows, Washington's regulatory environment provides a more detailed accounting of the activities of lobbyists attempting to influence the state government than do the Texas regulations.

Thinking Critically

- Which provisions of Washington's lobbyist regulations not found in Texas do you find the most attractive?
- How do you think such provisions would change the dynamics of money in Texas politics?

Lobbying in Texas and Washington State

ACTIVITY REGULATED	TEXAS (pop. 2.8m)	WASHINGTON (pop. 2.1m)
Register if lobbying executive	Yes	Yes
Register if lobbying legislature	Yes	Yes
Minimum spent to qualify as a lobbyist	$500	$0
Must provide photo with registration form	No	Yes
Must report compensation	Yes	Yes
Must itemize all spending	No (only over $25)	Yes
Campaign contributions disclosed on registration form	No	Yes
Lobbyists' employers must file spending report	No	Yes
Online registration and reporting allowed	No	Yes
State conducts audits of lobbyist reports	No	Yes

Source: Compiled by author from data available at The Center for Public Integrity, 2007, "Lobby Disclosure Comparisons 2003," www.publicintegrity.org/hired-guns/comparisons.aspx, accessed November 3, 2007.

i. The Center for Public Integrity, "In Your State—Washington" and "In Your State—Texas," www.publicintergrity.org/hiredguns/iys.aspx, accessed November 3, 2007.

Winners and Losers

One important debate in the area of organized interests is always who wins and who loses. One perspective on this issue is the **pluralist perspective** that looks at politics as a collection of interests and argues that democracy is best practiced when citizens participate through groups. When many interests are represented, pluralists see wide participation and a healthy democracy. The leading voice of pluralism was the political scientist Robert Dahl who, in his classic *Who Governs?* concluded that no single interest dominated and that politics was open to broad participation with organized interests representing the needs of real people.[24]

Critics of pluralism disagree with the idea that the presence of a large number of interest groups means that citizens are well served, because some people will be better represented by organized interests than others. C. Wright Mills argued that the

Pluralist perspective
a view of politics that argues that democracy is best practiced when citizens participate through groups; a greater number of organized interests means wider participation and a healthier democracy.

"power elite," the wealthy and powerful interests, were better represented than ordinary citizens.[25] As one scholar colorfully suggested, "the flaw in the pluralist heaven is that the heavenly chorus sings with a strong upper-class accent."[26] Most Texans don't have enough money to contribute to an interest group or hire the lobbyists and other staff needed to build support for their agenda. There are some groups that represent poor Texans but, ironically, these groups are generally funded and led by people who are not poor themselves. That is, poor Texans remain reliant on wealthy patrons to advocate for them.

One of the challenges to the pluralist view is that we have gone beyond simple pluralism and evolved into a system of **hyperpluralism,** in which many narrow groups are represented, often at the expense of the broader public interest. For example, the National Rifle Association may effectively represent many Texans on the issue of gun ownership, but that does not mean that NRA members are heard on other issues. As is evident from looking over the groups functioning in Texas, many businesses and groups labor in Austin on behalf of narrow interests while very few work on behalf of citizens in general.

Some of the arguments implicating organized interests have less to do with class or party. One view is that special interests have made it impossible to get rid of a government program that is no longer needed, whether it's a social program benefiting the poor or a subsidy benefiting businesses.[27] In this argument, organized interests have been successful at protecting their own spending, even if it is at the expense of everyone else's pocketbook. While all organized interests win in this state of affairs, they also all lose as taxpayers remain burdened with programs that are ineffective.

The ability of some groups to effectively organize while others remain unorganized produces clear winners and losers in the state. In Texas, businesses, and often businessmen, have effectively organized and exerted influence in the state. Once organized, the relatively loose laws governing lobbying make it easy for them to exert considerable influence in Austin. Other groups, perhaps due to lack of money, apathy, or both, fail to effectively organize and pay a high price. For instance, the vast majority of college and university students in Texas have been continuously uninterested in politics. In recent years, the Texas Legislature has approved increased tuitions, capped the number of hours students can attempt to carry or withdraw from, and in one case, the governor even vetoed Texas's community college health benefits. The veto, which would have forced community colleges across the state to raise tuition even more to make up the difference, was so unpopular that the governor backed down.

Conclusion

arties and organized interests can be both allies and enemies in the political process. While organized interests often support political parties, there are times when narrow interests will abandon the broader goals of the political parties and divide the parties. However, while the two political actors may at times clash, their impact on Texas politics is undeniable.

While their importance is not in dispute, their place in Texans' hearts is less certain. V. O. Key, who defined much of our understanding of Texas and southern politics, noted, "As institutions, parties enjoy a general disrepute, but most of the democratic world finds them indispensable as instruments of self-government, as means for the organization and expression of competing viewpoints on public policy."[28] Organized interests similarly generate little fondness among the citizens of Texas, but Texans show little hesitation to support interests that serve their personal needs. Tex-

Hyperpluralism

a view that the system today has evolved beyond simple pluralism and is now one in which many narrow interests are represented, often at the expense of the broader public interest.

ans may dislike interest groups, but few states have systems in which lobbyists play a stronger role. We may express frustration and proclaim our political independence, but the citizens of Texas have proved unswervingly loyal to first the Democratic Party and now the Republicans. Despite our disdain and doubts, we continually turn to these political institutions, ensuring them a place in the future of Texas politics.

Key Terms

astroturf lobbying
chronic minority
collective goods
conventions (caucuses)
county chairs
county or senatorial district conventions
delegates
disturbance theory
electioneering
electoral competition model
executive committee
expressive benefits
free-rider problem
grassroots lobbying
grassroots organizations
grasstop lobbying
hyperpluralism
intergovernmental lobby
labor unions
lobbying
organized interest
party platform
permanent party organizations
planks
pluralist perspective
political action committees (PACs)
precinct chairs
professional associations
public-interest groups
responsible party model
revolving door
runoff primary
selective incentives
single-interest groups
solidarity benefits
state party chair
temporary party organizations
trade associations

Explore this subject further at http://college.cqpress.com/lonestarpolitics, where you'll find chapter summaries, practice quizzes, key word flash cards, and additional suggested resources.

Houston highways, usually unable to keep up with the growth of the area, were emptied by the evacuation of residents as the state prepared for Hurricane Rita in September 2005. Highway maintenance and disaster preparedness are policy areas Texas politicians typically confront.

CHAPTER 9

Policy

Change creates all kinds of new challenges for government. For example, the advances of modern medicine, while yielding miracles in the lives of individual citizens, create their own challenges for government. The array of new medicines and advanced treatments that make Texans' lives longer and fuller have proven expensive, and often the costs of treatment have grown beyond the means of many families. One predictable outcome of miracle cures is that parents want them for their children and Texans, like all other Americans, do not want to see their children going without needed medicine. In 1997 Congress partnered with the states to create the State Children's Health Insurance Program (SCHIP) to help ensure that the nation's poorest children had access to medical care.

Ten years later the state of Texas and the national government were caught up in battles over children's heath care. In Washington D.C., Congress twice sent President George W. Bush legislation that would have expanded the number of families eligible for the SCHIP. Congressional Democrats, with the backing of some Republicans, wanted to raise the limits that state governments set on how much a family could earn and still qualify for the program. Each state establishes income limits within federal rules for its children's health program. In 2007 Texas and thirty-one other states had set limits at twice the poverty level (200 percent) or less, while seventeen states had limits from 220 percent to 300 percent of the poverty level. New Jersey, the only state with a higher limit, offers coverage to children with family incomes up to 350 percent of the poverty level, or $72,275 for a family of four. In some states with higher ceilings the coverage is not free and families are charged premiums and co-payments.

President Bush vetoed the legislation because this expansion of the program would have cost the federal government $35 billion dollars over five years. Opponents of the expansion also warned that the program would encourage some families to leave private insurers in order to join the federal program. Supporters of the expansion of the program pointed out the legislation would insure more than 3 million additional children. Congress voted to use a $0.61-per-pack increase in tobacco taxes to pay for the expansion of the program, recasting the debate as a battle between children and tobacco companies.

Earlier in the year, the Texas Legislature had grappled with the issue from their end, passing legislation that restored funding cut from the program in 2003. These funding cuts had led to enrollments dropping from a high of 529,000 children in May 2002 to 300,800 in the summer of 2007. While the state's task seemed relatively simple at first glance, about 30 percent of children who were eligible and without other health insurance had never been enrolled in the program. Many of the children in need of assistance were the hardest to reach, and Texas's re-enrollment rules may have compounded the problem by requiring families to re-enroll every six months.

The SCHIP battle reflects the complexity and high stakes of policy debates. Even with the federal government taking responsibility for much of the program, without effective implementation by the states, the program would never be completely successful. The SCHIP battle also shows how Texas must continually adapt to the changing needs of its citizens, even as federal policy changes.

Texas government finds itself attempting to manage a wide variety of challenges. Policy, the actions of government, can take a variety of forms. Some policies, like taxes, present a constant reminder of government and its activities. Other policies, like education, are subtler in their costs and in their benefits.

In this chapter we will describe the policymaking process and examine the types of policies in general, as well as some of the specific policies that emerge from the process. Policy comes to Texans from a variety of actors in Texas government. Some policies result directly from the action of the Texas Legislature as it gathers every two years to write new laws. Many policies result from executive orders and other actions of the governor or other elected executives. Other policies emerge from the bureaucracy as it interprets the laws enacted by the legislature. Finally, more localized policies result from the actions of city or county governments. Government is seldom tasked with problems that have easy solutions. As we'll see in the discussion of the issue of immigration at the end of the chapter, policy solutions are difficult because Texans often do not even agree whether or not there's a problem. Texas government under different flags and constitutions has been struggling for generations to find solutions to the problems Texans face. However, a rapidly changing population continually redefines our old problems and generates new problems as immigration from other countries and other states continues to bring new people and new politics into Texas.

As you read the chapter, think about the following questions:

★ What kinds of taxes do Texans pay?
★ Should Texas change its current tax system?
★ What are the problems with the current education system in Texas?
★ How can Texans prepare for current and future transportation needs?

Policy
the actions and activities of government.

Agenda setting
the stage in which policymakers prioritize the problems facing the state.

Policy formation
the stage in which possible solutions are developed and debated.

Policy adoption
the stage in which formal government action takes place.

Policy implementation
the stage in which the policy is carried out in state agencies.

The Policymaking Process

Scholars have identified five stages in the process of making **policy,** which are depicted in Figure 9.1. The first is **agenda setting,** in which policymakers prioritize the various problems facing the state. These policymakers may discover the problem themselves through sources ranging from their own everyday experiences to formal legislative hearings or it may be brought to their attention by individual citizens, interest groups, or media reports. In the next step, **policy formation,** possible solutions are developed and debated. Next, in the **policy adoption** stage, formal government action takes place with approval by the legislature or administrative action by a member of the executive branch. After approval, policies move into the **policy implementation** stage, in which state agencies follow up on the actions of elected officials. In this state bureaucratic agencies develop rules and regulations that detail the guidelines for how the policy will be carried out. In the final stage, **policy evaluation,** government agencies, the legislature, and interest groups examine the implementation of the policy to see if its goals are being met.

Political scientists have categorized policies into three types: redistributive, distributive, and regulatory. **Redistributive policy** moves benefits (usually in the form of money) from one group to another in an attempt to equalize society by taxing people with higher incomes to provide benefits to people with few resources. **Distributive policy** is similar except that it attempts to meet the needs of citizens without targeting any one group as the source of money. As a result, distributive policies are easier to implement because their costs are widely dispersed and such policies face less opposition since no group is identified as the source of funds. **Regulatory policy** attempts to limit or control the actions of individuals, including corporations. For example, businesses may face fines or other penalties as a disincentive for polluting or other socially undesirable outcomes. Thus, policy is at the heart of politics as the government resolves the question of who gets what from government.

Fiscal Policy: Taxes, Spending, and Budgets

Maybe the most obvious way of looking at who gets what from government is examining the money that Texas takes from its citizens (taxes) and puts into various programs (spending). While the intentions and effectiveness of spending merit specific discussion, we need to first look at **fiscal policy,** how government seeks to influence the economy through taxing and spending. This takes the form of policies to shape the health of the economy overall, as well as the taxing and spending policies the state uses to encourage some businesses and discourage others.

Policy evaluation
the stage in which the implementation of a policy is examined to see if its goals are being met.

Redistributive policy
moves benefits (usually in the form of money) from one group to another in an attempt to equalize society.

Distributive policy
attempts to meet the needs of citizens without targeting any one group as the source of money.

Regulatory policy
attempts to limit or control the actions of individuals, including corporations.

Fiscal policy
how government seeks to influence the economy through taxing and spending.

Figure 9.1 The Policymaking Process

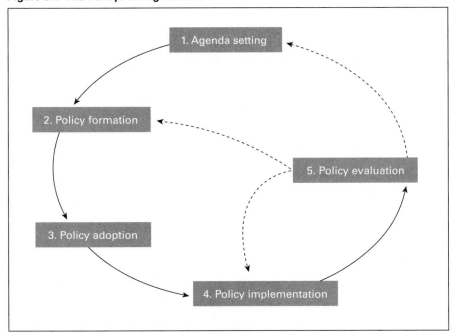

Source: Christine Barbour and Gerald C. Wright, *Keeping the Republic,* 2nd Brief Ed. (Washington, D.C.: CQ Press, 2006), 419.

Every year, the Tax Foundation, a nonpartisan tax research group based in Washington, D.C., calculates "Tax Freedom Day" to illustrate what portion of the year citizens must work to pay their federal, state, and local taxes. In 2007 they estimated that the average American works about 120 days out of the year to pay his or her taxes, making "Tax Freedom Day" April 30. By their estimate, Tax Freedom Day comes a little earlier (April 19) to Texans, placing Texas forty-second among the 50 states in terms of total state taxes paid per capita. The most heavily taxed state, according to the Tax Foundation, was Connecticut, although some of Connecticut citizens' heavy tax burden resulted from their prosperity, as a high average income in the state results in high federal income taxes.[i] Connecticut state taxes averaged $3,300 per person, compared to an average of $1,434 per person in Texas.[ii] Citizens of Connecticut face taxes of 5 percent on income over $10,000 as well as a 6 percent state sales tax (local governments are not allowed to add to that rate). One of the reasons for Connecticut's high taxes is that its citizens are relatively prosperous, with a median household income in 2005–2006 of $52,174, compared to Texas's median household income of $43,044 and the national average median of $48,203.[iii] Because households in Connecticut have higher in-

comes, this will naturally translate into higher federal income taxes.

Overall, the highest rates of taxation could be found in the Northeast, with Connecticut, New York, New Jersey, Vermont, and Rhode Island having the highest rates in the nation. In contrast, taxes were generally lower in the South, with Oklahoma, Alabama, Mississippi, Tennessee, and Louisiana among the least taxed states.

Thinking Critically

- Can you think of some advantages of living in a high-income tax state like Connecticut? What might these be?
- Can you also see problems in Texas that might be better addressed if the state of Texas had more revenue? What might these be?
- Can you think of other ways the state might raise revenue without imposing income taxes?

i. The Tax Foundation, *Special Report: Americans Celebrate Tax Freedom Day,* April 2007.

ii. The U.S. Census Bureau, "States Ranked by Total State Taxes and Per Capita Amount: 2005," www.census.gov/govs/statetax/05staxrank.html.

iii. The U.S. Census Bureau, "Two-Year Average Median Household Income by State, 2004–2006," www.census.gov/hhes/www/income/income06/statemhi2.html.

Subsidies

incentives designed to encourage the production or purchase of certain goods, to stimulate or support some businesses.

The state may also provide **subsidies,** incentives designed to encourage the production or purchase of certain goods, to encourage some businesses or industries. For example, the Texas state government encourages local governments to grant tax breaks to businesses that meet wage and benefits standards. Recently a proposal was made that would require NRG Energy to pay school taxes on only a tiny fraction of its planned $4 billion expansion of the South Texan Nuclear Project because of the quality of the jobs it would bring to the area. While bringing jobs to an area might seem popular at first glance, these incentives creating subsidies for new businesses shift the tax burden to existing businesses that may not enjoy paying the tax bill for their new neighbors. In addition, as the NRG case demonstrates, tax dollars might be used to bring in businesses that may be controversial (like nuclear power plants).

Taxes

Texans, not surprisingly, have never liked taxes. Settlers in Stephen F. Austin's colony complained about the 12.5 cents per-acre tax Austin charged to pay for survey fees and the militia needed for settlers' defense.[1] Today, Texans pay relatively little in state taxes. According to the Census Bureau in 2005, Texas taxes ranked forty-ninth out

Map 6: Tax Freedom Days

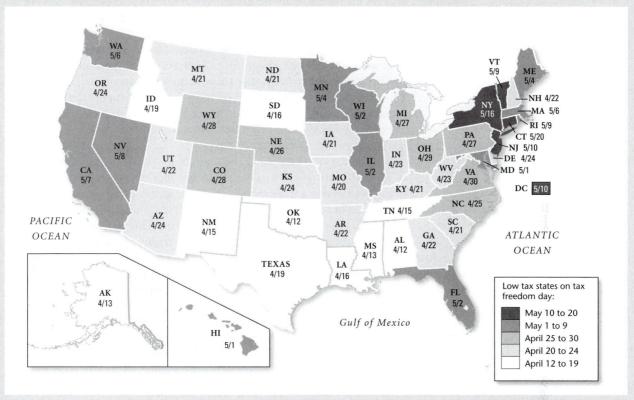

WA 5/6
OR 4/24
ID 4/19
MT 4/21
ND 4/21
MN 5/4
WI 5/2
MI 4/27
VT 5/9
ME 5/4
NH 4/22
MA 5/6
RI 5/9
NY 5/16
CT 5/20
NJ 5/10
PA 4/27
DE 4/24
MD 5/1
WY 4/28
SD 4/16
IA 4/21
NE 4/26
IL 5/2
IN 4/23
OH 4/29
WV 4/23
VA 4/30
NV 5/8
UT 4/22
CO 4/28
KS 4/24
MO 4/20
KY 4/21
CA 5/7
AZ 4/24
NM 4/15
OK 4/12
AR 4/22
TN 4/15
NC 4/25
SC 4/21
DC 5/10

PACIFIC OCEAN

MS 4/13
AL 4/12
GA 4/22

ATLANTIC OCEAN

TEXAS 4/19
LA 4/16

AK 4/13

Gulf of Mexico

FL 5/2

HI 5/1

Low tax states on tax freedom day:

	May 10 to 20
	May 1 to 9
	April 25 to 30
	April 20 to 24
	April 12 to 19

of fifty, with state taxes for each Texan in 2005 averaging $1,434, just slightly higher than South Dakota's $1,430 and well below the national average of $2,190 per person in state taxes.[2]

State Taxes

Today, Texas relies on a complicated mixture of taxes. Texas is one of seven states with no **income tax.** Two states (New Hampshire and Tennessee) have no general income tax but do tax dividend and interest income. While the idea of avoiding income tax is appealing, as Texas demonstrates, the lack of an income tax doesn't mean there will be no taxes since, as we're about to see, there are many, many other ways of raising revenue for the state.

In 1961 Texas implemented its first **general sales tax,** imposing a 2 percent sales tax on many goods sold. Over the next forty years that tax rate has increased to 6.25 percent and expanded to include more goods and services. In 1967 the Local Sales and Use Tax Act authorized cities to add a 1 percent local tax on all retail sales. Today, Texas cities, counties, transit authorities, and other special purpose districts have the option of imposing an additional local sales tax for a combined possible maximum

Income tax
a tax calculated as a percentage of income earned in a year.

General sales tax
an across-the-board tax imposed on goods and services sold within a jurisdiction.

for all state and local sales taxes of 8.25 percent. By 1967 the sales tax had become the largest source of tax revenue for Texas. In 2007 the state sales tax brought in over $20 billion, accounting for about 55 percent of Texas taxes, by far the biggest source of tax revenue for the state. Texas's sales tax of 6.25 percent is the fourth highest state sales tax rate in the nation, a full point behind California's 7.25 percent sales tax.

Comparing state sales taxes is difficult because each state uses a different mixture of state and local sales taxes. For example, the state of New York imposes a sales tax rate of only 4 percent, but counties in New York have local sales tax rates that allow them to add an additional percentage, from 3 percent to 5.75 percent. Other states, like Connecticut, have a state-level sales tax with no local add-ons.

In addition to the general sales tax, Texas has a separate tax of 6.25 percent on the sale and rental or lease of motor vehicles. There is also a tax of 3.25 percent on the sale of manufactured housing. These taxes bring in another $3 billion or 9 percent of the state's revenue.

Texas also taxes the sale of gasoline. The Gasoline and Diesel Fuel Tax charges consumers in Texas 20 cents on every gallon of gasoline they buy (on top of another 18.4 cents a gallon in federal taxes). Texas's gas tax is one of the lowest rates in the nation, (thirty-seventh out of the fifty states and the District of Columbia) half of New York's 49.5 cents a gallon but much more than Alaska's 8 cents. This generates almost $3 billion each year, or about 9 percent of the state's tax revenue. The Texas Legislature's refusal to raise the gasoline tax since 1992 has generated a good deal of controversy in the last few years. Since the gasoline tax has been used as one of the primary sources of revenue for highways, Texas has increasingly turned to toll roads to keep pace with the needs of a growing state.

After oil erupted from the Spindletop well on January 10, 1901, ushering in an era of petroleum, taxes on Texas's oil production became a huge source of revenue that has kept many Texans from having to pay much in the way of taxes. By 1905 the state was raking in $101,403 a year from oil production alone. Texas still taxes the production of oil and gas with a **severance tax,** a tax on natural resources charged when they are produced or "severed" from the earth. These severance taxes, similar to a value added tax (VAT), that is common in Europe, take the form of Texas's "Oil Production" tax that takes 4.6 percent of the market value of oil produced, while the "Oil Regulation" tax takes three-sixteenths of a cent from each barrel of oil produced. The state also taxes the production of natural gas at 7.5 percent of market value. In addition, liquefied gas is taxed at a rate of 15 cents a gallon. While once a much larger portion of the state budget, the state's tax on oil and gas production today accounts for only about 7 percent of all state taxes.

Texas's **franchise tax** is its primary tax on business. That tax was significantly revised in the 2006 special session in order to help fund Texas public schools by expanding the types of businesses taxed. At the same time, the calculation of the tax was changed and now the franchise tax is based on the "taxable margin" (a variety of measures approximating profit) of the company (70 percent of total revenue, total revenue minus the costs of goods sold, or total revenue minus compensation, whichever is less).

Like other states, Texas has a number of **sin taxes,** taxes on products or activities that some legislators want to discourage. The objects of sin taxes make inviting targets, as elected officials look for places to impose taxes on the least sympathetic products possible. While the federal government has its own **excise tax,** a tax paid at the time of purchase with the cost of the tax usually included in the price of the product, on alcoholic beverages, Texas has separate tax rates on liquor, beer, wine, malt

Severance tax

a tax on natural resources charged when the resources are produced or "severed" from the earth.

Franchise tax

the primary tax on businesses in Texas, which is based on the "taxable margin" of each company.

Sin taxes

taxes on products or activities, such as cigarettes or gambling, that some legislators would like to discourage.

Excise tax

a tax paid at the time of purchase, with the cost of the tax included in the price of the product.

liquor, and mixed drinks. While some alcohol is taxed by volume, mixed drinks are taxed at 14 percent of sales. In 2006 Texas's taxes on alcohol totaled just over $731 million. This is a small portion (2 percent) of the total state taxes, as a contribution of a single product, but Texans might be surprised to realize that they drink enough to average over $40 in alcohol tax for every Texan of drinking age.

The recent rise in the state's tax on cigarettes, passed in May 2005 to help pay for schools, illustrates the complexities of sin taxes. On January 1, 2007, the state's tax on a pack of cigarettes leapt a full dollar for a total tax of $1.41 a pack, driving the cost of most packs of cigarettes over $4 and making the state's tax one of the highest in the region. Some Texans contemplated quitting smoking, an effect intended by groups like the American Cancer Society that lobbied for the increase. Others saw the tax increase as a way of offsetting the health care costs to a state that sees over 20,000 people a year die from smoking-related illnesses. With about half of the revenue from the tobacco tax designated for funding public schools, the tax may seem to present an easy opportunity to raise some revenue at the expense of unpopular products. However, these taxes can be problematic. Because Louisiana's 36-cent tax per pack is one of the lowest in the nation, some Texans simply crossed the state lines to buy their cigarettes, just as New Mexico's smokers streamed into Texas when New Mexico increased its tax 70 cents per pack in 2003. With convenience stores claiming that cigarettes account for over one-quarter of their sales, the outflow of Texas customers results in a significant loss of revenue, depriving Texas merchants of customers and losing taxable sales to other states.

The general mixture of taxes is spelled out in Table 9.1 below. As the table demonstrates, while Texas's tax rates may be low, the system is far from simple as the state looks to a wide variety of sources for its tax dollars.

Table 9.1 Texas State Taxes by Source, Fiscal Year 2007

	2007 REVENUE (in thousands)	PERCENTAGE OF TOTAL TAX REVENUE	PERCENTAGE OF ALL SOURCES OF REVENUE
Tax Collections			
Sales tax	$20,270,476,222	55%	26.3%
Motor vehicle sales and rental taxes	$3,325,596,670	9%	4.3%
Motor fuels taxes	$3,053,812,019	8%	4.0%
Franchise tax	$3,144,059,392	9%	4.1%
Insurance taxes	$1,346,576,684	4%	1.7%
Natural gas tax	$1,895,487,909	5%	2.5%
Cigarette and tobacco taxes	$1,334,038,617	4%	1.7%
Alcoholic beverage taxes	$731,677,225	2%	0.9%
Oil production and regulation taxes	$835,025,116	2%	1.1%
Inheritance tax	$5,291,127	0%	0.0%
Utility taxes	$506,069,409	1%	0.7%
Hotel occupancy tax	$340,634,147	1%	0.4%
Other taxes	$166,885,345	0%	0.2%
Total tax revenue	$36,955,629,884		47.9%

Source: Comptroller, "Biennial Revenue Estimate, 2008–2009," Table A16, January 2007, www.window.state.tx.us/taxbud/bre2008/ BRE_2008-09.pdf; Comptroller, Revenue by Source for Fiscal Year 2007, www.window.state.tx.us/taxbud/revenue.html.

Note: May not sum due to rounding.

Property Taxes

Property tax

a tax on the value of real estate that is paid by the property owner; used by county and local governments to fund such programs as public schools.

While Texas's state taxes are lower than most other states', Texas imposes a significant local property tax burden on its citizens, although the Texas Constitution forbids a statewide **property tax.** While Texas does not officially have a statewide property tax, cities, counties, and local school districts charge property taxes that they rely heavily on for their revenue. In Texas, the balance of responsibility for public schools has been a major conflict, requiring special legislative sessions to resolve. In 2006 the Texas Legislature reduced school property taxes by one-third. The plan traded lower school property taxes for higher taxes on businesses, smokers, and used-car purchasers. While the legislature's reform promised significantly lower taxes, about two-thirds of local school boards in the state opted to increase the rates after the legislature had reduced them.[3] While the increases were relatively small and within the limits created by the law, they served to reduce the size of tax cuts the legislature sought.

These complications result from a mixed funding system that leaves local school boards dependent on the state for much of their money at the same time the boards remain subject to state rules on how they raise remaining revenues. Many local school boards are facing rising utility bills and staff costs even as the legislature has capped available funding. Locally elected school boards are left with few alternatives, having little choice but to raise property taxes.

Ad-valorem tax

a tax based on property value, which is subject to periodic appraisals.

Appraisal

the official estimate of a property's value.

Setting property tax rates may seem like a simple process. However, the property tax is an *ad-valorem* **tax,** a tax based on the value of property. Even if the property tax rates remain the same, governments may raise the tax on citizens by increasing their **appraisal,** the official estimate of a property's value. This problem is especially serious in growing areas like Dallas, which saw a 60 percent rise in property values from 2000 to 2005.[4] This creates what critics call a "stealth tax increase," even though the state government had no hand in increasing property values. Currently the state caps the annual increase in a home's taxable value to ten percent. Senior citizens and others living on fixed incomes may have trouble keeping up with the taxes on their property as values rise. Rising property values create a significant problem for seniors today, who, after paying off a $250-a-month thirty-year mortgage, for example, now find themselves paying that much in property taxes every month. To protect seniors, Texas offers a cap on school taxes and the Texas Constitution was amended in 2003 to allow (but not require) cities and counties to cap seniors' taxes. While this may give retired Texans a protection against rising rates, it shifts the burden for taxes to others and may present a serious problem for areas with high numbers of retirees.

Winners and Losers

Progressive tax

a graduated tax, such as an income tax, which taxes people with higher incomes at higher rates.

Regressive tax

a tax, such as a sales tax, that taxes everyone at the same rate, regardless of income, which has a greater impact on those with lower incomes.

he type of taxes Texas uses creates obvious winners and losers. **Progressive taxes,** such as the federal income tax, place higher rates on people with higher incomes. **Regressive taxes,** in contrast, take a higher proportion of income from people with lower incomes than from people with higher incomes. Sales taxes are often cited as examples of regressive taxes, even though everyone pays the same tax rate on purchases. Critics of sales taxes point out that people with lower incomes tend to spend a larger share of their income on the kind of items taxed at sale.

Some Texans have advocated an income tax like those used by other states to shift more of the state's tax burden to people with higher incomes. While critics complain about the complexity of an income tax system with exemptions and schedules of deductions, the vast array of current state taxes reflects that Texas has already created a complicates system without an income tax. Even some conservative legislators privately concede that replacing Texas's long list of taxes with a single income tax based on calculations already done for federal income taxes would actually simplify taxation in the state. These legislators are more worried that if the state did away with these small taxes in favor of an income tax, nothing would prevent the state from gradually reinstating these small taxes whenever the government needed more money.

So choosing who to tax and how to structure taxes is a clearly visible statement by the government of who wins and who loses. Thus, it is not surprising that the Texas Legislature, currently faced simultaneously with increased costs and statewide tax fatigue, has largely avoided the problem altogether. In some cases, creative but surreptitious alternatives (such as the growing number of toll roads or significant increases in university tuition and fees) are filling the gap. In other cases, citizens are left with an education system, healthcare system, and even basic infrastructure that are inadequate to their needs. As Texans grapple with the difficult issue of who pays, it appears everyone loses.

Other Sources of Revenue

While the taxes outlined so far generated over $33 billion dollars in 2006, they accounted for less than half (48 percent) of state revenue. This raises the question of where the state gets the rest of its revenue. As Table 9.2 indicates, tax revenues are only part of the funding picture.

Federal Grants

The large share of the state budget that comes from the federal treasury might surprise many Texans. In 2007, Texas received about $24.3 billion from the federal gov-

Table 9.2 Texas State Revenue by Source

	2007 REVENUE (in thousands)	PERCENTAGE OF ALL SOURCES OF REVENUE
Revenue by Source		
Tax collections	$36,955,629,882	47.9%
Federal income	$24,376,052,502	31.6%
Licenses, fees, fines, and penalties	$6,914,295,978	9.0%
Interest and investment income	$2,372,705,358	3.1%
Lottery proceeds	$1,551,975,844	2.0%
Sales of goods and services	$538,835,356	0.7%
Settlements of claims	$537,942,295	0.7%
Land income	$751,358,474	1.0%
Contributions to employee benefits	$237,887,499	0.3%
Other revenue	$2,952,608,025	3.8%
Total revenue	$77,189,291,212	100.0%

Source: Texas Comptroller, Revenue by Source for Fiscal Year 2007, www.window.state.tx.us/taxbud/revenue.html
Note: May not sum due to rounding.

ernment, accounting for about a third of the state's finances. As the federalism discussion in chapter 2 illustrates, some of these federal monies generally come with strings attached while others pay for programs in which the state and federal government partner. These large dollar amounts account for much of state leaders' willingness to accept federal rules.

Relative to other states, Texas has not fared that well with federal dollars. A study by the Tax Foundation found that in 2004 Texas ranked thirty-sixth out of fifty states on federal funds received relative to federal taxes paid by residents of the state. Overall, Texas received $0.94 for every $1.00 Texans paid in federal taxes.[5]

Licensing and Lottery Funds

Rounding out the revenue picture for Texas are various funding sources that together account for about one-fifth of all state revenues. Some of this money comes from the licensing of various professions and businesses. While these fees resemble taxes on certain professions, the argument that they simply offset some of the specific expenses associated with licensing justifies counting these fees as something different from taxes. In addition, the state receives money from fines paid by those found guilty of traffic and other offenses.

In 2007 the state received over $2.3 billion in income from returns on its bank balances and other investments. The largest source of investment income came from the state's **Permanent School Fund,** a fund set aside to finance education in Texas.

Permanent School Fund

a fund set aside to finance education in Texas; the state's largest source of investment income.

Texas also makes money from a state lottery. Half of the proceeds of lottery ticket sales go into the prizes, with the state and retailers dividing the rest. In 2007 the state brought in $1.6 billion based on $3.8 billion in lottery ticket sales. Of that $1.6 billion, just over $1 billion was used to help fund public education in Texas. While under attack from a variety of groups, the lottery remains a part of Texas state finances for the same reason as the other taxes, fees, and revenue sources mentioned here: no one has found a more popular way to replace the money it generates. For example, many conservative members of the Texas Legislature find the state's profits from gambling distasteful. However, eliminating the Texas lottery would require increasing taxes or cutting popular programs to offset the revenue lost. Thus taking this revenue source off the books would be politically difficult.

Spending and Budgeting

Texas government has not always been frugal. During the three years of Mirabeau Lamar's presidency, the government of Texas spent about $4.85 million while taking in only about $1.08 million.[6] Lamar had reversed Sam Houston's policy of cooperating with the Native American tribes, and the hostilities spawned by Lamar's desire to wipe Native Americans off the face of the state cost Texas dearly. By contrast, Houston's administration spent only about half a million dollars in the three years after Lamar's presidency.

As the Texas economy changes and Texans' expectations for government change, spending in Texas shifts. One of the fundamental causes of a growing state budget is a growing state population. For example, 2006 saw spending on public safety and corrections surge by 27.8 percent, in part because more Texans means more crime. As Table 9.3 details, Texas spends its money on a wide array of functions. While some

Table 9.3 State Spending by Function, Fiscal Year 2007

GOVERNMENT FUNCTION	AMOUNT	PERCENTAGE OF BUDGET
Executive departments	$1,970,160,437	2.6%
Legislative branch	$129,463,817	0.2%
Judicial branch	$225,340,159	0.3%
Education	$26,324,526,875	35.3%
Employee benefits	$2,836,431,787	3.8%
Health and human services	$27,894,746,580	37.4%
Public safety and corrections	$3,778,469,104	5.1%
Transportation	$7,609,018,395	10.2%
Natural resources/recreational services	$1,897,573,779	2.5%
Regulatory services	$233,153,863	0.3%
Lottery winnings paid	$389,758,161	0.5%
Debt service	$837,363,803	1.1%
Capital outlay	$374,808,786	0.5%
Total net expenditures	$74,500,815,546	

Source: Comptroller, *Texas Annual Cash Report, Fiscal Year 2007,* Table 7: "Net Expenditures by Function."

details of the policies in these areas will be discussed later in this chapter, our concern here is how overall spending is managed.

Texas has a **"pay-as-you-go" system** that requires a balanced budget and permits borrowing only under a very few circumstances. The Texas Constitution provides that state borrowing can only exceed $200,000 unless such borrowing is needed to "repel invasion, suppress insurrection, or defend the State in war" or unless such borrowing is approved by voters. The Texas Legislature may declare an emergency, but doing so requires getting a four-fifths vote of each house before the spending limit can be exceeded.[7]

While many Texans might assume that balancing the state budget is relatively simple, the system created to ensure that the budget stays balanced has spawned some unique features in Texas government, especially in the role of the Comptroller of Public Accounts. At the beginning of each legislative session, the Texas Constitution requires that the comptroller certify how much money will be in the state's accounts in the two years ahead that the legislature is budgeting for. For example, when the Texas Legislature convened in January 2007, Comptroller Susan Combs reported to the legislature that revenue "from all sources and for all purposes should total $156.8 billion."[8] This estimate from the comptroller effectively became the ceiling for state spending that the legislature had to operate under. The constitution also provides that a bill cannot be considered passed by the legislature unless the comptroller has authorized that the amount to be spent by the bill is available. If the comptroller finds that legislation would exceed the state's budget, the comptroller must notify the legislature so that additional revenue can be found or the appropriation in the bill reduced. These provisions put the Texas comptroller in a unique—and powerful—position. As former comptroller Carole Strayhorn pointed out, "The comptroller's office is a constitutional office; there's nothing like it in any other state.

"Pay-as-you-go" system
a fiscal discipline, adopted by Texas and many other states, that requires a balanced budget and permits borrowing only under a very few circumstances.

I tell the legislature what they can spend, and I certify that the budget is balanced. Unless and until I certify that budget, there is no appropriations bill, and there is nothing for the governor to line-item veto." [9]

The constitution does allow the state to sell revenue bonds to finance activities specified in Article 3. These bonds are sold to investors and then paid back with the revenue from the services they provide. For example, Texas often issues tuition revenue bonds that may pay for new buildings on college campuses with student fees being used to pay back the debt after the building is finished.

The Legislative Budget Board (LBB) was created in 1949 to help coordinate the budgeting process in Texas, a process that had previously been a haphazard collection of individual appropriations bills. As outlined in chapter 3, the LBB is co-chaired by the Speaker of the Texas House and the lieutenant governor. The presence of the presiding officers of both houses, as well as the chairs of key committees, ensures that the LBB holds tremendous political clout.

The LBB is responsible for budgeting, looking at the balance of taxing and spending as well as the performance of state agencies. While the LBB enjoys tremendous influence because it prepares the initial budget estimate that will be considered during the legislative session, its work continues beyond the initial proposal. During the legislative session the LBB staff provides analysis for the legislative committees involved in budgeting. Texas law requires each bill in the legislature to have a "fiscal note" prepared by the LBB staff that estimates the cost of the bill. Because elected officials tend to want to spend more than they have, many critics feel that the fiscal notes have become politicized and that they often ignore the true costs of bills favored by the leadership. At the end of the 2007 legislative session Governor Perry complained that fiscal notes were no longer providing accurate pictures of the costs of legislation and warned that he would no longer sign bills with inaccurate fiscal notes. [10]

Between sessions, the LBB or the governor may recommend prohibiting a state agency from spending money appropriated to it by the legislature. The LBB or the governor may also transfer money from one state agency to another or change the purpose for which an appropriation was made. Such recommendations by the LBB must be approved by the governor in order to go into effect while recommendations by the governor require approval by the LBB.

While the state's constitution establishes numerous barriers to state debt, these provisions have not always proved enough to stop increasing state spending. Despite the fact that Texas has been a conservative state, spending continues to rise. As Table 9.4 demonstrates, spending in the state has been increasing steadily for the past thirty years. Some of this increase can be explained by inflation and the fact that the state's population has roughly doubled in the same time frame. However, Texas's government has grown dramatically, under both Republicans and Democrats, and this growth reflects the increased demands of a growing and changing state.

Education Policy

During the 2006–2007 school year about 5.8 million Texans were in the educational system at some level. Over 520,000 were in nursery, preschool, or kindergarten, 1.75 million were in elementary schools (grades 1–5), another one million in middle school (grades 6–8), and 1.27 million in high school (grades 9–12). [11] In addition, 1.3 million people were enrolled in institutions of higher education.

Education is important even to those Texans not in school, because education contributes to the economy of the state by providing the state's businesses with the qualified workforce needed today while research conducted at the state's universities contributes to the innovations needed for the future. The importance of schools to the state's businesses was reflected in 2007, when a new group calling itself "Raise Your Hand, Texas" sought new educational reforms. Although the organization is chaired by the former lieutenant governor, Bill Ratliff, most of the board members are current or former heads of major corporations like Texas Instruments, Continental Airlines, and AT&T, reflecting the ongoing interest of business in public education.

Public Schools: Education in Grades K–12

Education policy in the state's public schools is especially complicated because it brings together the efforts, money, and rules of federal, state, and local governments. In the 2005–2006 school year, Texas public schools received 54.6 percent of their revenues from local taxes, 33.9 percent from the state, and 11.5 percent from the federal government. As the sources of money indicate, while federal laws like No Child Left Behind have continued to increase federal involvement in Texas public schools, the financial responsibility for schools remains mostly with state and local officials.

Combined, state and local government spent over $43 billion on Texas public schools, averaging $9,629 per pupil.[12] Given the large investment of tax dollars and the future of the state's children at stake, the education issue is primed for conflict. The possibility for conflict is increased as various political groups try to bring their concerns into the schools, triggering debates about emotional issues like prayer and contraceptives, as well as societal concerns and more technical issues about what math, science, and communication skills students need to equip them for their future in the workforce.

Political battles over education are nothing new. The political battles over public schools in Texas predate the state and even the Republic, as the authors of the Texas Declaration of Independence included in their list of grievances that Mexico had "failed to establish any public system of education, although possessed of almost boundless resources (the public domain) and, although, it is an axiom, in political science, that unless a people are educated and enlightened it is idle to expect the continuance of civil liberty, or the capacity for self-government." During his presidency Mirabeau Lamar earned the title of "Father of Texas Education"[13] by championing education in the new republic and setting aside three leagues of land for each county to support elementary schools. Despite Lamar's vision, the limited value of this land combined with Texans' reluctance to finance schools and the preference of many for private schools delayed realization of a public school system until the Constitution of 1868 centralized the public schools.

Table 9.4 Historical Trends in Spending

FISCAL YEAR	TOTAL EXPENDITURES
1978	$7,864,096,032
1979	$8,600,168,100
1980	$10,210,907,514
1981	$11,367,553,831
1982	$12,074,204,469
1983	$13,539,476,462
1984	$14,348,917,194
1985	$16,526,569,692
1986	$17,692,682,714
1987	$17,918,188,233
1988	$19,432,790,686
1989	$20,695,147,589
1990	$22,680,257,166
1991	$25,602,753,536
1992	$29,290,095,003
1993	$33,388,708,598
1994	$35,638,096,003
1995	$39,337,381,101
1996	$39,669,455,477
1997	$41,460,006,691
1998	$43,223,731,907
1999	$45,687,044,389
2000	$49,707,754,236
2001	$52,669,367,487
2002	$55,739,143,025
2003	$60,270,447,962
2004	$60,718,645,275
2005	$64,693,009,292
2006	$68,833,163,941
2007	$74,500,815,546

Source: Comptroller's Office, "Texas Expenditure History by Function, 1978–2006," www.cpa.state.tx.us/taxbud/expend_hist.html.

James Leininger

Dr. James Leininger is a man on a mission to transform education in Texas. Leininger began his journey to become the state's leading advocate of school vouchers twenty years ago when he discovered that some of the employees of his very successful hospital bed company were functionally illiterate despite having high school diplomas. Initially, he tried to help by personally sponsoring a mentoring program. When his mentoring program failed to produce change, Leininger became interested in vouchers, certificates given to parents that could be used to pay for education for their children at the school of their choice, as a means of allowing students to find their way into better schools. He began by offering scholarships to help poor students pay the $3,000 needed to attend public schools in other districts or private schools. Over the years, students in his privately funded scholarship program have enjoyed a 100-percent graduation rate and 95 percent have gone on to college.

In 1993 Leininger began working with the Texas Legislature to create a state-funded voucher system. In the years since, he has backed voucher-friendly candidates and worked directly with the legislature. In the 2006 election he pumped over $5 million into campaigns, backing Republican candidates who favored vouchers. In five races, Leininger backed Republican challengers to the Republican incumbents in that party's primary, in one race accounting for 96 percent of a candidate's campaign funds. While the flood of money was alarming to some, Leininger's massive spending generally failed to be decisive. Despite spending about $2.5 million in five Republican primary races, three of the five candidates that Leininger backed failed to unseat the incumbent.

In 2007 Leininger announced that he would be ending his privately financed voucher program for 2,000 students and urged the legislature to approve a state-funded system. While he has ended his own program Leininger plans on continuing to support pro-voucher candidates and a statewide voucher program in Texas.

While Leininger has not won approval for vouchers, he has been attacked for his efforts to reform education. Leininger attributes the bad press coverage he has received to misunderstanding and misrepresentation of the voucher issue. However, some of the concerns emerge from the fact of one person playing such a large role in an election.

The foundation of the modern public school system in Texas was laid in 1949 when the legislature passed the Gilmer-Aikin Act (named for Rep. Claud Gilmer and Sen. A. M. Aikin) that guaranteed Texas children twelve years of school with a minimum of 175 days of instruction per year. The legislation also redesigned the state's governance of public education by replacing the old nine-person appointed State Board of Education with commissioners elected by voters in districts.

Texas education was further transformed by the civil rights era, although change proved slow. In 1954 the U.S. Supreme Court issued the landmark *Brown v. Board of Education*[14] decision that declared segregated public schools to be a violation of the Equal Protection Clause of the U.S. Constitution. Despite the Court's unanimous verdict in the original decision and a follow-up decision known as *Brown II*[15] in 1955 calling for desegregation "with all deliberate speed," little progress was seen in Texas in the decade after the Brown decisions, and students in many areas remained separated by race. Eventually, the U.S. Department of Justice filed a lawsuit against the State of Texas resulting in a 1970 decision by Judge William Wayne Justice, the chief judge of the U.S. District Court for the Eastern District in Tyler, to desegregate the state's public schools and give the court authority to oversee the state's implementation of desegregation.[16]

Since that time Texas has labored to improve the quality of public schools through various reform movements, while still addressing the need for equality. In the 1980s the Perot committee, led by wealthy businessman H. Ross Perot, pushed for reforms and saw the Texas legislature adopt many of its recommendations in a special session in the summer of 1984. The **Education Reform Act** required that teachers and administrators take the "Texas Examination of Current Administrators and Teachers" (TECAT) to assure basic competency before being recertified. Students were also tested periodically, beginning Texas's long experimentation with standardized testing that would ultimately spread across the nation during the presidency of George W. Bush. The act also include the "no-pass, no-play" rule that kept students with an average below 70 in any subject from taking part in extracurricular activities. The new law also called for more funding for poor school districts that lacked resources because of the reliance on local property taxes to fund schools. Some of these reforms proved unpopular as "no pass" sometimes meant "no play" for high school football players. Additionally, poor school districts felt they did not receive enough money, while others resented the increased taxes needed to equalize school districts. While these reforms eventually cost then governor Mark White his reelection bid, most of the reforms he signed into law have endured.

Despite the end of legal segregation, the inequality between school districts remains one of the most vexing problems in Texas politics. Texas traditionally used a system of local control and local financing for its public schools. While the Texas Legislature mandated a statewide curriculum in 1981 and continues to dictate most of what local schools must teach, much of the financial responsibility for these mandates remains with the local school district. This reliance on local funding left the public schools largely dependent on property taxes, meaning that school districts located in areas with high property values were able to provide more resources for their students, while other school districts have had to get by with much less.

In 1989 the Texas Supreme Court's unanimous decision in *Edgewood Independent School District v. Kirby*[17] forced the funding issue, when the court ruled that Texas's system violated the Texas Constitution's requirement of free and efficient schools. The court noted that two schools in Bexar County illustrated the inequity, as the Edgewood Independent School District had $38,854 in property tax per student while Alamo Heights had $570,109 per student. After three failed special sessions of the legislature, the fourth session produced a bill to raise sales taxes one-quarter of a cent and increase taxes on cigarettes. While this financing scheme did not satisfy the court, it did hold off further reform (thanks to court appeals by the state) until the early 1990s. In 1993 the Texas Legislature passed a law that established an equalized wealth level for schools and created a process for redistributing money between districts. In subsequent years, this law became known as the "Robin Hood" plan because it took money from "rich" school districts and gave it to "poor" districts. The issue continued into a 2006 special session of the Texas Legislature called to try to solve the inequality. The legislature found additional funding for schools.

Education Reform Act
a 1984 statute that requires teachers and school administrators to take a test to assure basic competency before being recertified; students are also tested periodically to monitor progress and are required to pass an exam before being allowed to graduate.

In the 2006–2007 school year Texas had 8,061 schools in 1,222 school districts and charter schools. These schools educate about 4.6 million people, using about 311,000 teachers and another 302,000 administrators and support staff.[18] Today, the system is run by the Texas Education Agency overseen by a commissioner of education appointed by the governor, along with a State Board of Education (SBOE) composed of fifteen members elected from districts with the chair appointed by the governor. The SBOE meets every few months and decides broad education issues like curriculum and standards for passing state-mandated exams.

States, and increasingly the national government, have been demanding more accountability from local school districts, and Texas has become a focal point of the debate on accountability because of the state's early embrace of standardized testing and Governor Bush's rise to the presidency, based partly on his promise to do for the nation's schools what had been done for the Texas public schools. Actually, the assessment craze did not begin with George W. Bush. As mentioned earlier, the Education Reform Act signed into law by Governor Mark White in 1984 required students in odd-numbered grades to take tests in language arts and math. It also required students to pass an exam before they could receive their diploma. In 1990 the **Texas Assessment of Academic Skills (TAAS)** was implemented and used to create higher standards for state assessment. In 2003 TAAS would be replaced by **Texas Assessment of Knowledge and Skills (TAKS).** The TAKS exams tested students annually on reading in grades 3 through 9 and mathematics in grades 3 through 11. Students also are tested on writing in grades 4 and 7, on English Language Arts in grades 10 and 11, on science in grades 5, 10, and 11; and social studies in grades 8, 10, and 11. These tests are designed to create a standard by which student progress can be tracked and schools evaluated based on that progress. In 2006, 81 percent of Texas schools met the standards of the federal government's **"No Child Left Behind" Act (NCLB)**. However, 291 Texas schools faced penalties under NCLB for failure to demonstrate progress on test scores annually for two years in a row. After two years of failing to show progress, schools that receive federal money to help low-income students are required to allow students to transfer to another campus (and provide transportation). After three years without progress, schools are required to provide extra tutoring or other help for students.

These exams have spawned some unintended consequences. Studies funded by the *Dallas Morning News* found evidence of massive amounts of cheating on the 2005 and 2006 exams. According to the newspaper's analysis, more than 50,000 students' exams showed evidence of cheating. Evidence of cheating was three times as frequent in schools that had been underperforming—where the pressure to cheat would have been greatest. For example, in one previously underperforming school district, science scores went from 23 percent below the state average to 14 percent above, and half of the eleventh grade exams in science produced evidence of cheating.[19] Such results were eight times more common in the eleventh grade exams that determine graduation than at other levels. Confronted with these figures, Texas officials generally were content to call these results "anomalies" rather than proof of cheating.[20] Because schools see their ratings and teachers see their raises tied to test scores, concerns go beyond student cheating and extend to "educator-led" cheating, in which teachers or school administrators aid students or change answers after the exam to produce higher passing rates. Further, state officials have little incentive to follow up on the evidence of cheating, since it would undermine their claims to progress.

In 2007 the Texas Legislature removed the requirement that seniors pass the TAKS test before they could graduate after 16 percent of Texas seniors failed to pass the test by graduation, meaning that 40,182 students did not graduate with their classmates in the spring of that year. While some school districts allowed students who had met other requirements to participate in graduation ceremonies, many school districts rejected students' pleas to be allowed to walk across the stage with their classmates. Under the revised law, Texas high school students will no longer be taking the annual TAKS exams, and instead, will be required to take twelve separate end-of-course exams at the end of each year in high school in the four core subject areas: English, math, science, and social studies. Students will have to score an average of 70 on the tests in each subject in order to graduate, and the tests must count for 15 percent of a student's final grade in the class.

While the roots of the federal government's No Child Left Behind law may be in Texas, the state, like every other state, has battled parts of the federal policy. States have challenged federal standards and asserted their desire to use their own standards. NCLB was designed to provide accountability in public schools, but very few parents have taken advantage of rules which allow students to transfer out of low-performing schools. Texans in general have some doubts about the consequences of NCLB, with a 2006 poll finding 56 percent of Texans worried that there is too much emphasis on testing, 27 percent saying there is the right amount of testing, and a mere 13 percent preferring more emphasis on testing.[21]

Overall, Texas's record on education has been mixed. While scores on standardized tests have indicated some progress, Texas's graduation rate (67.3 percent) lags slightly behind the national average (69.9 percent), with pockets of lower rates in some areas, including Houston (54.6 percent) and Dallas (44.4 percent).[22]

In many ways, the struggles of Texas public schools dramatically reflect the basic dilemmas of public policy. Citizens want as much efficiency as possible, and in response, legislators create systems of accountability. However, accountability proves costly and generates unintended consequences, like cheating, which then leads to more oversight, more bureaucracy, and more expense.

Higher Education

The relationship between the state's politicians and the University of Texas has been a stormy one. There under the nose of the Texas government, the University has been an appealing target for political hotheads who sought to reach across town and squash troublesome academics. Governor James Ferguson battled with the University of Texas faculty, a battle that helped lead to his impeachment. In the 1940s the regents of the University fired four economics professors who had supported federal labor laws, eliminated funding for social science research, and banned John Dos Passos's *U.S.A.* trilogy shortly before it won a Pulitzer Prize.

Higher education in Texas has been aided by the **Permanent University Fund (PUF).** The PUF was created by the Constitution of 1876, which added one million acres to the one million acres previously granted to the University of Texas. Initially the land, spread over nineteen counties in West Texas, generated little money. Most of the value of that land was in grazing leases that netted about $40,000 in 1900. In 1923 the PUF changed dramatically when the Santa Rita well struck oil on university lands, and by 1925 the PUF fund was growing at about $2,000 every day. Today, the PUF totals over ten billion dollars and provides support for schools in the University of Texas and Texas A&M systems. The PUF is an endowment, meaning that

Permanent University Fund (PUF)

an endowment funded by mineral rights and other revenue generated by 2.1 million acres of land set aside by the state. Investment returns from this fund support schools in the University of Texas and Texas A & M systems.

the principal from this account cannot be spent and that only investment returns can be used. However, in recent years these returns have averaged about $350 million dollars a year that is available to the eighteen universities and colleges. PUF funds may be used only for construction and renovation projects or certain "academic excellence" programs.

Today, the term higher education brings together a wide variety of institutions seeking to serve students beyond K–12. While large institutions like the University of Texas enjoy the most visibility, the system involves a variety of institutions that may have widely different goals. As the Texas economy continues to become more diverse, higher education must meet not only the higher demands of the global market but also the increasingly diverse set of skills required for the state to remain competitive.

Much of higher education policy in Texas is overseen by the **Higher Education Coordinating Board,** made up of thirteen citizens appointed by the governor for six-year terms. The governor also appoints the chair and vice chair. No board member may be employed in education or serve on a community college board of trustees. The board selects a full-time commissioner of higher education to run the organization. The board meets quarterly and is responsible for setting the broad direction of education policy—within the boundaries established by Texas law. For example, in October 2000 the Higher Education Coordinating Board approved "Closing the Gaps," a long-term plan intended to guide higher education in Texas for the next fifteen years. It proposed adding 500,000 students to the rolls of higher education institutions, increasing the number of degrees awarded, while improving the quality of programs and research, by 2015.

Access

If a college degree is a ticket to a better future, a key question is who has access to higher education in Texas. The coordinating board reported in 2006 that African Americans and Hispanics made up about 55 percent of Texas's college-aged population, but only 36 percent of the students in higher education in the state.[23] The Texas appellate courts specifically addressed the issue of minorities in higher education in 1996 in *Hopwood v. Texas;*[24] the courts ruled that race-based admission violated the U.S. Constitution. That standard has been loosened by a subsequent U.S. Supreme Court case which ruled that although race couldn't be the sole deciding factor, it could be used as a plus factor in university admissions standards. The use of race in university admissions remains a complicated matter. In 1997 the Texas Legislature approved a law that guaranteed students in the top ten percent of their high-school class admission to any university in the state. While this allows every community in the state a chance to place their students in the most exclusive universities, critics complain that it overlooks some students from highly competitive school districts and demanding private schools. In 2007 the University of Texas and its allies launched a major effort to modify the law and restrict the number of students admitted to the University of Texas under the rule to 60 percent. In fall 2006, 71 percent of students entering the University of Texas came in under the top-ten-percent rule, limiting its ability to bring in students from out of state or those who have distinguished themselves through special abilities, like music, that are not fully reflected in a student's general academic performance.

The battle over college admissions reflects some of the issues of representation that can be found in many policy areas. The coalition that stood behind the ten-percent rule went beyond the representatives of minority and border districts that were initially the focus in an attempt to expand access and bring in a more diverse student body. In addition, legislators from rural districts saw this as a means of ensuring that their students had a chance to attend the University of Texas and Texas A&M.

Beyond the issue of admissions, tuition is a major issue, because tuition and fees pose a barrier to college for many students as costs rise. In 2003 the state legislature deregulated tuition, allowing each school to raise its tuition as it saw fit. Since then, colleges have responded to declining state funds for schools by turning to their students to make ends meet. For the 2006–2007 academic year, the average cost of tuition in state schools in Texas was $5,327, up 38 percent since deregulation.[25]

Texas must continue to invest wisely in higher education as Texas's students prepare to compete for jobs globally. Today, the newest wave of immigrants competing for jobs may arrive digitally, citizens of far-away countries like India and China, who, thanks to the Internet, may be in a position to compete for work as effectively as if they were living next door. These "digital immigrants" are already providing services for Texas firms, ranging from technical assistance in call centers for some of the state's high-tech firms to accounting outsourced from some of the state's largest corporations.

Health and Human Services

American federalism has brought state governments increasingly into national policy related to health and human services, albeit through partnerships with the federal government. Generally, Americans think of such policies as coming from Washington, D.C. However, the states play an important role in delivering many of the benefits, in partnership with the federal government. Further, each state faces a different set of challenges. In 2005 Texas had one of the highest rates of poverty (17.6 percent) in the nation, well above the national average of 13.3 percent and over twice the rate in New Hampshire (7.5 percent). Texas has three of the nation's five counties of 250,000 or more people with the highest rates of poverty: Cameron (41.2 percent), Hidalgo (41.0 percent), and El Paso (29.2 percent). All told, Texas spends over $25 billion on 200 different programs, with 46,000 state workers engaged in the broad category of health and human services. While there is not space here to describe (or even list) all these programs, a few of the state's programs merit some discussion here.

Texas provides assistance to some families through **Temporary Assistance for Needy Families (TANF),** which replaced Aid to Families with Dependent Children (AFDC). Under this program eligible households receive monthly cash payments and Medicaid benefits. Today, recipients must accept the terms of a Personal Responsibility Agreement that requires them to stay free of alcohol or drug abuse, seek and maintain employment, and take part in parenting and other programs if asked. In June 2007, about 55,000 Texas families were receiving TANF, including about 110,000 children and 22,000 adults, with the average recipient getting about $65 a month.[26]

Families may also qualify for the **"Lone Star Card" Program** (Texas's version of the Food Stamps program) that helps low-income seniors, people with disabilities, low income single people, and families in need buy food from local retailers. While the benefits are available to adults with no children, they must work at least twenty

Temporary Assistance for Needy Families (TANF)
federal program that provides eligible households with monthly cash payments and Medicaid benefits.

"Lone Star Card" Program
Texas's version of food stamps that helps low-income seniors, people with disabilities, and single people and families in need buy food from local retailers.

hours a week or meet other work requirements in order to qualify. Adults without dependent children that do not meet work requirements are limited to three months of benefits in a thirty-six-month period. These benefits cannot be used for hot ready-to-eat foods, cigarettes, alcoholic beverages, cosmetics, or paper goods. In June of 2007 just over 2.3 million Texans were receiving an average of $91 a month in benefits. The majority of recipients (1.3 million) were children under eighteen.

Health care is quickly becoming a major issue in American politics, and Texas faces an especially daunting task. In 2006, Texas had the highest percentage of people without health insurance (24.6 percent), well over the national average of 15.3 percent uninsured, and nearly triple the rate of Minnesota, the state with the lowest rate (8.5 percent).[27] Texas also led the nation in the highest percentage of uninsured children (21 percent).

Medicare
a federal health insurance program available to senior citizens who have worked and paid into the Medicare system for ten or more years.

A variety of programs address the health care needs of Texans. **Medicare** is a federal health insurance program that serves about 2.5 million Texans. Medicare is available to senior citizens who have worked and paid into the Medicaid system for ten or more years. This means that today about 86 percent of the state's Medicare recipients are age 65 or over, while the remaining are under age 65 but qualify for Medicare because of some form of disability. There are actually several components to Medicare. Part A covers in-patient hospital care, while Part B covers doctors' fees and other "out-patient" costs. Recently, the federal government added "Part D" that extends Medicare coverage to provide prescription drugs.

Medicaid
a federal program providing medical coverage for low-income people and some elderly and disabled people.

The **Medicaid** program provides medical coverage for people with low incomes and some elderly or disabled people. Currently, there are about 2.6 million people covered by Medicaid, with most (71 percent) under 19 years of age. Medicare has a fixed standard that is consistent across all states, while Medicaid allows each state some discretion in how funds are used. Texas shares the cost of coverage of its citizens with the federal government. For every dollar Texas spends on Medicaid, the federal government matches with about $1.50.

State Children's Health Insurance Program (SCHIP)
a federal–state program that offers health insurance and medical care to the children of families that make too much to qualify for Medicaid but not enough to afford private health insurance.

For those families making too much to qualify for Medicaid but not enough to afford private health insurance, the **State Children's Health Insurance Program (SCHIP),** a federal–state program, offers the children in these families health care, including regular checkups, immunizations, prescription drugs, hospital visits, and many other health care services.[28]

The Texas Health and Human Services Commission (HHSC), with an annual budget of $15 billion and 8,500 employees, is responsible for overseeing these policies in the state. Like many Texas agencies, the HHSC is overseen by a council of nine citizens appointed by the governor. The day-to-day operations of the commission are conducted by the executive commissioner, a professional administrator appointed by the governor, who works with the council to develop rules and policies for the commission.

One experiment in privatization in Texas has been in the area of social welfare. Texas has been experimenting with using private contractors to manage call centers and other tasks previously handled by state employees in HHSC. So far, the results have been less than clear. Critics say that service has suffered while the savings have been smaller than expected. Advocates of privatization argue that service in general has been good and that the long-term savings will be significant.

Environmental Policy

iven the wide open spaces of Texas and the individualistic nature of Texans, concern about the environment has been slow to develop. Even in a conservative state, there is some need for regulation. **Regulation** can be defined as government rulemaking and enforcement intended to protect citizens from harm by private firms. While federal regulations generally attract the most attention, much of the regulatory task is left to the states.

Texas's first environmental policies were passed after hundreds of Texas oil wells drilled in the late 1890s dumped unusable crude oil onto the ground. Air pollution made its first major appearance in Texas in 1901 when oil from an uncapped well was set on fire by a passing train, sending clouds of black smoke over Beaumont and generating a rain that damaged the paint of the houses in the town.[29] Still, environmental regulation has remained relatively low on Texas's priority list. Until recently, most of the state's environmental policy was focused on protecting the quality of water. Texas did not begin to address air quality until 1965 when the Legislature created the Air Control Board. The board, appointed by the governor, was empowered to look at air quality, but the law required that the board consider any adverse impact that its rulings might have on existing industries and economic development. In 1990 the Air Control Board was combined with the Texas Water Commission, effectively putting environmental policy in the hands of one agency, the Texas Natural Resource Conservation Commission (TNRCC). In 2002 the TNRCC's name was changed to **Texas Commission on Environmental Quality (TCEQ).** In 2007 the TCEQ had 2,900 employees working out of sixteen offices throughout the state. About 85 percent of the Commission's $480.7 million operating budget for the 2007 fiscal year came from fees it charged to clients, with about 10 percent of the budget coming from the federal government and only 1 percent from the state.

The surging Texas economy and the growth of Texas's major cities gave the state its share of environmental headaches. Houston and the Dallas-Fort Worth Metroplex have some of the highest ozone levels in the nation and smog warnings are not unusual in the summer. In 2000 Houston held the distinction of having the worst air quality in the nation, leading to new EPA emission standards for automobiles in those areas.

In the language of economics, government regulation protects citizens from negative externalities. An *externality* occurs when costs are imposed on someone who is not participating in a transaction. For example, a citizen who does not make, own, drive, or ride in an automobile still must live with the pollution created by cars. This is a problem in a free-enterprise system, which assumes that costs and benefits involve just those people buying and selling a product. Those people involved in a transaction express their desire for cleaner or safer products as they shop by favoring products with those qualities and avoiding those without them. An individual not taking part in a transaction has no influence on shaping the characteristics of a product through market participation, thus creating the need for government involvement. In short, if you're not buying or selling a product you have no way of dealing with its impact on your own life without regulation.

While environmental policy has most often been the concern of the federal government, many states have taken their own paths, even with regard to problems such as global warming that go beyond state lines. California, for example, has for

Regulation
government rulemaking and enforcement intended to protect citizens from being harmed by private firms.

Texas Commission on Environmental Quality (TCEQ)
the agency that oversees state environmental policy, including air and water quality.

Anyone who has watched a television game show like *The Price Is Right* with luxury car models being given away as prizes is familiar with the idea of "California emissions standards." While the U.S. government has enacted a series of minimum standards regarding auto emissions, California has long been at the forefront of this activity, regularly creating standards that exceed those required by the U.S. government. Since the 1970s, California has enacted the most restrictive standards regarding the gases coming out of the exhaust pipes on cars, trucks, and other automobiles. Eleven other states have also enacted auto emission standards beyond the minimum standards set by the U.S. government.

Several agencies in California are involved in the regulation of auto emissions including the California Environmental Protection Agency, the Department of Public Health, and the Department of Consumer Affairs—Bureau of Automotive Repair. Key pollutants subject to regulation include carbon dioxide, hydrocarbons, and ozone. These agencies in the past led the United States in developing additional equipment on vehicles to limit emissions, in requiring the use of unleaded gas, and in mandating routine inspections of vehicles. For example, Texas required the use of fuel injectors and catalytic converters long before they became standard across the United States. Current efforts by California include efforts to increase sales of zero-emission vehicles, to encourage the use of alternative fuels, and to boost the fuel efficiency of cars.

Opponents of California's efforts at regulation note that the result of such differing regulations is differences in automobile standards across states. This variation creates additional costs to makers of cars, which is then passed onto the people who buy cars and trucks. In the end, they argue, the United States government should be the appropriate level of government to regulate auto emissions.

Texas, in contrast, maintains little state legislation above and beyond the minimum standards established by the U.S. government. One of the few requirements in Texas is the imposition of annual auto emission standards in metropolitan areas like Houston with consistently high levels of air pollution linked to automobiles. Texas also requires all state, city, and county governments that own fifteen or more vehicles to purchase some low-emission vehicles

Thinking Critically

- How is California a leader in the regulation of auto emissions?
- How does California's attempt to regulate auto emissions affect the size and scope of government?
- Do you think that Texas and other states should set standards that are stricter than those set by the U.S. government?
- What do you think the advantage of Texas adopting stricter emissions standards might be?

NIMBY

comes from "not in my backyard," and refers to local efforts to prevent the location of potentially harmful activities, such as industrial waste disposal, close to citizens.

a long time aggressively pursued environmental policies that went beyond federal standards.

At the same time, Texans worry about the possibility of electricity shortages, resulting in the kind of rolling blackouts that crippled California a few years earlier. In response to the rising demand for power, in 2005 Governor Perry expedited the approval of new coal power plants. TXU, the state's largest energy producer, planned eleven new plants, citing the growing demand for electricity and Texans' fondness for large homes and air conditioning. Despite the power industry's claim that these new coal plants would be cleaner than their predecessors, many Texans resisted locating these plants near them. This triggered several **NIMBY** ("not-in-my-backyard") battles as communities lobbied to keep the plants away from them, even if the electricity flowed into their homes.

The Public Utility Commission of Texas is charged with protecting consumers. In 1975 the Texas Legislature passed the Public Utility Regulatory Act that created the PUC to regulate the rates and services of telephone companies everywhere in the state, as well as electric, water, and sewer utilities in unincorporated areas of the state. The PUC is headed by three commissioners appointed by the governor to six-year terms. While utility regulation is not an especially exciting topic to most Texans, the rising costs of electricity have awakened citizen interest and drawn the notice of Texas politicians.

Transportation

Transportation has always been an issue, given the need to connect the broad expanses of a large state and provide farmers a way of transporting their produce to markets. Texas's transitions have been borne on a transportation system that continues to evolve with the state. Today the state's growth demands more highways to convey goods coming and going north into other states and south into Mexico.

In the latter half of the nineteenth century Texas farmers, usually suspicious of railroads and other big companies, quickly realized that without railroads the state's economic growth would stall because Texas's rivers were not large enough to carry goods. The Constitution of 1876 had defined railroads in a way that allowed rate regulation, but the state quickly began looking for ways of bringing the railroads into the state. The Texas Legislature passed a Land Grant Law that offered over 10,000 acres of land for each mile of track the railroads put down. In addition, numerous Texas cities began offering deals to the railroads in hopes of bringing in the railroads and the prosperity and jobs they brought. Cities competed against each other and money was often passed under the table. As we saw at the beginning of chapter 6, some towns like Abilene thrived when the railroad arrived while cities like Buffalo Gap withered without the arrival of the railroad.

In 1890 Attorney General James Stephen Hogg decided that his office was not able to keep up with the enforcement of regulations on the state's railroads. Hogg advocated for the creation of a Railroad Commission, making the call for a commission a centerpiece of his campaign for governor. While the railroads labeled Hogg as "communistic," his reforms were appealing to voters and Hogg became Texas's first native-born governor in 1891.

Texas roads have played a vital role in the economic health of the state for generations. The state's "farm-to-market" roads helped Texas farmers and ranchers bring goods to towns and cities. Since the 1950s, highways have played a vital role in bringing products to store shelves. Today, most Texans tend to think about transportation policy in terms of rush-hour traffic and urban traffic jams.

Seeing what past investments in transportation have brought to the state, Governor Perry in 2004 proposed the next generation of transportation policy: the Trans-Texas Corridor. This system would include over 4,000 miles of roads, railways, and pipelines to move goods from Mexico to Oklahoma. The corridor would include ten highway lanes, six lines for rail travel, and a cost of about $183 billion to build it over the next fifty years.[30] To meet this ambitious goal, Perry has embraced privatization, turning over some of Texas's public roads to private companies who will build and maintain these roads in return for the right to charge citizens tolls to drive on them. Perry's plans have met with a mixed reaction. On one hand, handing some of Texas's

Texas Legends

Private Property and Takings

One of the most pervasive legends in Texas is that of private property. Most Texans view their property as coming exclusively under their own control. However, this is increasingly false.

The idea of "takings" emerges from the Fifth Amendment to the U.S. Constitution that prohibits the taking of private property "for public use, without just compensation." Traditionally, this clause has been examined in the light of eminent domain, the power of government to take property for public use. Generally, eminent domain has been used to take private property for government use for public functions such as roads. Recently, the limits of eminent domain have been tested as the government has taken private property for public uses like the Dallas Cowboys' new stadium in Arlington or toll roads operated by private firms. In this more expansive use of power, the taking of private property is justified for general economic development, even though privately owned, that will create jobs and other advantages for the entire community. Thus "public use," doesn't exclude private profit.

Other use of the takings label deals with the impact of regulation on the value of private property. One example of regulatory takings would be environmental regulations that place restrictions on the uses of private property designated as "wetlands." These rules restricting how individuals use their property may diminish the value of property. In this case, the government is restricting use of property to promote the general welfare, which is certainly a public concern. However, for many years the courts did not support compensating citizens for regulatory takings. Restrictions on land use are not unique to environmental regulation. Property owners in cities face restrictions on how they use their land. Zoning rules prohibit building businesses in residential areas. However, environmental regulations reach outside cities to the rural areas, where many people have retreated in their attempt to avoid rules imposed by government and their neighbors.

The problem of takings reflects a cost of government that frequently does not show up on the balance sheet of costs and benefits. Sometimes, government regulation requires costly action, like altering coal plants to produce less pollution, with the cost being passed along as higher utility bills. At other times, government policies restrict citizens' uses and enjoyment of their own property.

However, without some ability to extend its authority onto private property the government would lack the ability to create and enforce meaningful rules related to the environment or public safety, since pollution and other problems don't honor property lines. Without such rules, individuals could block the flow of creeks and cut off water supplies to or cause flooding for other citizens. Neighborhoods could find adult businesses placed next to family homes or schools. Thus, the matter of who wins and who loses involves a balancing act in which the government must weigh the public safety against the rights of individual property owners.

roadway over to private firms offers the potential of efficiency and savings as the profit incentive motivates private companies to find the least expensive way to provide roads. In addition, privatization would free up money that the state can invest in other uses, as it leaves some of the investment in roads to the private sector. Some Texans—both Democrats and Republicans—harbor doubts about Perry's proposal. 2006 Democratic gubernatorial candidate Chris Bell estimated the super highway would "destroy almost 1.5 million acres of prime farmland and will strip Texas landowners of over 150 square miles of privately owned property."[31] Critics worry about Texas farmers and eminent domain issues in what may be one of the biggest land grabs in the state's history. Some Texans would see their land claimed by the government through **eminent domain** and then handed to private firms. Resistance has been especially strong in light of the fact that the largest investor would be a Spanish company named Cintra. Because of the concerns about eminent domain and foreign investors, the conservatives most likely to back privatization of government services like roads are also those most likely to oppose the government's taking private land to build these toll road. This dilemma helped create the challenges within the Republican Party to Rick Perry in his 2006 reelection campaign and fed the legislative rebellion against his plan in the 2007 legislative session. While Perry has been largely successful in getting much of his plan through, he found himself facing compromises forced on him by both Democratic and Republican legislators.

The division among Republicans and Democrats on the Trans-Texas Corridor illustrates that state policy often fails to break down neatly as liberal versus conservative or Republican versus Democrat. While some conservatives embrace the potential for privatization, others resent the taking of privately owned land for private toll roads. Some liberal constituencies favor expanding roadways and opening the door to more trade with Mexico, while others hold doubts about free trade and worry about the flood of cheap goods and labor from Mexico. Transportation policy is an example of how Texas's economic growth and rapid change continuously redefine politics and create new challenges.

Immigration

Perhaps the most dynamic and challenging policy issue facing Texas today is immigration. It shouldn't be surprising that a president from Texas remained conflicted in the nation's debate over immigration. Coming from one of the largest destinations for illegal immigrants, some expected President Bush to be an avid advocate of tight border security and getting tough on illegal immigration. Because Texas provides education and other social programs for immigrants, you might expect an ex-governor of Texas to want to aggressively turn away immigrants at the border. However, the Texas economy's heavy reliance on immigrant labor convinced Bush that immigrant workers were an important part of the Texas and American economy. The fact that Bush has had more experience with the issue of illegal immigration than most people, but holds a less ideological view than most Americans, should be instructive. As is often the case, the immigration issue is more complicated than it would first appear and President Bush's approach reflects the complicated relationship between Texas and immigrants. Today, Governor Perry, another staunch conservative by most measures, rejects the idea of building a wall at the border, a favorite solution of some strident conservatives. Clearly, there's more to the immigration issue.

In some ways, the debate over illegal immigrants tells us more about Texas politics than immigration. In reality, immigration is a federal issue with the U.S. Citizenship and Immigration Services taking the lead in sealing U.S. borders and managing the flow of legal immigrants into the country. Despite this, many state and local officials continue to make public proclamations and pass new rules. In May 2007, the town of Farmers Branch, Texas, made national headlines by passing an ordinance that would punish landlords for renting to illegal immigrants.

Some of this conflict results from differences among Texans over the costs and benefits of immigration. Other debates emerge because the costs and benefits of immigration policy fall unevenly. It is estimated that while illegal immigrants

Eminent domain
the power of government to take private property for public use, generally for public functions such as roads.

WHAT GOES AROUND, COMES AROUND: TEXAS, 1830...

"ALL THESE AMERICAN IMMIGRANTS SHOULD BE SENT BACK HOME! THEY'RE A *THREAT* TO OUR *MEXICAN WAY OF LIFE!*"

cost the state of Texas $1.16 billion, they pay $1.58 billion in state taxes and fees. In contrast, local governments in Texas pay about $1.44 billion in costs like indigent care, law enforcement, and other services resulting from the presence of immigrants, while bringing in only $513 million in taxes. In addition, it costs local school districts about $957 billion to educate an estimated 151,000 children of illegal workers.

An increase in government taxing and spending is not the only impact of an estimated 1.4 million undocumented immigrants in Texas. The Comptroller's Office estimated that their absence would cost the state's economy $17.7 billion dollars.[32] The distribution of costs and benefits to the government and the private sector reflects the origins of some divisions. Clearly many Texas cities and school districts bear a disproportionate burden from illegal immigrants. At the same time, these workers were drawn to Texas by the promise of wages from businesses that benefited from their labors, as the forces of the free market drew these immigrants into the U.S. economy, if not into citizenship.

The fate of Cactus, Texas, after immigration raids illustrates the degree to which some businesses and local economies rely on immigrant labor. On December 12, 2006, Immigration and Custom Enforcement (ICE) officers raided the Swift meatpacking plants in Cactus, a small town of 2,639 in the Texas Panhandle, arresting 292 workers. Some of those arrested had lived and worked in Cactus over fifteen years, and their arrest left behind families and large numbers of job openings that Swift scrambled to fill. As these families and the community tried to patch themselves together, the plant, now woefully shorthanded, found itself offering employees who referred good job candidates a bonus of $650 for unskilled candidates and $1,500 for experienced ones.[33]

While the influx of people into the United States remains a federal issue, the border states like Texas bear the burden of following up on the promises of the U.S. Constitution. One of the most important legal cases in the dispute over illegal immigration occurred in Tyler, Texas. In the 1982 case, *Plyler v. Doe,*[34] the U.S. Supreme Court ruled that School Superintendent Jim Plyler could not charge illegal immigrants residing in Tyler $1,000 in tuition to attend public schools in Tyler. In the majority opinion written by Justice William Brennan, himself the son of Irish immigrants, the Court pointed out that the Fourteenth Amendment required that states provide equal protection of the law to "any person within its jurisdiction" and that the language of that amendment had been intentionally designed to protect the rights of aliens living in the United States. Reflecting on the decision more than twenty years later, in 2007, Plyler remarked, "It would have been one of the worst things to happen in education—they'd cost more not being educated."[35]

The issue of immigration captures the state's ongoing struggle with change and the two political parties' attempts to balance the new versus the old. The political dynamic behind one side of the immigration debate was illustrated by former Republican congressman Dick Armey, for years one of the state's leading conservatives, who complained that after years of Republicans courting Hispanic voters in Texas his party was throwing away its future on the immigration issue: "Who is the genius that said, 'Now that we've identified that [the Hispanic community] is the fastest growing demographic in American, let's do everything we can to make sure we offend them?' Who is the genius that came up with that bright idea?"[36]

Conclusion

While some Texans worry that immigration from Mexico will transform the politics of Texas, a broader view of our history reveals that change is the Texas way of life. Native American populations were challenged by the Spanish and later the Mexican governments; those governments would, in turn, see themselves pushed out by the Anglo settlers who first moved Texas to independence and then to statehood. Texas's union with the United States was quickly undone by secession and the decision to join the Confederate States. The end of the Civil War saw Texas's return to the United States, but under very different terms imposed by the Radical Republicans, whose Reconstruction government was rooted in the North. Eventually, Reconstruction ended, leaving Texas to find its way through a century that saw more demographic than political change. During the last century and a quarter Texas has seen its population explode as immigrants from all over the United States and the world converged on the state, once again seeking the opportunity promised by the area.

Texas has never stayed the same and it remains in the enviable position of being a place where people can find more opportunity. The promise of opportunities that draw one set of people to Texas today will inevitably draw others in the future, and the immigrants from Central and South America are only the latest chapter in the changes that define the state.

Occasionally, we become so engrossed in recounting our colorful and larger-than-life traditions that we don't notice that dramatic events like the Alamo are the markers of great change, but change has always been with us. This is not surprising. As each regime departs, it leaves behind a little of its legacy, its traditions, and its own legends. While not always entirely compatible, these myths form a kind of patchwork quilt that makes up the Texas of today.

Texas's myths and legends are often stories of change. Stephen F. Austin became the Father of Texas by bringing new settlers to Texas before he played a key role in the revolutionary movement that the new settlers brought about. The battle of the Alamo is a pivotal point in the transition from Mexican to American rule and immediately served as a powerful symbol that motivated the Texas army to defeat Santa Anna's army at San Jacinto.

What is especially appealing about many of Texas's legends is the degree to which we Texans all share them. Standing in the line to visit the Alamo, you will encounter people of every race. These people are not drawn to the Alamo because the battle there was between the Anglo and Mexican forces but because the battle defines a dynamic state that draws people of every race and nationality. The defenders of the Alamo took their stand for change rather than against it, and future generations of Texans will—each in their own way—do the same.

Key Terms

ad-valorem tax
agenda setting
appraisal
distributive policy
Education Reform Act (1984)
eminent domain
excise tax
fiscal policy
franchise tax
general sales tax
Higher Education Coordinating Board
income tax
"Lone Star Card" Program
Medicaid
Medicare
NIMBY
"No Child Left Behind" Act (NCLB)
"pay-as-you-go" system
Permanent School Fund
Permanent University Fund (PUF)
policy
policy adoption
policy evaluation
policy formation
policy implementation

progressive tax
property tax
redistributive policy
regressive tax
regulation
regulatory policy
severance tax
sin taxes
State Children's Health Insurance Program (SCHIP)
subsidies
Temporary Assistance for Needy Families (TANF)
Texas Assessment of Academic Skills (TAAS)
Texas Assessment of Knowledge and Skills (TAKS)
Texas Commission on Environmental Quality (TCEQ)

Explore this subject further at http://college.cqpress.com/lonestarpolitics, where you'll find chapter summaries, practice quizzes, key word flash cards, and additional suggested resources.

Appendix

Declaration of Independence of the Republic of Texas

UNANIMOUS
DECLARATION OF INDEPENDENCE,
BY THE
DELEGATES OF THE PEOPLE OF TEXAS,
IN GENERAL CONVENTION,
AT THE TOWN OF WASHINGTON,
ON THE SECOND DAY OF MARCH, 1836

When a government has ceased to protect the lives, liberty and property of the people from whom its legitimate powers are derived, and for the advancement of whose happiness it was instituted; and so far from being a guarantee for the enjoyment of those inestimable and inalienable rights, becomes an instrument in the hands of evil rulers for their oppression; when the Federal Republican Constitution of their country, which they have sworn to support, no longer has a substantial existence, and the whole nature of their government has been forcibly changed without their consent, from a restricted federative republic, composed of sovereign states, to a consolidated central military despotism, in which every interest is disregarded but that of the army and the priesthood—both the eternal enemies of civil liberty, and the ever-ready minions of power, and the usual instruments of tyrants; When long after the spirit of the Constitution has departed, moderation is at length, so far lost, by those in power that even the semblance of freedom is removed, and the forms, themselves, of the constitution discontinued; and so far from their petitions and remonstrances being regarded, the agents who bear them are thrown into dungeons; and mercenary armies sent forth to force a new government upon them at the point of the bayonet. When in consequence of such acts of malfeasance and abdication, on the part of the government, anarchy prevails, and civil society is dissolved into its original elements: In such a crisis, the first law of nature, the right of self-preservation—the inherent and inalienable right of the people to appeal to first principles and take their political affairs into their own hands in extreme cases—enjoins it as a right towards themselves and a sacred obligation to their posterity, to abolish such government and create another in its stead, calculated to rescue them from impending dangers, and to secure their future welfare and happiness. Nations, as well as individuals, are amenable for their acts to the public opinion of mankind. A statement of a part of our grievances is, therefore, submitted to an impartial world, in justification of the hazardous but unavoidable step now taken of severing our political connection with the Mexican people, and assuming an independent attitude among the nations of the earth.

The Mexican government, by its colonization laws, invited and induced the Anglo-American population of Texas to colonize its wilderness under the pledged faith of a written constitution, that they should continue to enjoy that constitutional liberty and republican government to which they had been habituated in the land of their birth, the United States of America. In this expectation they have been cruelly disappointed, inasmuch as the Mexican nation has acquiesced in the late changes made in the government by General Antonio Lopez de Santa Anna, who, having overturned the constitution of his country, now offers us the cruel alternative either to abandon our homes, acquired by so many privations, or submit to the most intolerable of all tyranny, the combined despotism of the sword and the priesthood.
It has sacrificed our welfare to the state of Coahuila, by which our interests have been continually depressed, through a jealous and partial course of legislation carried on at a far distant seat of government, by a hostile majority, in an unknown tongue; and this too, notwithstanding we have petitioned in the humblest terms, for the establishment of a separate state government, and have, in accordance with the provisions of the national constitution, presented the general Congress, a republican constitution which was without just cause contemptuously rejected.

It incarcerated in a dungeon, for a long time, one of our citizens, for no other cause but a zealous endeavor to procure the acceptance of our constitution and the establishment of a state government.

It has failed and refused to secure on a firm basis, the right of trial by jury; that palladium of civil liberty, and only safe guarantee for the life, liberty, and property of the citizen.

It has failed to establish any public system of education, although possessed of almost boundless resources (the public domain) and, although, it is an axiom, in political science, that unless a people are educated and enlightened it is idle to expect the continuance of civil liberty, or the capacity for self-government.

It has suffered the military commandants stationed among us to exercise arbitrary acts of oppression and tyranny; thus trampling upon the most sacred rights of the citizen and rendering the military superior to the civil power.

It has dissolved by force of arms, the state Congress of Coahuila and Texas, and obliged our representatives to fly for their lives from the seat of government; thus depriving us of the fundamental political right of representation.

It has demanded the surrender of a number of our citizens, and ordered military detachments to seize and carry them into the Interior for trial; in contempt of the civil authorities, and in defiance of the laws and constitution.

It has made piratical attacks upon our commerce; by commissioning foreign desperadoes, and authorizing them to seize our vessels, and convey the property of our citizens to far distant ports of confiscation.

It denies us the right of worshipping the Almighty according to the dictates of our own consciences, by the support of a national religion calculated to promote the temporal interests of its human functionaries rather than the glory of the true and living God.

It has demanded us to deliver up our arms; which are essential to our defense, the rightful property of freemen, and formidable only to tyrannical governments.

It has invaded our country, both by sea and by land, with intent to lay waste our territory and drive us from our homes; and has now a large mercenary army advancing to carry on against us a war of extermination.

It has, through its emissaries, incited the merciless savage, with the tomahawk and scalping knife, to massacre the inhabitants of our defenseless frontiers.

It hath been, during the whole time of our connection with it, the contemptible sport and victim of successive military revolutions and hath continually exhibited every characteristic of a weak, corrupt and tyrannical government.

These, and other grievances, were patiently borne by the people of Texas until they reached that point at which forbearance ceases to be a virtue. We then took up arms in defense of the national constitution. We appealed to our Mexican brethren for assistance. Our appeal has been made in vain. Though months have elapsed, no sympathetic response has yet been heard from the Interior. We are, therefore, forced to the melancholy conclusion that the Mexican people have acquiesced in the destruction of their liberty, and the substitution therefor of a military government—that they are unfit to be free and incapable of self-government.

The necessity of self-preservation, therefore, now decrees our eternal political separation.

We, therefore, the delegates, with plenary powers, of the people of Texas, in solemn convention assembled, appealing to a candid world for the necessities of our condition, do hereby resolve and DECLARE that our political connection with the Mexican nation has forever ended; and that the people of Texas do now constitute a FREE, SOVEREIGN and INDEPENDENT RE-PUBLIC, and are fully invested with all the rights and attributes which properly belong to the independent nations; and, conscious of the rectitude of our intentions, we fearlessly and confidently commit the issue to the decision of the Supreme Arbiter of the destinies of nations.

RICHARD ELLIS, president of the convention and Delegate from Red River.

Charles B. Stewart

Thos Barnett

John S. D. Byrom

Franco Ruiz

J. Antonio Navarro

Jesse B. Badgett

Wm D. Lacey

William Menefee

Jno Fisher

Mathew Caldwell

William Mottley

Lorenzo de Zavala

Stephen H. Everitt

Geo W. Smyth

Elijah Stapp

Claiborne West

Wm B. Scates

M .B. Menard

A. B. Hardin

J. W. Bunton

Thos J. Gasley

R. M. Coleman

Sterling C. Robertson

Benj. Briggs Goodrich

G. W. Barnett

James G. Swisher

Jesse Grimes

S. Rhoads Fisher

John W. Moore

John W. Bower

Saml A. Maverick from Bejar

Sam P. Carson

A. Briscoe

J. B. Woods

Jas Collinsworth

Edwin Waller

Asa Brigham

Geo. C. Childress

Bailey Hardeman

Rob. Potter

Thomas Jefferson Rusk

Chas. S. Taylor

John S. Roberts

Robert Hamilton

Collin McKinney

Albert H. Latimer

James Power

Sam Houston

David Thomas

Edwd Conrad

Martin Parmer

Edwin O. LeGrand

Stephen W. Blount

Jas Gaines

Wm Clark, Jr.

Sydney O. Penington

Wm Carrol Crawford

Jno Turner

Test. H. S. Kimble, Secretary

Notes

Chapter 1

1. V. O. Key, *Southern Politics in State and Nation* (Knoxville: University of Tennessee Press, 1984), 267.
2. John Steinbeck, *Travels with Charley: In Search of America,* (New York: Bantam Books, 1961), 231.
3. Randolph B. Campbell, *Gone to Texas,* (New York: Oxford University Press—USA, 2004), 15.
4. James L. Haley, *Passionate Nation: The Epic History of Texas,* (New York: Free Press, 2006), 6.
5. Campbell, *Gone to Texas,* 41.
6. Campbell, *Gone to Texas,* 85.
7. Campbell, *Gone to Texas,* 88.
8. Campbell, *Gone to Texas,* 80.
9. Campbell, *Gone to Texas,* 186.
10. Haley, *Passionate Nation,* 272.
11. Campbell, *Gone to Texas,* 207.
12. Campbell, *Gone to Texas,* 299.
13. Campbell, *Gone to Texas,* 350–351.
14. Campbell, *Gone to Texas,* 366.
15. Christine Barbour and Gerald C. Wright, *Keeping the Republic,* 2nd Brief Ed. (Washington, D.C.: CQ Press, 2006), 22.
16. Daniel J. Elazar, *American Federalism: A View from the State* (New York: Thomas Y. Crowell, 1966), 86.
17. Campbell, *Gone to Texas,* 15.
18. T. R. Fehrenbach, *Lone Star: A History of Texas and the Texans* (Cambridge, Mass.: Da Capo Press, 2000), 24.
19. Elizabeth Cruce Alvares, ed., *Texas Almanac, 2006–2007* (Dallas: Dallas Morning News, 2006), 519.
20. Jared Bernstein, Elizabeth McNichol, and Karen Lyons, *Pulling Apart: A State-by-State Analysis of Income Trends,* Center on Budget and Policy Priorities and Economic Policy Institute, January 2006.
21. U.S. Census Bureau, "Census Brief: Warmer, older, more diverse, State-by-state population changes to 2025," CENBR/96-1, December 1996.
22. James E. Crisp, *Sleuthing the Alamo: Davy Crockett's Last Stand and Other Mysteries of the Texas Revolution* (New York: Oxford University Press, 2004), 59.
23. Anna J. Hardwicke Pennybacker, *A New History of Texas for Schools* (Tyler, Texas, 1888), 49.
24. Crisp, *Sleuthing the Alamo,* 59.
25. Pennybacker, *A New History of Texas for Schools,* 49.

Chapter 2

1. Randolph B. Campbell, *Gone to Texas* (New York: Oxford University Press, 2004), 371.
2. Bruce Hight, "Proposed changes show constitution could use updating," *Austin American-Statesman,* May 21, 2001.
3. Statement of Rob Junell, quoted in Osler McCarthy, "Ratliff Predicting Success in Bid for New Constitution," *Austin American-Statesman,* March 3, 1999.
4. Bill Ratliff, quoted in Juan B. Elizondo, Jr., "Time to Rewrite Constitution," *Austin American-Statesman,* October 28, 1999.
5. Bill Stouffer, chair of Common Cause Texas, quoted in Elizondo, "Time to Rewrite Constitution."
6. Bill Ratliff, quoted in Elizondo, "Time to Rewrite Constitution."
7. David Schmudde, "Constitutional Limitations on State Taxation of Nonresident Citizens," *Law Review of Michigan State University–Detroit College of Law* (1999), 95–169.
8. Ibid, 125.
9. *South Dakota v. Dole,* 483 U.S. 203 (1987).
10. Thomas Dye, *American Federalism: Competition Among Governments* (Lexington, Mass.: Lexington Books, 1989).
11. Campbell, *Gone to Texas.*
12. Robert Calvert, Arnoldo De León, and Gregg Cantrell, *The History of Texas* (Wheeling, Ill.: Harlan Davidson Press, 2002).
13. Stephen F. Austin, quoted in John Cornyn, "The Roots of the Texas Constitution: Settlement to Statehood," *Texas Tech Law Review* (1995), 26.
14. Campbell, *Gone to Texas,* fn11.
15. Texas Constitution (1836), General Provisions, sec. 10.
16. Texas Constitution (1836), General Provisions, sec. 6.
17. Texas Constitution (1876), art. 6, sec. 2.
18. Cornyn, "The Roots of the Texas Constitution."
19. Campbell, *Gone to Texas,* fn10.
20. Cornyn, "The Roots of the Texas Constitution," fn15.
21. Texas Constitution (1845), art. 3, sec. 1.
22. Joe Ericson, "An Inquiry into the Sources of the Texas Constitution," Ph.D. Dissertation, Texas Tech University (1957). See also Janice C. May, *The Texas State Constitution: A Reference Guide* (Westport, Conn: Greenwood Press, 1996).
23. Campbell, *Gone to Texas,* fn11.
24. Texas Constitution (1866), art. 8, sec. 1.
25. Ericson, "An Inquiry into the Sources of the Texas Constitution," fn18.
26. May, *The Texas State Constitution,* fn18.
27. Ibid.
28. Texas Constitution (1876), art. I, sec. 1.
29. Originally a state treasurer was also included in the plural executive, but this office was eventually dissolved.
30. Oklahoma is the only other state to have two high courts.
31. Calvert, De León, and Cantrell, *History of Texas,* fn12.
32. Only the constitutions of South Carolina, Arkansas, and Alabama have been amended more times.
33. www.sos.state.tx.us/elections/historical/70-92.shtml.
34. May, *The Texas State Constitution,* fn18.

Chapter 3

1. April Castro and Liz Austin Peterson, "Texas House Speaker Refuses to Step Down amid Uproar," *Arkansas Democrat-Gazette,* May 27, 2007, 7A.
2. Ibid.

3. "Speaker Fight: Legal Arguments," *Daily Sentinel* (Nacogdoches), May 27, 2007.

4. Ibid.

5. James Madison, *Federalist* No. 51, ed. Clinton Rossiter, *The Federalist Papers* (New York: Penguin Putnam, 1999), 288–293.

6. 376 U.S. 186 (1962).

7. 377 U.S. 533 (1964).

8. Keon S. Chi, *The Book of the States: 2006 Edition,* vol. 38 (Lexington, Ky.: Council of State Governments, 2006), Table 3.2, 68–70.

9. Ibid.

10. Texas Constitution (1876), art. 3, sec. 8.

11. Texas Constitution (1876), art. 3, sec. 21.

12. National Council of State Legislatures, "NCSL Backgrounder: Full and Part-Time Legislatures," www.ncsl.org/programs/press/2004/backgrounder_fullandpart.htm, accessed August 2, 2007.

13. Ibid.

14. Chi, *The Book of the States,* Table 3.13, 94–99.

15. Texas State Constitution (1876), art. 3, sec. 6; art. 3, sec. 7.

16. Thomas M. Spencer, *The Legislative Process, Texas Style* (Pasadena, Texas: San Jacinto College Press, 1981), 20–21.

17. Texas Constitution (1876), art. 3, sec. 8.

18. Chi, *The Book of the States,* Table 3.2, 72–73.

19. Adapted from Kendra A. Hovey and Harold A. Hovey, *CQ's State Fact Finder* (Washington, D.C.: CQ Press, 2007), Table D-8, 109; Keon S. Chi, *The Book of the States,* vol. 36 (Lexington, Ky.: Council of State Governments, 2004), Table 3.4, 85.

20. Peter Slevin, "After Adopting Term Limits, States Lose Female Legislators," *Washington Post,* April 22, 2007, A04.

21. Steven Smith, Jason M. Roberts, and Ryan J. Vander Wielen, *The American Congress,* 4th ed. (New York: Cambridge University Press, 2006), 26.

22. Ibid.

23. Quoted in Iain McLean, "Forms of Representation and Systems of Voting," in David Held, ed., *Political Theory Today* (Cambridge: Polity Press, 1991), 173.

24. David M. Farrell, *Electoral Systems: A Comparative Introduction* (New York: Palgrave, 2001), 11.

25. Texas Constitution (1876), art. 3, sec. 2; art. 3, sec. 25.

26. "State and Federal Law Governing Redistricting in Texas" (Austin: Texas Legislative Council, 2001), www.tlc.state.tx.us/pubspol/redlaw01/redlaw01.pdf, accessed August 1, 2007.

27. *White v. Register,* 412 U.S. 755 (1973).

28. U.S. Department of the Interior, Census Office, *Report of the Population of the United States at the Eleventh Census: 1890* (Washington, D.C.: Government Printing Office, 1895), 41–42.

29. U.S. Census Bureau, "State and County Quick Facts: Nacogdoches County, Texas" (2007), http://quickfacts.census.gov/qfd/states/48/48347.html, accessed August 1, 2007.

30. U.S. Census Bureau, "State and County Quick Facts: Dallas County, Texas" (2007), http://quickfacts.census.gov/qdf/states/48/48113.html, accessed August 1, 2007.

31. 526 U.S. 541 (1999).

32. Texas Constitution (1976), art. 3, sec. 2.

33. Sam Attlesey, "Panel OKs Map Favoring GOP," *Dallas Morning News,* November 29, 2001.

34. 548 U.S. 204 (2006).

35. Spencer, *The Legislative Process,* 22–23.

36. Texas House of Representatives, *Texas House Journal,* January 9, 2007, 28.

37. Texas House of Representatives, *Texas House Journal,* January 12, 1999, 15.

38. Chi, *The Book of the States,* Tables 3.11 and 3.12, 90–93.

39. Keith Hamm and Robert Harmel, "Legislative Party Development and the Speaker System: The Case of the Texas House," *Journal of Politics* vol. 55, no. 4 (1993): 1140–1151.

40. Ibid., 62.

41. Rep. Wayne Christian, e-mail correspondence with the author, August 11, 2007.
42. Charles W. Wiggins, Keith E. Hamm, and Charles G. Bell, "Interest Group and Party Influence Agents in the Legislative Process: A Comparative State Analysis," *Journal of Politics* 54 (1992): 82–100.
43. Michelle G. Briscoe, "Cohesiveness and Diversity among Black Members of the Texas State Legislature," in *Politics in the New South: Representation of African Americans in Southern State Legislatures,* ed. Charles E. Menifield and Stephen D. Shaffer (Albany: State University of New York, 2005).
44. Rep. Jim McReynolds, interview with the author, Nacogdoches, Texas, August 8, 2007.
45. Hamm and Harmel, "Legislative Party Development," 1140–1151.
46. Kathryn Birdwill, "Bill Requires Universities to Limit Credit Hours Needed to Earn Degree," *Daily Sentinel* (Nacogdoches), January 6, 2006.
47. Chi, *The Book of the States,* Table 3.25, 125–128.
48. Chi, *The Book of the States,* Table 3.18, 109–110.
49. Spencer, *The Legislative Process,* 31–32.
50. W. Gardner Selby, "It's Not Every Day a Legislator Travels Oversees while Voting in the Texas House," *Austin American-Statesman,* April 27, 3007.
51. Chi, *The Book of the States,* Table 3.14, 100–101.

Chapter 4

1. Liz Austin Peterson, "Perry's Staff Discussed Vaccine on Day Merck Donated to Campaign," *Austin American-Statesman,* February 22, 2007.
2. Janet Elliot, "Perry Won't Veto Bill Blocking His HPV Order," *Houston Chronicle,* May 9, 2007.
3. Corrie MacLaggen, "Abbott: Perry's HPV Mandate Does Not Carry the Weight of Law, Senator Says," *Austin American-Statesman,* March 13, 2007.
4. R. G. Ratcliffe, "Court Limits Perry's Power over Agencies," *Houston Chronicle,* February 21, 2007.
5. Elizabeth Souder and Emily Ramshaw, "Coal Plant Order Blocked," *The Dallas Morning News,* February 21, 2007.
6. R. G. Ratcliffe, "Perry Muscle Flexing Falls Flat," *Houston Chronicle,* February 25, 2007.
7. Daniel Murph, *Texas Giant: The Life of Price Daniel* (Austin, Texas: Eakin Press, 2002).
8. Texas Constitution (1876), art. 4, sec. 4.
9. Texas Constitution (1876), art. 4, sec. 6.
10. Kenneth E. Hendrickson, *The Chief Executives of Texas* (College Station: Texas A&M University Press, 1995).
11. Ibid.
12. Jim Yardley, "The 2002 Elections: Races for Governor: In Texas, Republican Who Inherited Top Job Is the Winner Outright," *New York Times,* November 6, 2002.
13. Jim Yardley, "In First, Texas Hispanic Seeks to Be Governor," *New York Times,* September 5, 2001.
14. Andrew Knapp, "Governor's Salaries Range from $1 to $206,500," May 15, 2007, www.stateline.org.
15. Ibid.
16. Frederic A. Ogg, "Impeachment of Governor Ferguson," *The American Political Science Review* 12, no. 1 (February 1918): 111–115.
17. Cortez A. M. Ewing, "The Impeachment of James E. Ferguson," *Political Science Quarterly* 48, no. 2 (June 1933): 184–210.
18. Texas Constitution (1876), art. 4, sec. 10.
19. Texans for Public Justice, "Governor Perry's Patronage" (April 2006), www.tpj.org.
20. Ibid.
21. Polly Ross Hughes, "Senators: Perry Evading Law with Expired Appointments," August 29, 2007, www.corridorwatch.org.
22. Margaret R. Ferguson, "Roles, Functions, and Powers of the Governors," in *The Executive Branch of State Government,* ed. by Margaret R. Ferguson (Santa Barbara, Calif.: ABC-CLIO, 2006).
23. Texas Constitution (1876), art. 4, sec. 11.

24. Thad Beyle, "The Governors" in *Politics in the American States: A Comparative Analysis* (Washington, D.C.: CQ Press, 2008).
25. "Poll: Texas Governor Perry Job Approval Up Post Hurricanes," December 6, 2005, www.foxnews.com.
26. Kavan Peterson, "Governors Lose in Power Struggle over National Guard," January 12, 2007, www.stateline.org.
27. Ibid.
28. Beyle, fn 21.
29. Ibid.
30. Ibid.
31. Ibid.
32. Ibid.
33. Texas Constitution (1876), art. 4, sec. 1.
34. Keon S. Chi, *The Book of the States: 2006 Edition,* vol. 38 (Lexington, Ky.: Council of State Governments, 2006).
35. Texas Constitution (1876), art. 4, sec. 22.
36. Jonathan W. Singer, *Broken Trusts: The Texas Attorney General versus the Oil Industry, 1889–1909* (College Station: Texas A&M Press, 2002).
37. HB7 transferred the Texas Performance Review and the Texas School Performance Review to the Legislative Budget Board.
38. Steven Quinn, "Texas Tops in Wind Energy Production," *USA Today,* July 25, 2006.
39. MSNBC.com, "Texas Leases Offshore Wind Tracts," www.MSNBC.com, October 3, 2007.
40. Sunset Advisory Commission, "Guide to the Texas Sunset Process" (2007), www.sunset.state.tx.us/htm.

Chapter 5

1. "Hello? Hello?! Criminal Justice," *Fort Worth Star Telegram,* October 31, 2007; ABC News, "Judge, We Close at 5," October 12, 2007.
2. Ralph Blumenthal and Linda Greenhouse, "Texas Planning New Execution Despite Ruling," *New York Times,* September 29, 2007.
3. Texas Constitution (1876), art. 5, sec. 1.
4. Office of Court Administration, *Annual Statistical Report for the Texas Judiciary, Fiscal Year 2006* (Austin: Office of Court Administration, 2006).
5. Ibid.
6. Texas Constitution (1876), art. 4, sec. 19.
7. *Annual Statistical Report to the Texas Judiciary 2006.*
8. *Annual Statistical Report to the Texas Judiciary 2006.*
9. Texas Constitution (1876), art. 5, sec. 15.
10. www.courts.state.tx.us/pubs/2007_Judicial_Directory/Judge_Profile_March_2007.pdf.
11. Ibid.
12. Texas Constitution (1876), art. 5, sec. 8.
13. Texas Watch Foundation, "The Texas Supreme Court by the Numbers: A Statistical Analysis of the Texas Supreme Court, 2005–2006" a Court Watch Release, at www.txwfoundation.org.
14. Ibid.
15. Anthony Champagne and Greg Thieleman, "Awareness of Trial Court Judges," *Judicature* 76 (1991): 271–277.
16. Honorable Thomas Phillips, quoted in "The Texas Judiciary: Is Justice for Sale?" panel discussion in Tyler, Texas, sponsored by the League of Women Voters, broadcast as part of a PBS *Frontline* Special (September 25, 2007).
17. Texas Constitution (1876), art. 5, sec. 1A.
18. *Annual Report, Fiscal Year 2006* (Austin: State Commission on Judicial Conduct, 2007).
19. Texas Research League, "The Texas Judiciary: A Proposal for Structural-Functional Reform," *Texas Courts: Report 2* (Texas Research League, 1991), 25.
20. 1993 Citizens' Commission on the Texas Judicial System at www.courts.state.tx.us/tjc/publications/cc_tjs.pdf.

21. Texans for Public Justice, *Billable Ours: Texas Endures Another Attorney-Financed Supreme Court Race* (October, 25, 2006).
22. Ibid.
23. Texas Watch Foundation, "Hecht Votes with Mega-Donors to his Personal Legal Fund 89% of the Time: Judge's Actions Raise Serious Questions about His Impartiality," July, 17, 2007, at www.txwfoundation.org.
24. Ibid.
25. Gail Russell Chaddock, "U.S. Notches World's Highest Incarceration Rates," *Christian Science Monitor,* April 18, 2003.
26. *State Profile of Texas,* at www.pewpublicsafety.org.
27. Karen Brooks, "Jail Bill Targets Dallas: Legislature: House Wants Staffing Rules, Monitors for Poor Performers,"*Dallas Morning News,* May 11, 2007, at www.dallasnews.com/sharedcontent/dws/news/texassouthwest/stories/051107dntexjail.380a0e5.html.
28. Mike Ward, "Privately Run Prisons Come Under Fire at Capitol," *Austin American-Statesman,* October 13, 2007.
29. Gregory Hooks, Clayton Mosher, Thomas Rotolo, and Linda Lobao, "The Prison Industry: Carceral Expansion and Employment in U.S. Counties, 1969–1994," *Social Science Quarterly* 85 (March 2004): 1.
30. Ward, "Privately Run Prisons."
31. Holly Becka and Jennifer LaFleur, "Texas' Youth Jail Operators Have Troubled Histories," *Dallas Morning News,* July 30, 2007, at www.dallasnews.com/sharedcontent/dws/dn/latestnews/stories/072907dnmettyccontracts.37bfd89.html.
32. David Dobbs, quoted in "The Texas Judiciary: Is Justice for Sale?"
33. Max B. Baker, "Poll: Death Penalty Losing Support," *Fort Worth Star Telegram,* June 10, 2007; R. A. Dyer, "Poll Indicates Iraq War Is Texans' Top Concern," *Fort Worth Star Telegram,* June 14, 2007.
34. Ford Fessenden, "Deadly Statistics: A Survey of Crime and Punishment," *New York Times,* September 22, 2000.
35. Christy Hoppe, "Executions Cost Texas Millions: Study Finds It's Cheaper to Jail Killers for Life," *Dallas Morning News,* March 8, 1992.
36. *Atkins v. Virginia,* 536 U.S. 304 (2002).
37. *Roper v. Simmons,* 543 U.S. 551 (2005).

Chapter 6

1. Texas State Historical Association, "The Handbook of Texas Online: Buffalo Gap," www.tsha.utexas.edu/handbook/online/articles/BB/hlb60.html, accessed September 16, 2007.
2. James L. Haley, *Passionate Nation: The Epic History of Texas* (New York: Free Press, 2006), 388.
3. *Clinton v. Cedar Rapids and Missouri River Railroad Co.,* 24 Iowa 455 (1868).
4. *Hunter v. Pittsburg,* 207 U.S. 161 (1907).
5. Texas Constitution (1876), art. 9, sec. 1.
6. Paul Ciotti, "Money and School Performance: Lessons Learned from the Kansas City Desegregation Experiment," *Policy Analysis,* No. 298 (Washington, D.C.: CATO Institute, 1998).
7. Texas State Historical Association, "The Handbook of Texas Online: Loving County," www.tsha.utexas.edu/handbook/onlinearticles/LL/hcl13.html, accessed October 2, 2007.
8. Texas Constitution (1876), art. 9, sec. 1(1).
9. Texas Association of Counties, "Some Facts about Texas Counties," www.county.org/counties/fact.asp, accessed August 18, 2007.
10. National Association of Counties, "About Counties: Data and Demographics—Texas," www.naco.org, accessed August 18, 2007.
11. Texas Constitution (1876), art. 9, sec. 14.
12. Texas Local Government Code, chap. 158, sec. 158.001.
13. Stan Reid and Tim Brown, *Texas Counties with Civil Service Systems: Research Report* (Austin: Texas Association of Counties, 2004), 2.
14. Texas Local Government Code, chap. 118.

15. Greene County, Missouri, "Personal Property Tax: Frequently Asked Questions," http://www.greenecountymo.org/spane/personalproperty.htm, accessed October 4, 2007.
16. Texas Local Government Code, chap. 6, sec. 6.001 and chap. 22, secs. 22.031–22.042.
17. Texas Local Government Code, chap. 7.
18. Texas Local Government Code, chap. 24, sec. 24.021.
19. Texas Local Government Code, chap. 6, sec. 6.002; chap. 7, sec. 7.002; and chap. 8, sec. 8.002.
20. Texas Municipal Association, "Annual Survey of Members" (Denton, Tex.: Texas Municipal Association, Inc.: 2007).
21. Robert Brischetto, "Cumulative Voting at Work in Texas" in *Voting and Democracy Report: 1995* (Takoma Park, Md.: FairVote–Center for Voting and Democracy, 1995).
22. Emily Ramshaw, "State Law Would Usurp City Control of Zoning, Neighborhood Control," *Dallas Morning News,* March 2, 2007.
23. Texas Local Government Code, chap. 43, sec. 43.055.
24. Texas Constitution (1876), Art. 7.
25. Texas Education Code, chap. 11, secs. 11.301 and 11.303.
26. Texas Education Code, chap. 11, secs. 11.051–11.058.
27. Texas Education Code, chap. 11, secs. 11.151–11.170.
28. Texas Education Agency, "SBOE History and Duties," www.tea.state.tx.us/sboe/ sboe_history_duties.html, accessed September 5, 2007.
29. Texas Constitution (1876), art. 7, sec. 8.

Chapter 7

1. "Most Oppose Perry, But He Has Big Lead," (Poll conducted by Blum and Werpin Associates, Inc.), *Dallas Morning News,* October 6, 2006.
2. John Whitesides, "Is Texas Ready for Governor Kinky?" (*Reuters,* March 6, 2006) found on www.kinkyfriedman.com/2006/03/is_texas_ready_for_governor_ki.html.
3. Texas Election Code, chap. 11, sec. 002.
4. Texas Election Code, chap. 16, secs. 002–003.
5. Texas Constitution (1876), art. 7, sec. 3.
6. Ricky F. Dobbs, *Yellow Dogs and Republicans: Allan Shivers and Texas Two-Party Politics* (College Station: Texas A&M University Press, 2005), 80.
7. Michael J. Klarman, "The Supreme Court and Black Disenfranchisement," in Richard M. Valelly, ed., *The Voting Rights Act: Securing the Ballot* (Washington, D.C.: CQ Press, 2006).
8. Of course, the courts allow some limitations to exist, primarily where health and safety of citizens are concerned. Laws may discriminate on the basis of age; for example, statutes prohibiting children from driving. Imagine if three-year-olds were allowed to drive!
9. 383 U.S. 663 (1966).
10. 273 U.S. 534 (1924).
11. 321 U.S. 649 (1944).
12. 345 U.S. 461 (1953).
13. Klarman, 154.
14. Abigail M. Thernstrom, *Whose Votes Count?* (Cambridge, Mass.: Harvard University Press, 1987), 55.
15. Chandler Davidson, "The Voting Rights Act: A Brief History," in Bernard Grofman and Chandler Davidson, eds., *Controversies in Minority Voting* (Washington, D.C.: The Brookings Institution, 1992).
16. Thernstrom, 56.
17. Texas State Historical Association, "Civil Rights Movement," in *The Handbook of Texas Online,* www.tsha.utexas.edu/handbook/online, accessed August 7, 2007.
18. Thernstrom, 52.
19. Ruth P. Morgan, *Governance by Decree: The Impact of the Voting Rights Act in Dallas* (Lawrence, Kan.: University of Kansas Press, 2004), 50–51.
20. Thernstrom, 56–57.
21. Texas Constitution (1876), art. 6, sec. 5.

22. Donald P. Moynihan, "Building Secure Elections: E-Voting, Security, and Systems Theory," *Public Administration Review* 64 (2007): 515–528.

23. Ibid., 518.

24. Paul S. Herrnson, et al., "Early Appraisals of Electronic Voting," *Social Science Computer Review* 23 (2005): 274–292.

25. Jeffrey S. Connor, "Amended Texas State Plan Pursuant to the Help America Vote Act of 2002" (Austin: Elections Division, Office of the Secretary of State, 2005), 3.

26. Ibid., 15.

27. 530 U.S. 567 (2000).

28. John F. Bibby and Thomas M. Holbrook, "Parties and Elections," in Virginia Gray and Russell Hanson, *Politics in the American States: A Comparative Analysis,* 8th ed. (Washington, D.C.: CQ Press, 2004), 63.

29. Dobbs, 70.

30. Ibid., 88.

31. Alexander Heard, *A Two Party South?* (Chapel Hill: University of North Carolina Press, 1952), 104–105.

32. John G. Matsusaka, "2005 Initiatives and Referendums," in Keon S. Chi, ed., *The Book of the States: 2006 Edition,* vol. 38 (Lexington, Ken.: The Council on State Governments, 2006), 307.

33. In some rare cases, voters do mark local and state races and leave "higher" offices, such as U.S. Senate or U.S. House of Representative races, unmarked. However, this pattern is much, much rarer than "roll off." As a result, political scientists do not really have a term to describe the phenomenon, but "roll on" seems a bit silly.

34. Samuel L. Popkin, "Information Shortcuts and the Reasoning Voter," in Bernard Grofman, ed., *Information, Participation, and Choice* (Ann Arbor: University of Michigan Press, 1993), 19.

35. Popkin, 22–27; Anthony Downs, *An Economic Theory of Democracy* (New York: Harper and Row, 1957), 85.

36. Karlheinz Reif and Hermann Schmitt, "Nine Second-Order Elections: A Conceptual Framework for the Analysis of European Election Results," *European Journal of Political Research* 8 (1980): 3–44.

37. U.S. Census Bureau, "Voting and Registration in the Election of November 2004" (Washington, D.C.: U.S. Department of Commerce, 2006).

38. William H. Riker, *Liberalism against Populism* (Prospect Heights, Ill.: Waveland Press, 1982), 5; Robert A. Dahl, *A Preface to Democratic Theory* (Chicago, Ill.: University of Chicago Press, 1956), 132.

39. James Endersby, Steven Galatas, and Chapman Rackaway, "Closeness Counts in Canada," *The Journal of Politics* vol. 64, no. 2 (2002): 610–631. Specific cases finding a link in the United States at the state level include Harvey J. Tucker, "Contextual Models of Participation in U.S. State Legislative Elections," *Western Political Quarterly,* vol. 39, no. 1 (1986): 67–78; Gregory A. Caldiera and Samuel C. Patterson, "Contextual Influences on Participation in U.S. State Legislative Election," *Legislative Studies Quarterly,* vol. 7, no. 3 (1989): 359–381; and Samuel C. Patterson and Gregory A. Caldiera, "Getting Out the Vote: Participation in Gubernatorial Elections," *American Political Science Review,* vol. 77, no. 3 (1983), 675–689.

40. Earl Black and Merle Black, *The Rise of the Southern Republicans* (Cambridge, Mass.: Belknap Press, 2002), 88.

41. Ibid., 23–24.

42. Bibby and Holbrook, "Parties and Elections," 87–88.

43. *Buckley v. Valeo,* 424 U.S. 1 (1976).

44. *McConnell v. Federal Election Commission,* 540 U.S. 93 (2003).

45. *Federal Election Commission v. Wisconsin Right to Life,* 551 U.S. ____ (2007).

46. National Institute of Money in State Politics, "State at a Glance: Texas 2006 Candidates," www.followthemoney.org, accessed June 16, 2007.

47. Because Carole Strayhorn competed first in the Republican primary and then as an independent candidate in the general election, the figures include her spending in both the primary and general elections.

Chapter 8

1. Alwyn Barr, *Reconstruction to Reform: Texas Politics, 1876–1906* (Dallas: Southern Methodist University Press, 2000), 5.
2. T. R. Fehrenbach, *Lone Star: A History of Texas and the Texans* (Cambridge, Mass.: Da Capo Press, 2000), 618.
3. Ibid., 624.
4. Lewis L. Gould, *Progressives and Prohibitionists* (Austin: University of Texas Press, 1973), 39.
5. Fehrenbach, *Lone Star,* 415.
6. Gould, *Progressives and Prohibitionists,* 39.
7. Randolph B. Campbell, *Gone to Texas* (New York: Oxford University Press—USA, 2004), 350.
8. Edmund Burke, *Works,* vol. I (London: G. Bell and Sons, 1897), 375.
9. Leon Epstein, *Political Parties in Western Democracies* (New York: Praeger, 1967), 9.
10. *Eu v. San Francisco County Democratic Central Comm.,* 489 U.S. 214 (1989).
11. Paul Allen Beck, *Political Parties in America,* 8th ed. (New York: Longman, 1997), 67–68.
12. Marc J. Hetherington and William J. Keefe, *Parties, Politics, and Public Policy in America,* 10th ed. (Washington, D.C.: CQ Press, 2007), 21.
13. John Kenneth White and Daniel M. Shea, *New Party Politics: From Jefferson and Hamilton to the Information Age* (Boston: St. Martin's Press, 2000), 174.
14. V. O. Key, *Southern Politics in State and Nation* (New York: Knopf, 1949), 307.
15. Anthony J. Nownes, *Pressure and Power: Organized Interests in American Politics* (Boston: Houghton Mifflin Company, 2001).
16. Ibid., 8.
17. Campbell, *Gone to Texas,* 313.
18. David Truman, *The Governmental Process: Political Interests and Public Opinion,* 2nd ed. (New York: Knopf, 1971).
19. Tara Copp, "State Lobbyist Bid Fell Short," *Austin American-Statesman,* January 25, 2006, 1A.
20. 548 U.S. 204 (2006).
21. Laylan Copelin, "Wined, Dined and Rubbed the Right Way," *Austin American-Statesman,* January 30, 2007.
22. Center for Public Integrity, "Statehouse Revolvers: Study Finds more than 1,300 Ex-legislators among 2005 State Lobbying Ranks," October 12, 2006, www.publicintegrity.org/hiredguns/report.aspx?aid=747.
23. Pete Slover and Robert T. Garrett, " 'Kinfolk' lobbyists prospering," *Dallas Morning News,* May 5, 2005, 1A.
24. Robert A. Dahl, *Who Governs?* (New Haven, Conn.: Yale University Press, 1961).
25. C. Wright Mills, *The Power Elite* (New York: Oxford University Press, 1956).
26. E. E. Schattschneider, *The Semisovereign People* (New York: Holt, Rinehart and Winston, 1960) 34–35.
27. Jonathan Rauch, *Government's End: Why Washington Stopped Working* (New York: Public Affairs, 1999).
28. Key, *Southern Politics,* 11.

Chapter 9

1. James L. Haley, *Passionate Nation: The Epic History of Texas* (New York: Free Press, 2006), 81.
2. U.S. Census Bureau, "States Ranked by Total State Taxes and Per Capita Amount: 2005," www.census.gov/govs/statetax/05staxrank.html.
3. Laurie Fox, "School Districts Opt for Extra Tax," *Dallas Morning News,* September 22, 2006.
4. Kevin Krause, "Senior Property-tax Freeze Considered," *Dallas Morning News,* July 31, 2007.
5. Tax Foundation Special Report No. 139, "Federal Tax Burdens and Spending by State," October 19, 2007.

6. Haley, *Passionate Nation,* 231.

7. Texas Constitution (1876), art. 3, sec. 49.

8. Comptroller, "Biennial Revenue Estimate, 2008–2009," January 2007, 3, www.window.state.tx.us/taxbud/bre2008/BRE_2008-09.pdf.

9. Evan Smith, "One Ticked-Off Grandma," *Texas Monthly,* December 2003, 163.

10. Rick Perry, "Message," May 26, 2007, www.governor.state.tx.us/divisions/press/bills/letters/letter3-052607.

11. Texas Education Agency, *Pocket Edition, 2006–2007 Texas Public School Statistics,* www.tea.state.tx.us/perfreport/pocked/2007/pocked0607.pdf.

12. Ibid.

13. Haley, *Passionate Nation,* 232.

14. 347 U.S. 483 (1954).

15. 349 U.S. 294 (1955).

16. Judge Justice's order in the *United States v. Texas* case is generally referred to as "Civil Order 5821."

17. 777 S.W. 2d 391 (Tex. 1989).

18. Texas Education Agency, "2006–2007 Texas Public School Statistics."

19. Joshua Benton and Holly Hacker, "Analysis Shows TAKS Cheating Rampant," *Dallas Morning News,* June 3, 2007.

20. Joshua Benton, "TAKS Analysis Suggests Many Graduates Cheated," *Dallas Morning News,* June 11, 2006, 1A.

21. Terrence Stutz, "Most Say School Testing Overemphasized," *Dallas Morning News,* February 22, 2006, 3A.

22. "Diploma Counts: Ready for What," *Education Week,* June 2007.

23. Texas Higher Education Coordinating Board, "Closing the Gap by 2015: 2006 Annual Progress Report," July 2006, 3, www.thecb.state.tx.us/reports.

24. 78 F.3d 932 (5th Cir. 1996).

25. Liz Peterson, "Bill Aims to Stabilize Tuition, Fees," *Dallas Morning News,* December 10, 2006, 3A.

26. Texas Health and Human Services Commission, "TANF Cases and Recipients by County, June 2007" www.hhsc.state.tx.us.

27. Carmen DeNavas-Walt, Bernadette D. Proctor, and Jessica Smith, *Income, Poverty, and Health Insurance Coverage in the United States: 2006* (Washington, D.C.: U.S. Census Bureau, August 2007).

28. Associated Press, "Heal Program Enrolling Fewer Kids," *Dallas Morning News,* March 1, 2006, 4A.

29. Randolph B. Campbell, *Gone to Texas* (New York: Oxford University Press—USA, 2004), 326.

30. Pamela M. Prah, "Wanna Buy the Brooklyn Bridge? Some States aren't Joking," *State of the State Report: A Stateline.org Report,* 2007, 16, http://archive.stateline.org/flash-data/Stateline's_State_of_the_States_2007.pdf.

31. Jonathan Blundell, "Candidates take stand on TTC," *Waxahachie Daily Light,* April 4, 2006.

32. Comptroller's Office, *Undocumented Immigrants in Texas: A Financial Analysis of the Impact to the State Budget and Economy,* December 2006.

33. Isabel C. Morales and Al Dia, "Swift Plant Raid Devastated Cactus," *Dallas Morning News,* February 11, 2007, 1A.

34. 457 U.S. 202 (1982).

35. Katherine Leal Unmuth, "Tyler Case Opened Schools to Illegal Migrants," *Dallas Morning News,* June 11, 2007.

36. "Texas Monday Talks: Dick Armey," *Texas Monthly,* January 2007, 66.

Glossary

Administrative federalism the national government sets up guidelines for policy, then expects the state government to pay for the programs without additional money. (6)

Ad-valorem tax a tax based on property value, which is subject to periodic appraisals. (9)

Advanced or early voting a voting system that allows a voter to cast a ballot before an election without giving a specific reason, thus making voting more convenient for the voter. (7)

Agenda setting the stage in which policymakers prioritize the problems facing a state. (9)

Amendment a formal change to a bill during the committee process. (3)

Annexation adding areas adjacent to a city into the city limits. (6)

Appellate jurisdiction the authority to hear the appeal from a lower court, which has already rendered a decision; appellate courts review the court record from the original trial and do not hear new evidence. (5)

Appointment power the ability to determine who will occupy certain key positions within the bureaucracy. (4)

Appraisal the official estimate of a property's value. (9)

Astroturf lobbying a simulation of grassroots support, usually conducted by specialized lobbying firms and involving spending large sums of money to generate the appearance of public support to advance a group's agenda. (8)

At-large elections elections where a county is treated as a single district and candidates are elected from the entire district as a whole. (5)

Auditor the county officer appointed by the district judge, who oversees county finances. (6)

Beyond a reasonable doubt in a system where the defendant is presumed innocent, this is the standard for the burden of proof of a defendant's guilt in criminal trials. (5)

Bicameral a legislature that consists of two separate chambers or houses. (3)

Bills proposed new laws or changes to existing laws brought before a legislative chamber by a legislative member. (3)

Blanket or wide-open primary a primary for which voters do not register party affiliations and receive ballot papers containing the names of all candidates from all political parties running for office; usually voters may choose only one candidate per office, rather than one candidate per political party. (7)

Block grant created by Republicans, these national funds are given to state and local governments for a broader purpose and they impose fewer restrictions on the states regarding how the money is to be spent. (2)

Blocking bill a bill regularly introduced in the Texas Senate to serve as a placeholder at the top of the Senate calendar. (3)

Budget power the executive's ability to propose an annual budget that the legislature then considers; the Texas governor has very limited power over the budget process, since there is a Legislative Budget Board. (4)

Casework solving problems for constituents. (7)

Categorical grant national money given to states and local governments that must be spent for specific activities. (2)

Ceremonial duties being the most visible officeholder, the executive makes appearances at events and performs ceremonial duties; such exposure can become an important source of power. (4)

Chronic minority a group that rarely wins elections or achieves majority status, and thus sees few reasons to become actively engaged in politics. (8)

Citizen initiatives citizen-initiated petitions, which force consideration or votes on certain legislation and amendments, rather than having the impetus for these actions coming from the legislature. (3)

Citizen legislature a legislature that attempts to keep the job of being a state legislator as a part-time function that many or most citizens can perform. Normally it provides minimal compensation, offers few staffing resources, and operates with short or infrequent legislative sessions. (3)

City charter in home rule cities, a plan of government that details the structure and function of city government, similar to a constitution. (6)

Civil cases cases in which an aggrieved party sues for damages claiming that he or she has been wronged by another individual. (5)

Closed primary an electoral contest restricted to party loyalists and excluding supporters of other political parties and independent voters. (7)

Closed rider a rider that is not made public until after the legislature has voted on the bill, either when the bill goes to a conference committee for reconciliation or when the governor prepares to sign the bill into law. (3)

Cohesion members of a political party or special caucus voting together on a bill or resolution. (3)

Collective goods benefits that, once provided, go to everyone and cannot be effectively denied to others, even those who did not contribute to the effort. (8)

Commissioners court the governing body for Texas counties, consisting of four elected commissioners and the judge from the county constitutional court. (6)

Committees formally organized groups of legislators that assist the legislature in accomplishing its work, allowing a division of labor and an in-depth review of an issue or a bill before review by the entire chamber. (3)

Compensatory damages monetary damages designed to compensate the injured party. (5)

Concurrent jurisdiction a system where different levels of courts have overlapping jurisdiction, often resulting in a confusing and ill-defined system. (5)

Concurrent powers powers such as taxing and spending, the ability to establish courts, and charter banks that are shared by the national and state governments. (2)

Concurrent resolutions express an opinion of the legislature and must pass in both houses. (3)

Confederal system a type of government where the lower units of government retain decision-making authority. (2)

Conference committee an official legislative work group that meets on a limited basis to reconcile the different versions of a bill that has passed in the Texas House and Senate. (3)

Constitution a written document that outlines the powers of government and the limitations on those powers. (2)

Contract outsourcing when a government entity contracts with a private company to perform a service that governments traditionally provide, such as a contract to collect trash and garbage. (6)

Conventions (caucuses) meetings that usually occur on the same day as primary election day at which party members participate in a range of party business. (8)

County attorney the county official who represents the county in legal activities and offers legal advice to the county government. (6)

County civil service commission the agency administering the county's civil service system, by developing job definitions, qualification processes, employee classifications, and other aspects of the system. (6)

County clerk the elected county official who maintains county records and in some counties oversees elections. (6)

County or senatorial district conventions held on the third Saturday after the primary election, these conventions select delegates to the statewide convention. (8)

Credit claiming the advantage derived from incumbents' ability to point out positive outcomes for which they are responsible. (7)

Criminal cases cases in which an individual is charged by the state with violating the laws and the state brings the suit. (5)

Crisis manager the responsibility to act as a policymaker, coordinator of resources, and point person during a variety of natural and man-made disasters that might befall the people of the state during the executive's tenure. (4)

Cross filing a system that allows a candidate to run simultaneously as a Democratic and a Republican candidate, essentially competing in both parties' primaries. (7)

Cumulative voting a system that allows voters to take the total number of positions to be selected in a district and divide the votes among one or a few candidates. (5)

Defendant (civil) the party alleged to have committed the wrong at issue in the suit. (5)

Defendant (criminal) a person charged with committing a crime. (5)

Delegate (theory) this approach sees elected officials as agents of the majority who elected them to office and believes that officials should carry out, to the extent possible, the wishes of the majority. (3)

Delegated powers the powers listed in Article I, Section 8 of the U.S. Constitution that are expressly granted to the national government. (2)

Delegates party members elected to attend their party's conventions at the county level or the Texas senatorial district level. (8)

De novo to hear an appeal with a new trial, most commonly taken in the absence of an official case record. (5)

Dillon's Rule the principle that regardless of the type of local government, all local governments are creatures of the state government and have only those powers specifically granted to them by the state. (6)

Direct primary an election in which the winning candidate directly receives the party nomination. (7)

Disclosure the reporting of who contributes money and how much is contributed by an individual or corporation. (7)

Distributive policy policy that attempts to meet the needs of citizens without targeting any one group as the source of funding. (9)

Disturbance theory a theory of group formation that suggests that as societies become more complex and more diverse, new interests will emerge to voice their concerns and established interests will mobilize to protect the status quo. (8)

Education Reform Act a 1984 statue that requires teachers and school administrators to take a test to assure basic competency before being recertified; students are also tested periodically to monitor progress and are required to pass an exam to graduate. (9)

Electioneering method used by organized interests to try to shape public policy by influencing who is elected to office, especially by serving as sources of campaign funding. (8)

Electoral competition model the view that parties make a pragmatic move to the center of the political spectrum as they attempt to win votes, sacrificing the more purely ideological positions. (8)

Emergency clause language that makes the bill effective immediately upon being signed into law, rather than being subject to the customary ninety-day waiting period. (3)

Eminent domain the power of government to take private property for public use, generally for public functions such as roads. (9)

Empresario an entrepreneur who made money colonizing areas of the Mexican territories. (1)

En banc an appeal that is heard by the entire court of appeals, rather than by a select panel of judges. (5)

Equal Protection Clause this clause of the Fourteenth Amendment to the U.S. Constitution requires that state laws and state constitutions treat all citizens the same. (7)

Excise tax a tax paid at the time of purchase, with the cost of the tax included in the price of the product. (9)

Exclusive jurisdiction a particular level of court with the sole right to hear a specific type of case. (5)

Executive committee this group, selected at the state party convention, carries on the activities of the party between party conventions; by law, the committee consists of one man and one woman from each state senatorial district. (8)

Expressive benefits benefits that arise from taking action to express one's views; serves as another motivation for group membership. (8)

Extradition the constitutional requirement that states deliver someone suspected or convicted of a crime in another state back to that state so they can face trial or sentencing. (2)

Federalism a form of government based on the sharing of powers between the national and state governments. (2)

Filibuster an effort to kill a bill by engaging in unlimited debate, refusing to yield the floor to another member and preventing a vote on the bill. (3)

Fiscal federalism use of national financial incentives to encourage policies at the state level. (2)

Fiscal policy how government seeks to influence the economy through taxing and spending. (9)

Floor debate when a bill is brought up before the entire chamber for debate for and against the measure. (3)

Floor whips individuals who remind legislators of their party's position on a bill and encourage members to vote with the rest of the party caucus. (3)

Franchise tax the primary tax on businesses in Texas; based on the "taxable margin" of each company. (9)

Free-rider problem occurs when citizens who do not contribute to the effort of a group enjoy the results of the group's efforts. (8)

Full faith and credit clause the constitutional requirement that court judgments or legal contracts entered into in one state will be honored by other states. (2)

General election the interparty election in which candidates from two or more political parties compete for actual political office. (7)

General law city the default organization for Texas cities, with the exact forms of government, ordinance powers, and other aspects of city government specified in the Texas Local Government Code. (6)

General revenue sharing transfers of money from the national government to the states with no rules on how the money is spent. (2)

General sales tax an across-the-board tax imposed on goods and services sold within a jurisdiction. (9)

Gerrymandering the practice of incumbents creating very oddly shaped electoral districts to maximize their political advantage in an upcoming election. (3)

Grandfather clause the granting of voting rights only to those citizens whose grandfathers had the right to vote; used to bar African Americans from voting in the South after the end of Reconstruction. (7)

Grand jury a panel of twelve that reviews evidence, determines whether there is sufficient evidence to bring a trial, and issues an indictment. (5)

Grassroots lobbying attempts by organized interests to influence legislators through public opinion; an extension of democratic principles in which groups of citizens spontaneously mobilize to build support for a cause. (8)

Grassroots organizations groups in which power and decision making reside with average citizens; average citizen participation is the foundation of these groups' legitimacy. (8)

Grasstop lobbying the attempt to influence legislators through key constituents or friends. (8)

Help America Vote Act (HAVA) federal statute enacted after the 2000 presidential election to effectively standardize election procedures. (7)

Higher Education Coordinating Board a group of thirteen appointed by the governor for six-year terms to oversee higher education policy in Texas. (9)

Home rule city a city that has been granted greater freedom in the organization and functioning of city government, and can make changes without seeking permission from the state. (6)

Horizontal federalism refers to the relationship between the states. (2)

Hyperpluralism a view that the system today has evolved beyond simple pluralism and is now one in which many narrow interests are represented, often at the expense of the broader public interest. (8)

Impeachment formal procedures to remove an elected official from office for misdeeds; passage of the articles of impeachment by the House merely suggests that there is sufficient evidence for a trial, which is then conducted by the Senate. (4)

Income tax a tax calculated as a percentage of income earned in a year. (9)

Incumbency advantage advantages enjoyed by the incumbent candidate, or current officeholder, in elections. Incumbency advantages are based on greater visibility, proven record of public service, and often better access to resources. (5)

Incumbent the candidate already holding office. (7)

Independent candidate a candidate running for office without a political party affiliation. (7)

Indictment a document that formally charges a defendant with committing a crime. (5)

Indirect primary primary in which voters elect delegates to a party convention; delegates are pledged to support a specific candidate seeking the party nomination. (7)

Individualistic political culture the idea that individuals are best left largely free of the intervention of community forces like government and that government should attempt only those things demanded by the people it was created to serve. (1)

Informal powers attributes of personal power based on factors such as the electoral mandate, political ambition ladder, personal future as governor, and performance ratings, rather than constitutionally enumerated powers. (4)

Initiative a mechanism that allows voters to gather signatures on a petition in order to place statutes or constitutional amendments on a ballot. (2)

Instant run-off if no candidate receives a majority at the initial election, the second place votes are considered, and a winner is determined by adding the first and second place votes. (3)

Intergovernmental lobby the lobbying that occurs between different levels of government, such as between the state and national government or between local governments and the state government. (8)

Interim committee legislative work groups that are created during periods when the legislature is not in session to provide oversight of the executive branch and monitor public policy. (3)

Introduce [a bill] to officially bring a bill before a legislative chamber for the first time. Introducing a bill is the first step in the formal legislative process. (3)

Jessica's Law a law, adopted in several states, that provides for the death penalty or life imprisonment without parole for repeat sexual predators whose victims are underage, in Texas, defined as under the age of fourteen. (5)

Joint committee a temporary legislative work group created by agreement between the lieutenant governor and Speaker of the Texas House of Representatives for a special purpose; sometimes called a select committee. (3)

Joint resolution the format for all amendments to the Texas Constitution. (3)

Judicial federalism a system in which judicial authority is shared between levels of government. (5)

Jurisdiction the court's sphere of authority. (5)

Justices of the peace and constables elected county officers who act as judicial officers for minor criminal and civil cases. (6)

Killer amendment language added to a bill on an unrelated or controversial topic in order to make the bill unacceptable to the majority of the legislature who will then vote against the bill. (3)

Labor unions organizations that represent the interests of working people seeking better pay and better working conditions. (8)

Legislative Budget Board (LBB) the group that develops a proposed state budget for legislative consideration. (3)

Legislative Redistricting Board (LRB) created by a 1948 amendment to the Texas Constitution, this group steps in if the state legislature is unable to pass a redistricting plan or when a state or federal court invalidates a plan drawn by the legislature; this group comes into play only for plans to redistrict the state legislature. (3)

Legislative role the executive's role in influencing the state's legislative agenda. (4)

Lieutenant governor the presiding officer of the Texas Senate, elected directly by the voters. (3)

Line-item veto the ability of the executive to selectively veto only some parts of a bill; in Texas available only on spending bills. (3)

Literacy test a test of a prospective voter's ability to read and understand aspects of American government; used to bar African Americans from voting in many parts of the post-Reconstruction South, but not widely used in Texas. (7)

Lobbying direct contact with members of the legislative or executive branch to influence legislation or administrative action. (8)

"Lone Star Card" Program Texas's version of food stamps that helps low-income seniors, people with disabilities, and single people and families in need buy food from local retailers. (9)

Long ballot a system in which almost all of the positions in a state are elected rather than appointed. (2)

Machine politics political organizations that are led by a local party boss who uses a patronage system of city jobs, government contracts, and other benefits to run the city for personal power and gain. (6)

Magistrate functions the authority to conduct the preliminary procedures in criminal cases, such as issuing search and arrest warrants, conducting preliminary hearings, and setting bail for more serious crimes. (5)

Majority election an election where a candidate is required to receive 50 percent of the vote, plus one additional vote to be declared the winner. Winning the most votes is not sufficient. (3)

Majority-minority districts an election district in which the majority of the population comes from a racial or ethnic minority. (3)

Manifest Destiny the belief that U.S. expansion across the North American continent was inevitable. (2)

Mark-up when the committee goes line-by-line through a bill to make changes without formal amendments. (3)

Medicaid a federal program providing medical coverage for low-income people and some elderly and disabled people. (9)

Medicare a federal health insurance program available to senior citizens who have worked and paid into the Medicare system for ten or more years. (9)

Merit or civil service system a system in which people receive government jobs based upon a set of qualifications and formal training; job promotion and pay raises are based upon job performance. (6)

Moralistic political culture rare in Texas, in this view, the exercise of community pressure is sometimes necessary to advance the public good; it also holds that government can be a positive force and citizens have a duty to participate. (1)

Motor Voter Act the National Voter Registration Act that allows citizens to register to vote when applying for or renewing their driver's license. (7)

Multi-Member District (MMD) an election system in which the state is divided into many election districts, but each district elects more than one person to the state legislature. (3)

Municipal bonds certificates of indebtedness, in which there is a pledge to pay back the loan over time with interest, issued by cities to raise money for services and infrastructure. (6)

Municipal utility districts special districts that provide water, sewer, and similar services to individuals and businesses outside city limits. (6)

Name recognition making a voting choice based on familiarity with or previous recognition of a candidate's name. (5)

NIMBY comes from "not in my backyard," and refers to local efforts to prevent the location of potentially harmful activities, such as industrial waste disposal, close to citizens. (9)

"No Child Left Behind" Act (NCLB) the federal education act, based on the Texas standardized testing statutes, which requires schools to institute mandatory testing to track student progress and evaluates schools based on that progress. (9)

Nonpartisan or bipartisan independent commissions a system of drawing electoral district lines that attempts to remove politics from the process of redistricting. (3)

One person, one vote shorthand term for the requirement by the U.S. Supreme Court that election districts should be roughly equal in population. (3)

Open primary an electoral contest in which voters do not have to declare a party affiliation to participate, but must request a specific party's ballot at the primary, and are then barred from participating in the other party's primary. (7)

Ordinance a law enacted by a city government. (6)

Organized interest an individual, group of people, or group of businesses that organizes its efforts to influence public policy. (8)

Original jurisdiction courts with the authority to hear the initial case; this is where the evidence and the case record are established. (5)

Oversight when the legislature reviews policies and decisions of the executive branch to make sure that the executive branch is following the intentions of the legislature. (3)

Pardon an executive grant of release from a sentence or punishment in a criminal case. (4)

Partisan elections elections in which candidates compete for office, with both candidates' names and party affiliations appearing on the ballot. (6)

Party affiliation a candidate's identifiable membership in a political party, often listed on an election ballot. (3)

Party caucus the organization of the members of a specific legislative chamber who belong to a political party. (3)

Party caucus chairs the party leaders, whose main job it is to organize party members to vote for legislation on the floor. (3)

Party-line or straight-ticket voting when voters select candidates by their party affiliation. (7)

Party platform the document that officially spells out the issue stands of a party; written and approved at the convention. (8)

Party primary an electoral contest to win a political party's nomination for the right to appear as their candidate on the ballot in the general election. (3)

Patronage when individuals who supported a candidate for public office are rewarded with public jobs and appointments. (4)

"Pay-as-you-go" system a fiscal discipline, adopted by Texas and many other states, that requires a balanced budget and permits borrowing only under a very few circumstances. (9)

Permanent party organizations the party officials selected by the temporary organizations to conduct party business between the primaries, caucuses, and conventions. (8)

Permanent School Fund a fund set aside to finance education in Texas; the state's largest source of investment income. (9)

Permanent University Fund (PUF) an endowment funded by mineral rights and other revenue generated by 2.1 million acres of land set aside by the state. Investment returns from this fund support schools in the University of Texas and Texas A & M systems. (9)

Petit jury a trial jury, which attends a trial, listens to evidence, and determines whether a defendant is innocent or guilty. (5)

Plaintiff the party claiming to have been wronged and bringing the suit. (5)

Planks the individual issue positions of the party platform. (8)

Plural executive an executive branch in which the functions have been divided among several, mostly elected, officeholders, rather than residing in a single person, the governor. (4)

Pluralist perspective a view of politics that argues that democracy is best practiced when citizens participate through groups; a greater number of organized interests means wider participation and a healthier democracy. (8)

Plurality election the candidate with the most votes wins the election. (3)

Policy the actions and activities of the government. (9)

Policy adoption the stage in which formal government action takes place. (9)

Policy evaluation the stage in which the implementation of a policy is examined to see if goals are being met. (9)

Policy formation the stage in which possible solutions and policies are developed and debated. (9)

Policy implementation the stage in which a policy is carried out in state agencies. (9)

Political action committees (PACs) the fundraising arms of interest groups that have been organized to meet the requirements of state and federal campaign finance laws. (8)

Political ambition ladder how a political figure has come up through the ranks, working through various levels of state governmental offices and positions on the way to the top position; climbing several levels on the ladder can increase a politician's contacts, allies, and political savvy. (4)

Political culture the shared values and beliefs of citizens about the nature of the political world that give the public a common language as a foundation to discuss and debate ideas. (1)

Politico this approach is a hybrid of the trustee and delegate theories and holds that on important issues, representatives should follow the wishes of the electorate, but on other issues, the representative has leeway. (3)

Poll tax an annual tax paid before one was allowed to vote; allowed by a 1902 amendment to the Texas Constitution and used to legally bar African Americans from voting. (7)

Popular mandate the claim that a newly elected official's legislative agenda is the will of the people based on a high margin of victory in a general election. (4)

Popular sovereignty a government where the power to govern is derived from the will of the people. (2)

Position taking an incumbent's advantage in having an existing record of positions on issues from previous elections and in the context of decisions made while in office. (7)

Post-adjournment vetoes vetoes that occur after the legislature has adjourned, thus giving the legislature no way to overturn the veto. (4)

Precinct and county chairs precinct chairs are selected by party members in each voting precinct by majority vote; county chairs are selected by countywide voting. These party officials are responsible for managing the local affairs of their party for the next two years. (8)

Preference primary primary in which voters indicate their choice to hold office, but the actual selection is left to the political party elites. (7)

Preponderance of evidence the burden of proof in a civil case, which is lower than that in a criminal case; the plaintiff must show merely that the defendant is likely to have committed the wrong. (5)

Presidential republicanism the practice in the South of voting for Republicans in presidential elections, but voting for conservative Democrats in other races, a practice that continued until animosity over Reconstruction faded and the Republicans demonstrated their electability in the South. (1)

President pro tempore a presiding officer elected by the members of the Texas Senate, who takes over when the Lieutenant Governor is unavailable. (3)

Primary elections intraparty elections in which candidates compete to determine who will win the party's nomination in the general election. (7)

Private financing occurs when citizens, interest groups, labor unions, and corporations make donations to candidates and political parties to cover the cost of an election. (7)

Private prisons private, for-profit prison corporations that staff and run the prison facilities in a state. (5)

Privatization when a government entity sells assets or services to a private company, such as a school district selling its buses to a private company and allowing the private company to provide busing. (6)

Privileges and immunities the constitutional requirement that states may not fundamentally treat citizens of other states differently than their own citizens. (2)

Professional associations organizations that represent the needs of professionals not represented by unions. (8)

Professional legislature a legislature that meets annually, often for nine months a year, compensates its legislators with a professional-level salary, and provides generous allowances to hire and keep support and research staffs. (3)

Progressive tax a graduated tax, such as an income tax, that taxes people with higher incomes at higher rates. (9)

Property tax a tax on the value of real estate that is paid by the property owner; used by county and local governments to fund such programs as public schools. (9)

Prosecutor a lawyer who represents the government and brings a case in criminal trials. (5)

Public financing a system of campaign financing in which the government covers the cost of elections for political parties and candidates. (7)

Public-interest groups organizations that pursue noneconomic policies on behalf of the general public, even if all members of the general public do not agree on these issues or policies. (8)

Punitive damages larger monetary awards designed to punish the defendant and, perhaps, send a message to the larger society. (5)

Recess appointments gubernatorial appointments made while the Senate is not in session; these require Senate approval within ten days of the next legislative session. (4)

Recidivism a former inmate's return to crime after being released from prison. (5)

Redistributive policy policy that moves benefits (usually in the form of money) from one group to another in an attempt to equalize society. (9)

Redistricting the periodic adjustment of the lines of electoral district boundaries. (3)

Referendum a mechanism that allows voters to cast a popular vote on statutes passed by the state legislature; the legislature can place measures on the ballot for voter consideration. (2)

Regressive tax a tax, such as a sales tax, that taxes everyone at the same rate, regardless of income, which has a greater impact on those with lower incomes. (9)

Regulation government rulemaking and enforcement intended to protect citizens from being harmed by the actions of private firms. (9)

Regulatory policy policy that attempts to limit or control individual or corporate actions. (9)

Removal powers the power of the governor to remove an appointee; in Texas the governor may remove his or her own appointees, but must obtain two-thirds support of the state Senate. (4)

Representation the relationship between an elected official and the electorate. (3)

Reserved powers the specification in the Tenth Amendment that all powers not delegated to the national government belong to the states. (2)

Resolutions a legislative act expressing the opinion of the legislature on a matter or changing the organizational structure of the legislature. (3)

Responsible party model the theoretical view that each party should hold firmly to a clear and consistent set of policies with a coherent ideology distinct from that of other parties to present voters with clear choices. (8)

Revolving door the phenomenon of legislators and members of the executive branch moving easily from government office to lucrative positions with lobbying firms. (8)

Rider an addition to a bill that deals with an unrelated subject such as changing some aspect of law or public policy or spending money or creating programs in a specific member's district. (3)

Roll call votes votes, usually important, for which a permanent record of each member's vote is created. (3)

Roll off occurs when a voter marks off only the "more important" offices on a lengthy ballot—usually the national or statewide offices—and leaves the county or local office choices blank. (7)

Run-off election an election to decide the winner that is held after a majority election fails to yield a clear 50 percent winner in the initial balloting. (3)

Runoff primary primary that occurs if no nominee receives the required majority of the votes in a primary; the top two finishers face off in a second primary to determine the nominee for the general election. (8)

Second order elections elections for offices below the national executive level in countries with presidential systems like the United States or the national legislature level in parliamentary countries like Great Britain; generally seen as less important in scope and impact on a country. (7)

Selective incentives benefits exclusively available to members of an organization. (8)

Senatorial courtesy the informal requirement that any gubernatorial appointee have approval of their own state senator in order to get support of the entire Senate. (4)

Severance tax a tax charged on natural resources when they are produced or "severed" from the earth. (9)

Sheriff the elected county official who oversees county law enforcement. (6)

Simple resolutions address organizational issues and may be limited to a single house. (3)

Sin taxes taxes on products or activities, such as cigarettes or gambling, that some legislators would like to discourage. (9)

Single-interest groups groups usually organized around one side of a single issue, such as pro-choice or anti-abortion groups. (8)

Solidarity benefits the social interactions that individuals enjoy from joining a group and from working together for a common cause. (8)

Speaker of the House the presiding officer of the Texas House of Representatives. (3)

Speaker pro tempore akin to the president pro tempore in the Texas Senate, this House officer presides when the Speaker is unavailable. (3)

Special caucuses organizations of members of the state legislature who share a common interest or have constituencies with a common interest. (3)

Special session the ability to require the out-of-session legislature to meet; in Texas the governor can invoke this power "on extraordinary occasions" for a thirty-day period to consider an agenda the governor has predetermined. (4)

Standing committees permanent, chamber-exclusive formal work groups that typically exist across sessions and across elections. (3)

State Children's Health Insurance Program (SCHIP) a federal–state program that offers health insurance and medical care to the children of families that make too much to qualify for Medicaid but not enough to afford private health insurance. (9)

State of the state address the requirement that the governor address the state legislature about the condition of the state; the state of the state address occurs at the beginning of each legislative session as well as at the end of the governor's term. (4)

State party chair individual selected at the state party convention to head the state executive committee; state law mandates that a man and a woman be chosen. (8)

Straight ticket voting allowing a voter to select all of the candidates running under a party label by simply checking off a box with the party label. (5)

Structuring the vote the way in which political parties align support or opposition to bills. (3)

Subsidies incentives designed to encourage the production or purchase of certain goods to stimulate or support some businesses. (9)

Succession a set order, usually spelled out in the constitution, of which officeholder takes over when the sitting governor resigns, dies, or is impeached. (4)

Suffrage the legal right to vote. (7)

Sunset review process a formal assessment of the effectiveness of all statutory boards, commissions, and state agencies. (4)

Sunshine laws laws designed to make government transparent and accessible. (4)

Supremacy clause the section in the U.S. Constitution that guarantees that the national government is the supreme law of the land, and national laws and the national constitution supersede state laws and state constitutions. (2)

Tax assessor the elected county officer who collects county taxes and user fees. (6)

Temporary Assistance for Needy Families (TANF) federal program that provides eligible households with monthly cash payments and Medicaid benefits. (9)

Temporary party organizations gatherings, such as primaries, caucuses, and conventions, at which ordinary party members meet. (8)

Term limit a legal limitation on the number of terms an elected official can serve in office. (3)

Texas Assessment of Academic Skills (TAAS) a standardized test implemented in 1990 to create higher standards for state educational assessment. (9)

Texas Assessment of Knowledge and Skills (TAKS) replaced TAAS in 2003; annually given to students starting in grade 3 to assess reading and math skills; also mandates periodic tests in writing, language arts, science, and social studies. (9)

Texas Commission on Environmental Quality (TCEQ) the agency that oversees state environmental policy, including air and water quality. (9)

Trade associations organizations of similar businesses, which work together to advance shared goals. (8)

Traditionalistic political culture the idea, most prevalent in parts of Texas most like the old South, that government has a limited role concerned with the preservation of the existing social order. (1)

Treaty of Guadalupe Hidalgo signed on February 2, 1848, this agreement between the United States and Mexico ended the Mexican American War and recognized the Rio Grande as the boundary between Texas, now part of the United States, and Mexico. (1)

Trustee this approach holds that the electorate has entrusted their elected officials, who understand the issues more broadly than the electorate, to act in their best interests. (3)

Turnover when current officeholders step down from office and are replaced by new office-holders; turnover may result from retirement, defeat in an election, or term limits. (3)

Unfunded mandates when legislation is passed by the national government imposing requirements on state and local governments, in which those governments bear the costs of meeting those requirements. (2)

Unitary system a type of government where power is vested in a central governmental authority. (2)

Vertical federalism the distribution of power between the national and state governments. (2)

Veto power the formal power of the executive to reject bills that have been passed by the legislature; in Texas, a veto can be overridden only by a two-thirds vote in both houses. (4)

Voter turnout the number of people casting ballots in a given election. (7)

Voting Rights Act of 1965 (VRA) a federal statute that eliminated literacy tests as a qualification to vote, greatly increasing African Americans' access to the ballot box. (7)

White primary the attempt by the Democratic Party in Texas to limit the voting in party primaries only to party members. (7)

Zoning policy policy in which the city restricts what individuals and entities may do with their property, usually by designating certain areas of the city for industrial, commercial, and residential uses. (6)

Index

NOTE: Page numbers with *b* indicate boxes; with *f*, figures; with *n*, endnotes; with *t*, tables, respectively.

Image Credits